MORE THAN A GRAIN OF TRUTH

MORE THAN A GRAIN OF TRUTH

The Official Biography of Gareth Jones

DR MARGARET SIRIOL COLLEY

with

Additional Material and Editing
NIGEL LINSAN COLLEY

Second Edition Edited by
NAOMI FIELD

LUME BOOKS

LUME BOOKS

First published in 2005 by Nigel Linsan Colley.
Reprinted in 2006.

Revised edition published in 2020 by Lume Books.
This edition published in 2021.

ISBN 978-1-83901-476-5

Printed and bound by Ingram Lightning Source.

Typeset using Atomik ePublisher from Easypress Technologies

www.lumebooks.co.uk

In Memoriam

I have endeavoured to write this story in memory of my grandparents, Taid and Nain, Major and Mrs Edgar Jones of Barry, Wales. The silent minority must be remembered; those who have suffered at the hands of ruthless dictators and the millions of Ukrainians and others in the Soviet Union whose plight moved Gareth to pity.

Were we to dance upon the dust of love's security,
Were we to kiss beyond the lust of life's embrace,
Might we then understand the meaning of impermanence,
And put asunder the illusion of the face?

For to know that every window,
Holds the frozen eyes of ghosts,
And every door the footsteps of the past,
Is to shine within the shadow of our destiny,
In a world where even mountains do not last.

Philip Colley, 2005

About Gareth Jones

Gareth Jones was a prominent young journalist and former Foreign Affairs Secretary to David Lloyd George, who, in 1935, on the eve of his thirtieth birthday, died in Inner Mongolia. He was murdered by bandits under unknown circumstances.

Gareth's personal letters, diaries and newspaper articles tell the social and political story of the tumultuous period in world events in the 1930s.

He covered the Depression in the USA as well as the famine that spread across the Soviet Union as a result of Stalin's Five-Year Plan. In 1933 he witnessed first-hand the effects of Soviet policy in Ukraine which allowed millions to starve to death and was the first named journalist to expose this tragedy to the Western World.

The rise of Hitler is described by Gareth who was one of only two foreign journalists to fly with Hitler to a rally in Frankfurt and saw his influence over a frenzied crowd.

He upset many important figures with his honest reporting and this book also includes his encounters with major political and public figures of the time including David Lloyd George, Randolph Hearst, Frank Lloyd Wright, Maxim Litvinov and Eamon de Valera.

'Les premiers jours de printemps ont moins de grâce que la vertu
naissante d'un jeune homme.'

*The first days of spring have less grace than the
budding virtue of a young man.*

Dr H. F. Stewart, Fellow of Trinity College, Cambridge,
The Times, August 19, 1935.

For supplementary background material, errata and any matters
relating to this book please visit garethjones.org

This edition dedicated to the memory of
Margaret Siriol Colley (1925-2011)
and
Nigel Linsan Colley (1960-2018)

Contents

Preface to the First Edition

(Incorporating Method of Research)

Gareth Richard Vaughan Jones, the son of Major Edgar and Mrs Annie Gwen Jones was born in Barry, South Wales on August 13, 1905 and died in mysterious circumstances in Inner Mongolia. As a budding young journalist, he paid the ultimate price in his search for the truth. On finding Gareth's diaries in my Aunt Gwyneth's (Vaughan Jones) house in 1990 after a burglary there, I was determined to investigate the circumstances of his death and this inspired me to write the book *Gareth Jones: A Manchukuo Incident*, which was published in 2001. At that time, I believed the story started in Japan and not in China as most people thought, but with further investigation, aided by Nigel Colley, it is possible that the seeds were sown much earlier in Gareth's career.

Since completion of the first book I have slowly transcribed his early letters to his family, his diaries and studied his newspaper articles. These included those written in the United States in late 1934 whilst on his 'Round the World Fact Finding Tour'. Following this I endeavoured to merge them into the biography prior to his arrival in Japan in February 1935. Mrs Sheila Sellars transcribed those diaries relating to the Far East in 1935.

This biography traces Gareth's story from his college days at the University of Wales, Aberystwyth College, his three years at the University of Cambridge, his experiences with the former First World War Prime Minister, David Lloyd George, to his time in the United States during the Great Depression, when he was employed by Ivy Lee, the publicity mogul. It describes Gareth's observations on the rise of Nazism and his revelations on the iniquities of the Soviet Five-Year plan. It also touches on his visits to Austria, Czechoslovakia and to Italy where he reported on Mussolini's dictatorship. His observations on his short visit to Ireland are still pertinent today. His final adventure took him to the Far East, where his investigations into Japan's interests in China were to cost him his life.

The period of Gareth's short life is set against the backdrop of the tumultuous world events of in the early 1930s, a time when nations feared the advent of a second war, following so soon after the catastrophic Great War. This terrible war had killed a generation of young men leaving elderly politicians to rule the countries of Europe. Gareth, who had been employed by David Lloyd George, a signatory to the Treaty of Versailles, understood the ensuing acrimony following this Treaty, and the terrible consequences of the failure to revise it.

Using the rich legacy of his diaries, newspaper articles, and letters to his family, it has been possible to trace the blossoming of an exceptional young man emerging from his college days, into an increasingly respected journalist, energetically going In Search of News.

Perusing a scrapbook containing clippings of most of Gareth's newspaper articles dating from 1930 onwards was invaluable, and Dr Alun Jones at the National Library of Wales dated many of these. Without his help the task of tracing their source would have been impossible. Other articles by Gareth were researched in the National Library of Wales and the newspaper collection of the British Library at Colindale has been consulted for the London, American and Foreign newspapers of the 1930s. Many books have been read and many archives approached that had documents referring to Gareth, and these are recorded in the Appendix. The internet, which has become accessible since the publication of the first book, has been extremely useful in research. The whole task has been a voyage of discovery and innately interesting if Gareth's death had not been such a tragedy to the family. There have been many ramifications to Gareth's story and many paths have been followed to investigate what might have been the cause of his death.

The Public Records Office (now known as the National Archives), the UK Parliament, Parliamentary Archives for David Lloyd George's papers, and the Seely Mudd Library in Princeton for Ivy Lee papers have all proven to be fruitful sources of research. The Wheaton College library staff and James Peters at the Manchester Guardian Archives have also been of great assistance with Malcolm Muggeridge's documents. The public library at Beeston, Nottinghamshire has been particularly helpful in obtaining books from the British Library and it has been possible to peruse the Times microfiche at the Public Library, Angel Row, Nottingham. The private library, Bromley House, Nottingham has many old books of extreme and valuable interest. Many other archives have been researched, some without success, and often it has not been possible to trace the papers of the people with whom Gareth came in contact.

My son Nigel has devoted his time to researching the Holodomor section of this story, and the colleagues and characters that Gareth met during his three visits to the Soviet Union, including Soviet Ukraine. He has investigated a basis for a possible Soviet Secret Police connection with Gareth's demise and looked into the connection that Gareth might have had with the creation of the books *1984* and *Animal Farm* by George Orwell. Gareth's friend, Paul Scheffer has been another line of enquiry.

Gareth's predictions of impending hostility in the danger zones of the world were uncannily accurate. He foresaw the advent of war with Germany, a country for which he had so much affection, as well as the later conflicts in such places as Czechoslovakia and Pearl Harbor. Tragically, his promising career was brought to an untimely end before he had truly made his mark in the world. He died on the eve of his thirtieth birthday on August 12, 1935, in the wilds of Inner Mongolia, but Gareth had managed to accomplish more than most manage to in a whole lifetime. His extensive knowledge and wisdom were lost with his death, and the memory of Gareth was airbrushed out of history until this biography was written.

There must be further archival material as yet untouched and which will come to the fore after the publication of this book. The final interpretation of Gareth's death is my own opinion. On commencement of the transcription of his diaries and letters I presumed that the story was to be a personal one but have found that as it has evolved it has become one of political intrigue. "Mr Gareth Jones was", as Lloyd George said, "a man who knew too much".

Preface to the Second Edition

More Than a Grain of Truth has been out of print for many years and after the death of his mother in 2011, Nigel Colley wanted to update and republish the book. This was not to be, as he had barely started on the revision when he died in early 2018.

It had been Nigel's intention to undertake a comprehensive overhaul of the book to reflect the growing international interest in Gareth Jones since the first publication of *The Manchukuo Incident*. It was largely thanks to the initial research undertaken by Siriol and later on by Nigel, both of whom gave many lectures to audiences in Europe, the USA and Canada, that Gareth became better known in academic circles and to the wider public, particularly the Ukrainian diaspora. This resulted in a major exhibition about Gareth at Trinity College, Cambridge in 2011, and a BBC and a BBC Storyville documentary Hitler, Stalin and Mr Jones in 2012. Gareth's reporting on Russia was the focus of Ray Gamache's book *Gareth Jones: Eyewitness to the Holodomor* published in 2013. Ray Gamache has also transcribed facsimile volumes of Gareth's diaries from both 1931 and 1933 with which Nigel collaborated. Several important books have been published which analyse the historical backdrop to some of the events that Gareth reported on first-hand and which include those by Professors Tim Snyder and Anne Applebaum. These have been all been added to the updated Bibliography.

Rob Phillips and the staff of the South Reading Room at the National Library of Wales have been very helpful, giving generously of their time, during my various visits in the summer of 2019.

Finally, my love and thanks go to Nigel's family who have been so supportive of this project, especially to Philip Colley who read through the revised text, with suggestions for corrections and improvements. While I have tried to remove all errors from the text, any remaining are my own. I hope that Siriol and Nigel would have approved of the changes.

Editor's Note

I set out intending only to correct typographical errors and improve the rather old-fashioned layout of the book. However, it became clear that a more extensive edit would help to make the book more useful to academic researchers and hopefully more accessible to a wider readership. The footnote system of the first edition, and its reprint, has been rationalised with shorter footnotes, such as translations of foreign phrases, being incorporated into the main text. In the case of longer footnotes they have added to the notes at the end of each chapter. Chapter titles have also been rationalised, and small sections of chapters have been moved to the previous or following chapter to make for more logical reading (e.g. the end of Chapter 3 was previously the beginning of Chapter 4). There has also been some reordering of the content within chapters, usually to make more chronological sense, or to bring a particular subject together in a single location to aid the flow of the story. Chapters 23-25 are about contemporaries of Gareth Jones and have been identified as a new Part 6, resulting in renumbering of the final parts of the book. Chapter 30 has been split into two, resulting in a change to the subsequent chapter numbers. More radical changes have been made to Chapters 32-36. The 'new' Chapter 35 'The King of Kalgan' comprises material that was originally in the Will o' the Wisp chapter, with a slightly expanded section relating to the circumstances surrounding Gareth's death, for those who have not read the companion volume *The Manchukuo Incident* where a more detailed account may be found. The section on the complex politics of the area has benefited greatly from Philip Colley's expert eye. The final chapter (Chapter 34 in the former edition) contained a long section that was a summary of the preceding chapters. This has now been mostly deleted with small parts being incorporated into appropriate locations within earlier chapters of the book.

A few additions have been made to the thumbnail biographies of people that Gareth either knew, met, or referred to in his letters and diaries (Appendix IV).

People are now in alphabetical order rather than grouped by their nationalities, which I hope will make them easier to find. The index in the printed version of this edition has been expanded to include subjects and places as well as people.

Spellings have been altered to follow modern usage, but no attempt has been made to alter place-names to their modern equivalent — for example Czechoslovakia, rather than Czecho-Slovakia unless quoted in a letter, newspaper article or diary entry; but Czechoslovakia not the Czech Republic or Slovenia. The city of Kharkiv was spelt both Kharkoff and Kharkov in various of Gareth's letters and newspaper articles.

Gareth used the terms 'Negro' and 'Red Indian', as well as other racial descriptions in his letters. While not acceptable today these have not been altered when quoting his letters verbatim. No offence was intended at the time and it is hoped that no offence is taken by the modern reader.

Since the first edition was written the Public Records Office (PRO) in London has changed its name to the National Archives.

Since 2005, personal papers of Gareth Jones that were still in the hands of his family have all been donated to the National Library of Wales, Aberystwyth. The Gareth Vaughan Jones Papers comprise letters, diaries, miscellaneous personal papers, newspaper cuttings and photographs and are made up of three separate bequests. Series 1-21 covers correspondence, with further letters being in Series B6 and elsewhere. Items are organised in chronological order but have yet to be separately numbered. Series B1/1-16 contains his diaries. Further details may be found on the National Library of Wales website. Funding is now in place with digitisation of these important documents beginning in 2020, to make them more accessible to researchers both in the UK and across the world.

Proceeds from the sale of this book will be used for the upgrading of the official Gareth Jones website garethjones.org.uk that was first created by Nigel Colley back in 2001.

Naomi Feld
Lincoln
December 2019

Gareth Jones Timeline

August 13, 1905	Gareth is born in Barry, S. Wales
1916-1922	County School for Boys, Barry.
1922	Wins County Scholarship.
1922-1923	University College of Wales, Aberystwyth.
1923-1925	University of Strasbourg: Diplôme Supérieur des Etudes Françaises.
1925-1926	University College of Wales, Aberystwyth. First Class Honours in French, University of Wales.
1926	Entrance Exhibition, Trinity College, Cambridge.
1927	Medieval and Modern Languages Tripos, Part I. First Class Honours in French and German, with distinction in the Oral Examination. College Prizeman.
1928	Senior Scholar & Prizeman, Trinity College, Cambridge.
1929	Medieval and Modern Languages Tripos, Part II. First Class Honours in German and Russian, with distinction in the Oral Examination. College Prizeman.

August-September 1929	1-month internship, *The Times* of London
October- December 1929	Supervisor of Studies, Trinity College, Cambridge.
January 1, 1930- April 1931	Private Secretary for Foreign Affairs to David Lloyd George, O.M.
April 21, 1931	Visited New York to study the economics of American business and to work for Ivy Lee.
August- September 1931	Visits the Soviet Union with Jack Heinz II
October 4, 1931	Returns to New York and the employment of Ivy Lee
May 1932	Returned to his former post with Lloyd George, due to financial cutbacks at Ivy Lee.
July 1932	Visited Italy in official capacity to report the measures adopted for the relief of the unemployed in the draining of the Pontine Marshes.
January 30, 1933	In Germany on the day Adolph Hitler became Chancellor
March 5, 1933	Arrived in Moscow to study living conditions in the USSR.
March 11, 1933	Five British engineers arrested and imprisoned in the Lubyanka.
March 13, 1933	Gareth arrives in Kharkov on the day that *Izvestia* announces the arrests

March 17, 1933	Arrived back in Moscow following visit to Ukraine
March 23, 1933	Interviewed Maxim Litvinov, Soviet Commissar for Foreign Affairs.
March 29, 1933	Gareth holds press conference in Berlin and issues his press release on the Soviet famine.
March 30, 1933	Famine articles published in USA and Britain
March 31, 1933	*London Evening Standard* first famine article with Gareth Jones's name attached
April 1, 1933	Famine article in the *Berliner Tageblatt* by Paul Scheffer
1933	Awarded Master of Arts, University of Cambridge.
April 1, 1933	Joined the staff of the *Western Mail*.
June 1, 1933	Visits Randolph Hearst at St Donat's Castle, Wales
October 1934	Left for Round-the-World Fact Finding Tour.
November 26, 1934	Arrived in New York on *SS Manhattan*.
December 4, 1934	Interviewed Frank Lloyd Wright at his home Taliesin.
January 1, 1935	Stayed at Randolph Hearst's Ranch, San Simeon.
January 18, 1935	Embarked from San Francisco on *SS President Monroe* for Hawaii.

March-July 1935	Toured the Pacific visiting the Philippines, Dutch East Indies, Singapore, Siam, Cambodia and French Indo China, Hong Kong, and Canton, eventually arriving in Peking on July 4, 1935.
July 11, 1935	Left Peking to visit Prince Teh Wang's Palace before proceeding on his fateful journey.
July 15, 1935	Gareth leaves Peking to visit Prince Teh Wang's Palace before continuing on his fateful journey.
July 23, 1935	At Larsen's Camp where Dr Müller and Gareth saw Sir Charles Bell.
July 25, 1935	Gareth and Müller arrive in Dolonor.
July 26, 1935	Final entry in Gareth's diary.
July 28, 1935	Gareth and Müller captured by bandits.
August 12, 1935	Gareth murdered in Inner Mongolia on the eve of his 30th birthday.

PART 1

University Life (1922 — 1929)

Chapter 1

Aberystwyth — The College by the Sea

1922-1926

In the South Wales town of Barry, during the early hours of August 13, 1905, the lusty cries of a baby could be heard echoing throughout an Edwardian home. Mrs Edgar Jones had been safely delivered of a son, Gareth Richard Vaughan Jones. The proud father, Edgar Jones, woke his two daughters to announce that he had a surprise for them. Gwyneth, aged ten, was very excited at the news, but Eirian, aged six, did not appreciate the arrival of a brother — as she had hoped that it was a bicycle.

Edgar was born in the village of Llanrhaeadr-ym-Mochnant, close to one of the seven wonders of Wales, the waterfall of Pistyll Rhaeadr, amid the beautiful countryside of Montgomeryshire. He was the eldest son of Richard Bellis Jones, the local schoolmaster, and Hannah Vaughan Jones who managed the village post office. Only five boys out of nine children survived into adulthood. His brother, Dr Raymond Jones, was killed in the Battle of the Somme in 1916 whilst tending the wounded and dying, close to battle area of Mametz Woods.

Edgar was a pupil at Oswestry High School during the period that Owen, the famous Welsh educationalist, was headmaster. Edgar left the school in 1885 to become an undergraduate at the newly established University College of Wales, Aberystwyth, a particularly sad year for the college as a disastrous fire destroyed a great part of the College, and its precious contents of books and manuscripts.

The town of Aberystwyth is situated on the long curve of Cardigan Bay. In 1860, Thomas Savin, an entrepreneur who had pretensions of it becoming a Victorian seaside resort built a neo-gothic hotel at the enormous sum of £80,000. The enterprise failed and in 1867 it was bought for £10,000 by David Davies of Llandinam, to establish a university in this picturesque setting, which became known affectionately as the 'College by the Sea'.

Edgar excelled both academically and on the sports field (being Victor Ludorum).

He graduated in Celtic studies in 1890, by which time the number of students at the college had reached about 200.

Annie Gwen Jones, Gareth's mother, was born in Dowlais in the mining district of the Rhondda where her father, Tom Jones, was a mining deputy. Later the family moved a few miles away to Fochriw where Esther, her mother, ran the small general store. Annie Gwen was one of eight children, two of whom died in infancy, but it was only Annie Gwen and her sister, Winnie, who reached a ripe old age. A brother and a sister died of tuberculosis in their twenties. History does not tell us what became of her other two siblings. A gifted student, Annie Gwen Jones was one of the first women to attend University of College of Wales, Aberystwyth.

Edgar and Annie Gwen, scarcely into their twenties, met as students in Aberystwyth. Their romance blossomed and they became engaged in 1889 — a partnership that lasted nearly 60 years, until Edgar's death in 1953. Following her engagement, Annie accepted the position of tutor to the grandchildren of John Hughes[1], the steel industrialist who founder of the town of Hughesovka, now the city of Donetsk, in Ukraine. Bravely leaving Wales for the first time, Annie Gwen journeyed to a far-away land. She remained with the family of Arthur Hughes for three years from 1889 until she left fled with them during the cholera riots of 1892.

It was not until December 1894 when Edgar, at the age of 25, was appointed headmaster of Llandeilo Secondary School that Annie Gwen and Edgar were in a financial position to get married. The seaport of Barry was expanding from the profits of coal exports, and the population was rapidly increasing from what had been a small. village into a large and flourishing town. Young families were moving in with children who needed educating, so in 1896 Barry County School opened with one hundred and eleven pupils. Three years later a youthful and enthusiastic Edgar became its headmaster and remained head of the school until his retirement in 1933.

Annie Gwen Jones standing top right with Arthur Hughes and his family in Hughesovka.

On moving to Barry, the family lived near the school in a house called 'Eryl', which at that time was bordered by fields. Gareth had a very contented childhood in his home, surrounded and loved by four women. His mother doted on him, his aunt Winnie spoilt him, and his two sisters were devoted to him. He was a lively character and roamed freely about the bustling town. Down at the Barry docks, Gareth would listen to the adventure stories of the sailors who travelled to distant shores. This must have fostered his imagination and his desire to see the world outside the narrow sphere of Wales. In particular, he heard his mother's accounts of her exciting life in Russia. In contrast, Gareth's well-respected father immersed himself in the Classics, for he was a cultured gentleman of a bygone Victorian era who read widely, enjoying poetry, Latin and Greek prose, Welsh literature, architecture, and archaeology.

Edgar Jones, M.A., Ll. D.

Higher education was of paramount importance in his family, as it was in Wales as a whole. As a young child, his mother taught Gareth at home until the age of seven years, and as a youth, he attended his father's school. His mother was a woman of great intellect with a strong personality. She was an early suffragist and actually convened a meeting at her home, to which Chrystabel Pankhurst was invited, but the conventions of the day prevented her from fulfilling her full academic potential, so instead she channelled her wide interests into Gareth's education. From school Gareth gained a County Scholarship to the University of Wales, Aberystwyth in 1922. 'Aber' was held in great affection and respect by the Jones family, for not only had Gareth's parents been undergraduates, but later, so were his two elder sisters, Gwyneth and Eirian. Without doubt, Gareth would regularly have heard his family sing the praises of Aberystwyth; its wonderful education and its academic glories, as well as stories about the eminent men which the College produced it its early days. This may well have fostered his ambition to attend the College.

4

Gwyneth, Eirian and Gareth circa 1911.

His happy childhood at Eryl richly prepared the fertile ground for Gareth's future, but it was during his carefree years at University that the seeds of Gareth's adult life were sown. He had the potential to enjoy the social activities at college to the full and worked hard and played hard. Those letters that remain of Gareth's earlier years, written from Aberystwyth to his proud mother, describe what a wonderful time he was having. Gareth savoured every moment of his very active student life. He regularly played a round of nine holes on the local golf course and always enjoyed watching the 'Aber' Rugby matches. Remarkably, he still found time to study, and he succeeded in winning a number of academic prizes. Every week he attended the Welsh Tabernacle, often twice on Sunday, where he heard the Rev. Principal Preece preach — Gareth had a devout Methodist temperate upbringing, and his family were exemplary Welsh Non-Conformists.

Gareth wished to see a better world rise out of the political chaos that followed the Great War and he carefully planned his academic career with this in mind. He wanted to study modern languages, including Russian, so that he might follow his mother's footsteps to the land of the Tsars. He spent seven years at university studying the French, German and Russian cultures and learning to speak these languages fluently, adding to his native tongues of Welsh and English. The First World War had left great bitterness within the countries that had lost many men, the flower of their youth. In June 1919 the world's victorious nations, with the exception of the United States, signed the Treaty of Versailles. The consequences of this treaty were to have a profound influence on the course of the world, and his life.

Aberystwyth Union Committee (Gareth is standing at the back).

In 1923, as part of his first degree, Gareth spent two years studying abroad in Alsace at the University of Strasbourg, where eventually he would leave in June 1925 with distinction, being awarded the Diplôme Supérieur des Études Francaises. His experiences in France were to influence his views on French life, but despite his love of the French language he never became enamoured with the country. His affection and sympathies always leant towards Germany, where he had many friends and was to visit every year from 1921.

It was during these two years of study in France, that Gareth's intended future direction in international affairs became affirmed. Some thirty-five years after Annie Gwen stayed with the Hughes' family at the Hotel Europeska in Warsaw on her way to Hughesovka, Gareth at the same age of 19 years old was a congress delegate in the Polish capital. The Congress of the International Students (CIE), was convened by the National Polish Students Union, and, by its multi-national nature, Gareth was to learn first-hand the political grievances of young men across Europe, and which had a marked influence on his outlook on life.

On his arrival in Warsaw on September 14, 1924, Gareth, was appointed a guide, and taken to the home of a Mrs Skorupka, one of many hostesses in Warsaw who had offered accommodation to visiting students. Mrs Skorupka had spent a year in Oxford as a student, spoke very good English, and was to become one of Gareth's close friends.

According to Gareth, the Conference was a great success. The Conference president, a Swede, concerned that there was no German representative present, persuaded Herr Zimmerman to attend. He was the president of the German students' union, the Deutsches Studentschaft, which represented all the German-speaking students in Austria and Czechoslovakia. It was apparent that the Swedish president was extremely pleased with the results of the conference, and an enthusiastic Gareth was invited to meet Zimmerman. Both the presidents were strong personalities, and according to Gareth, were delighted that French domination of previous congresses was coming to an end.

The Commissar of the Conference, who was assigned as a guide to Gareth, explained some of the perceived reasons for the Nationalism and conservative sentiments of the Polish students. He believed the nationalistic spirit of Poland was a result of the oppression by the Germans and the Russians. Warsaw had been under Russian domination, but Posen and West Poland were dominated by Germany until an Independent Polish state was re-established in 1918 after the fall of the Russian, Austrian, and German Empires. The Russians suppressed the Poles by keeping them ignorant and had forbidden the teaching of Polish in the few schools there. Their museums were shut, and any trace of their national culture disallowed. The Polish language was banned in Public Offices. Gareth's mother had described to him "how terrible was the depth and breadth of hate for Russia and indeed, the Poles were most harshly and unjustly treated, especially after the rebellion of 1862".

The Germans in the West endeavoured to force their own Teutonic 'kultur' upon the Poles. They, too, forbade the use of the Polish language in schools, and attempted the policy of complete Germanisation. There was no mercy for the native-language speaking minorities. Gareth's mother was greatly influenced by the three years spent in Russia in the early 1890s, and she fostered her liberal views on her son, gained from her own Eastern European experiences. She was deeply moved by the pogroms, the restrictive measures, and the persecution of the Jews. East Poland was under Russia occupation until the end of the Great War, and she imparted to Gareth, her concern for the plight of the Polish Jews who were kept in a state of poverty. When she was lost in the city of Warsaw, she described meeting "Jews on all hands, and Polish Jews are the most unprepossessing in appearance". The new Polish State that emerged after the Great War was not much kinder to the Jews. While in Warsaw, Gareth was prompted to visit the Jewish quarter with a Jewish delegate, Caplan, and found it to be squalid and dirty; kept so purposely by the Polish Health Department.

The Warsaw conference culminated in a magnificent League of Nations candlelit ball in a marble hall, which began at midnight and ended at dawn. After the conference, the delegates had the choice of an excursion, either to Posen (Poznan) or Vilna (Vilnius). Gareth chose the latter as it was his ultimate aim to visit Russia, and the town was only 120 miles from the Russian frontier. Following a long overnight train journey, the students had a great surprise on their arrival. The station was crowded, and flags and decorations were everywhere. The dignitaries of the town were present and drosckes (carriages) were waiting to escort the delegates through town amidst cheering students.

The group stopped outside part of an old wall spared from destruction by the numerous armies that had ravaged the town of Vilna. Passing through the archway of the town wall they saw a marvellous sight, for in the wall was an open-air chapel. Mass was being held; melodious music and the singing of a soprano haunted the air while crowds of peasants were kneeling in the street. Leaving this scene, the students climbed a hill to an old castle where there was a wonderful view of the town. Trees were everywhere. Gareth's letter to his family gave the following description: "Several golden mosques glistened in the sun and the river wound itself in and out to the North of the town in direction of Russia. In one direction a beautiful white church with red scarlet dome could be seen, and on another hill stood three large white crosses in memory of three Vilna Martyrs."

Returning to the town square, Gareth noted that the walls of the cathedral, its towers and other buildings were riddled with bullet holes. A Pole who spoke excellent French said that until 1921 there had been bloodshed and fighting, and that each time Vilna had changed hands between the Bolsheviks, Germans, and the Poles, the bridges were blown up. It had been extremely dangerous to go out in the streets. The conduct of the Bolsheviks had been unmerciful. The German troops had also behaved badly, with the exception of a few cultured people, but not as barbarously as the Bolsheviks. The medieval town of Vilna, which had seen so many tragedies, appeared oriental to Gareth.[2]

Gareth, along with the other delegates and the Polish students, whom he found charming, left the cathedral, and continued to a beautiful church, St. Anne's. He was told Napoleon had expressed a wish to take the church back to France. Thirty-five years previously, when Gareth's mother was lost in the Polish capital, she had been shown the house where the French general stayed in Warsaw in 1812, prior to his disastrous march into Russia.

In Gareth's regular Sunday letter home, he described his experience:

> *Every minute is booked for us, we have a programme of visits, receptions and banquets, and we rarely have minute free. I have never felt so important in my life. A Cinema operator has come with us from Warsaw and has taken us in all attitudes — leaving the train, entering our carriages, shaking hands with the mayor, arriving at the University, visiting the cathedral etc.*
>
> *There is a banquet at 10.30 to-night, and I have to speak on behalf of the English delegation. There are only six of us here and I shall speak in English. I am very tired, having travelled all night by train and been on our feet for 21 hours yesterday, banqueted and danced until 3.15 this morning. And up again at nine o'clock. We have been going about all day walking, in a car or droscke. We are all fagged out, but we must go to the banquet to-night given by the Mayor of Vilna.*[3]

Nearly all the impoverished Polish students worked through the day and studied at night. Many students had lost their property in Russia following the Bolshevik Revolution and had come to live in Vilna, as had numerous other Russians. One aristocratic-looking student, handsome, tall, fair-haired and with excellent manners, turned out to be a Russian émigré who had had all his estates confiscated. All these former Russians inhabitants had similar terrible stories to tell of terror and of the awful deeds that the Bolsheviks had committed. Several of them told of remarkable escapes, and many had seen their friends shot before their eyes. Gareth's hostess, Mrs Skorupka, whom he was to visit on a number of occasions in the coming years, told of her father's (an army doctor), lucky escape. He was condemned to death by the 'Bolshevists' for carrying an anti-Communist letter to his friends, but he was fortunate that a young student saved his life.

Gareth's father was concerned about his son's future and wished to direct him towards an academic profession. Gareth barely 19 years old had, however, already formed a very different vision of his future which he set out in a letter from Alsace, where he was undertaking part of his university studies:

I was very interested in Dada's [father's] suggestions about a fellowship and perhaps a lectureship. But I'm sorry, it does not tempt me very much. I am much more interested in people and countries and in modern Europe especially. I would a thousand times prefer to use my knowledge of languages with an aim to obtaining a position where I could meet interesting people of all nationalities, and where I could really find out the characteristics of the nations of today; why there are wars, and how they could be prevented; how national, Semitic and religious prejudices can be destroyed, and why they exist; why there are certain movements, literary or political in certain countries; why people of races have certain ideals; why certain nations have their characteristics reflected in their literature. All that — and especially learning all these things by travelling and trying to make people speak out their ideas and meet interesting men — interests me much more than study for study's sake. I would much prefer a career, which comprehends a knowledge of men. I can judge men much better now than before I came to Strasbourg; and I think I can observe now their traits — national or political much more thoroughly, since Strasbourg, with the students of all nations here, has been an excellent experience for me in this respect. Also I do not want to specialise on one language alone as I could have to do if I were a professor or something of the sort, and I would certainly not like to specialise in French, since I have very little in common with the French or with their literature. I am going to continue Russian. I find that in general I get on well with people and can usually accommodate myself to different milieus. I have succeeded quite well in getting their ideas out of the Alsatians, who usually keep their ideas to themselves…

So I would much prefer of course, if I can (I don't know if I am capable enough) something in the League of Nations, Foreign Office, Diplomacy (? this is too costly) or Consular Service… I want to travel, and I want to learn languages. I find the world much more interesting from the human point of view than I did two years ago.[4]

In order to achieve his ambitions Gareth need to further his academic studies. During his final year at Aberystwyth, Gareth attended Whewell's Court, Trinity College, Cambridge to sit the examination for the Common Entrance Exhibition. As soon as he arrived, he described his visit to his parents:

Everything is going well in Cambridge. I have excellent rooms, a very comfortable sitting room with blazing fire all day and a bedroom. They belong to someone

*called Hoffman who has left most of his belongings here. From the photographs
on the wall, he was cox of the Trinity eight; from his books and a human skull on
the bookcase I suspect he is a medical student... The chairs and the sofa are most
comfortable in blue... I doubt whether I shall get an Exhibition. I have been
told that Trinity is rather snobbish and gives preference to public school men...*

*This morning, I went to King's Chapel to the service at 10.30. It is a wonderful
chapel especially the roof and the stained-glass windows. Tomorrow the exams
begin earnest... The results will be out in a week. Don't expect too much.*[5]

Despite his doubts, Gareth received an Entrance Exhibition at Trinity College,
Cambridge and he planned to commence his studies at the University in the autumn
of 1926. Had he not had an offer at Trinity, Mr Debenham, senior tutor of Caius,
(who had been with the South Pole Expedition) had offered him a provisional
place at Caius College.

Gareth graduated in the summer of 1926 from the University College of Wales,
with a First Class Honours degree in French and in September 1926, shortly before
going up to Cambridge, Gareth was in Geneva as an interested bystander to witness
the events that led to Germany being admitted to the League of Nations.

The delegation of students from Aberystwyth, including Gareth, was present at the
plenary session of the International Universities League of Nations Federation. The
'Aber' students visited the International Labour Office of which Albert Thomas was
the Director. Albert Thomas, Professor Goldscheidt from Austria, and others spoke
at an International Economic Conference on the 'League of Nations'. According to
Gareth's reports, the lecturers said that "The danger of war in the future will come
from economic reasons, that the only thing to avoid war was to have the economic
conditions of the world controlled by the League of Nations."[6]

Gareth saw many of the leading figures and politicians of the period, including
Albert Einstein (who in 1921 had won the Nobel Prize for Physics); Joseph Wirth
(Chancellor of Germany 1921-22); President of the German Reichstag, Paul Löbe;
and Walther Schücking, 'the greatest German pacifist'. Other delegates present
outside the council meeting included the British Foreign Secretary, Sir Austen
Chamberlain (Nobel Peace Prize winner of 1925); Aristide Briand (the ex-Prime
Minister of France and member of 11 French Governments between 1909-1929);
André Paul-Boncour (Prime Minister of France in 1932-33); Viscount Ishi, former
Foreign Minister from Japan; Unden from Sweden, and Lord Robert Cecil, one of
the architects of the League of Nations.

Leaving Geneva, Gareth decided to go home via the Auvergne and stay with Mr

Jannelle, a French friend he made while in Strasbourg. Gareth wrote to his parents asking for permission to stay longer abroad:

> *I do hope you don't mind. I am very keen on learning to speak French perfectly. As a language for conversation and a diplomatic career French is a hundred times better than German and a much more beautiful language... I can imagine no better preparation for the Cambridge oral examination, and it will be an insight into French life...*

Notes on Chapter 1

1
John Hughes was a Welsh engineer from Merthyr (Tydfil), who caught the attention of the Tzar Alexander II and the Russian Government, through his technical skill, whilst he was a superintendent at Millwall Docks, London. The Russian Government was keen to expand its railways, and to develop its steel and coal works.

2
Vilna, now Vilnius, the capital of Lithuania, is sometimes called 'the city built on human bones'. It stands in the main Berlin to Moscow corridor, which for over 200 years has been the battlefields of the armies of Napoleon, the Tsars of Russia, Hitler, and Stalin, as well as Poles, and Prussians — hence its sinister description.

3
Gareth Vaughan Jones Papers, National Library of Wales. Correspondence Series 1-21, File 6.

4
Gareth Vaughan Jones Papers, National Library of Wales. Correspondence Series B6/1. January 1925.

5
Gareth Vaughan Jones Papers, National Library of Wales. Correspondence Series 1-21, File 1. December 13, 1925.

6
Gareth Vaughan Jones Papers, National Library of Wales. Correspondence Series B6/1. September 9, 1926.

Chapter 2

A Fresher at Cambridge

1926-1927

In the autumn of 1926, Gareth went up to the University of Cambridge to read French, Russian and German, remaining an undergraduate for another three years. At Trinity College, he was given rooms in New Court, which was built between 1823-25 during the time of the Master of Trinity, Christopher Wordsworth (brother of the poet, William Wordsworth).

New Court, Trinity College, Cambridge.

Gareth was always an excellent correspondent and soon after he had left Wales for Cambridge, his family were eagerly awaiting his news. On October 12, they received what was to be the first of a ritual of weekly Sunday letters; a routine he was to strictly observe to the end of his days:

13

My rooms are high up a flight of stairs, but splendid. From my bedroom I look out on the red brick buildings of Trinity Hall. I can see the Senate House and Caius College. King's Chapel looks splendid and towers above the others. My bedroom is fine, and my bed is very comfortable with blankets and rugs. I have three carpets in the bedroom, which cover nearly all the floor. The sitting room has two windows which look out on the parapets. By getting on a chair and scrambling out I can get on the ramparts and have a fine view. The Backs [a mile-long section of the River Cam in the centre of Cambridge] are within a few yards.[1]

My first week in Cambridge is over and I have enjoyed it thoroughly. I have settled down splendidly and shall be very happy here. It is a lovely day today; crisp and autumnal it is grand having rooms in College and I have a fine blazing fire. I have plenty of coal and I shall not be cold.[2]

It was not long before Gareth sent the following invitation to his parents inviting them to visit him at college:

Mr Gareth Vaughan Jones of Trinity College, Cambridge requests the pleasure of the company of Major and Mrs Edgar Jones to lunch in his rooms on Saturday, November 13.

R.S.V.P. F7, New Court, Trinity College.

What would you like for lunch — cold ham and cake or the 2/6 hot lunch from the kitchen sent up to one's room to see what hall lunch is like? It would be a more economical plan to have ham and cheese.[3]

When his parents visited, Gareth showed them around the colleges of Cambridge. Returning to his room he discovered that he had been 'ragged' (had a practical joke played on him) and he found mince pies in his bed. The culprit was one of his Welsh friends.[4]

Gareth quickly made new friends and acquaintances as well as his keeping old colleagues from Aberystwyth. They were varied in their interests; some were from Grammar and some from Public Schools, though he was equally happy to make overseas contacts in order to practise his skill in speaking foreign languages. His social calendar was always full of appointments for lunch, tea, and dinner — and Gareth steadily built up a formidable network of personal contacts, and these were described in considerable detail in his letters home.

The first lunch that Gareth gave was for his friends who were with him at Aberystwyth. He invited B. A. Edwards, Seabourne Davies, and Llywelfryn Davies.

Everything is on the table, the cold chicken, salad, rolls, the serviettes, all look fine. On one small table are the bananas and cream, dates and cakes and over the cupboard, the coffee pot is standing with four cups. I am surveying it all very proudly. It will be a Welsh lunch as everybody speaks Welsh.[5]

A staunch and lasting friend was Norton, later the second Baron Rathcreedan, who early in his days at Cambridge invited Gareth to tea. His familiar name was Patrick, but few students called their friends by the first name, a custom which survived until well after the Second World War. Norton had spent seven months in Hanover and was now anxious to meet a particular German student, Schmorl, who was hoping to enter the German Diplomatic Service, so Gareth facilitated a meeting in his rooms for coffee. On another occasion, Gareth and Norton went to hear the Don Cossacks' Choir, which Gareth described as being the best choir he had ever heard who were 'excellent basses and beautiful tenors'.

In the summer term of 1927, Gareth hosted regular weekly meetings, where he invited a foreign student to come and speak on his home country. Amongst those who came was Prince Lubomirski, a subject of the USSR (whose Polish ancestors' reputations were apparently not wholly spotless and who used continually to revolt against the king). A German spoke about the Polish Corridor problem, and Prince Arthit of Siam told the group in a most diplomatic fashion what a wonderful place Siam was. A few years later Gareth endeavoured to call on the Siamese prince. Another 'fresher' at Trinity, one of several Germans from well-known families, was Count Lichnovsky, whose father was the German Ambassador to London from 1912 to 1914.[6] An Albanian friend, Meta, had an interesting upbringing. During the First World War, he had wandered from village to village in the mountains of Albania, and only first went to school when he was 14 years old in 1919. In his first year of education, he had learnt to read and by 1928 spoke English fluently. Meta informed the student group, about what he would do if he became dictator in Albania.[7]

Gareth undertook many student activities. As a true Welshman he loved to sing, in particular airs from his native Wales. He soon became an active member of the Trinity Madrigals as a tenor. Each year the Madrigals performed at the London Coliseum and Gareth contemplated the thought of becoming an 'artiste'. He also became a member of the *Cercle Littéraire*, the French reading circle. The leader,

Marchant, asked him to speak third in a debate in the French Society. The debate was "Est ce que La République est le Gouvernement idéal pour La France?" ("Is the Republic the ideal government for France?") He joined the Hare and Hounds society and went on a 'man-hunt' organised by them and remarked, "I regained my Boy Scout enthusiasm. While we were running the gigantic airship R33 flew over us — a fine sight." Gareth owned a bike, which was indispensable in Cambridge, where the narrow streets of the city were full of students darting along with their black gowns flowing in the wind.

Taking part in so many university activities, it might appear that Gareth had little time for study. This was not the case, for although he mentions very little about his work in his letters home, he must have studied extremely hard. He had boundless energy and declared, "I am going to work like anything at translation, composition and essays to get a First and hanged if I don't get a First."

At the end of his first year, Gareth did indeed gain First-Class Honours in French, and German in his Medieval and Modern Languages Tripos part I, with distinction in the Oral Examination, and was the College Prizeman.

Term was nearly over, and Gareth started to plan his vacation. Still beholden to his parents, he was dependent on them for financial support. On June 5, 1927, he wrote:

> I should like to go abroad this summer. Norton is spending three months in Spain. I should like to earn money in Berlin by giving English lessons and living, if possible, with a Russian family... I shall try to save money by finding a boat in Barry or Cardiff to Bremen or Hamburg.[8]

However, Gareth had a change of plans for his summer vacation...

Notes on Chapter 2

1
  Gareth Vaughan Jones Papers, National Library of Wales. Correspondence Series B6/1, October 12, 1926. The Backs is a mile-long section of the River Cam in the centre of Cambridge, so called because of the University Colleges, which 'back' onto it and is one of the most beautiful stretches of river in England.
2
  Gareth Vaughan Jones Papers, National Library of Wales. Correspondence Series B6/1 October 17, 1926.
3
  Gareth Vaughan Jones Papers, National Library of Wales. Correspondence Series B6/1.
4
  Ibid. letter to his aunt Gwyneth November 18, 1926.

[5] Ibid. October 31, 1926.

[6] In 1935, Gareth was to meet the Count Lichnovsky's sister at the German Legation in Peking.

[7] Rose Wilder Lane took a lifelong interest in Meta, sponsoring his attendance at the American Technical School in Tirana and later at Cambridge University, UK. He appears in Miranda Vickers' book *The Albanians: A Modern History*, 2004 I.B. Tauris & Co., Ltd.

[8] Gareth Vaughan Jones Papers, National Library of Wales. Correspondence Series B6/1. June 5, 1927.

Chapter 3

A Working Passage to Riga

(Summer of 1927)

In its heyday many millions of tons of coal were exported from Barry to countries all over the world. An extensive railway system was built to carry the coal to the port, and great viaducts were constructed, including the impressive one at Porthkerry. It was still a busy port in the 1920s, when Gareth made his plans to obtain a working passage with a cargo ship to the continent of Europe for his summer vacation. His intention had been to go to Moscow, but these plans had to be altered because the British Government had just broken off diplomatic relations with Russia.[1] He had considered going to Germany, but through a contact by the name of Mr Fetler, he decided to go instead to Riga in Latvia, to improve his Russian, with the intention of covering his living expenses by teaching English.

Always mindful of economising, and ever-thoughtful of his parents, the confident Gareth sought out the captains of cargo ships and enquired as to whether he could obtain employment as a deckhand, or, as his Auntie Winnie thought, that of the job of a stoker. Gareth, eager for adventure, was fortunate to be given work on a ship carrying coal to Stavanger. On 8 July 1927, he boarded the *SS Vesta*, and from a 'compass point' in North Sea, between Hull, North Holland and Germany wrote to his parents:

> *Thursday morning, about five am, the pilot left the ship just outside the Docks [Barry]. The weather was fairly fine, and I could see the coast clearly, Ilfracombe, Hartland Point. We could imagine from the map where Tintagel ought to be and Trevose. We passed Land's End about midnight.*
>
> *We took a long time to go up the English Channel. Friday, we passed the Isle of Wight, and about evening we saw the Île de France, the biggest liner built since the war. It looked splendid. We have passed a number of steamers, and as we passed Dover, I could see the White Cliffs quite clearly.*

I am having a splendid time on board and am quite a privileged person. I have food with the captains' family, sleep on a sofa in the small saloon (which Dada saw) where we have our meals, do nothing except stroll about read, play with little seven-year old Ella, who is a little Tartar. She likes fighting with everybody and scrambles on deck everywhere. I have not even wiped dishes, leave alone painted the ship, and as for stoking I haven't even been down to the engine room. The crew take their hat off to me! So, my vision of working my passage has disappeared.

The food is excellent — bread, butter, three kinds of cheese and three hot meals a day. Capt. Thorbjornsen is very jolly, laughing and joking all the time. Mrs Thorbjornsen is quiet, but she is confined to her bunk most of the time. The Chief Officer has been teaching me a little Norwegian. He told me that Britain is losing a lot of trade through breaking off relations with Russia.[2]

Two days later, Sunday was a fine day and the sea was calm. Only one steamer had been seen all day. In two days' time the ship would sight the lighthouse on at Egersund. So early on the following Tuesday morning Captain Thorbjornsen called Gareth at 4.30 am with a cup of black coffee and brought him out to see the Norwegian coast. He described the scene in his next letter:

Land at last! It was a wonderful view. There were rows of jagged mountains one on top of another and the sun rising up behind — one of the finest views. We followed the coast from Egersund, the lighthouse, until we turned into the Stavanger Fjord. We are now passing the Granary of Norway, a very fertile stretch of land. This tiny patch of land produces most of the corn for Norway. There are little farms dotted everywhere which we can see since we are only 1½ miles from the coast. Then behind rise the mountains, now covered with clouds. We shall call, but I am not allowed to land at Stavanger, but I shall enjoy the trip up to Sauda right through wonderful fjords, some of the finest scenery in Norway.

Later that day he continued his letter:

We are now sailing up the Stavanger Fjord. In the distance there are snow-clad mountains. There are hundreds of little islands to be seen. White wooden houses with red roofs are scattered everywhere, dotted here and there. The sun is shining beautifully and lighting up the hills. Most of the low-lying islands are bare rocks with just the odd a patch of grass or moss, but some of the hills are wooded. It is hard to believe that the population is only 2½ millions, and most of them live on the coast.

After lunch: We have just entered Sauda Fjord. Gulberg, the captain's elder daughter is dressed in a gorgeous Norwegian costume with plenty of rich red about it; some of the crew are playing the guitar, accompanied by a kind of tambourine and bells and singing at the front of the boat. Going through this fjord is wonderful and this glimpse with the music and the glitter of the Norwegian costume with red, green and all colours, the strong smell of the forest, adding the just right atmosphere to the mountains, the water and the trees.

Five o'clock. Hurray! Just arrived this moment in Sauda after a wonderful sail up the Sauda Fjord. The town is small, situated at the very end of the fjord, snow-capped mountains all round and a tremendous number of waterfalls reminding me of Pistyll Rhaeadr.[3]

According to Gareth, there was an iron ore refinery in the beautiful surroundings of Sauda. The factory employed about a thousand men producing steel that when refined was exported to the USA. The manganese and iron ore were brought from Africa to the factory in Norway, where electricity was relatively cheap. The coal, transported from Barry, was unloaded by the biggest crane in the world, after which the boat sailed on to Bergen. Captain Thorbjornsen invited Gareth to accompany him to visit his parents and all his family at Sandied:

I was lucky to meet a Norwegian family. Norway gives the impression of being very contented. Nobody complains as in France against the Germans as in Germany against the occupation of the Rhine, and Poland against the Jews. The only sad feature seems to be the sardine industry. It is heartbreaking to hear the shrieks of the young sardines as he struggles in vain to get through the mess. It does not compare with the yells of the bristlings as they are called, and their outbursts of anger and pain as they are forced one by one into the tins.[4]

In his last letter from the *SS Vesta* Gareth exclaimed, "Hurray! I have done some dish-wiping at last. I have helped the steward wipe dishes twice today. So, I can say I have worked a little. Aren't I lucky to get such a fine voyage to Norway?" After farewells all round, he went ashore in a small boat and made his way to Bergen station to catch the early morning train to Oslo. He had a delightful journey through a 100-miles of snow-covered country and described the mountain scenery to his family:

dazzlingly breath-taking, with the sun shining brightly upon long stretches
of snow'. The snow came right up to the railway and here and there were lakes
with ice-floats in the centre. In many places the railway had shed-like structures
to prevent the snow covering the lines. In one station the passengers even went
out and had a snow fight.[5]

Arriving in Oslo he found a bed for the night at the YMCA. With the day free, he spent the time exploring the city, and in the evening caught the night train to Stockholm. To his disappointment he found there was only one boat a week to Riga from Stockholm, and, as it left that very day, he decided to depart immediately. He felt he was unable to spend time in the Scandinavian city, as it was his intention to learn Russian in Latvia. With little time to spare, he boarded the *SS Angermanland* to continue his journey to Riga. Economy always in mind, he travelled third class across the Baltic Sea, he slept well in a hammock that he had to put up himself on the lower deck.

On his arrival in Riga, Gareth wrote to his family: "I came straight here, and met Mr Fetler, who said I could stay until I found a family. I have been have given a room with a sofa bed in the Mission." He continued his letter:

I have just come back from an English prayer meeting which lasted from
10.30 am until 12.50 pm with which I was heartily fed-up. At some periods
of the prayer meeting some people were praying for such a long time, and we
had to stick down on our knees for over an hour. They are very, very kind to me,
but I shall be glad to get into another atmosphere. I hope I shall get an answer
to my advert tomorrow.

…I have been to another prayer meeting until quite weary of it!! Luckily, I am
enjoying it as I can see the funny side. This evening when we were all standing
at prayers, (we have prayers three quarters of the day here) Pastor Fetler said:
"Brother Jones will now lead us in prayer!" May I pray in Welsh I said. I started
off with "Ein Tad yr hwnwyl yn Nefoedd" [Our Father who art in Heaven], got
half way through and could not remember the rest. I then started, "Beth sydd i
mi yn y byd" [What is there for me in this world, but great adversity]. After a
few lines I gave, "O Arglwydd bendithio'n bwyd" [O! Lord bless our meal]… a
few words of "Wrth fyned efo Deio I Dywyn [As we went with Tom to Tywyn-a
traditional Welsh folksong]. It was the first thing that came into my mind,
and I repeated "O blotia, Arglwydd ein an wireddau o lyfr dy gofadwriaeth"
[Erase O! Lord, our transgressions from your record book] twice, and finished

with a few words of Hen Wlad fy Nhadau [Welsh National Anthem: 'Land of our Fathers'. Thank goodness there was no one who could understand Welsh.[6]

Gareth's last evening at the Mission was on July 21, 1927, when he wrote:

Tomorrow morning, I move to my new abode. I am sure if I remain here much longer, I should become an absolute heathen, despite all the kindness.

The workers call Mr Fetler "Papa". Pastor Fetler is an autocrat and, I think, narrow-minded. The rest of the people I like very much, if they did not ask me whether I was learning Russian to be a missionary and if the Lord had called me to do this or that. At meals Pastor Fetler aged about 50 with a black-grey beard strides in singing or rather bellowing:

"Blessed be the name, Blessed be the name of the Lord,
Blessed be the name, Blessed be the name,
Jesus is the name. Blessed be the name of the Lord".

And so the curtain goes down on my life in the Mission. I am glad to get into a less sanctimonious atmosphere (although please don't think I have not been happy in the Mission. They could not be nicer. The fault lies with me.)

I haven't told you anything about Riga. The town is about an hour by boat from the sea. Imagine heaps of streets with huge pebbles and cobblestones, placed here and there in sand. When you go in a droscke you are rattled and shaken to bits. There are lots of tiny dirty wooden houses and ramshackle buildings. Next you may find a splendid stone building or big house with six or seven stories [sic]. Everything in the streets seems uncared for; no proper gutters. It is a tremendous contrast from clean well-built Scandinavia, where the wooden huts are spotlessly white. There is a difference between Britain, Germany and Scandinavia and Eastern Europe. But then the people must have suffered a lot here. I have never seen so many disabled, deformed, ragged dirty people. Last night when I was returning back to the Mission, I saw an old woman in a corner crying. I felt sorry for her and I gave her a lat (coin). She burst out crying and grabbed hold of my hand and kissed it. The faces of the children look so ill. Life is cheap here.[7]

The Consul at the British Consulate gave Gareth the name of a Russian lady from Petrograd, who was the widow of a Russian Naval Officer; now a poor refugee, being a Russian émigré. Her husband, a hereditary noble, and an officer in the navy, had been killed during the Great War. Gareth went to the address, and found a tall, dignified lady aged about 54, Madame Krzyzanovki; and her daughter, Olga Nicolaevna. He was given a lovely room at her house. Madame Krzyzanovki and her daughter were excellent teachers of Russian, and they could not have been nicer people. They called him by his patronymic name, Gareth Edgarovitch.

Gareth tried to advertise in the Riga Times to teach English but had no replies. He apologised to his parents that it was so expensive, but he expected to learn 'heaps' of Russian:

I buy a Russian (Riga) newspaper every day and it is full of Russian news. The situation in Russia must be very bad; fiery war speeches by Stalin, and Voroshiloff. [People's Commissar for military and navy affairs and chairman of the Revolutionary Military Council of the USSR]. The latter says war will probably come next year, 1928. Every leader is calling on every citizen to arm. There is quite a panic in some parts of Russia. But here in Riga people are quite calm. It seems a political move on the part of the Communist leaders. There will probably be a bust up between the two sections before long. It is interesting to see detailed speeches from Russia instead of the snippets in English newspapers.

I have not had much opportunity to meet Latvians as Madame and her daughter look down on them as a race of peasants… Madame Krzyzanovki has German-Baltic blood and her relations are of German-Baltic nobility, all 'vons'. She is related to Count von Witte who was once Prime Minister of Russia. Here in Latvia, the Germans used to be the aristocracy and ruling class, the Germans who are descended from colonists arrived here in the 13th century. There are thousands of Germans in Riga and this part of the city looks like a German town. Now since the war and since the formation of the Latvian Republic, the Germans are still the aristocracy, but are poor, their lands having been partly confiscated and given to the peasants, and they are no longer the ruling, privileged class.

I was lucky to buy heaps of Russian books recommended by Mr Goudy and I have sent them to Cambridge. I am very pleased with my purchases. I bought them all second-hand here. It would be impossible to get them in Cambridge, quite a foundation to a small Russian library. All the books are essential for the Tripos. I got them very cheaply.[8]

On August 11, Gareth's stay in Riga was nearly over and a week later he would be in Germany, where he expected to feel at home since he knew more people there. He would be able to improve his German, and afterwards he would go to

23

France to refresh his French. His plans were to sail from Riga on a passenger boat to Stettin, and then travel straight on by train to Waldheim via Berlin. All being well he expected to be in Waldheim at 10.20 pm on Thursday.

Gareth left his Russian family in Riga and on the deck of the *SS Ostsee* sailing through the Baltic Sea, some miles off the Pomeranian Coast, he wrote on August 18:

> *You will be glad to hear that I have just been talking to a German sailor who was a prisoner in Cardiff and in Flat Holm Island during the beginning of the War. He said he had a splendid time, remembers Dada and said that Dada was a fine man He said that the Germans asked Dada if they could do their own cooking instead of having the same food as other nationalities, and that Dada was very decent about it and allowed them to. The sailor said that he was wonderfully treated during the war and did not want to go back to Germany. He had served on British boats and much preferred being on British boats than German...*
>
> *... The Ostsee is a German steamer, which sails once a week from Riga to Stettin and also carries a few passengers. I am travelling Upper Deck, the cheapest way, 20 marks (i.e. fourth-class). There are first-class, second-class, Lower Deck and Upper Deck.*
>
> *Tuesday was a pouring wet day in Riga. Madam Krzyzanovki and Olga were very sorry to see me go... When I arrived, I had a surprise. I found the Upper Deck passengers had to stay in the open air all the time. Since it was pouring, this was impossible. So, the steward let me down to the lower deck (this is a small boat) and there I found a kind of hold with a few wooden beds, which was much better than spending two days in the open air. A Wandervögel [German hiker] came on board and I discovered that he also was travelling Upper Deck. So, we made friends and both of us went down to the Lower deck without paying extra... Then we met another fellow traveller, an East Prussian, who is travelling Lower Deck, and the three of us soon became friends. They have been wonderfully kind to me. The Prussian has shared all his food with me and insisted that I should have his blanket because the wooden bed was hard, and because he had brought a mattress. So, I have been very lucky and slept two nights on a thick warm blanket. The East Prussian is very keen on politics, and we have talked a lot together. He has lived many years in Latvia, and says that the political corruption is incredible, that when the land was taken from the big landowners, the politicians took the valuable land (e.g. the land with a factory) for themselves. No man is allowed to have more than 50 hectares; so*

the politicians took the valuable land where there was a factory or something
worth having, then sold it again.[9]

Gareth reached Waldheim, Saxony on Friday, August 19, 1927 after stopping briefly overnight in Berlin. The Haferkorns gave him a very warm welcome and he felt quite at home with the family.

Three days later a group including the Haferkorns set out on a walking tour in the mountains. Dr Reinhard Haferkorn, whom Gareth had known at Aberystwyth, lent him authentic German 'wander-suit' breeches for the walking tour, and he felt the part with his German companions. From Bohemia they penetrated Czechoslovakia and down the mountainside into the Eger Valley. After crossing into Czechoslovakia, they slept in a village on the frontier before they reached a place called Gabrielahütten.

After a few days at Waldheim, Gareth left the Haferkorn family, stopping briefly in Leipzig, before arriving in Geneva on August 31, 1927, to attend the British Dominions' Conference. The delegates from Cambridge joined him at a League of Nations Conference at Geneva during the first week in September 1927. He was also fortunate to meet a family friend, the Rev. Gwilym Davies; a member of the Welsh League of Nations Union and the founder of the Welsh Book Festival, who gave Gareth a ticket for every meeting. Gareth had such a pleasant surprise to find a friend from Strasbourg University, Pierre Winkler sitting in the gallery. Gareth attended the meetings daily and regularly went to hear Herr Zimmer lecture. The chief events of the Assembly were the speeches of Foreign Ministers of Germany, France and Great Britain, Gustav Stresemann, Aristide Briand and Austen Chamberlain.

To perfect his French, Gareth left Geneva and travelled on to stay at Charvot par St. Jean des Ollières, Puy de Dôme, in France with a family he had known during his student days at Strasbourg University. He wrote of his trip:

> *This is a charming place, but what a journey to arrive here! Imagine a tiny little place in the middle of the mountains about 20-miles or more from a toy railway station and 40-miles or more from a real station! The last part of the journey was in a rattling bus, and when I arrived Mr and Mrs Janelle gave me a very warm welcome. On a hill just near there home are red roofed houses of St Jean des Ollières, all the villages are charming with their pretty roofs, the vine climbing over the doors, dark faces and black hair of the inhabitants. You can realise how far away we feel from civilisation, nestling right in the heart of the mountains. We are so high up, that the mountains around just look like small hills. It gives me a wonderful insight into French village life, and I am delighted to notice that my French is improving rapidly. After hearing the French speeches*

in the assembly, I want to be able to speak well. You cannot beat French for attractiveness and elegance. German sounds so clumsy in comparison.

Notes on Chapter 3

[1] On May 12, 1927, the British police raided the London premises of the Soviet Trade Delegation and of the Arcos Trading Company with close links to Russia that had been obtaining military information. The Soviet Chargé d'Affaires was asked to leave Britain, and relations were broken off for two and a half years.

[2] Gareth Vaughan Jones Papers, National Library of Wales. Correspondence Series 1-21, File 8. July 8, 1927.

[3] Ibid. July 12, 1927.

[4] Ibid.

[5] Ibid.

[6] Ibid.

[7] Ibid. July 21, 1927.

[8] Ibid.

[9] Ibid. August 18, 1927.

Chapter 4

Second Year at Cambridge

1927-1928

In early October 1927, Gareth returned to Trinity College after a very full and adventurous vacation. The following month, returning from the Union building to his rooms he found a parcel waiting for him on the table in his sitting room, containing a publication of German songs:

> *It is a wonderful book with splendid illustrations and piano accompaniment and one of the nicest things is that each of the 'wanderers' — Dr Haferkorn, Haferkorn's father and others- have written a piece of poetry dedicating the book to me. Some verses humorous and some serious and with the songbook is a copy of a song I liked very much on the walking tour and which is not in the book.*[1]

It was Gareth's second year at Cambridge and he became friendly with Gustav Stresemann's son, who was also at the university, and continued to host tea parties in his rooms. His aunt regularly baked fruitcakes, and these were duly sent to appreciative students up at Trinity College. Gareth wrote home:

> *The cake was lovely. Thank you, Aunty Winnie, ever so much for it. Stresemann's son had some yesterday and enjoyed it thoroughly. He will be writing home to his father, the Foreign Minister, how nice the cake was. Stresemann [senior] will spread the news throughout Germany and in the next League of Nations Council Meeting will perhaps tell Austen Chamberlain who will tell Briand. And so, the fame of Aunty's cake will spread around the world.*[2]

Aunty Winnie's fame may not have spread round the world, but it certainly reached Germany. At Christmas, Aunty Winnie cooked a plum pudding, and this was duly posted to the Haferkorn family in Waldheim. Reinhard Haferkorn replied in verse that the plum pudding had arrived safely, and a party had been arranged to celebrate its arrival from Wales. Apparently, so many people wanted to taste it that they almost had to divide the basin and the cloth as well as the pudding so that all might have a share.

Gareth interests were numerous and varied. He soon introduced himself to members of the Cambridge University League of Nations. Gareth's father was a friend and supporter of David Davies, who had been so prominent in the formation of the League of Nations. This fostered Gareth's active interest and within days of arriving in his first term he joined the League of Nations at the university. During the collegiate year, the branch in Cambridge organised a series of lectures on "The International Organisation of Peace, 1919-1926" by J.R.M. Butler [later to become deputy Master of Trinity College]. Butler then proposed Gareth as chief Secretary of the Cambridge League of Nations. Albert Thomas, the Director of the International Labour Office in Geneva presented an excellent lecture in French entitled; 'Labour and the League of Nations'.

Gareth had a wide circle of friends, and so he was able to introduce a Canadian, Gerald Graham, to a number of people including Laurie Bunker, an Irishman and Harvard man. Graham was very grateful as it was only through Gareth that Graham had any connection with undergraduate life. Both men became close friends of Gareth's. Another was an American, Pierpoint Stackpole from Harvard, whom Gareth described as very funny person. On one occasion before they went for walk, he kept Gareth waiting for a long time while he fetched his coat. Eventually he re-appeared and remarked "When I deliver my address to the American Nation, I shall exhort young Americans to emulate the astuteness of Bismarck, the courage of Lincoln and the patience of Jones."

The Madrigal Choral Society met regularly to practise for the performance at the Coliseum Theatre in London, which the group were presenting at Christmas. Gareth described the rehearsals as "being enjoyable… did not take up much time and the choice of songs was very beautiful". In the previous year the Cambridge singers had been well-paid for their performance, and received £100, sharing it between 14 of the group.

Gareth's Strasbourg friend, Pierre Winkler, visited him, and they were invited to Prof. Breul's, (Gareth's German professor), 'At Home'. It was an afternoon party in held in the university rooms and according to Gareth, it turned out to be a very swell 'thé dansant' with ices, lemonade and delicious refreshments. Despite the fact there was a jazz band, there were not many girls with whom they could dance. As was the convention, the following day he left his card with Mrs Breul. Pierre Winkler joined him at a lecture at 10.00 the next morning, and he created a sensation with the students by arriving in full morning dress and yellow spats — the complete outfit. Later the Frenchman went to lunch and sat at High Table at Newnham Women's College in the same ensemble where he caused a 'stir' among the 200 to 300 girls.

The Trinity Madrigal Society 'singing' at the London Coliseum.
[Gareth is at the front in the centre].

Gareth was beginning to think of his future career after he had left Cambridge, and he applied for a job in America but was not optimistic, as many other people had applied. On the first Tuesday in May, he had an interview with Civil Service Commissioners for permission to sit the exam for the Diplomatic Service and wrote in his weekly letter home:

It will be most interesting whether they will pass me. The idea of being a lecturer and then a professor is very amusing. I would dislike being a professor intensely and have been fortunate to have done so well so far, considering my complete lack of original ideas and thinking. It will be interesting whether they pass me or not. The board are sure to pass me for the consular service. I shall call on consuls in Germany when I am there in the summer.[3]

On June 24, 1928, the Madrigal group left for their tour in Germany:

In Cologne we went to see the cathedral, which made a great impression on me. It is the finest interior I have ever seen. We shall have a lovely trip leaving Cologne as I believe the train will go near the river Rhine. I had a conversation in the train with one of the leaders of the Rhine Sailors Trade Union — a very sensible clever, working-man who said he was a colleague of the leader of the German Communist party. He was a big internationalist. I enjoyed the journey, and I have had plenty of opportunity to speak German.

When we reached Frankfurt, we were met by number of German students who led us into tea in an impressive dining hall, and we were given a fine meal. We toured the old part of Frankfurt which was beautifully clean. It is the nicest town I have seen in Germany. The Römer, where the Holy Roman emperors were crowned, was most interesting. The houses in Frankfurt are charming. We climbed the cathedral, and went to a lot of fascinating museums, and finally the Goethe House. Then we had an excellent lunch in a room overlooking the Main in the very same room where Mendelssohn celebrated his engagement in 1837. We all stayed with the leading families of the town.

Karlsruhe performance was a great success, and the students gave us a hearty welcome. In each concert I have had to announce the changes in German, and I always acted as interpreter. The press notices of the concert were excellent, and we were given great praise. We were taken on a wonderful excursion by charabanc right into the Black Forest to a place called Württemberg. It was a beautiful ride.

We left Karlsruhe Station on Thursday July 5, 1928, to start off for Heidelberg where we had a further concert at night. The hall was almost packed. We had numerous receptions. The German students were tremendously grateful for the help received from the British students and did their outmost to pay us back. They made wonderful use of the money we gave them.

We have already been 14 days in Germany, and I leave for Leipzig on Saturday. I shall spend some time with the Haferkorns before returning home.

Notes on Chapter 4

1
   Gareth Vaughan Jones Papers, National Library of Wales. Correspondence Series 1-21, File 2. October 1927.

2
   Gareth Vaughan Jones Papers, National Library of Wales. Correspondence Series B6/1. October 23, 1927.

3
   Ibid. April 28, 1928.

Chapter 5

Final Year at Cambridge

1928-1929

Gareth returned to Trinity College on October 9, 1928, for his last year at Cambridge University. It was an important year, for not only did he wish to do well academically, but also there were consultative plans with his family as to his future career path. From the replies to his parents' letters, it appears that he was not always in agreement with them as what he should do with his life. Since his time in Strasbourg, Gareth had revelled in his frequent travels abroad, which gave him a much wider interest in world events. It was still his intention to seek a position within the diplomatic service, rather than follow in the footsteps of his father's cloistered world of academia. However, in contemplation, he wrote to his parents:

> *I thought a year ago that I should be miserable with a Tripos and a Civil Service examination to do, but strangely enough the effect is exactly the opposite. In spite of the foggy weather, which I don't really dislike, it is so nice to sit beside a fire. I am enjoying myself this term more than any time I had in Cambridge. One reason is probably the fact that I am a Scholar. In my first year, I had an undercurrent of fear all the time lest I should let Aber down and also lest I should not prove worthy of a Trinity Exhibition. The letter I wrote home after my French exam when I thought I had done so badly was probably an accumulation of those fears, which I believe I had been unconscious of most of the time.*[1]

During his first year Gareth remained faithful to his Welsh Calvinistic roots, and as a Methodist regularly attended the Welsh service in Wesley House. He was unsure of himself at Trinity Chapel and felt quite miserable and self-conscious whenever he attended the Anglican service not knowing when and where to go down on his knees. He longed for the end of Chapel because of his discomfiture. In the autumn term of his final year, Gareth met a bright and interesting young man, the Chaplain of Trinity who persuaded him to read in the early morning Trinity Chapel Service. Gareth wrote home:

> *I must really say I enjoy it. It makes me get up early and I feel fresh. Great Court and the Backs are in their glory at that time of the day and there is a very peaceful atmosphere in the Chapel, which takes you away from everyday thoughts. I shall continue early morning rising though there are very few peoples in Chapel at that time.*[2]

On March 1, Gareth tried to buy a small leek to wear on St David's day, but he was unable to find one so wore a daffodil instead. He had been elected Cambridge president of the Welsh Society and noted that the membership had gone up in number. The society invited Judge Ellis to lecture, who gave 'an excellent paper 'Hywel Dda's Laws,'[3] although it was technical and in legal language'.

Dinner at the Pitt Club. Gareth is standing, second from the left in the back row.

A close friend, Ludovik Stewart, son of Professor Stewart, arranged a dinner at the Pitt Club. Gareth described it as; "one of the jolliest and merriest dinner parties imaginable. The dinner was excellent, everyone was in a good humour, and story after story was told". All those present thought Gareth an excellent raconteur, and he thought this was funny, "because I can only tell stories to a few people and on a few occasions when I am in the mood." Gareth continued:

As we were having dinner in the elegant dining room of the Pitt, a Harrovian man came in whom I had often seen. 'Who is that man?' I asked. 'Oh, that's Tennant' said Berry. 'He's some relative of Asquith's [Prime Minister of Great Britain 1908-16] and the biggest snob in Trinity. There is a wonderful story about him. Some people in Pitt wanted to pull his leg. So, they called him and said, 'Come and join our new game.' You open the peerage book at any page, and the person who knows most peers must pay for drinks all round! And who had to pay for drinks all round? Of course! It was Tennant who knew all the peers!' And he had to pay for all the drinks, which was exactly what they wanted.[4]*

Gareth was a very popular student, and he had a wide circle of friends including a Russian by the name of Volkov. Gareth believed that Volkov must have been a noble, as he had been in the 'Adventurers' cavalry company that was described in Pyotr Krasnov's book *From Double Eagle to Red Flag*. Volkov recognised a number of officers in the book as his colleagues. Volkov was a supporter of the Secret Police and of the OGPU and considered that they are absolutely essential. He thought that the OGPU was much cleverer than the Secret Police, because it acted from the principle that everyone was suspect.

When Volkov, his mother, and a Russian girl came to tea, one part of conversation struck Gareth because it sounded just like a novel. They were talking about General Deniken, who was the Commander of the White Russians in the civil war against the Red Army in 1918-19, when the Russian girl said:

"They say Deniken killed Romantsov".
"No he didn't." Said Volkov.
"Why do you say that?" [said the girl.]
"Because I know who killed Romantsov", said Volkov.
-and then complete silence…[5]

Later that summer Gareth was to express compassion for the father of another of his Russian émigré friends:

Yesterday I met Reavney's father. His character was the saddest I have ever seen. He seemed a man who once was cheerful and humorous but had been absolutely crushed by life. He was once a flax specialist in Russia but was absolutely ruined by the Revolution and cannot find work. He had long white hair and his face was one of the palest I have ever seen. He made a deep impression on me by the sense of suffering he gave one and by his attempts to smile.[6]

Gareth took his studies very seriously but did not miss an opportunity to enjoy himself. He recounted an incident on a river trip with seven of his friends to Byron's Pool, just beyond Grantchester. According to Gareth, after they had eaten a picnic his college friends from Aberystwyth, Llywelfryn Davies and Gwyn Jones, said they would take the punt into deeper water while the others walked along The Backs. The punt was moored in a shallow spot and Gwyn Jones pushed with the pole; Llywelfryn Davies with the paddle. The punt swerved round but would not move forward. They redoubled their efforts but with no result. People gathered to watch them, and everybody laughed at the pair, as they were the only ones who did not realise that the punt was still tied to the bank.

Gareth had described an earlier humorous incident to his parents:

The ice is back again, and there is wonderful skating. We had a tremendous amount of fun yesterday. Ludovik [Stewart] took me in his car to Lingay fens. On the way, he called to take a girl he knew with us. Before going into the house, he said; 'let me introduce you as a Frenchman. What shall I call you?' 'Oh! Call me Count Louzac' I said. I was introduced as a Frenchman and was a great success. Ludovik's friend spoke French really quite well and I pretended to speak French as Pierre speaks English. She told Ludovik and Peter Lewis when I was skating far off. 'Your friend Count Louzac is an absolute dear. Where did you pick him up?'[7]

Gareth's last term at Cambridge was mainly occupied in studying for the Final examinations. He described the papers as 'splendid especially the history'. Despite the anxiety of the examinations Gareth had enjoyed his final term immensely.

On June 3, he wrote to his parents while sitting on The Backs (of the river Cam):

They are putting up the marquee for the Trinity Ball, which will altogether cost £3,000. Cambridge is quite a different place this week — 'May Week'[8]. There are hosts of cars, beautifully dressed people in evening dress and dinner jackets — all floating about the place.

Last night about 9.15, I heard a din on The Backs. I went out and saw the

Trinity group. Gareth is far right in the back row. Peter Lewis is in the centre and Ludovik Stewart is seated at the end of the front row.

first Trinity playing rounders! It is a tradition before the May races. Then they rushed along the Backs and upset the punt. All the men fell in the water. Two men started wrestling for fun on the bank and they fell in. Then another man dived in to rescue the cushions, which had fallen from the punt. A few minutes later about 20 men from another college dressed in evening dress, but with pyjama coats of different colours came along. They took a punt, started pushing each other about and some of them fell in.[9]

Gareth was invited through Gerald Graham to join the personal party of Mrs Fowler, daughter of the famous scientist Sir Ernest Rutherford, at the Trinity Ball at the end of term.[10] The two Chapple daughters (one of whom had been told that Gareth was Count Louzac) were Ludovik and Gareth's partners at the ball. Gareth described the May Ball setting as being:

unrecognisable; a tremendous marquee has been erected, and corridors are covered with awning stretching right from the Backs to the College. There are wonderful lighting effects, and the Backs look like a fairyland with thousands of coloured lights and Chinese lanterns…
…I looked quite elegant and wore a buttonhole of a red carnation. We first went to Mrs Fowler's house where there were eight of us for dinner, and

35

then we drove to Trinity. Hundreds of people stood around watching the guests arrive. The dance band conducted by Ambrose with at least twenty musicians was excellent and Ambrose, the great man himself signed my programme.[11] *Our party was extremely jolly, we danced all night; the refreshments and supper were perfect. We saw dawn come, and I managed to get to bed before seven o'clock.*[12]

Cambridge Trinity May Ball 1929. Gareth is seated in the front row to the right-hand side, between two girls

With Gareth's hard work at his studies throughout his time at Cambridge he eventually achieved his goal of First-Class Honours in German and Russian in the Medieval and Modern Language Tripos, Part II, with distinction in the oral examinations. He was also College Prizeman receiving the princely sum of £5 for the award. His parents were delighted with their son's success.

In the previous autumn of 1928, Gareth had looked up the Civil Service results, and noted that about ten or twelve candidates had been accepted to the Home Civil Service and seven for the Consular Service. He had consulted the Adviser on the Civil Service and asked him if he had a chance of a place and the reply was, "An excellent chance. You seem to be mopping up Firsts at a terrific rate, monopolising them in fact". So, Gareth sat the Consular exams after his finals. All had gone extremely well.

I did marvellously in the orals. I have never spoken French so fluently. The examiner was a charming man and knew some of my Strasbourg friends. I enjoyed it and when the 20 minutes were over the examiner said he was really sorry that our conversation had to come to an end. In the German oral I spoke all the time. The German fellow who examined me seemed so afraid of me that it gave me confidence. I spoke about the German youth movement without stopping for almost 20 minutes.[13]

Despite his apparent success neither Gareth nor any of the other students who had applied for the Consular or Diplomatic Service in 1929 were offered places by the Commission. Clearly hiding his disappointment, Gareth continued in the same letter:

You will be glad to hear that I shall never have to spend years in South America or Liberia, and that I shall probably spend a great part of my life in Britain or at least in Europe within a few hours flight of London. You will be sorry at the same time to hear that all this exam, all the preparation, the journey going to Strasbourg, all the money have been in vain because this morning I had a notification from the Civil Service Commission that there are No vacancies in General Levant Consular Services!!! The Commission informs the candidates of this fact… when the exams are nearly over. A Cambridge man I know, Cattle of Sidney, has been months in the hands of coaches. And when all the work is done and the £8 entry fee paid, Cattle and heaps of others are just told that there are no vacancies. Usually there are seven, eight, sometimes ten vacancies. It will be a big blow to a lot of candidates. Strangely enough I feel it is a relief more than anything else. Luckily, I have the chance of The Times post, but a lot of the others were relying on the Consular.[14]

With his ever-optimistic nature, a few days later Gareth was to write:

I am delighted not to be going into the Consular service. It would probably mean spending all my life in a place like Chile or Timbuktu or Belgium Congo and the prestige of the Service isn't so high as it used to be, so I think everything in the garden is lovely.

… Please don't forget to have a family group photo.[15]

The resulting family photo taken in Barry. [From left to right; Gwyneth, Annie Gwen, Edgar, Siriol, Gareth, Eirian and 'Aunty Winnie'.]

Gareth left Cambridge with the following glowing academic testimonial references from his College tutors:

Dr Stewart, Fellow of Trinity wrote:

> *Mr G.R.V. Jones, Scholar of this College is a young man of real ability and quite exceptional linguist. He is one of the most competent and satisfactory pupils that have passed through my hands. With nimbleness of mind and rapidity, he reached a high first class standard in every language he studied. His grasp of history and principles of literature is remarkable. He has a clever head and a retentive memory, and I have no doubt that whichever way he turns his intellectual attention he will succeed and reach a commanding position. His moral character is above reproach. He is exceedingly popular with his fellows and for responsibility. He has common sense and good humour and is delightful to work with.*[16]

Dr Breul, Fellow of King's College and his German Professor, wrote on July 29, 1929:

> *I have pleasure in testifying to Mr Gareth R.V. Jones of Trinity College, that I have known him well for several years and have formed a very high opinion of his character and abilities. He attended my University Lectures and my advanced*

Seminar and struck me as a very keen and intelligent student. Mr Jones understands and speaks German easily and has travelled extensively in Germany and German speaking countries. He is exceptionally well informed about modern German life and thought, politics, social and educational questions and conditions, and has been for several years in intimate touch with the "Youth Movement" in Germany and other continental movements. He has taken a deep and intelligent interest in international questions and was for a time Assistant Secretary to the Cambridge University League of Nations Union. Apart from his proficiency in German, he speaks French and Russian, and besides of his travels in German speaking countries, he has visited France, Switzerland, Poland, Czecho-Slovakia, Latvia and the Scandinavian countries and made a study of the conditions and characteristic features of these countries. I am convinced that either as Foreign Correspondent to a leading newspaper or as a member of the Consular Service, or working on the staff of the League of Nations, Mr Jones would be sure to do most valuable work, and I strongly recommend him for any post of this or a similar nature.

Notes on Chapter 5

1
  Gareth Vaughan Jones Papers, National Library of Wales. Correspondence Series 1-21, File 2
2
  Ibid. Correspondence Series B6/1. October 24, 1928.
3
  Hywel Dda (Hywel the Good) or Hywel ap Cadell (c. 880 - 950) was a King of Deheubarth who eventually came to rule most of Wales.
4
  Gareth Vaughan Jones Papers, National Library of Wales. Correspondence Series 1-21, File 2
5
  Ibid. Correspondence Series B6/2. May 25, 1928.
6
  Ibid. August 7, 1928.
7
  Ibid. February 26, 1929.
8
  Since the late 19th century the 'May Week' festivities at Cambridge have taken place in June after the end of exams.
9
  Gareth Vaughan Jones Papers, National Library of Wales. Correspondence Series 1-21, File 2. June 3, 1929.
10
  Ibid. Correspondence Series B6/2. April 26, 1929
11
  Bert Ambrose & His Orchestra was one of the top dance orchestras of the 1920-40s, with a residency at the Mayfair Hotel in London.
12
  Gareth Vaughan Jones Papers, National Library of Wales. Correspondence Series B6/2 June 13, 1929.
13
  Ibid. Correspondence Series B6/1. October 24, 1928.
14
  Ibid. August 7, 1929
15
  Ibid.
16
  Ibid. Correspondence Series 1-21 File 14. Dated June 1929.

Chapter 6

A Trial at *The Times*

Autumn 1929

Soon after finishing at Cambridge, Gareth attended a one month's trial with *The Times* in London. He was still without a guaranteed wage despite his excellent examination results. Nevertheless, with his usual buoyancy, he was quite hopeful of gaining employment with this prestigious newspaper. On August 27, 1929 he wrote:

> *My first night at The Times was intensely interesting, and I enjoyed the work immensely. My hours of work will be 5 pm to 12 am and Saturday will be a free day. I shall thus have to work on Sunday. Usually however I shall be able to leave soon after 11 o'clock, unless there is a lot to be done.*
>
> *You will be glad to see some of my work in The Times today. One of the items I arranged is entitled 'Attacks on women in Dusseldorf'. Another piece of my work is 'Paris-Warsaw Express Accident'. But I had better begin from the beginning.*
>
> *At one o'clock, I met Reinhard [he had just arrived in London on a tramp steamer from Germany] outside the British Museum and we had a lunch together in a splendid restaurant next door to the British Museum. The lunch was only 1/6 and was first-class. We had cheese soufflé, roast veal with bacon, roast potatoes and cabbage and sultana pudding. There was plenty of choice.*
>
> *After lunch I went to have my haircut and at 4.15, I stood outside The Times office. I strolled along to pass the time as far as Blackfriars station, but the minutes passed slowly. At 4.25 I entered the door of The Times and told the porter that I had to report to Mr Pearson at 4.30 in Room 1. An office boy took me up in a lift to the first storey and knocked at a door, which had Room 1 on it. We went into a place, which had a very large table in the middle and about eight chairs around it. In front of each chair, there was a green blotting pad with a book of white paper on it. All around there were guide-books, reference*

books, huge brown cutting books with 'RUSSIA', 'LEAGUE OF NATIONS', 'POLAND', 'CRIMINALS' and Atlases and Who's Whos of all the leading countries in the world.

A man with a beard, who made me think that he was from Devonshire — (I don't know why) and with a collar and tie which reminded me of Mr Frost, was standing near the door and came up smiling. He shook hands very warmly and asked me: 'Have you had tea? because I'm just going down to have some. We don't begin work in this department, which is the Imperial and Foreign Department until five o'clock. Come down and have some tea.' Then he said: 'My name is Cana. Mr Pearson is away this weekend, and I have to look after you until he returns next Monday.' Mr Cana seemed a very kind-hearted old boy. He took me through the corridors, across a court, where plays used to be performed in the reign of Queen Elizabeth, and finally we got to a room furnished in a very old-fashioned way, like a dining-room in a commercial travellers' hotel. The room was not big, but the table in the middle was round and vast. On the walls, there were old photographs and caricatures.

It was 5 o'clock. There were three other men besides Mr Cana and myself having tea. One said: 'I have no idea what I shall write a leader about. I think I shall write something on floods and droughts.'

They talked about the riots in Jerusalem.[1] 'Did you see the letter from Mr '___' [intentionally unnamed] Special Correspondent in the Near East) this morning? I was very surprised that he referred to some Jews as 'loudly dressed in gents' natty sports suits.' It doesn't sound like a Times correspondent.'

Everybody had a sense of humour and they took the news very lightly. Then Mr Cana and I returned to room number one; a man was writing in shirtsleeves on the 'Wailing Wall'. Mr Cana told me to take the seat next to him and handed me a long telephone message from the Riga correspondent. 'Our Riga correspondent has an abominable style. Just lick that into respectable English.'

The man in the shirtsleeves turned to me and said: "I'm sub-editing. You must begin from the principle that all our foreign correspondents except one, write abominably. And, by the way, you'll be much more comfortable if you take your coat off."

Telegrams and telephone messages kept arriving. They were either brought by messengers or fell through a tube into a message-receiver. I had to write out two telegrams. One about Ambassadors in Constantinople, another about Rykoff.

'What rotters those Evening Standard people are!' said the Wailing Wall man. 'They have pinched our map of Jerusalem without acknowledgement. We'll get 5 guineas out of them.'

At about 11.15 pm, I was told I could go. I walked down Fleet Street with
an Australian also on trial. Then I turned up Chancery Lane into Holborn,
Gray's Inn Road, got into bed and slept well.[2]

The trial period finished on the September 20, 1929, and Gareth and the
Australian, Hood, were told that Barrington-Ward would let them know his decision. There had been a dozen people on trial during the summer. Gareth said he
would not have missed the experience for the world that it had been most enjoyable,
and that the Times' men were splendid people.[3] On the last night Gareth was called
in by a very tired man called Graves, who had been writing a leader all the evening.
He said Gareth showed great promise, but he lacked journalistic experience. The
policy of *The Times* was not to take men who had no previous experience. Gareth
was advised to spend a year on a provincial newspaper. There would then be a good
chance of being accepted by the newspaper.[4]

So Gareth was still without employment, but a few days later Dr Stewart offered
him a post to remain at Trinity College, Cambridge as a coach. This he accepted. His
scholarship would be renewed at £100, and he would be able to make about £100 by
coaching. The post would be temporary. He attended an interview with Sir Bernard
Pares of the School of Slavonic and East European Studies with whom he spent a
number of hours at lunch discussing Russian history. Sir Bernard gave him a subject
for his Ph.D thesis, "The Russian Press during the Revolution". Gareth was then
given a bibliography, and a pile of Russian newspapers to commence his research.[5]

Despite having been turned down for a Civil Service post in the summer, Gareth
received an urgent letter from the Civil Service Commission asking him to report
at his own expense to be medically examined on October 7, 1929. Gareth quoted
part of the letter from the Commission to his family, setting out the conditions for
acceptance before telling them that he had declined the offer:

'You will be required to pay a fee of two guineas to the medical examiner. By
declining an existing vacancy in the Consular service, a candidate removes his
name from the list of that Service.' Therefore, by declining China and Japan I
remove my name from the list of the Consular Service. That is what they told
me in the Foreign Office. I replied I cannot attend for the medical as I have
accepted another position.[6]

Gareth received another disappointment when he discovered that the estimate
of £350, which he had been expecting for his coaching in German, was far too

optimistic. 16 pupils had been transferred to another man for supervision, which meant Gareth would earn £32 per term less than he had expected. He only had 13 girls from Newnham, the Women's College to coach. Nevertheless, Gareth promised to repay his parents the £40.14s.0d. that he owed them from his earnings.[7]

Gareth soon settled down into the academic life that he had previously resisted. He said in his usual cheerful way that everything was going along splendidly. He acquired a number of effects for his room, intending to remain for some time. He sent home for some etchings; one of Oxford was by a family friend, Fred Richards. Dr Stewart lent him a huge picture of Queen Victoria, an etching that used to hang in the Lodge and had been presented to him by the late master, Dr Butler. Gareth reflected on his current lot in life, "it is very comfortable on my sofa in front of a blazing fire and far better than being in a lonely flat in Wei-ha-wei or Tokyo or in the sub-editors' room of *The Times* on a Sunday evening."[8]

His cosy life in academia was to prove short-lived because a family friend Dr Thomas Jones, CH, who was deputy British Cabinet Secretary, introduced him to David Lloyd George, the former Prime Minister on October 21, 1929. This was to become the turning point in Gareth's life.

> *Just a rapid note before the 12 o'clock post. Mr Lloyd George has offered me either a 12-month or a 6-month trial and said he wouldn't think of giving me less than £400 per year. I am to decide before next Wednesday, and I feel tempted to take it for six months for the following reasons. It is exactly the subject I am interested in, I shall gain varied experience, and the salary is excellent. It will not debar me from trying the Diplomatic Service again in August if I get another interview. I can continue on with research as I shall be resident in London and should be able to join the London University to take my Ph.D., though I am not really keen on Academic work permanently. I am free to the drop the post should I not like the position*
>
> *Mr Lloyd George praised very highly the notes I had to write on Germany. He was very pleased with them and said that he had learnt a great deal from reading them. I wrote on the 'present political situation in Germany', a kind of trial run. Everything was done for me; a fine room was put at my disposal with Asquith's picture on one wall.*
>
> *I feel therefore very keen trying for six months, but I do not want to decide anything before getting your advice. So, will you please write and let me know everything you think. Lloyd George looked tired and said in Welsh, 'Mae eich Tad a Mam yn Cymory da' [Your mother and father are good Welsh people].*[9]

On the following day, October 22nd, Gareth sent a further rushed note:

Thank you very much for your telegram. I hope you will finally agree that I shall do well to accept a six-month trial. Dr Stewart said that he was sorry I would have to leave Trinity, but that it was an offer I could not possibly refuse. He said it was an opening for many things.

I must be a very calm and balanced character, because all this bustle and deciding does not affect me in the slightest. It does not worry me at all, because I know that I am pretty sure of having a good post, and that I have a cheerful disposition. I can be happy whatever I am doing.

Lloyd George said I would be stationed in London and would have to prepare notes for debates in the house, for his articles and his speeches. It is funny to think so, but I would have an influence on Foreign Affairs through Lloyd George. I shall probably have to go abroad now and then.[10]

Events and decisions were moving rapidly, and on October 28, 1929, Gareth posted another rushed letter from Trinity College, replying to his very concerned parents:

I have definitely decided to accept Lloyd George's offer. Everybody in Cambridge is absolutely unanimous in advising me to accept. I am going to accept six-month's trial beginning on January 1.

Please do not worry about it. It is not going into politics, and I shall not bind myself to any fixed political rules. Therefore, I shall be able to be independent and non-political. At the end of six months, I shall be entirely free to do what I like. Think of Sir Edward Grigg. He was Lloyd George's secretary up to a few years ago and he is now Governor of Kenya. Sir Edward is not politically labelled. I am very fond of Cambridge, but I shall be better off in London on £400 than in Cambridge. It is also the work that Philip Kerr did.[11]

Two days later, a telegram arrived from A. J. Sylvester, Lloyd George's secretary informing Gareth that his salary would be £500, and it was decided that Gareth would take up his position as Foreign Affairs Adviser on New Year's Day, 1930.

Notes on Chapter 6

1
The Times August 26, 1929. Riots were reported at the Wailing Wall in Jerusalem when Muslims came out of the walled City attacked the Jewish quarters. The Wall itself and the surrounding pavement were actually the property of the Muslims. On 28 August there were further riots, and, in total, 83 Jews and 36 Arabs were killed.

2
Gareth Vaughan Jones Papers, National Library of Wales. Correspondence Series B6/2 August 27, 1929.

3
Ibid. September 19, 1929.

4
Ibid. September 22, 1929.

5
Ibid. September 24, 1929.

6
Ibid. October 8, 1929

7
Ibid. October 13, 1929.

8
Ibid. October 20, 1929.

9
Ibid. October 21, 1929.

10
Ibid. October 22, 1929.

11
Ibid. October 28, 1929. Philip Kerr was private secretary to Lloyd George between 1916-20. He became 11th Marquess of Lothian in 1930.

PART 2

Lloyd George's Secretariat (1930-31)

Chapter 7

The First Month

Considering the international economic depression that had begun in 1929, Gareth was fortunate to secure a well-paid position with David Lloyd George. His happy carefree student life was over. Gone were the days of college pranks, the humorous lunches and the convivial tea parties. Before leaving Trinity College he purchased a bowler hat and acquired a rolled-up umbrella, the essential apparel for a London City gentleman. He would no longer wear the grey flannels and the sports jacket so favoured by Cambridge undergraduates. Gareth still met his friends for a quiet lunch at such places as Craig's Court in Whitehall, but the dinner parties were more serious, and did not echo with laughter as they did in Cambridge. He would soon be at ease with the men of influence and the academics of London, but his humour would become more subtle. He was delighted to accept the responsible appointment of Foreign Affairs Adviser to his boyhood idol, David Lloyd George, who was to keep him fully occupied researching briefs on current political problems.

On Wednesday, January 1, 1930, Gareth took the underground to St James' Park and then walked to his office at Old Queen Street, Westminster, for his first day at work. Mr Malcolm Thomson explained to him the workings of the office. There were two sections; personal staff of which he was a member, and the campaign staff or what remained of it. Gareth was shown his room and settled down quickly. On his desk was a memorandum written by two Croat politicians appealing for a better treatment of their citizens, which had just been presented to Lloyd George, the Prime Minister, Mr Ramsay MacDonald and the Foreign Secretary, Mr Arthur Henderson.

The following morning, Mr Sylvester, Lloyd George's Secretary, informed Gareth that Lloyd George had an article to write on India's demands for Independence for the Daily Mail. "Will you prepare a brief on this before 6 o'clock tonight?"[1]

To complete this task, Gareth studied the newspaper reports on the All-India Congress at Lahore, which expressed doubt that the Labour Government would honour its pledge to India of eventual Dominion status. Hastily, Gareth prepared the cuttings about India and then went along to the RIIA (Royal Institute for International Affairs) to collate some more information. There, he spoke to Mr Zimmern, a former Aberystwyth professor of Law, who was pleased to offer some 'sound advice'. Zimmern believed Lloyd George's December 4 disarmament speech in Parliament was a great mistake:

> *You can't make the French disarm by attacking them. You merely create the*
> *wrong impression implying that these armaments are worthwhile and are useful.*
> *In France they say: 'C'est seulement Lloyd George!' [It's only Lloyd George].*
> *Lloyd George has been too rash in his articles and has aroused distrust in many*
> *countries. He does not weigh up sufficiently the consequences of his words upon*
> *other countries.*

Mr Zimmern also impressed upon Gareth the responsibility of his position with Lloyd George but, on the subject of India, he was not very enlightening. Returning from the RIIA he found on the table a note marked: "'Important'. Mr Lloyd George wants you to see Lord Meston[2] and get his views, so as to include them in your brief." After some difficulty, Gareth contacted Lord Meston at his Holborn office, the Calcutta Electrical Supply Company, and arranged to meet him at Lloyd George's office.

A little before five o'clock, the messenger boy knocked and announced the arrival of Lord Meston, who Gareth described as "a youngish-looking man [who] came in acting with pleasant manners; at home and at ease". Gareth explained that Lloyd George required some information on India by that evening. Meston, who was Chairman of the Joint Indian Committee of both Houses of British Parliament, expounded his views on Gandhi's influence and the future of India for Gareth's brief. He feared a second Amritsur, a lot of sporadic trouble, but he hoped the government would be firm.

On his first Saturday at work, on arrival at the office, Miss Frances Stevenson telephoned Gareth to tell him that Mr Lloyd George wanted to see him in his room. He met Lloyd George's assistant and former tutor to his daughter Megan, Miss Stevenson, whom he thought was pleasant although he was later to note in his diary "Mae Mrs Lloyd George a Megan yn cashau ysgrifennyddes Lloyd George, Miss Stevenson." [Mrs Lloyd George and Megan (Lloyd George's daughter) do not like Miss Stevenson.]

While he was waiting, Dr Macnamara, a former Cabinet Minister, came in, a 'jolly fellow' who called Gareth "Old Boy," when he offered to take his coat! He seemed very friendly with Miss Stevenson; they had been to 'Iolanthe' the night before. The doctor seemed a great talker, and they discussed singing — Trinity Madrigal Club and folk songs. Soon Lloyd George opened his door, and greeted Gareth with "Happy New Year," but then it was soon to work. Lloyd George said: "I have to write an article for the *Daily Mail*. I'm sorry now [that] I have promised. *The Manchester Guardian* has a very good article today, saying that we shall have to let go of India. I've no doubt that we shall have to someday. But I can't take that line".

Lloyd George seemed hesitant about what line to take. Gareth read him the important part of Lord Meston's views. Later, he was asked to prepare the figures on the number of 'Mohammedans and Hindus', to get the figure of races and religious languages in India and China and the number of people under the rule of the Princes. Gareth had a great deal of difficulty finding the facts and rang the RIIA, the High Commissioner for India and the Chinese Legation, for help. Finally, he gathered all the necessary background research and took them across to Lloyd George's town house in Addison Road, riding upstairs of an open-top bus in the rain!

When Lloyd George had completed his *Daily Mail* article on India, Miss Edwards, the typist, brought it in for Gareth to read. Gareth thought it was on the whole disappointing, although sound in the last paragraph. The article contained an attack on Wedgwood Benn, which Gareth considered in poor taste for the 'great statesman', a veiled attack on Lord Irvine, the Viceroy of India, stating that he ought to command more support from politicians. A paragraph on Mr Stanley Baldwin, the former Conservative Prime Minister, gave the impression that the British leaders were muddled and confused. Gareth mentioned his considered views to Miss Stevenson when she asked him what he thought of the article. He added that he was surprised Lloyd George did not bring in Ireland, as this would suggest to the British public that since (in Gareth's opinion) Lloyd George had solved the Ireland problem, so he could solve the India problem as well.

Gareth also discussed his concerns about his brief on India, and his other research work, with Sylvester who told him that it was most difficult to persuade Lloyd George to do things that he should. He was impatient and inattentive when Sylvester talked about subjects that Lloyd George was not interested in, and he always wanted everything done at short notice.

Returning to his room, another secretary, Miss Magda Gellan, came in, and to Gareth's surprise, told him that Miss Stevenson had repeated all that he had said to Lloyd George. In confidence, Miss Stevenson had said that Gareth was disappointed with the article. Lloyd George had replied rather gruffly, "Oh IS he!" Miss

Gellan said that everything mentioned to Miss Stevenson went straight back to Lloyd George, and counselled silence as the best policy.

Nonetheless Miss Stevenson soon telephoned Gareth to come and see her. She informed him that Lloyd George wanted to know what newspapers he was scanning for news. His employer was clearly not satisfied with the number, so in future the Gareth would have to read seven French, one Swiss, two Italian, three German, four Russian and the *Chicago Tribune*. In addition, he had to write a weekly report on the foreign and Welsh Press.

No sooner had Gareth finished one brief than there was further work to do. He found there was a note from Sylvester awaiting him when he arrived at the office. On January 6, 1930, a Syro-Palestinian delegation had written a letter to Lloyd George drawing attention to the pledges made to the Arabs during the First World War, and stating that the Balfour Declaration was in total opposition to these pledges. It pointed out that: "the Mandate was in opposition to Article 22 of the Covenant. The enquiry Commission suggested in Balfour, Lloyd George and Smuts' letter to *The Times* could merely aggravate the position. Why were pledges to the Jews honoured and those to Arabs disregarded?" Sylvester wished him to study the letter in *The Times*.[3]

Around the same time Miss Stevenson told Gareth that Mr Lloyd George was preparing an article on the prospects of the London Naval Conference. "Would Gareth prepare a brief before his return tomorrow evening?" On the following day, he arrived in the office early, and started work on the "Prospects of Five Power Conference". He telephoned the *Chicago Daily News* offices, and asked for Mr Constantine Brown, the London correspondent, who said he would be glad to see him. Gareth immediately rushed to the newspaper office and found 'a friendly man — easy to get on with, frank, and willing to give his views'. Brown said he had great admiration for Lloyd George. It was in Brown's office, that the then Prime Minister, Ramsay MacDonald's visit to America had been suggested and arranged. The newspaperman was apparently a close friend of Mr MacDonald and General Charles Dawes. Brown gave his views:

> *MacDonald wants to go down in history as the greatest British Prime Minister for centuries. President Hoover is set upon the success of the Conference; therefore, there is bound to be some result. It will probably not be a Five Power, but three Powers [excluding France and Italy] or even a Two Power agreement. [Confidentially] MacDonald has made many blunders and so have the Americans."*

This is the last chance Great Britain has of sharing the supremacy of the seas with the United States. If you miss that chance, then America will rule the waves and no more Britannia. The Japanese ratio [of capital ships] is a matter between Great Britain and the United States. The US is willing to drop the abolition of submarines. Italy and France will never come to an agreement. Conflict in the Mediterranean is extremely possible. America will never join in a Mediterranean Pact. I told General Dawes that the Freedom of the Seas must be settled before there can be any reduction. He said, "Don't touch it." I told him they were putting the cart before the horse. I said, "You must settle the Freedom of the Seas." but obviously I am a darned fool.[4]

After the interview, Gareth rushed back to the office in a taxi, and immediately dictated Constantine Brown's appraisal, as there were urgent instructions that the brief was to await Lloyd George at Euston station on his return from Wales. Four typists were busy doing the work. He managed to get it finished and Philo, the messenger, called in at Gareth's room to fetch the completed brief — and was just in time to meet the arrival of the Welsh train.

On January 15, 1930, Gareth lunched at Craig's Court with two friends of his father — Dr Thomas Jones (formerly Cabinet Secretary to Lloyd George and who had introduced Gareth to Lloyd George), and Sir Percy Watkins who had lectured to the University of Cambridge Welsh Society just before Gareth graduated. Tom Jones, as he was often known, was keen to discover the contents of Gareth's brief for the forthcoming Naval Conference.[5]

On Monday, January 20, a few minutes before 10 o'clock, Gareth saw the delegates of the Naval Conference entering 10 Downing Street — the French, Briand and Tardieu; the Japanese, Watsuki; the American, Stimson; the Italian, Grandi, whom Gareth described as, "sly, with cunning little eyes, and a pointed beard" and finally the Canadian delegates. After lunch, Gareth went to hear Lloyd George's speech, which he described as a masterpiece of restraint, humour and wit. Lloyd George made an appeal to Lord Grey to help the Liberals and realised that the three-party system (Labour, Conservative and Liberal) had come to stay. Gareth was disappointed not to be personally present at the proceedings of the Conference, as the places for journalists were limited to 20.

The following day, in his letter home, Gareth noted there was a thick London fog:

I groped my way along the railings of St James' Park; ventured across the Mall, arrived far right of the steps [in the Mall] and finally got to the RIIA to hear the King, whose diction was excellent, speak on the Naval Conference. I heard MacDonald, Stimson, Tardieu. The fog was worse than night, but after the lunch it suddenly cleared.[6]

In his next letter, he related:

Miss Stevenson told me on Friday that Mr Lloyd George was very pleased with my brief on the Naval Conference. I have settled down very quickly and feel quite at home and get on very well with everybody. You'll be tickled to hear that I have my own secretary now; Miss Edwards who does my typing, stamps my letters. I dictate to her and she does my cuttings, etc... She is the typist who does Lloyd George's articles. She answers the phone for me when I am away.[7]

Later in the month, Lloyd George saw Gareth and asked, "Have you been following the Conference in the French Press?" "Yes, Sir." "Do you think they'll stick to their guns?" Gareth replied, "Definitely, I think they would keep to their guns." Later David Lloyd George was to say, "The Naval Conference is a farce, an absolute farce!"

Gareth was given some free time from work and wrote, "Yesterday I had the morning off and I enjoyed myself skating in Hammersmith." He lunched with Reavney, Norton, Pentland and other old Cambridge friends at a favourite restaurant.

Gareth had continued his friendship with the Russian émigrés, Volkov and his mother. He met Volkov's father, Admiral Volkov, who usually resided in Paris (whom he had wrongly presumed was dead), describing him as, "a fine-looking military man with a hard face and grey hair". Gareth met many fascinating Russians at the Volkovs' home in London and the conversation was often in Russian, which he remarked as always interesting and sometimes strange.

Irina Suyatoslavna Wolodimeroff, a singer, invited Gareth to join a group attending the Russian Ball. In the party were Sandra Volkov, her daughter Alice, and a Mr Lees Smith, First Secretary at the British Legation in Belgrade. Gareth observed "Alice Volkov danced perfectly and was very pretty. Had it not been for the Revolution she would have been one of the beauties of the Russian Court."[8]

According to Gareth's diary there were many pleasant faces at the ball and the costumes were lovely, especially those of the Boyar, Cossack and peasant. The entertainment was 'splendid'. After the dance, Irina, Alice and Gareth returned to Alice's house, near Kensington Gardens, where they had tea. Gareth was struck by some interesting photos in the room. All were signed. Gareth described them as being that of the Grand Duke Nicholas wearing a gold crown, of the Grand Duchess Helen, of Anastasia, and of Admiral Kolchak. One he noted was a woman with striking face, perfect features, but hard and domineering. Irina told him "it was one of Princess Yussopov, the most beautiful woman she had ever seen. She was the niece of the Emperor and daughter of Prince Yussopov who had killed Rasputin." Irina said that she hated Prince Yussopov, and she thought that Rasputin ought to have been killed, but to put poison in his cup was not the way to do it.[9]

Back at the office, Gareth commenced a brief on the Russian Five-Year Plan. At Charing Cross, he met Nicolai Yemshikov from the Soviet Embassy and they dined at Le Dîner Française. Gareth listened to Yemshikov attentively; describing it as one of the most interesting conversations he had ever heard. Yemshikov said:

> So far, the Five-Year Plan has been a success. But oppression in Russia is terrible; much worse than before the revolution. There are numbers of Chekists (secret police) in London; in the Foreign Office, in Scotland Yard, everywhere. If the Cheka knew I was dining with a Secretary of Mr Lloyd George, I would be imprisoned when I returned to Russia. If it were known that I was acquainted with the Volkovs, I would be shot.

Yemshikov asked Gareth "not to mention his name to anyone. The OGPU had great power. If Lloyd George went to Russia he would be entertained royally, but if he [Lloyd George] went to see any old friends they would be arrested as soon as he left."[10]

Gareth noted Yemshikov's views in his diary:

> The standard of life in Russia was being reduced in order get money to buy exports; that there was great suffering; only children were allowed milk; a grown-up was allowed two eggs per week. A peasant revolt was possible, but the Soviet Government had aeroplanes, troops, and guns; everything to crush it.[11]

A week later, so as not to be overheard, Gareth strolled through St James' Park conversing with Yemshikov. The Russian was afraid since he was not a Communist that he might lose his job and that it would be given to a party member. Confidentially, he told Gareth:

> England is encouraging a separatist movement in the Ukraine, Turkestan and the Caucasus. There will be Civil War in Russia if this continues. There is

a rumour that the Foreign Secretary is giving money to Ukraine and Caucasian separatists. The Ukrainian propaganda is far cleverer than Russian propaganda and is much more active. I hate the Bolsheviks, but if there were a War between the Bolsheviks and the Ukrainians I would fight for the Bolsheviks. Riga is absolutely pro-Russia and the Latvians would not mind coming back to Russia, though they do fear the Bolsheviks. The Russian peasants understood Lenin, but they did not understand Milyukov. If Lenin only had crossed himself, and worshipped God the peasant would have followed him en masse. Many Jews say they are Communists in order to obtain a post. My daughter may find it difficult to get into university, because preference is being given to the children of Communists. Some peasants may be willing to join the Collective Farms to get the grain, but when the crops come, they say, "Oh no, this corn is ours."[12]

Returning to the RIIA after his conversation with Mr Yemshikov, Gareth continued to work on his brief about the Five-Year Plan. In the evening he listened to a stirring account in the RIIA lecture hall of how America was trading with Russia and how the Five-Year Plan would to be a tremendous success. During the discussion following the lecture, a gentleman whom Gareth guessed was Mr Metcalf, a director of the large British engineering firm, Vickers, made an emotional speech, and Gareth asked him, whether he had written on the need for Export Credits.

The following morning Gareth made a point of interviewing Mr Vickers in Vickers House, who told him that £2,000,000 of Soviet orders had gone to other countries, because the Government would not guarantee 60% to 80% credit. This was mainly due to the disastrous breakdown in Russo-British diplomatic relations (caused in 1927 by the MI5 instigated police raid at the offices of Arcos Ltd, a company that had been suspected of spying for the Soviets).

Gareth had a long talk with Mr Somerville, the Head of the Russian Department in the Office of the American Commercial Attaché, who told Gareth that his outlook for Russian trade was not optimistic. He disagreed entirely with his fellow American, the journalist, Louis Fischer, who had been gripped by the enthusiasm of Moscow. The Americans had no faith in the Five-Year Plan. The Russian Department of Regional Division of Commerce in the US did not advise firms to lengthen credits to the US. He did not believe, like Fischer, in the stability of the Soviet Regime and he considered the Five-Year Plan might eventually crash.

Gareth regularly met Sir Bernard Pares at the School of Slavonic and East European Studies and clearly enjoyed his intellectual company whilst they discussed Soviet literature and politics. However, Pares was most dissatisfied with the little work

Gareth had so far done for his doctoral thesis. On the subject of the Five-Year Plan, Pares was most indignant about Stalin's oppression of the kulaks. He said that Lloyd George should protest against the enslavement of liberty. The new policy towards the peasants was the reintroduction of serfdom and Pares criticised the armchair economists like Maurice Dobb.

As an aside, on one occasion when he called on Sir Bernard Pares, he met a well-known writer and lecturer of Russian literature, Prince Mirsky. (After a privileged Russian upbringing, Mirsky had converted to Communism and following a decade of exile in London, returned to the Soviet Union in 1932. He was permitted to write for five years but was arrested in 1937 during Stalin's Terror and eventually died in a gulag in 1939.)

Gareth found his work varied but interesting, and continued to widen his sphere of political knowledge, through his research on other briefs which he was undertaking for the former Prime Minister. He called on Professor Seto-Watson to enquire into the 'Macedonian problem and Yugo-Slavia'. He visited the Polish Embassy, where a Mr Skokowski introduced him to Count Potocki, a 'tall aristocratic looking young man, and a member of one of Poland's aristocratic families. Gareth was informed that Lloyd George's prejudice against Poland had originated through the bad personal relations between the Polish leader, Roman Dmovski[13] and Lloyd George during the Versailles Peace Conference. The Count asserted that Lloyd George had failed to give the Poles moral support against the Bolsheviks.

Gareth arranged to call at the Czechoslovakian Legation, and was taken up to see Mr Hyka, First Secretary, whom he described as, "not so diplomatic looking as Mr Skokowski of the Polish Embassy". He gave the Gareth many books and explained the favourable position of the German minority in Czechoslovakia. He was indignant that Lloyd George had called his country: "a vassal state of France. Czecho-Slovakia was quite independent, but of course their interests in many ways went hand in hand".

The ever-demanding Lloyd George requested information on diverse topics, and he wished to write an article on the "Fall of Primo de Rivera" (Miguel, Second Marquis de Estella). Gareth prepared a brief on the "Fall of the Spanish Dictator." and when it was ready, he took it up to Miss Stevenson. By the next day, Lloyd George wanted to see him. The Spanish memorandum was returned by Lloyd George, 'well-marked'. Gareth was quite pleased by one phrase he had written in the brief, "the problems which confront statesmen change from decade to decade, but the qualities of leadership are constant."

On February 2nd 1930, Gareth wrote:

> *My first month is over and I am delighted with it and highly satisfied with everything; no work could suit me better or make me happier. I can't think how I possibly thought of going on as a don all my life. Last Tuesday, Lord Astor introduced General Smuts by saying: "General Smuts might have been many things. He was at Cambridge and could have stayed there all his life as a don." "What a prospect!" interrupted General Smuts.[14]*

Despite Gareth's new job, his family in Barry were concerned for his welfare. Aunt Winnie was sending him regular parcels of homemade cakes that he kept in his office drawer to have a slice with his tea. His anxious mother wrote to ask him to find a secure job with a pension in the field of academia. His parents' life revolved around the narrow sphere of a scholastic life; safe but limited in its outlook. Gareth reminded his mother that she had left Wales in her 'teens to go to Russia, and that his father had been plucky on the football field, that he loved his work so much that the only single drawback to his post was the fact that his parents worried about his future.

His spirited reply continued:

> *And now for my future.*
>
> *I should consider myself a flabby little coward if I ever gave up the chance of a good and interesting career for the mere thought of safety. I have no respect for any man whose acceptance or judgment of a post depends on the answer to the question: Will it give me a pension? Is it safe? And I have not the slightest desire to be a lecturer for all the safety and security in the world. No man ever got on or did the slightest bit of good by putting the L.s.d., [pound, shillings and pence] he will receive at the age of 60 before considerations of public good, love of work, overwhelming interest; and to think of myself spending my life talking about German literature in which I have not the slightest interest saying the same thing every week, every year, makes me prefer any kind of adventure with a little excitement into how the world moves.*
>
> *A term in one of the greatest universities of the world was quite enough for me — although I enjoyed the experience, what would it be like in some provincial university like Manchester where I should be finally stuck?*
>
> *I have come to the conclusion that the only life I can live with interest, and which I can really be of use is one connected with foreign affairs and with men and women of today; not with the writers of two centuries ago.*

You talk of anxiety about my future? If I got drunk, you would be justified. If I ran from one stage door to another there would be some cause for anxiety. If I had been sent down from Cambridge, if I'd had a Third. If I had no testimonials, if people disliked me and if I were easily depressed and always unhappy, if I'd stolen something, then I should quite understand your position. If there were no hope for the future, if I were earning about £3 — £4 per week- and millions of people can get no work- then you'd be right in being unhappy.

Tell me why you have no confidence in my future? Why do you want a son of yours to have no courage and just stick in the mud, for the feeling of security?

Security? Wasn't I offered a post in the Consular service? Then immediately after wasn't I made a supervisor in TRINITY COLLEGE, CAMBRIDGE? Then a couple of weeks later I was offered a post of great responsibility at £500 per year. How many people in Cambridge got £500 a year straight after leaving? You may not think much of my job, but in the view of people in Cambridge and in the RIIA it is most important. It brings me in touch with people of international repute.

Notes on Chapter 7

1
Gareth Vaughan Jones Papers, National Library of Wales. Correspondence Series 1-21, File 18 January 5, 1930.

2
The Rt. Hon. The Lord Meston of Agra and Dunottar: The dispute with regard to the number of seats to be reserved for Non-Brahmins in the Legislative Council led to the appointment of Lord Meston as Arbitrator. He gave the award which secured 28 reserved seats for non-Brahmins. In 1925, Lord Meston was elected Chairman of the Joint Indian Committee of both Houses of British Parliament.

3
On December 20, 1929, *The Times* printed a letter from Balfour, D Lloyd George and J C Smuts, "The Balfour Declaration of 12 years ago pledged a Policy of a home for the Jews" and the letter showed anxiety for the present situation. "The Palestine Mandate entrusted the Government with vital administrative duties but the causes of which are still obscure and have impeded the task of administration and consequently the full carrying out of the policies." The letter "urged the Government to appoint an authoritative Commission to investigate the whole working of the mandate. The present commission has limited terms of reference and considerable readjustment of the machine was desirable.

4
Gareth Vaughan Jones Papers, National Library of Wales. Correspondence Series B6/2.

5
Gareth recorded the following anecdote -Tom Jones was going to give a lecture on "the 15 most decisive books he had read". When he asked George Bernard Shaw for his thoughts, he replied; "Well, there's half a dozen of mine to begin with!"

6
  Gareth Vaughan Jones Papers, National Library of Wales. Correspondence Series B6/2. January 21, 1930.

7
  Ibid. January 26, 1930.

8
  Ibid. January 15, 1930.

9
  Gareth Vaughan Jones Papers, National Library of Wales Diary Series B1/3.

10
  After a five-day visit to Ukraine in August 1933, the former French Premier, Herriot's interpreter, Professor Seeberg of the Ukrainian College of Linguistic Education in Kiev, was reported to have been arrested and sentenced to five years in a Karelian camp for 'close connections' with the Frenchman..

11
  Gareth Vaughan Jones Papers, National Library of Wales Diary Series B1/3.

12
  Ibid.

13
  Roman Dmovski. Leader of the Duma in Poland. David Lloyd George said of him; "Dmovski is a fool and the most dangerous of fools is a clever fool."

14
  Gareth Vaughan Jones Papers, National Library of Wales. Correspondence Series B6/2. February 2, 1930.

Chapter 8

Spring in Old Queen Street

After his first month Gareth was still enjoying his work despite the heavy demands from Lloyd George. Gareth regularly attended the House of Commons where he was given a ticket to the Special Gallery from the Liberal Whip's runner. One evening Gareth went to Sylvester's room at the House to talk over a proposed scheme for foreign policy. Sylvester commented, "The Americans were rapidly ousting our trade in South America". At that juncture, Winston Churchill came in and said, "Is he back yet?" "No, Sir. There's a party meeting, but he'll be back before long". replied Sylvester. "And soon we heard Lloyd George's voice and heard a loud discussion between Winston Churchill and Lloyd George."

On February 12, 1930:

> I rang Sir Percy Watkins who had previously phoned me. He asked me to call at the Board of Trade at ten to four. I went, and he explained to me that the Elphin Jones Memorial Fund Committee was meeting in the House of Commons in Mr Baldwin's room where we were introduced to Lord Astor, Sir Geoffrey Fry, (the Permanent Secretary to the Prime Minister), Dr Thomas Jones and Mr James Morton were there.
>
> I liked Baldwin very much. He was very witty. I naturally said nothing all the time and when Dr T.J. announced in proposing me as secretary that I had only heard about it a half-hour before. He said, "Well, he kept the secret very well."
>
> When one clause was being considered — that persons should be eligible whose course of study had been interrupted by economic or other causes, Mr Baldwin asked, "Does that include being sent down." Afterwards I had a chat with Stanley Baldwin.[1]

On Monday, February 17, 1930, Miss Stevenson rang Gareth at 10.20 am saying that Mr Lloyd George wanted the latest facts about the persecution of religion in

Russia. Lloyd George was going to see the Soviet Ambassador on Thursday, but it was to be kept secret, and Gareth was asked: "Would I go and see Dr Rushbrooke, the Secretary of the Baptist World Alliance?" Dr Rushbrooke, an English Non-conformist, whom Gareth considered a tolerant and broadminded man, invited him to lunch. Gareth was given the sad details about the sufferings of Baptists in Russia. He was shown a letter written by a Baptist that had been smuggled across the frontier and had been posted in Vienna. The Baptists in Russia had increased ten-fold since before the War. Gareth learnt that his so-called friend, Pastor Fetler in Riga was, "a wild adventurer, shifty, and that more than one man had been shot in Russia because of Fetler's incompetence in smuggling money across the frontier". Fetler's history seemed a murky one.

The following day, Gareth had an interview with the Chief Rabbi of Britain, J H Hertz, who showed Gareth a telegram from Vilna which stated: "The Rabbi in Minsk is in danger of his life. Make haste to save us. Use all your influence." Then Gareth went to the Jewish Telegraphic Agency, and invited Dr Jochelmann to see him. He was at college with Lenin and Trotsky, and very nervous about the visit. He made Gareth promise not to have his name written on a memorandum for fear there was a spy in Lloyd George's office. He conveyed to Gareth that the terrible persecution in Russia was moral rather than physical; by indoctrination rather than by atrocities.

Later in the year, Gareth interviewed M. Chenkeli, the Prime Minister and Foreign Minister of the Georgian Republic who described to him the character of Stalin,. Gareth recorded this in a memorandum for David Lloyd George:

> *The dictatorship has become personal, STALIN — all power is concentrated in the hands of Stalin. I knew Stalin; he is a countryman of mine, and his real name is Djugashvili. He is not such a brain as Trotsky or Kamenev or Zinoviev. He is not of first-class intelligence, but he is a brilliant organiser.*
>
> *He is disinterested, has no material ambition, is very honest, absolutely ruthless and brutal; very brave and a first-class intriguer. He sits in his room in the Kremlin and handles men like pawns. He moves one man from one position and raises another.*
>
> *He knows his men. He continually receives reports about party men throughout the country. His father was a shoemaker and his mother a washerwoman. Stalin is the real chief of the G.P.U. an army numbering over a hundred thousand men, which is better armed than the Red Army. He is continually changing the leaders of the Red Army and moving them from place to place. Menzhinsky (head of the OGPU) is the servant of Stalin.*[2]

Lloyd George was considering whether to write on India or on the religious situation in Russia for the United Press Association. He finally chose Russia and Gareth arranged to meet Dr Rushbrooke immediately, and the two men talked about the situation for about an hour. Gareth returned to his office to work hard on the brief, when at 11 am, Miss Edwards came in to say that Lloyd George had changed his mind, and was going to write on Admiral von Tirpitz instead. However, Gareth had already arranged an interview with Professor Onou, Secretary to Kerensky's Government. As he wished to continue writing the brief on the religious situation in Russia he decided not to cancel and went to see the Professor at his home as arranged. "Poor old Professor Onou! He is a funny, nervy man with a goatee beard. I was sorry for him. Nobody seems to consult him about Russia, although he once played an important part. He feels himself neglected, and I was glad I went to ask him for his opinion."[3]

At 3.45 pm Miss Edwards phoned the Professor's home to tell Gareth, "Mr Lloyd George wants you to get a biographical notice of Admiral Scheer and General Hoffman[4] ready by 5.30 pm"[5] Gareth rushed back to Old Queen Street in a taxi, but finding no information there he took another taxi to the German Embassy; where he met the Count Bernstorff's son before proceeding to the RIIA. There, Philip Kerr, a former wartime secretary to David Lloyd George, told him if he needed any help with Lloyd George's briefs, he would only be too pleased to help. Gareth finally assembled all the facts just in time for his impetuous employer.

Later that week Gareth was suddenly called to see Lloyd George, who said; "The Chancellor of Austria is coming to see me today. Schoo — What is his name?" "Schober, Sir," replied Gareth. "What's the political situation in Austria now?" So, Gareth briefed his elderly master about the Austrian army, the Heimwehr, but Lloyd George much preferred to talk about the Sängerfest in Vienna, instead.

Gareth often had to write messages on behalf of Lloyd George. On one occasion he wrote to the National Library of Wales, Aberystwyth in reply to an invitation from Sir John Ballinger:

It is with deep regret that I find I shall be unable to be present at the coming of Age Celebrations of the National Library of Wales. Since that memorable day, twenty one years ago, when my old friend the late Sir John Williams made to Wales from the generosity of his heart his priceless gift of Welsh Manuscripts and books, the library has added treasure after treasure to its store and has steadily, but surely enriched the intellectual and spiritual life of Wales. It stands proudly today as a barrier against the menace of materialism, and as a tribute to all those lovers of learning who have toiled and striven for the good of the Welsh Nation.

One quiet morning in the office, Gareth began the review of the book, *In the Evening of my Thought* by France's former Prime Minister, Clemenceau. Later that day at the RIIA he heard a Jean Marel speak on Clemenceau. He referred to the 'subtilité fugante de M. Lloyd George'[The cunning of Lloyd George]. When asked if Clemenceau had been 24 hours in Germany, he said "Non, mais l'Allemagne a été quatre ans chez nous!" [No, but Germany has been here (in France) for four years!]

Gareth was still busy undertaking briefs, including one on "The situation in India, Palestine and Egypt" and another on the results of the "Naval Conference compared with Washington Conference." He later prepared memoranda on Briand and American tariffs.[6]

Gareth continued to enjoy meeting his Cambridge friends. He dined with Pentland at Craig's Court restaurant where their discussions turned to politics. Lord Pentland had dined with Lord Beaverbrook the night before and he told Gareth "Beaverbrook started the Empire Party to force Stanley Baldwin's hand, and Baldwin had given in. The party wondered how long it would be before Baldwin would capitulate."[7] He lunched with some of his numerous college friends; Norton, Reavney, Seabourne Davies, Ludovik Stewart, and also his French friends, Janelle and the Winklers, who often came to London. Pierre Winkler had just won a Rockefeller Scholarship.

On March 19th 1930 Gareth noted:

Yesterday was an exciting day. At five minutes to one, the phone went, and Sylvester's voice came through very excitedly: "Come up to the floor at once! Mr Lloyd George wants to know something about Intermediate Education in Wales!" I dashed up to the room next to George Lloyd's room on the sixth floor. "Get your hat and coat, quick!" said Sylvester, "You're going in the car!" I got my hat and coat from my room and put some cuttings on education in my pocket and got upstairs just in time to enter the lift with Lloyd George wearing a dark blue coat and black hat. We went out and got into the beautiful Rolls Royce. Smith, the man at the door, put the rug over LG's and my legs. "Where to, Sir?" said the Chauffeur. "11, Downing Street," said Lloyd George.

Then as we were gliding past the Board of Trade, down Parliament Street, Lloyd George told me what he wanted. He asked me to get him figures for the number of pupils in Secondary Schools in Wales, the percentage to the population and comparison with the numbers in England, Scotland and Germany [for his speech in Caernarfon]. Finally, the car drove up to 11, Downing Street. Lloyd George got out, and entered the, [Philip] Snowden's house [Chancellor of the Exchequer] and the Chauffeur drove me back in great style near the Houses of Parliament and Westminster Abbey to 25, Queen Street. I got the information ready by the evening. So everything was OK.[8]

At the end of March, Gareth attended the Young Liberal Dance, which he said he enjoyed immensely:

Lloyd George was there and talked to me, as well as his wife, Margaret Lloyd George. I liked her very much and I spoke Welsh to her. She had a natural, simple North Wales accent and she sent greetings to you [Edgar and Annie Gwen Jones]. I met Sir Thomas and Lady Carey-Evans. I sat at their table for a while, also the Chief Whip, Sir Robert Hutchinson and a lot of others.[9]

Gareth still maintained his interest in the problems of India, and met Srivinasa Sastri whom he described as, "modest, humble and polite". He was an Indian member of the Legislative Assembly and the First Agent of the Indian Government in South Africa ensuring fair treatment of Indians in the country.

Miss Edwards who had worked for Lloyd George for a long time remarked on Lloyd George's character:

It is sheer cussedness on Lloyd George's [part]. He is a strange mixture of extremes. Sometimes he can be amazingly kind, as he was when her father died. He phoned to see if he could do something. Sometimes he can be absolutely cruel, and give you the worst dressing down possible. You never know how he takes news. Sometimes he takes bad news extremely angrily and peevishly for instance, Nottingham by-elections yesterday. Sometimes much worse news may come in, and he may say, 'Oh, it doesn't matter. We'll do better next time.' He takes sudden likes and dislikes or if he takes a dislike then everything you do is bad.[10]

On May 3, 1930, Gareth visited the Soviet ship *Felix Dzerzhinsky* with Miss Gellan from the office.

I was most impressed with the cleanliness, and had a long chat with the sailors, all of whom did their best to persuade me how excellent everything in

Russia is. The next day at 4.30 I drove up to the Soviet Embassy in a taxi; went inside Mayfair House, at Grosvenor Square. I met Joelson and Neymann from the Soviet Embassy. A car [later] drove us through Hyde Park, past Buckingham Palace and drove up to the Trocadero where we had a capitalistic tea.

Gareth's diary continued with a résumé of their conversation:

Russia is in now in a state of war, but in a state of a war of construction, not of destruction. We are to evolve a new collectivist psychology. We are battling for the Five-Year Plan, which is sure to succeed because the whole country is in exactly the same state as Great Britain during the last War. Of course we cannot tolerate defeatists; that is why we oppose any counter-revolutionary force. The spirit of competition between factories increases the production in a 'spirit of war'. Russians are being asked to sacrifice for the present to gain in the future.

The American big firms are able to trade with Russia, because they control so much capital themselves. In Britain, the companies rely too much on the banks. We should like the Export Credits Scheme to be extended from one year to five years. We should like to have £15,000 to £20,000 in credits.[11]

Gareth discussed with Malcolm Thomson the errors he had found in Lloyd George's speech on Russia in Hansard [the record of the daily speeches in the House of Commons]. Lloyd George spoke of, "enormous increase in production of grain" whereas in Gareth's translation of Stalin's speech published in *Izvestia* only 5% increase over the 1913 figures was expected. Thomson said that Lloyd George often found it hard to distinguish between millions and thousands, and that he trembled whenever he sat behind him in a speech for fear Lloyd George would misquote the figures.

On June 4, Sylvester came down and was furious about his boss. He grumbled:

I've been following him round with a bag for 10 days. If I ask him a question he just walks away. He won't say, 'Yes or No'... He's in a terribly difficult mood these days. He's going to Derby today. He wanted to go in a new blue suit, so he had new blue suit made for him. He said he was not going in a top hat. Today he asks, "What should I wear?" I said, "You should be going in a top-hat." "Well, I am going to wear this suit." Now what if the King talks to him! So finally at the last minute he says: "Very well; why weren't the clothes ready." And now we have to search all the corners of London for clothes for him.

About Russia he says he only wants to do about the Russia of today. If only he'd say 'yes' or 'no'. And when someone asks him about anything I've been trying to tell him for days and he hasn't listened, he says: "Why haven't I been told? Nobody tells me anything."

Notes on Chapter 8

1
   Gareth Vaughan Jones Papers, National Library of Wales Diary Series B1/3. Lloyd George Diary, 1930.

2
   Parliamentary Archives, The Lloyd George Papers. Gareth Jones. 'Soviet Russia and the Caucasus', December 9, 1930. LG/G/26/1/33.

3
   Gareth Vaughan Jones Papers, National Library of Wales Correspondence Series B6/2. March 7, 1930.

4
   General Hoffman was successful on the German 1917 Eastern Front against the Russians. The campaign was planned by Hoffman, but Hindenberg was given the credit. The trans-Germany transit of Bolsheviks was approved, facilitated, and financed by the German General Staff. Major General Hoffman wrote, "We neither knew nor foresaw the danger to humanity from the consequences of this journey of the Bolsheviks to Russia." Consequently, on April 16, 1917, a trainload of thirty-two, including Lenin, his wife Nadezhda Krupskaya, Grigori Zinoviev, Sokolnikov, and Karl Radek, left the Central Station in Bern en route to Stockholm. When the party reached the Russian frontier only Fritz Plattan and Radek were denied entrance into Russia.

5
   Gareth Vaughan Jones Papers, National Library of Wales Correspondence Series B6/2. March 7, 1930.

6
   Parliamentary Archives. The Lloyd George Papers. Mr Gareth Jones, LG/G/26/26. June 27, 1930.

7
   Gareth Vaughan Jones Papers, National Library of Wales Correspondence Series B6/2. March 7, 1930

8
   Gareth Vaughan Jones Papers, National Library of Wales Correspondence Series 1-21, file 18. March 19, 1930.

9
   Gareth Vaughan Jones Papers, National Library of Wales Correspondence Series B6/2. March 30, 1930.

10
   Gareth Vaughan Jones Papers, National Library of Wales Diary Series B1/3. Lloyd George Diary, 1930

11
   Ibid.

Chapter 9

Hughesovka 1930

Diplomatic relations with Great Britain had been restored on October 1, 1929, and tourists were now encouraged to visit the USSR. Gareth was therefore able to obtain a Soviet visa, and made plans for a pilgrimage to the town of Hughesovka where his mother had been tutor to the grand-daughters of John Hughes.

Gareth perusing his new passport.

By chance, before he left for the Soviet Union, he went to a lecture at the RIIA entitled the 'Permanent Court.' Afterwards, a Dr Gerald Merton spoke to him and they travelled home together. He was Chairman of the Executive of the Air League.[1]

Gareth mentioned that he was going to Russia. Merton thought Gareth might be able to get information on Soviet aviation and that he would put him in touch with Col. Thwaites, who was in the intelligence service during the WWI.[2] Merton further informed Gareth that "the best way to find out about Russian aviation was to talk to the German engineers about meteorology."

On the morning of July 24, 1930, Gareth went to the Air League offices on the sixth floor of Astor House. Col. Thwaites was waiting for him in a small room, in morning dress, a top hat hanging on a peg. He had "keen dark eyes; not a very attractive personality, absolutely unscrupulous and cold". Gareth confided his conversation with Thwaites to his diaries as to how unprincipled governments were about propaganda:

> *It was difficult to get the facts about Soviet aviation and he [Thwaites] had heard they were advancing very quickly. The Air Ministry had men in Helsingfors, Warsaw and Rumania to watch Russia; and it was very probable that they had men in Russia. He considered that Russia was aiming at India. The Colonel was on the black list of the Soviets, and could not get into the country though he had travelled in Poland and the Balkans to get information about Soviet aviation. He had been as far as the Soviet Frontier, and learnt that the Russians were training pilots near the Western Frontier. Poland was very nervous she was going ahead in aviation. Aeroplanes were being built in the Puilov works. The Sigorski plane was being used — an excellent plane and the Soviets were boasting about their planes. He would write to the Admiralty about me.*
>
> *But if I was going to do anything for them, it had better be at the end of my trip, and to be very careful. Sydney Reilly[3] got shot going across the frontier, at least so they say. He knew Reilly well — a wonderful man. He never forgot when his little widow came with the rumour that Reilly had been shot, and he had to take her to the House of Commons where it was stated that he was, "in the clutches of Tcheka." The news came out that Sydney Reilly was a prisoner of Tcheka and had not been shot.[4]*

Thwaites remarked that he "could have had Trotsky and Zinoviev arrested in 1917, but that silly ass Kerensky stopped them, objecting to the arrest of Russian Citizens." Whether Gareth undertook any data gathering for Thwaites is not known, but there are no further references in any of his diaries or papers relating to any covert involvement with the British Government, nor has any evidence been discovered hitherto within any Foreign Office records.

Less than two weeks later Gareth set off on his travels and on August 5, 1930, whilst en route to Moscow, he wrote his first letter home from Warsaw:

Here I am, feeling fresh after a most enjoyable and interesting journey. Mrs ----- [Skorupka]⁵ is not here, but her mother and brother are very kind, and I am staying the night with them before starting early tomorrow morning to travel to Moscow…

…In Berlin, I changed and after a bath I waited for the Paris-Niegorologe express (Niegorologe — Soviet frontier)… When the train left Berlin, I went to the restaurant car, and who sat opposite me but Saul Bron, the Soviet Trade Representative for Great Britain! We had a chat on Soviet business, etc.. He had awful manners, eats like a horse, bangs his plate with his knife, snorts, has a bullet wound in his face, cannot stop smoking between courses, the most unpolished man you could ever imagine.

Bron said that the Russian debt negotiations were beginning in September. I gathered from his expressions — although he said nothing definite — that he did not expect them to be a success. He said that there would be a drive against the Kulaks, and in favour of collective farms as soon as the harvest was in. He said that commercial aviation was being developed rapidly… He greeted the extension of the Export Credit Scheme for Russia to two years.

Two American engineers were sitting just near. One was helping to build oil pipes in Baku and said that the oil industry was getting on well.

…After dinner, I went back to the train compartment where there was a little man from Hughesovka! who had been studying mining engineering in America. He told me that he thought the Five-Year Plan was going along too quickly. 'What on earth was the government exporting food to buy machines when there was not enough to eat in the country?

The other Russian in the compartment, well dressed and a gentleman, turned out to be a Professor at Moscow University. He was afraid that a pair of boots would be taken from him at the Soviet frontier, because he had one more pair than he was allowed. He could only take one pair.

Some Poles pointed out the new airport, the finest in the world, built regardless of price, with the best machinery and concrete that money can buy. 'It will hold 40 huge military planes' they said with great pride. There are soldiers here everywhere. At the same time Poland is terribly poor.

We crossed the Polish border about 11 pm at night. I noticed how strict and rude the custom officers were with the Jews. One of them was bundled out of the train with a lot of ladies' clothing. The customs officer had to confiscate them, I believe. Whether the Russian came back to the train I do not know. The following morning I woke up to find myself looking out of the window at very flat and monotonous country three-quarters of an hour from Warsaw.

Mrs S-------'s brother said that [Josef] Pilsudski is in a weak position and that he is treating the minorities (e.g. the Ukrainians) better, to get their support. Pilsudski wants a still bigger Poland with Lithuania and Ukraine. Absolutely mad ideas here, nothing, but war and fear and everybody is bad except the Poles. To blame everybody else seems a sign of weakness.[6]

Gareth's next letter was from Stolpce station on the Polish frontier, a day later:

The Poles have been telling me how bad things are here in Poland — peasants cannot get good prices for their corn and coal; industry is hit a tariff war with Germany — terrifically high tariffs and a tendency to raise them even higher and they are raising a big army. It all sounds absolutely mad. Before long I shall be in the USSR. There are Polish soldiers tramping up and down in the station here.[7]

And not long after leaving the Polish Frontier station Gareth saw on an archway over the railway a poster, which read, "Welcome to the Workers of the West". Five days later from Moscow, Gareth wrote:

I am having an intensely interesting time, and really don't know where to begin telling you all that has happened.

After writing to you on Thursday, I thought I'd go, and see the Kremlin and then go to a cinema. The Kremlin is most impressive place. There were posters everywhere such as, "In an illiterate country it is impossible to build up a communist society". ... The film was good, but short. Then I decided to go to the circus, which began at nine pm.

Yesterday (Saturday) I met Mr Petrov, head of the Russian Tourist Company and walked around. Today has been a wonderful day. I have had a fine car and an excellent guide at my disposal all day. We went to a factory, saw excellent crèches for babies, workmen's homes — splendid. Some children took a fancy to me near the factory. I talked to them and then they followed me and wanted me to play with me. When I went they shouted, "Take us with you" and waved until I was out of sight. I saw a workers club; then was taken by car all over Moscow, went to the Tretyakovskaya Gallery, but it was closed; then to the Anti-religious Museum.

Tomorrow I go to see the Izvestia and Pravda offices; also to meet the Head of the Press Department at the Foreign Office.[8]

A few days later, Gareth sent this postcard to his family of the Public Library from the Hotel Metropole:

I have just treated myself to a good lunch after a most interesting two-hour interview at the Ministry of Agriculture. I have an introduction to a State Farm and a Collective Farm near Rostov, so I may miss the Volga and go direct to Rostov, i.e. if I get my passport back with my exit visa. I got the letter you sent to the Vons this morning.

And the following afternoon August 15 from Kupk Station, he sent the postcard picturing Stalin:

In one hour my train leaves for Rostov right in the South 32 hours away, where I shall see State and Collective Farms. On August 24 (Sunday) I shall be back in Moscow, leave Moscow for Berlin on 25 Waldheim (Bei Herr Haferkorn). I am enjoying myself immensely.

From Karkov Station at 8.45 am on August 16:

Here I am halfway to Rostov. The time has passed very quickly in Russian trains and I slept excellently on my hired mattress, clean sheets and pillows, lying full length. The train left Moscow at 4 o'clock yesterday afternoon and in Tula Station, I had a real treat, cheese sandwiches, cakes and lemonade. A Cossack Communist with the Order of the Red Flag told me a lot of things about present day Russia, and I listened to a discussion about factories and engineers. So now I am in the Ukraine. Most people travel here with kettles and rush out on every station to get hot water.[9]

In a station not far from Hughesovka at half-past five in the morning of Sunday, August 17, 1930, after he had been travelling since Friday afternoon a very dirty, and unshaven Gareth wrote to his family, but especially to his mother;

Dawn found me sitting on the floor here in a small station in the Donetz Basin called Yassinovataya. (Train is now leaving.) In about 12 minutes I shall be in Hughesovka. My journey from Moscow has been full of experiences. I wish I had time to tell you now.[10]

And later, after a three hour delay:

Hughesovka!!

Here I am in Hughesovka! It's taken a long time to get here, but I did not want to miss it. I am sitting in the gardens just near the church. I wish I had time to go and see Mr Hughes' house, but the only news I can get about it is that was Mr Balfour's house, and that it is out of the town and I must catch the 11 o'clock train. I am delighted to be here where you lived. It would be hard to find someone you knew. So all I can do is to send you my Sunday letter from here. And now I am going to Rostov.

I had an excellent ride with three other people on a funny droschke. The droschke driver remembered the Hughes', Albert, etc. and someone told me that she had heard of a Miss James.

There are a number of new buildings here. And now I am going to catch a tram back to the station, having performed my pilgrimage. I shall be passing through Taganrog… They are repairing the church here. The droschke took me down the main street where I expect you were very often. I have just seen the factory where Mr Hughes' house used to be before he moved.[11]

At the Hotel Dyelovoy, Rostov-on-Don, on August 20:

Tonight I am leaving for the Caucasus. I want to see the mountains there. On Monday in Moscow I shall catch the 9.30 pm Moscow-Berlin train, via Warsaw. I shall [then] go to Waldheim and I shall really be delighted to be there. So a week Monday I shall be back again after the most interesting journey I have ever had. I shall be ever so glad to have news of you when I arrive in Moscow next Sunday.

Yesterday I went in a car to a State Farm, Gigant No.2. It is amazing to see how they have converted the desert steppes into a vast farm covering a hundred thousand acres and run by the most modern agricultural implements. In less than a year and a half they have built a town where nobody had ever sown or worked before. We went through a Cossack town. In the State farm I had excellent meals. I also saw a Collective Farm.

There are new buildings everywhere, and industrially the USSR is going

73

ahead at a rapid rate. This hotel is very clean. In a few hours I leave for a small place in the Caucasian mountains, called Kislovodsk. Won't I have travelled miles by the time I have returned! It will be very pleasant to have a comfortable home to return to after work.[12]

From the tone of all Gareth's previous correspondence from the Soviet Union, to his parents, all would have appeared to have been rosy in the garden of the 'Workers' Paradise'… However, from the uncensored safety of Germany, Gareth painted an entirely different picture of conditions:

Berlin,
Near the Station for Saxony,
12.30 pm Wednesday,
August. 26 , 1930[13]

Hurray! It is wonderful to be in Germany again, absolutely wonderful. Russia is in a very bad state; rotten, no food, only bread; oppression, injustice, misery among the workers and 90% discontented. I saw some very bad things, which made me mad to think that people like XXX [deleted and illegible] go there and come back, after having been led round by the nose and had enough to eat, and say that Russia is a paradise. In the South there is talk of a new revolution, but it will never come off, because the Army and the [O]GPU (Soviet Police) are too strong. The winter is going to be one of great suffering there and starvation. The government is the most brutal in the world. The peasants hate the Communists. This year thousands and thousands of the best men in Russia have been sent to Siberia and the prison island of Solovki. People are now speaking openly against the Government. In the Donetz Basin conditions are unbearable. Thousands are leaving. I shall never forget the night I spent in a railway station on the way to Hughesovka. One reason why I left Hughesovka so quickly was that all I could get to eat was a roll of bread — and that is all I had up to 7 o'clock. Many Russians are too weak to work. I am terribly sorry for them. They cannot strike or they are shot or sent to Siberia. There are heaps of enemies of the Communist within the country.

Nevertheless, great strides have been made in many industries and there is a good chance that when the Five-Years Plan is over Russia may become prosperous. But before that there will be great suffering, many riots and many deaths.

The Communists are doing excellent work in education, hygiene and against alcohol. Butter is 16/- a pound in Moscow; prices are terrific. Boots etc. cannot be had. There is nothing in the shops. The Communists were remarkably kind to me and gave me an excellent time.

Last Sunday I flew from Rostov to Moscow as their guest. You will get this letter probably before my Sunday letter. Germany is a fine place. I am looking forward so much to seeing the Haferkorns and getting your letters there, because I have had very little news. Thank goodness I am not a Consul in Russia — not even in Taganrog.[14]

Just had a fine lunch. When I come back I shall appreciate Aunty Winnie's dinner more than ever.[15]

By September 5, 1930, Gareth was back home in Britain and in his diary is a fascinating entry:

When I had arrived at Vickers[16] *and walked through the carpeted corridor, past photos of battleship, liners, cruisers and submarines, Sir Mark Webster Jenkinson's secretary said that there was a very important call for me. I rang Miss Edwards who said, "They want you down at Churt [Lloyd George's country residence in Surrey]." I took the first-class train to Farnham where I was met by car and taken to Churt. It was a beautiful place. I was given a room with a beautiful view facing the lawn. I went downstairs to the drawing room and then on to the library from where I heard Lloyd George's voice coming from the garden. He came in and said, "Hullo, Gareth!" Then Mr Rowntree joined us and Lloyd George said, "I am going to change, but you needn't, because you have a dark suit."*

Mr Rowntree and I sat down and he said: "I gave such a glowing account of your talk with me that they said they must have you down. I said that it was more thrilling than any novel I'd read, not only being very valuable, but that you have the gift of a raconteur."

We then strolled in the garden and met Wallace Stewart and Lord Lothian (Philip Kerr). Lloyd George joined us in a purple velvet coat and he was in an excellent humour. He asked me about the peasants. I told him about the kulaks. [Lloyd George,] "Well I suppose I'm a kulak and you Lothian, you are a super kulak."

At dinner they made me talk all the time. Mr Rowntree: 'We want to hear about the waitresses.' They pulled my leg about the blue-eyed Komesomolti [Young Soviet Brigade].

'Poor devils', said Lloyd George when I told him about Donetz. Tell us what would they do with us if we had a Soviet Government here?' I replied, "You would be shot Sir." 'And what about Lothian?' 'Oh, he'd be sent Solovki or the Dokery Islands.' 'And Rowntree?' 'Oh he'd be put in charge of the Soviet chocolate industry with a Communist looking after him. As soon as he had given all his knowledge and experience to another man he'd be sent away.'

We went to the fine large, sitting room where they made me talk for hours, from about 8.30 until 10.45. Lloyd George went to bed at about 10.15.

'Good God!' Lloyd George agreed that the Government in Russia was a tiny minority, coercing the rest.

When I said about the tear bombs on Russian towns, Lloyd George said, "There are some places in London I'd like to drop bombs on." "10 Downing Street," said Wallace Stewart. "Yes, I would like to wake them up a bit."

When I referred to the energy and enthusiasm of the Communist Party, Lloyd George said, "Well I know some ministers who have neither energy or enthusiasm." Lothian was very pessimistic. He was afraid that the 16th century might repeat itself. We had got used to the idea that there was only one Great War in a century. Perhaps the 20th century would be series of religious wars — religion or Communism. Lloyd George said that Poland was in great danger. The feeling of the company was very pessimistic about the future of Europe.

After Lloyd George had gone to bed, Wallace said: "I've never heard Lloyd George listen like that. Usually it's we who listen to him all the time."

There was a lovely view when I woke up. I had a cup of tea, got up and went downstairs. I slipped down the last step, but one. Lloyd George was there without a collar. "Hullo. That was a narrow shave." He went out and then I heard a shout, "Gareth. Let's go for a stroll."

We discussed foreign affairs. I told him that the German Reichswehr had secret relations with the Red Army. "Quite right. That's exactly what I would do if I were a German. I've always foreseen that. If they did that they make themselves independent of France. In spite of your libellous attack on Soviet Russia, I feel that they will make something of it some day. Of course the Five-Year Plan will not be a success. They can't possibly build up a prosperous Russia in two or three years. Bessarabia[17] was going to give trouble. Poland is going to cause trouble. They're so irresponsible. The time will come when we'll have to take them in hand."

At breakfast Lothian was pessimistic and thought that the armaments of Europe were sure to lead to war, that the day would come when the two camps, *the revisionists and the non-revisionists, would be pitted against one another. Lloyd George said with scorn in his voice: "Germany will go on, but I think there is bound to be revision. France will not be able to stand isolated with Czecho-Slovakia, Yugoslavia and Rumania. Then Great Britain will stand firmly on the side of revision. Then disarmament will follow."*

Rowntree: "Do you like Baldwin?" Lloyd George: "No. That is, I don't dislike him, but I have contempt for his ability. And he is not the honest fellow people take him for. He poses as the honest English gentleman, just as if the rest of us were low-down fellows and adventurous scoundrels and he is cunning and underhand. I could give you chapter and verse for what I say. I asked Winston [Churchill], 'What do you think of Baldwin?' He said, 'Very crafty.'"

Rowntree: "What do you think of Baldwin?"

Lloyd George: "He's very ambitious. Balfour once told me: 'There are two men who to the public appear ambitious, but who are really very retiring and conscientious. They are Asquith and Curzon.' Then, there are two who appear retiring and modest and who really very self-seeking and cunning."

Rowntree: "Who were they?" Lloyd George: "Baldwin and well, you will never guess? Lord Grey was very, very ambitious. I was staggered when he came to spend a weekend before the formation of the Government in 1906. He did nothing between 1896 to 1906, but did everything to be Foreign Secretary."

Rowntree: "What will his [Grey's] part be in history?"

Lloyd George: "He'll play a very contemptuous part in history. He made some great mistakes, which could have shortened the War. He could have kept Turkey out of the War. He could have kept Bulgaria out of the War. A million pounds would have done it. If only he could have bribed Ferdinand. That would have had a tremendous effect on the War. Then he persuaded Greece to keep out of the War. Greece had some 200,000 trained men. He could have saved the Gallipoli disaster. I was dead against the War. So were a lot of others until Belgium was invaded."

"Is Stalin a great man?" asked one of the group.

Lloyd George: "Trotsky was the only great organiser that Russia produced. The future of Russia depends on the springing up of a great personality. Germany is the real barrier against Bolshevism, not Poland.

Lord Lothian, impressed by Gareth's in-depth knowledge of Soviet affairs, put him in touch with Geoffrey Dawson, the editor of *The Times*, with the object of writing some articles for this highly respected London newspaper. Unlike most

"Enemies of the 5-Year Plan" - Art by Viktor Deni 1929. Poem by Denyan Bedny.
[Poster purchased in Moscow by Gareth in 1931.]

other prestigious newspapers, *The Times* was not prepared to be subjected to the Soviet Censor's pencil, and consequently their Russian correspondent was actually based outside the USSR in Riga. This allowed Gareth the platform to present an independent and considered appraisal of the Five-Year Plan, which remains arguably the most accurate reporting to have emanated from the Soviet Union at the time. In October 1930, a series of three unsigned articles by Gareth appeared in *The Times* entitled, 'The Two Russias'. Extracts from these articles may be found in Appendix II. In addition to the three articles in *The Times*, Gareth wrote another series for the Cardiff *Western Mail*, entitled 'Communists' Five-Year Plan', which appeared in April of the following year.[18] A youthful Gareth, only one year out of university was to predict 'It might make the twentieth century a century of struggle between Capitalism and Communism'.[19]

On September 23, 1930, Gareth surprised his father with an early telephone call, with the exciting news that Dr Ivy Lee, had been to see him. Ivy Lee was a great force in American public life and had many interests amongst which he was Vice-President of the American League of Nations Union, with a special concern was Russia. Gareth had only returned from his visit from Russia three weeks previously. His articles about the Soviet Union had not yet been printed in *The Times*. Mr Lee offered him a post beginning at £800 plus expenses, with a conservative estimate of the eventual total of £1500 after one year — a great sum of money for

1930. The work was to be exactly the same as Gareth was undertaking for David Lloyd George; memoranda on foreign affairs and reading foreign newspapers. The position would entail living in New York, but he would travel occasionally to Europe to undertake his research. Gareth was free to start the job whenever he liked. Sir Bernard Pares who had introduced Gareth to Ivy Lee, strongly recommended Gareth to take the position.

Notes on Chapter 9

1
  The Air League was founded in 1909 in recognition of the role that the aeroplane would come to play in the transport industry and, above all, national security.

2
  In 1916 Captain, later Colonel, Norman Thwaites went to New York to join Lt. Col. Sir William Wiseman who had established a branch of MI Ic, Section V, also known as the Secret Intelligence Service (SIS, later M16) there.

3
  According to M15 documents Reilly was tricked by Stalin's secret police, OGPU into returning to Russia supposedly to join an anti-Bolshevik organisation, The Trust. In fact, this was a front for the OGPU. National Archives files say Reilly was arrested several days after crossing the border with Finland into Russia. The Bolsheviks, in order to escape the possible demands by the English for his release, murdered him when he was taken out for exercise, after first putting into practice their methods of torture. The story of Reilly's shooting by a border guard was a cover-up planted in the press by the Russians.

4
  Gareth Vaughan Jones Papers, National Library of Wales Diary Series B1/3 1930.

5
  Written in Welsh to protect the identity of his hostess. For some unknown reason Gareth mentions that he had deliberately deleted her first name from the letter.

6
  Gareth Vaughan Jones Papers, National Library of Wales Correspondence Series 1-21 File 9. August 5, 1930.

7
  Ibid. August 6, 1930.

8
  Gareth Vaughan Jones Papers, National Library of Wales Correspondence Series B6/2. August 10, 1930.

9
  Gareth Vaughan Jones Papers, National Library of Wales Correspondence Series 1-21 File 11. August 16th 1930.

10
  Gareth Vaughan Jones Papers, National Library of Wales Correspondence Series B6/2. August 17, 1930.

11
  Ibid.

12
  Ibid. August 20, 1930.

13
  See Appendix I for the facsimile of the letter.

14
  This is a reference to a family joke when Gareth as a small child dressed up with top hat and walking stick and called himself the Governor of Tagenrog.

15
  Gareth Vaughan Jones Papers, National Library of Wales Correspondence Series B6/2. August 28, 1930.

16
  Metropolitan-Vickers. In the 1920s Metrovick made technical advances in the manufacture of turbines, generators, switching gear and industrial motors.

[17] A region between the Prut and Dniester rivers (Romania / USSR)

[18] Gareth Jones, The *Western Mail*, 'Force's Behind Stalin's Dictatorship' April 9, 1931, p. 14.

[19] Ibid., 'Mixture of Successes and Failures', April 11, 1931, p. 12.

Chapter 10

The Victim of 1930

Gareth was not to take up his appointment with Ivy Lee for another six months, remaining employed by Lloyd George until April 1931. His work for Lloyd George did not prevent him from continuing to write the occasional newspaper article and on New Year's Eve 1930, the *Western Mail* published a review article entitled, 'The Victim of 1930'. Gareth summed up the world disillusionment of the year that had just passed, while considering the outlook for 1931, with the maturity and insight of a man far beyond his 25 years.

A man is slouching down a street. The ends of his trousers are frayed and his boots want repairing. His face reflects a medley of feelings — emptiness, boredom, fear, disgust, and, above all disillusion. He has no name for he exists in nearly all countries. He is the victim of 1930; the Unemployed. In Merthyr and New York, in Cardiff and in Hamburg, in Swansea and Rome, in Newport and Tokyo, this tragic figure curses against the world order as he hears of over-production of wheat and butter, of cloth and manufactured goods, and cannot get any himself. He is the symbol of the world crisis, which the first year of the Thirties has heralded.

In America, this man has between six and eight million fellow — sufferers, who feel the blow all the more because a year ago nearly all of them had their own Ford and were saying that American prosperity could never melt away. Each newspaper boy as he has shouted the collapse of another bank has hit hard the national pride of the American passer-by. Decent young fellows who used to earn £7 a week are now glad to have a chance of selling a few apples in the streets. For they get no dole and no relief, except from charity. The gambling which had almost gone into the blood of the Americans has made the shock still worse. Disillusion is the dominant note in the United States.

In Germany, the workless man has 3,700,000 colleagues in distress, and before the winter is over it is expected that four million industrious men and women will find the factory door or the mine barred to them. Besides these there are the university students who cannot get the dole, there are the clerks, the teachers, the lawyers, and the young men who want to go to the colonies, but have no colonies to go to. No wonder that the Communists are cheered when they appeal to the working class to rise against a system that leaves them idle in the winter snow.

In Italy, in Japan, the workless are increasing. But nowhere is the problem of bread and work more pressing than in South Wales, where it is not a sudden apparition, but is eating into our very bones.

What effect has this had on the affairs of the world? It has made 1930 a year of fear, hatred, Depression, and despair in the dealings of nations with one another as well as in industry. There are but a few bright streaks to illumine the gloom. Europe had an attack of the 'jumps', and from the peasant homes of France to the Red clubs of Soviet Russia, there has been talk of WAR. A French Reserve officer wrote in a letter: "I am now going manoeuvres. I shudder to think that before long our mock warfare will be real and that Germany and Italy and Russia are preparing to attack us. Poor France! My poor children!"

As I was travelling through Poland not long ago and looking out of the window, a young Pole tapped me on the shoulder and pointed out an aerodrome. 'Do you see that? That's one of the finest military aerodromes in the world, which we are going to fill with first-class fighting machines. You see, the Russian have their airport across the frontier and God know how many planes have to bomb us at any moment. Then there are the Germans, who want revenge. They want their Polish Corridor back again and any time they may hurl their troops against us. If I had my way I'd hang thirty million Germans.'

In Soviet Russia everybody agreed that war was bound to come with a knowing nod people would say, 'Ah, yes, the English and the Americans, the capitalists, are preparing for war on us.' And a Red Army officers said to me with a smile: 'When the inevitable war comes I'll come and visit you in London.'

A German expressed what all Germans are thinking when he said: "The French promised to disarm and they are as powerful as ever. We cannot stick any longer being treated as we are and kept prisoners by the French generals and politicians. Every German would willingly die to win the Polish Corridor back."

The first effect of this fear and Depression has been to multiply the nationalists in all countries. Hitlerites with their hooliganistic methods and their aims of a powerful armed Germany are growing from day to day and are going to be before long a real menace.

The second effect has to be to make the world sick of Parliaments. Everything is going wrong, so blame the Government. 'What we want is a Mussolini.' How often are these words heard not only in German beer gardens and Polish drawing-rooms, but even in the home of Parliaments, Great Britain! Everywhere Liberalism and Democracy are rolled in mud, and everywhere the herd is shouting for the strong guidance of one firm leader. Liberty, for which fighters in Britain have struggled for centuries, is now considered pre-Victorian humbug throughout the world.

Thirdly, fear and Depression have made statesmen form new alliances. The last few months have seen Europe split into two camps as before 1914. On the one hand France with her satellite States stands out for the treaties, as they exist. No changes of frontiers! Germany must not arm! Germany must pay the reparations to the last penny! That is what time French camp says.

On the other hand Mussolini — and he is backed by Germany — says: — 'We must change the frontiers. Germany must have some of her territories and colonies back. Italy must have more land in Africa. Reparations cannot go on much longer.' This year Mussolini has been triumphant, for he has enrolled into his camp not only Germany but also Austria, Hungary, Bulgaria, and Turkey, and he is on excellent terms with Soviet Russia.

And France already hears the tramp of German, Italian, and Russian feet on sacred soil.

So great is France's fear that, the League of Nations is hindered in its work and its very life is endangered. Next year will be a critical one for the League. If it does nothing to countries, to persuade the nations to disarm and if it leaves Germany weak amidst powerful States, then hatred of the League will become violent in Germany and might even force Germany to leave. Is the League doomed? We shall see in 1931 or 1932.

That is a picture of black-threatening clouds. But there are bright rays here and there, and perhaps before long the sun will shine through. One hopeful ray is the work which the League of Nations is doing behind the scenes ... Modest and unspectacular as it is, it is bettering the health of the world, and it is putting the finance of many countries on its feet. Again, there is the help which countries, formerly enemies, are giving each other in Eastern Europe and in the Balkans. They are learning the lesson that loving one's neighbour is practical politics. Then the fact that the hard-headed businessman is on the side of peace and is developing international cartels is a bright sign.

But the most hopeful gleam of all is our friendship with America. It is not long ago that people were predicting war with America. How foolish that all sounds now! Ever since the London Naval Conference in the spring we have been on the best of terms with the United States, and that augurs well for the future.

Will the storm break or will the sun shine through? That is the enigma of the Thirties.[1]

By January 2, 1931, Gareth was in Germany having a successful visit, and meeting numerous politicians. He had met Dr Meissner[2], Hindenburg's right-hand man and was about to see Dr Curtius, the Foreign Office Minister. While waiting, he had seen the leading Ministers of the German Foreign Office and all the diplomats from a window in the President's Palace[3]. On the previous day, he had been at a reception at which President Hindenburg was present. This event was reported in the press and Gareth kept cuttings which he sent to his family.

Die Ehrenwache präsentiert.

Gareth's annotated press cutting:
'President's reception. X = self in window. Can you recognise me?'

Gareth's newspaper cutting following his visit to Wilhelmstrasse. 'XX My taxi stopped here and the whole crowd stared as if I were an Ambassador.'

Gareth spent the weekend in Saxony before proceeding to Poland for another series of interviews with politicians. He wrote of his success in Berlin:

> *Here am I in Waldheim again. I had an interview with the Foreign Minister of Germany, Dr Curtius at the Villa of the Foreign Minister. He spoke very, very openly. You can see that his patience is over... He seemed a sound reasonable man, but without the spark of Lloyd George or Winston Churchill. There will be fireworks in Geneva if he says openly, against the Poles, one tenth of what he told me. The interview lasted 40 minutes and I have sent a report on it to Mr Lloyd George. After the interview with the Foreign Minister, Hans von Haeften (who was at Trinity) and myself walked through the private park to the Foreign Office in the Wilhelmstrasse.*
>
> *I had heaps of interviews with the Ministerial directors at the Foreign Office, with Dr Gaus, who was responsible for Locarno[4]. On Friday also I had a long interview with Count Harry Kessler, a very well-known ex-diplomat, writer and gentleman. All are exceedingly pessimistic about the state of Europe. I lunched with Dr Wolfers, who is principal of the College for Politics. He was*

very interesting. Then on Friday night I went to the Wannsee (equivalent of Richmond Park or Windsor) and dined with the family of Kurt Hahn, who was secretary of Prince Max of Baden, the last Imperial Chancellor of Germany.[5]

Gareth's diary notes in the interview with Dr Curtius that he was adamant that no compromise was possible in the question of Polish Corridor. "There was no Foreign Minister in Europe who had to have a travel permit to cross to a province of his own country. When I went to East Prussia before Christmas my 16-year-old daughter said, "Father! The Poles will arrest you in the Corridor."" Dr Curtius continued:

The province will not survive if East Germany does not reunite with Germany. There is only one solution and that is to give the Corridor back to Germany. Until November 1918 Wilson was all for internationalisation of Vistula, but Dmovski who wanted East Prussia, persuaded Wilson to change his policy by saying that 'three and half million Poles will not vote for you if Polish Corridor to goes to Germany'. In the Versailles Conference, the Poles put forward falsified information.

Germany has no interest in partitioning Poland, but Poland must not fall into Asiatic methods of elections. The Polish government have put their own people in all election places. 100 leaders of the opposition have been put into prison suppressing all resistance. There were brutal methods carried out to influence the vote and all the Poles voted openly, so that it was not secret ballot. Fascism would be better than the brutal methods that were used. It is of the greatest interest to have a well-governed Poland next to us. We have not had incidents so far on the frontier in spite of unprecedented provocation. The dictator, Pilsudski, is not in a powerful position.

It has been a difficult task for me especially to carry through the Young Plan in the Reichstag — a big struggle against my own party, but it was carried with a small majority [the plan to reduce and re-schedule Germany's reparation payments. It did not reduce Germany's humiliation]. We carried it through but the Poles have done nothing. They have not ratified the Young Plan. I must send them an ultimatum. We have always tried to be on good terms with our neighbours, but we can't expect our patience to last forever. My patience is exhausted.

The Poles have never reached international control in Danzig, but we cannot give up the Corridor. Once there was a German majority in the region of the Corridor, but now there is a minority as 750,000 Germans have been thrown out of the area.

There must be an international conference as quickly as possible. It is a Treaty problem — other nations have pledged by the Treaty [of Versailles] to disarm. We must have our Treaty rights as quickly as possible. We cannot possibly remain unarmed if the French are armed. It is a terrific danger if we are bound to the Treaty then it will be a terrible source of unrest.

Germany must think of her security as we are not in a position to defend ourselves against Poland, who have an army of 200,000 to 300,000. What would happen if Poles suddenly attacked us from inside Poland? Pilsudski attacked Vilna so why not Danzig. We must have our security.[6]

Gareth recorded a conversation he had with an out-of-work young Nazi, Karl Oehne, who told Gareth:

The Nazis are bound to triumph. We can't stick it any longer and are desperate. Take our town of Olbernhau. Practically everything is at a standstill. The toy industry has been ruined by foreign competition. Everybody is going over to the Nazis or Communists. If a worker becomes a Communist he gets relief from the party since they get money from Moscow. There have been uprisings here in Olbernhau. I have lot of friends who have gone over from the Social Democrats to the Nazis. The Steel Helmets [an extreme right-wing and anti-Semitic organisation] are bound to join with the Nazis. All Nationalists will unite.

There is bound to be a dictatorship either left or right, probably right. The Nazis say all must have work. We must arm and have a Volkswehr with conscription. The situation will become worse. The towns are all going bankrupt. They cannot pay wages and even some officials only pay half. There is a great deal of Depression and many suicides.

"Krieg wird kommen" [War will come].[7]

When Gareth wrote home on January 9, 1931, it was from the Hotel Monopol, Katowice in Poland. It would appear that Sylvester (Lloyd George's Secretary) had contacted Gareth's family in Barry to find out how to contact him in Poland. Neither Gareth nor his parents knew why:

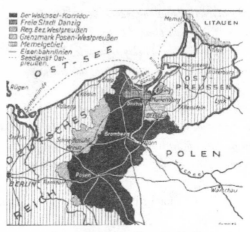

The Polish Corridor (shown in black).

Thank you very much for the postcards. I haven't heard from Mr Sylvester yet, but sent him a wire telling him my next address. It's certainly nothing to do with the article. It's probably about a matter I wrote to Mr Lloyd George and Sylvester about last week. The son of Prince Max of Baden is going to England and wanted an interview with Lloyd George. Probably it was about that. Or, Lloyd George suddenly decided he wanted me to study some special problem.

He went on to describe the situation:

Last night there were hunger demonstrations here. Large numbers of unemployed crowded through the streets- I with them- and shouted 'Bread! Bread! Hleba! Hleba!' Then the mounted police came and scattered the crowd."[8]

In the event the letter from Sylvester arrived the next day informing him of a 'reorganisation of staff' that affected him. Mr Sylvester had wanted to inform Gareth of the situation as soon as possible in case he wanted to curtail his European trip. Gareth guessed correctly that the economies being talked about in the office before Christmas were to take effect. Not for the last time in his life Gareth was to lose his job as a result of financial constraints.

With the same post I received a letter from Miss Edwards saying that she was leaving the office last Thursday, and that there has been talk of economy all along the line. ... I wonder who else will have to leave. Malcolm Thomas has been nervous about it too, but I don't think he will go, because he is such an all-round man ... Miss Edwards says 15 people were leaving Lloyd George's — one had been there 30 years. Sylvester has been anxious about the financial situation and we have had instructions to economise. However, he reassured his parents saying "*Please don't worry. I am quite all right because I can go straight away to Ivy Lee. I am very sorry for the others [in the office] though.*" And later in the same letter "*Please don't worry. If you had a tenth of the misery what there is here and in Germany and if you'd been one of the people shouting 'Bread! Bread! In Kattowitz, you would have something to worry about.*[9]

During Gareth's busy trip to Poland he had a long interview with the Governor of Katowice, Mr Grazynski. This meeting formed the basis of an article entitled 'Poland's Foreign Relations', which was later published in the July 1931 edition of The Contemporary Review. This article remarkably foresaw the secret addendum to the August 1939 Molotov-Ribbentrop Pact in which Germany and Russia agreed to carve up Poland:

The eternal fear of a German-Russian Alliance makes the Poles cling more tenaciously than ever to the Corridor. "If Germany regains her pre-war territory," said a politician in Warsaw, "then she will be able to join with Russia through Lithuania and we will be like a nut in a nutcracker, surrounded on almost all sides by hostile neighbours. We are willing to do anything to have good relations with Germany except commit suicide."

After five days in Danzig, Gareth arrived back in his London office on January 16, 1931. He was disappointed he could not visit his family in Barry for the weekend, but there was so much work to do on his return from the continent. There was a brief to be done by the end of the week for Lloyd George, and Megan wanted one on a "Month in Wales" by the following Saturday. He also had a lecture at the RIIA, which would take a lot of time to prepare.

Gareth continued to work with Lloyd George until the end of February, 1931. He told his parents that he had come to a fair arrangement with the office, especially as Lloyd George's financial situation was very low. Gareth had received a cheque for £45 for February, and he would receive another two cheques for £30 each until the end of April.[10]

Gareth's personally inscribed photograph from Lloyd George.

On March 30, 1931, Gareth received a cable that his visa for America had been approved. He would, therefore, place himself at the disposal of Ivy Lee any time from April 1, 1931. Mr Ivy Lee was due to arrive at the Carlton Club, London that evening, but Gareth had no idea when they would be sailing.

> *I went to say goodbye to Lloyd George and he was charming. We motored from the House of Commons together to near Victoria. He said in an emphatic way; 'you have been most helpful. You must write to me now and then'. He wants me to send information about America. Then he gave me a photograph (which I had already by the way) and wrote on it, "With sincere recognition of the intelligent help and best wishes for your future. D. Lloyd George.*[11]

Gareth went to say his other farewells. He saw his sister, Eirian, and her new baby, John (the author's brother). He called at Board of Trade where he saw Sir Percy Watkins, and Dr Thomas Jones. Finally, he visited Sir Bernard Pares. He was ill and his voice was husky. His children had not been told about his illness for a fortnight. His house was cold and miserable "a house of the past. So, I was very sorry for Sir Bernard. He is going to give me some excellent letters of introduction in America."

Notes on Chapter 10

1
  Gareth Jones, 'The Victim of 1930', the *Western Mail*, December 31, 1930, p. 12.

2
  Dr Meissner informed Gareth that the whole country was socially and economically dissatisfied. He considered that there would soon be a split in the Coalition government of the five political parties. [The Social Democrats had the greatest number of seats.] It would be best for the Parliament to continue to govern, but the situation was very serious. The Government had the support of President Hindenburg and the Reichswehr, and the Defence Minister was loyal, but it was quite possible that the Generals would go over to the Nazis. There might even be a coalition between the Nazis, the Social Democrats, and the Volkspartei (The People's Party), that would cause anxiety at first, but it would be right from the economic point of view. The French would certainly increase rearming, and the Poles would become hysterical. Meissner believed that the Nazis would rearm but would not start a war. The Volkspartei had become more right wing and was now a minority party.

3
  Gareth Vaughan Jones Papers, National Library of Wales Correspondence Series B6/3. January 2, 1931.

4
  Locarno Treaty (1925). An International Treaty which attempted to solve Europe's problems after the Treaty of Versailles. It resolved the borders of Germany and Germany joined the League of Nations.

5
  Gareth Vaughan Jones Papers, National Library of Wales Correspondence Series B6/3. January 4, 1930.

6
  Gareth Vaughan Jones Papers, National Library of Wales Gareth Jones Diary Series B1/6.

7
  Ibid.

8
  Gareth Vaughan Jones Papers, National Library of Wales Correspondence Series 1-21 File 12. January 9, 1931

9
  Ibid. January 10, 1931

10
  Gareth Vaughan Jones Papers, National Library of Wales Correspondence Series B6/3. March 5, 1931.

11
  Ibid. March 30, 1931.

PART 3

With Ivy Lee Public Relations, New York (1931 — 32)

Chapter 11

New York 1931

The *Île de France*, one of the finest, most luxurious liners on the Atlantic, sailed from Plymouth for New York at 6.30 am on Thursday morning, 16 April 1931. The evening before, Gareth had called to say farewell to his friend, Patrick Norton. He was now Lord Rathcreedan, having succeeded to his father's title, after his recent death in 1930. Gareth visited the RIIA to pick up his mail and said goodbye to the hall porter. Arriving at the station in plenty of time he registered his bags and those of Mr Ivy Lee that he had picked up from the Carlton Club. The railway porter took him to a first-class sleeper glistening with 'nothing but silver knobs and mirrors!'[1] It was most comfortable, though he slept fitfully. The attendant woke him very early the following day with tea and biscuits.

The ship lay in the 'Roads', several miles off the English coast. A tender took 40 or 50 passengers away from the shores of England to the fine-looking liner with her green and red funnels. They approached, looking up at the ship towering above them. Entering through a small door in the side of the ship, a little uniformed boy took Gareth to his cabin where a lovely surprise was waiting. There were telegrams with "Cheerio Boy". "Good-Luck". "Bon Voyage" and "Best of Luck from the McKenzie clan".[2] Soon he was up on the deck watching the tender return to Plymouth, and the gorse on the headland disappearing from view.

According to Gareth the dining room was a wonderful room, and bigger than it seemed in the advertising. It was ten to fifteen times larger than a 'favourite haunt' of his, the Carlton Club. The menu was exquisite. Every day the interesting company at Gareth's table dressed for dinner, and their conversation was cosmopolitan and lively. The ship offered all kinds of amusements and entertainment; deck games, dancing in the vast ballroom, cinema programmes, and concerts in the huge tea saloon. Every so often there was a loud bang of shooting at 'clay pigeons' — a kind of disc thrown into the air, he explained to his parents. Gareth most enjoyed watching the Punch and Judy Show and the small children shrieking with laughter.[3]

After breakfast on the first morning, Gareth sent a visiting card to Mr and Mrs Lee's cabin. The Lees had boarded the liner in France at the onset of the liner's journey. The American entrepreneur came and said, "I've told them to give you a better cabin." The new cabin was much bigger than the previous one with a porthole looking out on the Atlantic.[4]

Ivy Ledbetter Lee. Personally inscribed photo to Gareth, April 24th 1932.

The following morning Gareth had a long talk with Ivy Lee in his suite about Gareth's work, and about Russia. Ivy Lee was going to write a book called *What of Russia Now?* and Gareth was to undertake the research, and, in particular, study the history of the Russian Revolution and the Policies of Lenin. Some work would be undertaken in the New York libraries where Gareth would follow the Russian Press. Ivy Lee was fair in his judgment of Russia and tended to be sympathetic towards the Communists. Gareth's additional duties would be to follow any developments in the oil and sugar trades.[5]

Gareth's could barely contain his excitement at the sights and sounds of New York and his new job. He spent his first night in the great city at Ivy Lee's elegant apartment on 5th Avenue, with its vast rooms and a first-class library.

A taxi drove me from the boat to the elegant apartment of Mr Lee in Fifth Avenue, the Park Lane of New York, overlooking Central Park…Jimmy Lee,[Mr Lee's son] showed me to my bedroom. Then he suggested showing me New

York in his car. Broadway was a wonder, blazing with light far more than I expected. It is hard to realise that the buildings are so high until one is under them... Notices of Sales were everywhere: "Giving up after 40 years business." "The business is being liquidated," "Forced to sell." [6]

...Jimmy Lee suggested going up the Chrysler Building, which was until recently in the highest building in the world, over 1000 feet [in height] I believe and over 70 stories (sic). I have never seen anything so terrific as the view from the top when you look down on the dazzling red lights and the streets almost straight down. (The view from the Chrysler Building is by far the most impressive thing I have ever seen in my life. The second is I think the view of Mont Blanc I had with Dada.). Mr Lee is public relations counsel of the Chrysler Building and Company. [7]

The following day Mr Lee took Gareth to the Metropolitan Club.

It is known as the "Millionaires' Club". We drove beneath the skyscrapers for miles into the city. Mr Lee showed me everything, where Tammany[8] was etc etc. Finally, we got into WALL ST, skyscrapers towering all around. 15 Broad St is almost on the corner of Wall Street and is itself a tremendous skyscraper! I [had] imagined it to be quite a small building. The lift took us up to the 34th floor! We got out and I saw a dignified brass square: IVY LEE and ASSOCIATES [9]

Mr Lee asked Gareth to wait while he attended to some correspondence. His Secretary brought some letters for Gareth, including one from Mr Rowntree, enclosing letters of introduction. Soon Gareth overheard a conversation:

"Are the public still selling?" "How many Associate shares do I hold?" "Send this telegram to General Atterbury." Atterbury was the president of the Pennsylvania Railroad, and, one of the greatest business magnates of the US."

I was then taken round the office and given a fine room to myself with a wonderful view over New York, the [Hudson] river, New Jersey, Empire State Building (the biggest building in the world)". [10]

After lunch he went back to see Mr Lee and "discovered what a tremendous power he is in the world. I was astounded by what happened". The Minister of Nicaragua waited outside his office. On entering he bowed to Ivy Lee, "as if he were God".

He was terribly humble. "I am deeply honoured to meet you... You know how our country has suffered; first the earthquake and then the world Depression. We want to appeal to Mr Rockefeller. We want to restore our country. We know what wonderful things the Rockefeller Foundation has done in the way of charity. To help Nicaragua would be a humanitarian act if Mr Rockefeller would grant us some money. We want a loan but we cannot pay a high interest, so we want to avoid going to Trusts or Banks".[11]

Mr Lee treated him in a very condescending way. "He [Rockefeller] would never think of giving a loan as charity. When he does business, he does it for business's' sake; when he is philanthropic he does it for the sake of philanthropy. He would never camouflage a gift as a loan."[12]

Gareth hardly had time to settle in before he was sent to Washington DC. There had been some confusion about where his first assignment would be — Washington or Cuba — but after the meeting with the Nicaraguan minister Gareth notes in his letter that "it would be more valuable for me to go to Washington".[13]

He took the 6.40 [pm] train, arriving in Washington shortly after midnight, and registered The Willard, a hotel near the White House. The hotel was full of important women in glasses who talked about committees and wore badges and ribbons. They turned out to be a group of Nationalists calling themselves the 'Daughters of the American Revolution'.

The following day Gareth came across the Daughters of the American Revolution again near the White House with their badges and now carrying banners. There were a few young men with them. He followed them, by-passing the policeman at the White House gate, and walked with the crowd into the gardens of the White House by the side-door and into President Hoover's private grounds. The women started clapping and the President Hoover himself appeared, smiling benignly. The group collected for a photo which Gareth gate-crashed, standing behind Hoover in the centre. On Thursday evening Gareth writes:

My dearest All,
During my first day in the capital of the United States I have:
Disguised myself as a Daughter of the American Revolution
Been admitted into the private gardens behind the White House and
HAD MY PHOTOGRAPH TAKEN WITH THE PRESIDENT OF THE UNITED STATES! (a lot of other people in the photo of course!) [14]

Gareth was in the White House two weeks later when he got into the private gardens of the President and strolled around. "The White House pleased me very much, a cross between private house and a palace with best points of each. I met State Secretary Stimson at the garden party, but I was one among many hundreds who shook hands with him and Hoover. President Hoover told me he was 'very glad to meet me!' It is strange that the President of the United States makes the impression of being just an ordinary Tom, Dick or Harry, and has none of the dignity of a King or a Prime Minister of Great Britain."[15]

Gareth standing behind President Hoover in the gardens of the White House.

The following day Gareth noted in his diary:

> *After spending time in research at the Soviet Information Bureau, I became a tourist. The parkland is very green in colour with trees and gardens. I climbed the 500-foot Memorial Tower where I saw a magnificent view of Washington and Potomac River, and I visited the Lincoln Memorial where I read the message 'Government of the people, by the people, for the people'.*

On April 29, 1931 Gareth wrote home:

I have just been watching the four-funnelled Cunarder, the Mauritania sail for Great Britain… and I shall nearly always be able to see the liners arrive carrying letters from you. I am still staying at the Princeton Club at £13 a month and I find everything very expensive. I am looking for room with a Russian family to speak Russian; everywhere is very expensive.

I have just played a part in the Great Oil War here in Mr Lee's office, and we are in the centre of the war. Ivy Lee is one of the commanders of Rockefeller's side (Standard Oil), and he is fighting against Royal Dutch. (Under Deterding).[16] The latest move in the game is a book to be launched against Royal Dutch, who, according to this office has been guilty of malpractice. Royal Dutch is the company which sells Shell. Ivy Lee hopes the book will make American petrol users abandon Shell and use Standard Oil product. The reason for the book, my chief work, on Russia is that Mr Lee is favourable to the Soviet Union, probably because his clients, Standard Oil are keen on good relations. Standard Oil buys a lot of Soviet Petrol and sells it in Asia.

In the next room to me, a young man looks after the interests of American Tobacco (a monster company). He writes articles for them and does their publicity. Ivy Lee gets $50,000 (£10,000) a year for publicity alone. Young Jimmy Lee is studying Chilean Nitrates and doing their advertising.[17]

Gareth was never without friends and he frequently met Laurie Bunker, who had now returned to the States from Cambridge University and was a budding young lawyer. Gareth did not forget his other friends from Cambridge. One weekend, he took a ship from New York to Boston to visit Gerald Graham and Pierpoint Stackpole.

Gareth was also in touch with Pierre Winkler in New York. As part of his scholarship, he was studying American Foreign Policy in the Caribbean (Cuba, Puerto Rica) which he says is "revolting. The [American] oppression of the nations he says is terrible. Nearly all the land for sugar cultivation is in American possession that they had bought for a song."[18]

Gareth and Winkler met for dinner and discussed the collapse of Law and Order in the United States. He told Gareth of an experience that illustrated how bad justice was in the United States. A policeman had come up to him, accompanied by two women who accused him of molesting him, and threatening him with prison. Another policeman came and joined them: "I'll see to him. You seem a decent fellow. I don't want to take you to jail." Pierre took out his pocket book

Gareth and Laurie Bunker in November / December 1934.

which only had five dollars. "That will do." The policeman nodded, took the 5 dollars, smiled and said: "Well you can go now. Good-bye!"[19]

Gareth was introduced to the Washington Correspondent of the *Berliner Tageblatt*, Paul Scheffer. Scheffer had spent many years in Moscow as a correspondent, but in 1929 was the first journalist to be refused a re-entry visa as a result of his negative reporting of Five-Year Plan.[20] Scheffer invited Gareth to lunch on April 27th, as he was keen to hear what the Gareth had recently observed in the Soviet Union. From this initial meeting they were to become close colleagues.[21]

On the morning of May 3, 1931, the telephone phone rang and Gareth was invited at very short notice by Ivy Lee to attend the International Chamber of Commerce congress in Washington DC, where there would be representatives from 35 different countries, including some of the leading manufacturers of the world. He had to be at the Pennsylvania Station by 10.50 am. That evening he reported to his parents, "Life is such a rush. This is a wonderful opportunity for me to study the world situation from all the best experts in world trade. This morning I heard Hoover make a speech, the opening speech. All said it was a pathetic failure. He missed a great opportunity and showed himself a weak and broken man. He looks much older. He had a feeble reception. I felt very sorry for him." [22]

One of Ivy Lee's assistants told Gareth that "Mr Lee says he likes new blood all the time in his office and follows the American method of 'rapid turnover' in his assistants. Most of the staff are young and are snapped up very soon by all kinds of professions (journalism, university, lecturing, foreign affairs, economics, and business). To have been with Ivy Lee is considered to be a good recommendation and training in itself. So, you have no need to worry about my future." [23]

> I have seen a lot of Sir George Paish, the economist who is the most loveable and gentle man I have ever met in my life. Mr Lee said; 'He is a man of beautiful character'. He is strikingly like Dada in a very large number of ways; looks, manners, attitude to people. I know nobody so similar to Dada. Sir George is a perfect product of the best of British education and which is gentleness, kindness and polish and naturalness which cannot be beaten by any kind of man in any country… Sir George is most pessimistic about the future. He hinted that Mussolini might be overthrown and that the man who would have to be at the head of affairs in a liberal government Italy would be Prof. Ferraro. [24]

At the conference Gareth dined with Mr Lee, Mr Leo Pasvolsky (a Russian émigré economist and expert on Russian affairs who Gareth had first met in London) and his wife, together with Sir Harry Britain (owner of the *London Illustrated News*, Director of Napiers):

> He is an exact opposite [of Sir George] jolly, frivolous, popular, and a self-made man. … [He] was most amusing, and telling us how he'd had adventures everywhere except Tibet and in a few of the South Sea Islands…
> … There is deep gloom about the world crisis here. Private conversations show few signs of hope. Public utterances are on purpose optimistic. It is difficult for anyone who is not in business or production to realise how the world has crashed in the last year or two. [25]

Gareth continued on the same theme in a letter five days later:

> The Congress in Washington was exceedingly pessimistic. Whatever the newspapers say, the businessmen of the world are looking forward to a very long period of depression and trouble. All the world over there is chaos in trade

and industry. The Congress seemed to cow-tow terribly to the United States. They were very weak in the resolutions, and there was a general atmosphere of failure. The unemployed all over the world are having an awful time, and all the countries are having the same problem. Nobody out of work gets such a good time as in Great Britain…

I met one of the American advisers who had been at the Versailles Conference in 1919. He said David Lloyd George made a fight for fair play, and that his instincts were right, but the pressure from the Members of Parliament in England were too great for him to use his influence.[26]

Gareth's letter writing was always timetabled to catch the boats that carried the mail to the UK. He saw many of them docked on the river from his office window and he often mentioned which boat his latest letter would travel on. On May 10, 1931 it was the *Bremen*, "the fastest boat in the world."

My work could not possibly be better or more interesting. I have moved to my new address with the Savicliffe's to speak Russian and go to the Russian club to read newspapers.

Yesterday evening, I introduced myself to David Davies [later ennobled as 1st Baron Davies of Llandinam] as Dada's son.[His father, had met him on many occasions in the cause of peace and their mutual interest in the New Commonwealth Movement][27] *I said how much Dada had appreciated receiving his book. He said, "You're the fellow who writes those wonderful articles, aren't you."*

Thursday morning [May 7th], I had breakfast with David Davies whom I liked exceedingly. He is very earnest and sensitive about his scheme for international peace. He presented me with his book. He is anxious to see Mr Ivy Lee and is looking for a rich American to finance an organisation for world peace. But everyone is hard up here so I am afraid he will have little success.[28]

During my visit to Washington, I went to see several people about Russian research. Tomorrow, I begin in earnest on the Russian work, and I shall go ahead at full speed, because Mr Lee wants his book in the hands of the publisher by August 1st. So, I shall concentrate on that, for the next couple of months. It will be most valuable work for me because I shall be studying the origins of the Russian Revolution and the events of the first few years. That is just the stuff I know little about. So, it will increase my knowledge.[29]

On May 20, 1931, Gareth was delighted to meet Col. Davies again.

Today, there was a knock at the door, and in came Col. David Davies. He had an appointment with Mr Lee, but Mr Lee had not yet come back. We had a long talk and I gave the Soviet Govt's attitude towards war. Then Roy, the black doorman, came and said that Mr Lee wanted to see both of us... I had not seen Mr Lee since Washington. Mr Lee asked both of us down to lunch... and while there he left us for a few moments to talk to a man rather like Gwilym Davis, who was seated by the window. When he came back he said, "Just take a look at that man. He is a future President of the United States" We glanced over and David Davies said, "Who is he?" "That's Newton D. Baker who was Secretary for War. He is a statesman, that man. You watch. He will become the President."

Talk at lunch was very interesting. David Davies is very shy and self-conscious. I believe Mr Lee is afraid of a very serious economic collapse. Unless something is done within three months he fears the worst. Some leading men including Mr Lee are going to bring pressure to bear on the President to make a dramatic gesture to restore the confidence of the world. But what is he to say? That is what is worrying Mr Lee. He was asking David Davies what action by Hoover would have such a psychological effect as to turn the tide and avoid disaster.[30]

Railroads are very weak, and there is a great fear about them. US Steel (which is a barometer of the economic situation here) is down to 98. It was the surest and safest stock and stood once at 261. So Wall Street (which is underneath my window) is very nervous.

Just about an hour ago, I saw the Mauritania going fast down Hudson River on its way to England. It was much smaller than I expected. Colonel David Davies was on board.[31]

Laurie Bunker invited Gareth to dine with Mrs Dorr, the wife of Judge Dorr who defended Standard Oil in a then famous merger case. At the Dorrs' dinner party, they discussed the alarming disregard of the Law. Apparently, there were racketeers in every aspect of life: in liquor, in milk, in sugar and in the trade unions.

Gareth heard of many other instances of the breakdown of Law and Order. He regularly had breakfast at the "Coffee Pot," and one morning the Italian proprietor said, "That man Hindendorff [Hindenburg] that is like the Kaiser, he says there will be war. I am not so sure he isn't right. But, we get enough killings here without a war. Last night, two gangsters were shot two blocks away in my district." [32]

Gareth, a teetotaller, once stopped to talk to a man on the street a few yards from his rooms who was arguing with some people about the liquor racket. Aware that the prohibition regulations were broken freely, it was explained to him, what "taking the rap" meant:

> A guy would have 'paper ownership' of a drug store selling illicit liquor. He would take the 'rap' for selling the liquor in the store and not the owner, who accordingly did not lose his license. The police who were bribed by the owner would turn a blind eye to booze being sold at 'speakeasies'. The 'bootlegger', who delivered it, was paid-up as well. [33]

On one particular day, two unemployed men approached Gareth for money. He had long chats with them, and found it was very sad. One man had come all the way from Virginia by lorry. The other poor man was an office worker who had been out of work for four months. This pale and dejected fellow was afraid of seeing any of his friends because he had borrowed money from them. The food they got after standing four to five hours in bread line was miserable — only rotten soup. He told Gareth that there were probably a million unemployed in New York.

Gareth spent the weekend of June 12-14 in Boston, sailing there and back, where he met some of his relatives of his brother-in-law, as well as his old friends Stackpole and Gerald Graham. At dinner they discussed the political situation and Gareth noted:

> America is in a mood of self-criticism. People here are a thousand times more depressed and our attacking their weak points more than in England. And they have heaps of weak points. It must be awful to be an unemployed worker here, no dole, no health insurance, nothing...
>
> ...Are you glad that I am having experience of life in the heart of the capitalist world? It's not many people who have had their office first near the mother of Parliaments and the in the centre of finance Wall St? [34]
>
> Last night I went to have supper at Mrs Jukoff's, a Russian lady who lives in the same street as I do. She is noble, about 65 years of age and has a very nice son who was an officer... He lost his job and is now doing some translation. I help him in the translating and in exchange they talk Russian to me...
>
> I went to Pond's Lecture Agency this week to get fixtures for the winter. They are the leading people. They seemed very impressed with my testimonials. The

Lloyd George on performs wonders. The very fact that I was with LG gives me a fine status here.[35]

Oh LG referred to me in his Free Trade Speech (not by name of course) I wrote to LG and had a reply from Sylvester, saying that LG had used my stuff. He enclosed a cutting. LG refers to me as a 'a friend of mine in America, an able man in touch with some of the leading industrialists in America…[36]

…Please don't worry about the summer school etc etc. Think of the worries people are having here; millions without work; most people having lost heaps of money. It's lucky I've got a job.[37]

On June 20, 1931, a month after the lunch with David Davies, President Hoover proposed a one-year moratorium on inter-governmental war debt payments. Ivy Lee wrote on June 23, 1931 to President Hoover congratulating him. "I am one of those who threw my hat in the air when I read of your proposal proposed plan for the German moratorium. This was a great step and in the nick of time."

On June 29th as a PS to his Sunday letter Gareth wrote in large handwriting, underlined twice, "Hurray! Hurray! Everything fixed up. I am going to London and Russia with the son of Mr Heinz (57 varieties) and to get information for Mr Lee. Shall write again.[38]

On July 3, 1931, full of excitement, Gareth told his family more about this unexpected opportunity:

My visit to Europe. Isn't it splendid! I am lucky. I am having a wonderful almost 2-month trip abroad, first-class expenses and a great view of what is happening in Russia and Europe…

I wish I had time to give the details but I shall write more fully over the week-end… It will be splendid to see you all. I tried to imagine how you got my cable, and how unexpected it was. Were you glad? Or just pleasantly surprised?[39]

True to his word, Gareth wrote on July 7 setting out the circumstance of his meeting in more measured tones.

A fortnight ago Mr Lee called me in to his room, and there was a good-looking dark-haired young man with intelligent eyes. 'This is Mr Heinz who has just graduated from Yale and who is going to go to Russia. I have just been giving him some tips about the journey.' We talked about the trip and then young Heinz said afterwards that he was going to Trinity College, Cambridge. I said that was

106

my college and he was very pleased 'Shake hands', he said. I asked him to come and lunch with me, and then left him in the office with Mr Lee.

In the afternoon Mr Lee called me in again. "That was the son of an old friend of mine, Heinz of the 57 varieties. I told Heinz, the father, that his son would learn very little going with guides, but that a member of my staff knew Russian. Mr Heinz was very keen on you accompanying his son. I said I would ask you? 'What do you say to it?'" "I'd jump at it," I said. "I thought you would. Very well we'll see. Prepare an itinerary for three weeks to a month straight away and show it to me and we'll send it to Mr Heinz."

I returned to my room and nearly danced at the prospect of a voyage to Europe and Russia.

Well, here is my trip: Wednesday July 29th I sail on the Aquitania, (Cunard) with a First Class cabin. On Tuesday August 5th, I arrive in London where I shall join Jack Heinz and stay at the Dorchester Hotel, Park Lane (the finest hotel in Europe, newly opened). That tickles me. Such a change from 31, Doughty Street [where Gareth had lived in his frugal days in London]...

On Saturday August 8, Jack Heinz, a college friend of his, and I will sail from London Bridge on a Soviet steamer to Leningrad where we arrive on my birthday. Then follows a fine Russian trip to Moscow, Nizhni-Novgorod, down the Volga on a steamer to Stalingrad, thence to Rostov, then to Kharkov, Dnieperstroy, Kiev and into Poland (arriving between September 7-12th). At Crakow I say goodbye to Jack Heinz, and go through Germany to Berlin, getting interviews at the President's Palace and Foreign Office and big companies for Mr Lee. Then, a First Class sleeper to Paris, where I interview some people for Mr Lee. Then London (about Sept 16-18th, see a lot of people and then best of all home for 2 days about Sept 18th, 19th or 20th.[40]

In a more wistful vein he continued:

This morning from my office window I saw the Scythia, a handsome one-funnelled Cunarder steam up the Hudson River. It is not a fast boat. About an hour later I saw a fine sight — the Majestic very close to the shore, huge, with the yellow funnels of the White Star Line. And three weeks tomorrow on Aunt Winnie's birthday at 11 pm I shall be saying goodbye to the lights of New York and heading for the Atlantic, Southampton, London and Barry.

"Tomorrow I am going with Mr Lee to Montauk Point, right on the tip of Long Island. He is going to write his book on Russia in one week; so he says. We

shall stay in a place which is very "high hat". Montauk Point looks out towards the Atlantic and is one of the most healthy spots in America. [41]

On July 12, 1931, Gareth's Sunday letter home was written on the beach:

I am lying on the sand watching the huge breakers coming in from the Atlantic. Not far away, the US air ship Los Angeles is moored. I saw her arrive last night. One could see the red and green light in the sky.

Mr Lee, two secretaries, and myself, are here at one of America's super hotels right on the furthermost end of Long Island. Mr Lee is escaping from New York and is going to do his work in the country where is it cool and pleasant... Mr Lee is going to begin work on the Russian book before long. We came out Thursday. The Pennsylvania Railroad kept the train waiting 4 minutes especially for Mr Lee. Tonight I am returning to New York to look into the Bolshevik archives in the Public Library.

Notes on Chapter 11

[1] Gareth Vaughan Jones Papers, National Library of Wales Correspondence Series 1-21 File 12. April 4, 1931.

[2] Gareth Vaughan Jones Papers, National Library of Wales Correspondence Series B6/3. April 21, 1931.

[3] Gareth Vaughan Jones Papers, National Library of Wales Correspondence Series 1-21 File 12. April 19, 1931.

[4] Gareth Vaughan Jones Papers, National Library of Wales Correspondence Series B6/3. April 21, 1931.

[5] Ibid.

[6] Gareth Vaughan Jones Papers, National Library of Wales Correspondence Series 1-21 File 12. April 22, 1931.

[7] Gareth Vaughan Jones Papers, National Library of Wales Correspondence Series B6/3. April 23, 1931.

[8] Tammany. A charitable institution run by the Democrats. Corruption in city politics was investigated by a committee headed by Samuel Seabury (1930–31), of the city magistrates' courts which completely discredited Tammany Hall and this ultimately brought about the resignation (1932) of Mayor James J. Walker.

[9] Gareth Vaughan Jones Papers, National Library of Wales Correspondence Series B6/3. April 23, 1931.

[10] Ibid.

[11] Ibid.

[12] Ibid.

[13] Ibid.

[14] Ibid.

[15] Ibid. May 9, 1931.

16
  Shell Oil, headquartered in The Hague, Netherlands, properly named Royal Dutch/Shell Group, was founded in 1890 by Jean Kessler, along with Henri Deterding and Hugo Loudon, when a Royal charter was granted by the Queen of the Netherlands to a small oil exploration company known as "Royal Dutch."

17
  Gareth Vaughan Jones Papers, National Library of Wales Correspondence Series B6/3. April 29, 1931.

18
  Ibid. April 30, 1931.

19
  Ibid.

20
  He reported in May 1928 that there had been bread riots in Ukraine, the Don region and along the Volga. In June 1929 he warned that the food shortage was growing daily and by early 1930 he was anticipating catastrophe. His articles were read with appreciation at the Foreign Office and was called the finest journalist ever to work in the Soviet Union'.

21
  Ibid.

22
  Gareth Vaughan Jones Papers, National Library of Wales Correspondence Series 1-21 File 12. May 3, 1931.

23
  Ibid.

24
  Ibid. May 5, 1931.

25
  Ibid.

26
  Gareth Vaughan Jones Papers, National Library of Wales Correspondence Series B6/3. May 10, 1931.

27
  In 1941 Lord Davies published a book entitled *The Foundations of Victory*, a copy of which he gave to Gareth's father. He inscribed it 'To my friend Edgar Jones, in appreciation of his services to the Cause of Justice and the Temple of Peace and his efforts to lay the "foundations" with the sincere gratitude of the author. 4th April 1941. D.'

28
  Gareth Vaughan Jones Papers, National Library of Wales Correspondence Series B6/3. May 10, 1931.

29
  Gareth's research on Russia for Dr Ivy Lee, which covered the following topics:

  1. Lenin in Germany in 1917. The myth of Lenin as a German Agent.

  2. Russian repudiation of debts.

  3. Private properties in Russia

  4. The terror and Soviet Justice.

  5. Religion and Social Code. Anti-Bolshevik Propaganda, Zinoviev letter.

  6. The Communist International.

30
  Ivy Lee Papers, Seeley G. Mudd Manuscript Library, Princeton, University of Pennsylvania, USA (Box 2 Folder 22 entitled 'Herbert Hoover May 1931') of his letter of July 29, 1933 to President Hoover on improving the economic depression:

  'I feel strongly convinced however, that the measures which had been taken up are only temporary and that unless fundamental measures are taken to correct the situation at possible moment we will be faced with an even more serious crisis in the not distant future.

  '1. United States would have to assume some kind of political relationship with the other countries of Europe either through membership in the League of Nations implementing the Kellogg Pact or otherwise as will give France a sense of security.

  '2. The problem of German reparations and inter-allied debts must be faced realistically with due regard not merely to the financial and economic but also to the social and political considerations involved.

The sooner we go about this fundamentally the sooner will trouble be out of the way.'

31 Gareth Vaughan Jones Papers, National Library of Wales Correspondence Series B6/3. May 20, 1931.

32 Ibid. May 31, 1931.

33 Ibid. June 4, 1931

34 Gareth Vaughan Jones Papers, National Library of Wales Correspondence Series 1-21 File 12. June 14, 1931.

35 Ibid. June 19 1931

36 Ibid. June 21 1931

37 Ibid. June 23, 1931.

38 Ibid. June 29, 1931.

39 Gareth Vaughan Jones Papers, National Library of Wales Correspondence Series B6/3. July 3, 1931.

40 Ibid. July 7, 1931.

41 Ibid.

Chapter 12

In 'Russia' with Jack Heinz

Gareth commenced his journey to the Soviet Union, sailing in luxury on the RMS *Aquitania*. He described his stateroom on the Cunard ship as excellent, a great contrast to the accommodation he had experienced on the 'tramp' steamers in his impoverished student days. The voyage was even better than the one on the *Île de France*, and he was very fortunate to meet the most distinguished people. At his dinner table of eight he had pleasant company including the Staff Captain, who had 'a great sense of humour'. Another dinner companion was the wife of Sir Auckland Geddes, at one time the British Ambassador in Washington. The current British Ambassador, Sir Ronald Lindsay was also on board. Exploring the ship's library, Gareth found a 1931 copy of *The Contemporary Review* with his article on Poland. He anticipated meeting his family in Barry after four months absence with great excitement.[1]

In London, Gareth joined Jack Heinz II at the Dorchester Hotel before embarking from the Port of London on their journey. His sister Eirian met them on the ship, the *SS Rudzutak,* at London Docks to wish them "Bon Voyage". Many years later, when in her ninetieth year, she recalled seeing Jack Heinz's suitcase bulging with the '57' varieties including tins of Heinz baked beans. On board the ship, using a sheet of headed notepaper taken from the luxurious London hotel, Gareth wrote, "The Height of Capitalism" and below the ship's name was written "The Height of Communism." The note just said, "Saturday, August 8, Sitting on board this Soviet boat, *Rudzutak*. My dearest all, we sail soon for Russia. We shall have a fine time. Jack Heinz is a great sport. This will be a good trip. I hope you have a good August." Heinz later compiled Gareth's diary notes into a small book which was published anonymously in the following year, entitled *Experiences In Russia — 1931: A Diary* and is long out of print. Gareth wrote the preface. Page numbers after a quote in this chapter are all from the book. [2]

That evening Gareth and Heinz sailed from London on the Soviet steamer, which Heinz described at the start of his book:

The Heinz Family 1931. Inscribed to Gareth, "On the eve of your dramatic departure for Europe."

A 5,000-ton cargo and passenger steamer, neat and clean; and the lounge and dining saloon were nicely decorated. We had expected to get a good meal on board, but got only tea, served in a glass mug, and bread, cold ham, sausage, and cheese. (p.15)

Roaming about the boat, they discovered a "Lenin Corner" in the crew's quarters, where there stood a fine bust of Lenin. On the walls were several photographs of Karl Marx, Joseph Stalin, and other Party leaders and generals. Nearby, a bulletin board was plastered with Communist propaganda. A statement regarding the current world depression was entitled, "Two Worlds — The World of Capitalism' and 'The World of Growing Socialism" which Gareth translated:

August 1 [sic], is the International Red Day of the struggle of the revolutionary proletariat against the dangers of imperialist wars and the threats of attack on the USSR.

August 1st is the eve of a deepening of the world economic crisis, and of an unprecedented embitterment of conflicts between Capitalist countries, and especially between the systems of building Socialism and decaying Capitalism. (pp. 16-17)

The ship was delayed twenty-four hours by calling at Hamburg to load a cargo of German machinery. Heinz noted that the *Rudzutak* had previously dumped 2,000 tons of butter in England in order to obtain foreign credit to pay for Stalin's Five-Year Plan — this would have undersold the English or Danish product by 30%.[3]

They eventually reached Leningrad, where Gareth and Jack were met at the dock by an Intourist man and an interpreter, a young lady who had accompanied George Bernard Shaw on his visit to Russia the previous month.[4] The following day, they joined some American tourists visiting the Winter Palace, the Hermitage, and a sanatorium for the workers' sick children. Soviet propaganda posters were everywhere in the institution and such lines in big red letters, which read as; "Defenders of the USSR," was accompanied by pictures of guns, battleships and soldiers. Yet another poster said: "The Shock Brigade work is our method; the Five-Year Plan is our aim."[5]

'Komsomol Members (Soviet Youth) - Go into the front ranks of the Bolshevik Shock Brigade for sowing,' (1930). [Purchased by Gareth in Moscow in 1931.]

About his experiences in Leningrad, Heinz wrote:

The trains are filled to overflowing — packed. Everywhere there are long queues of persons waiting for their oil, soap, bread, or other food ration... The workers' Co-ops sells cheaply, but one must have a card or pay five times as much as one does so in the private market... Torgsin, the name given to the new State shops where one can buy only with foreign currency, is the latest development in cheap buying. Here one can buy food, cigarettes, and a few simple commodities, at a price comparable to American prices plus about twenty per cent. One article was quite cheap — cigarettes ten cents, but they were of an inferior quality. A notable feature of the streets was the number of drunks ... They say the reason for so much drunkenness was the lack of food, for the Russian is accustomed to drink vodka with his meals. (pp. 49-50)

Gareth and Heinz spoke to a woman about the cost of living:

Butter in private markets costs ten roubles [One pound sterling] eggs sell at ten for five roubles while in the Co-ops they cost only seventy kopecks. In the Co-ops one can buy one pound of butter per month, eggs once a month, but not regularly. In the winter there are no eggs. Meat, mostly salted, is given out in Co-ops at the rate of 200 grams, three times during the month... There is not enough bread, 200 grams a day... It is almost impossible to get fats... for two months we have not been able to get soap except at the highest prices. (pp. 57-58)

After several days in Leningrad they took the train for Moscow, travelling first-class. At the station there were crowds of people surging in and out, and many more sitting on their boxes and bundles, just waiting.[6] It was mid-morning on the eleventh day of their visit, when Gareth and Heinz arrived in Moscow, after a 12-hour train journey from Leningrad, and they were taken to the Metropole Hotel.

They visited the Park of Culture and Rest, where the workers would go in the late afternoon, and on their rest days for movies, sports, lectures, and swimming. About the park were radio speakers from which they heard propaganda songs blaring from speakers:

'We must have more and more Shock Brigade workers'... A poster showed a group of silk-hatted Capitalists seated around a table on which there was a sheet of paper bearing the word "Crisis." On the table was a sign reading, "The

114

Hoover Plan." Towering above this scene was a great red figure of a worker brandishing a rifle. (p. 73)

'The Road to Worldwide October (revolution) By Viktor Deni, (1931).- The placard says Hoover Plan – and the paper on the table Crisis. A copy of this poster was given by Gareth to Lloyd George.

That evening they met Lady Muriel Paget at the British Embassy and accompanied her to the cinema with her friend Madame Litvinov, an English woman and the wife of the Soviet Foreign Affairs Commissar (whom Gareth would meet on a later visit to Moscow in in 1933). After the cinema, Madame Litvinov refused to return to the hotel with them by taxi, as she had previously been reprimanded for associating with bourgeois foreigners. Leaving them quickly she jumped on to a tram crowded with people. [7]

While in Moscow Gareth and Heinz had breakfast with Maurice Hindus,[8] author of *Humanity Uprooted* who considered that:

> *The peasants are not so well off from the point of view of food, as in 1926, or before the Revolution, but that they now have education, entertainment and care for their children [under the Five-Year Plan]... They joined the collective farm movement because they realised there was no future for them as individualists... many feared the threat of being called a kulak. (p. 81)*

Later that same morning Gareth and Heinz had an appointment to visit Louis Fischer, a correspondent for the left-leaning American newspaper, *The Nation*, who had also written a book called *Why Recognize Russia*. He told Gareth and Heinz, "Russia is a 'bull' country. Exports and imports will not decline. Resources are so tremendous that the country will produce more than the people need."[9] Like Hindus, Fischer felt that, "the Comintern is declining... The personnel now consists of revolutionary bureaucrats," and Fischer finished by saying, "This country is starving itself great."[10]

Shortly after this interview, they called upon Walter Duranty,[11] *New York Times* Moscow correspondent. Almost every foreigner who visited the Soviet Union called on him. Perfectly charming to everyone, he was seen as the unofficial American Ambassador. Duranty, aware that there were American engineers working in the Soviet Union, reported to his two visitors, "There have been cases of sabotage where the Russian Engineers remained silent and afraid of reporting it, but things are now changed". He believed that the party would stick to the two Marxist principles:

1. Production by the state and the corollary that no individual make a profit for himself.
2. Only the workers have a voice in running things. (p.87)

Duranty further noted:

> *The secret of Stalin's power has been a matter of recent comment. It is amazing how he put out [of office] Trotsky, a man of equal, but of a more fiery and self-assertive nature. Stalin has maintained his position and advanced his strength by a special technique — achieving by seeming to put aside. He cloaks himself with the authority of the Party when it makes declarations. Yet, at the same time,*

those are always his opinions and coincide with his will. W. H. Chamberlin
tells of an amusing incidental example of this technique. It seems that a foreign
journalist put in an application to see Stalin when they were both at the same
summer resort. The answer came back, "Stalin never gives interviews unless the
Party commands him to do so." Thus, does the 'man of steel' identify himself
with Party discipline and play upon the Communist rule that is opposed to any
kind of self-assertive flamboyant leadership. (pp. 88-89)

During their time in Moscow, Heinz and Gareth had the privilege of visiting
Lenin's widow, Madam Krupskaya, in the Commissariat for Education. Her heart
was in her work in the schools, and she had a great love of children.

Gareth described her in a newspaper article:

I recognised at the table the woman whose image I had seen reproduced all
over Russia. Over 60 years of age, she had greyish white hair, which was brushed
tightly back over her head, and she wore a very simple check dress. Her manners
indicated a person in whom kindness and courtesy were natural. Her smile was
full of sympathy, and she made an impression upon me of complete unselfishness,
of hard work, self-sacrifice, and absolute absence of care for worldly comfort.
Her facial features were irregular, for she had big overhanging eyelids and her
lips were slightly twisted.[12]

One evening, after an early dinner, they visited Red Square and Lenin's Tomb;
"There lies the great man in state. All was quiet, except for the shuffle of feet. We
passed out, thrilled by the sight of the body of a man dead seven years."[13]

Gareth spoke to a peasant girl, the servant of two old Russian noblewomen who
were living quietly in Moscow:

The peasants are terribly dissatisfied. They have been forced to join the
Kolkhozi; they want their own patch of land, their own house, their own cattle
and pigs, and to work for themselves. My two cousins worked day and night.
With their own hands, they made bricks. They built houses, and what happened?
They did not want to join the collectives, and they were taken away to the Urals,
where it is very bad. My other cousin had two cows, two pigs, and some sheep;
he owned two huts. They called him a Kulak and forced him to sell everything.
Only three hundred roubles did they give him. In the Kolkhozi, nobody wants
to work. In my village, I hear they have murdered two Communists.

The peasants cannot kill their cows or their pigs without getting permission from the Natchalnik, the village boss. They were told that if they did not join the Kolhozi, everything would be taken from the, Many were sent to Archangel. They eat very little now; they used to have meat, but not now.

A worker they met told them; "Only when we are dead will conditions be better. The peasants are very angry. We only get salt fish, but in the Kremlin they get everything."[14]

The young men walked down a side street where they entered an open gate into a courtyard, and knocked on the door, to ask if they might look around. "Here lived, in the greatest squalor, forty persons in thirteen rooms, and only one kitchen."[15]

Gareth and Heinz went to call on an old Russian gentleman they had met on the street. "They walked miles, up dark streets and down dirty alleys, and finally discovered the building where he lived. They climbed several flights of dark, creaking stairs and knocked on a dilapidated door. No one came. They knocked again. The door opened a few inches, and a bedraggled woman asked what they wanted.

Gareth: Is Mr 'N' at home?
Woman: No, he is not here now.
Gareth: Could you tell us-?" he questioned.
Woman: Well, you see, he has moved!" she interrupted.
Gareth: Where?
Woman: Oh! It is far away, quite far.
Gareth: But where?"
Woman: Well, he has gone to the Urals, but not of his own accord." (p. 121)

Gareth later met Karl Radek editor of *Izvestia* on August 25, 1931 and sent a report of their meeting to Ivy Lee:

For the next twenty years, we in the Soviet Union will be absolutely occupied with our internal development and markets. The masses need so much. The peasants also want to have better clothing and commodities. ... There is now an argument for a more quiet policy. We are growing stronger in Russia. Every year more peasants realise that a tractor is better than a horse. The greatest danger for England is not the English Communism, but American capitalism.[16]

Gareth and Heinz also met Eugene Lyons, a correspondent for the Associated Press in Moscow, who told them during the course of their conversation, "There is a complete absence of organized opposition. The Party has never been so unified."[17]

On the 20th day of their trip Gareth and Heinz took the night train from Moscow, travelling east to Nizhny-Novgorod (a journey of around 260 miles) and arrived on the following morning where Mr Davis, of the British Austin Car Company, met them and who took them out to a building site in a company car.[18]

They spent the following day of their visit 'tramping'. In the first village they came across, they heard the familiar story repeated of how the villagers had been deprived of their land and that no one was allowed more than one cow. The villagers had no meat, butter or eggs, and it was difficult to feed the children.[19]

Just outside the village, Gareth and Heinz came to a milk farm under construction with 1,000 cattle in ten buildings — "adequate but nothing fancy" was Heinz's opinion. They wanted to eat in the dining room there, but it was so dirty and smelly with many flies that they changed their mind and persuaded someone on the superintendent's office to heat some of their baked beans. [20]

Gareth and Heinz continued their journey through potato fields and rolling country until they came to a charming little village with trees growing in the middle of the street. They at the priest's house, a simple cottage like the rest in the village. He was most hospitable and they talked until tea-time. The priest told them stopped how the villagers had disobeyed a decree forbidding the ringing of church bells the week before Easter. "They could not arrest the whole village, so I was arrested and put in prison for two weeks."[21] The priest continued, "No libraries are allowed in the churches except the books for the service. The penalty for distributing religious books or pamphlets is very severe."[22]

The priest suddenly changed his tone, his face became serious, his voice lowered, his eyes burned with emotion, "We hope to have help form foreign countries. We are hoping for war... If there were intervention, the peasants would rise in revolt, but now there are no leaders, amna all are afraid. Do not buy from these people who are crucifying Russia-poor Mother Russia!" [23]

After all this disheartening discussion, Gareth and Heinz took a walk and entered a Co-op. store to find out what it had for sale. They were greatly surprised to see a lot of lamb hanging from the ceiling. The meat was only for children, they were told, but Gareth flippantly remarked said, "Jack was nine years old and I am eight." As Gareth and Heinz were foreigners, the clerk smiled and gave them two kilograms for two rubles, fifty kopecks. They bought the meat and with some butter took it back to the delighted priest. [24]

At the priest's house, his mother was getting supper ready. "She offered us some excellent cherry and apple preserves, good cabbage soup with sour cream, boiled *kasha* [oatmeal] with butter, and some cream cheese with milk and sugar on it — all very good."[25]

On day 25 after a day's delay, they finally sailed down the Volga to Samara. Gareth began talking in Russian to a doctor's wife on the boat:

> *The peasants have been sent away in thousands to starve. They were exiled just because they worked hard throughout their lives. It's terrible how they have treated them; they have not given them anything; no bread cards even. They sent a lot to Tashkent, where I was, and just left them on the square. The exiles did not know what to do and many starved to death. (p.159-60)*

The steamer stopped at Kazan en route:

> *As usual, the people swarmed down to the boat to get on. It seemed impossible that so many could ever squeeze on with all their huge boxes, and bundles, and children. The usual case of someone who gets left, or a child who gets separated from its mother, makes each stop a tragedy...But we saw a real tragedy on the bank near our wharf, a group of about a hundred- men women and children-sitting sullenly and gloomily upon the bank waiting-for exile! They were Kulaks, the hated and hounded Kulaks. It was a pitiful sight; I have never seen such a dejected group. (p. 162-3)*

The morning after their arrival in Samara, on day 28, they took a train to visit a Kolhoz. "This was a Stalin Kolkhoz, a village of 4,000 persons. The village Soviet had fifty-two members, of which about one-third were Communists. From all sides they asked such questions as: 'When will there be a revolution in America?' 'Is it true that the English want war?' 'Why not let the Soviet Union live in peace?' 'Aren't there thousands of workers dying in England and America?'[26]

They met the president, a young man with a little military cap, and the vice-president, a jolly unshaven fellow with a big voice. After all these questions the vice-president took them to his house for supper. There they met his wife and five very dirty children. Though there was a lack of beauty and cleanliness, there was nothing missing in hospitality. They heated their baked beans, and were given watermelon, and tea. The President's wife poured out her woes:

Oh, it is terrible! We used to have three cows, two horses, sheep, and ten chickens: now look around. The devour [farmyard] is empty, and we only have two chickens. Now we only get half a litre of milk a day. We used to have as much as we liked; one cow used to give fifteen litres a day. That is why my children look so pale and ill. How can it get better, when we have no land and no cows? (p. 175)

The vice-president came in to say goodnight, and stayed to talk. He told them:

There were forty Kulak families in this village… and we've sent them all away. We sent the last man only a month ago. We exiled the entire families of these people because we must dig out the Kulak spirit by the roots! They go to Solovki or Siberia to cut wood, or work on the railways. In six years, when they have justified themselves, they will be allowed to come back. We leave the very old ones, ninety years and over, here, because they are not a danger to the Soviet power. Thus we have liquidated the Kulak!

In June and July we had a campaign against illiteracy; there were a lot of illiterates. We have liquidated the illiterates and now there is none at all. (p. 176)

Gareth and Heinz were offered the vice-president's bed for the night, but they said they preferred the floor. In spite of tucking their trousers in their socks, the fleas and bugs meant they did not sleep well. The following day, the president who the night before had been so enthusiastic for the Party regime had a complete change in attitude. "It is terrible. We can't speak or we'll be sent away [to Siberia]. They took away our cows and now we can only get a crust of bread. It is much worse than before the Revolution. But in 1926-7 — those were fine years." Heinz remarks, "It was an amazing reversion, but I think it significant that this is typical in many cases of enthusiastic supporters; they have many grave doubts and secret miseries."[27]

By September 7, Gareth and Heinz were reaching the end of their arduous and extensive tour of the Bolshevik State. Everywhere they heard the same sad tale of hunger and brutality towards the better-off peasants. Leaving Samara, they made a brief visit to the Autonomous Republic of Mordva. On stopping at a station, "Immediately, a bunch of ragged little lads, like the 'homeless boys' of Moscow, came up to the train, begging for bread. They were tough-looking little characters."[28]

Leaving Mordva they returned to Moscow and from there, Gareth and Heinz, escorted by an Intourist guide, boarded another train for Kharkov and the South.

The Dnieperstroy Dam from one of Gareth's glass slides – probably acquired from a Soviet Photo Library.

They arrived at Alexandrovsk, where they were met and from Dnieperstroy were driven by car to the dam. The next day, Mr 'M', chief engineer, took them over the dam. They described the Dnieperstroy dam as an amazing project in size and concept, but, as yet, unfinished.[29]

The following day Gareth went to see a German Kolhoz, where he talked with a Communist. There was only one member of the Party there, because the Germans were Mennonites. The Party man explained how the Germans sent workers to the factory. The man who went became a member of the Kolhoz. If he earned 150 rubles there, he must give from three to ten per cent to the Kolhoz. People did not mind going to work on the construction job, but nobody wanted to go to the Donetz Basin.

One German said:

They sent the Kulaks away from here and it was terrible. We heard in a letter that ninety children died on the way — ninety children from this district. We are all afraid of being sent away as Kulaks for political reasons. We had a letter from one, saying they were cutting wood in Siberia. Life was hard and there was not enough to eat. It was forced labor! They sent all the grain away from our village and left only 1,000 pounds. I heard that in a village thirty versts away they came to seize the grain, and the peasants killed three militiamen. They wanted to have enough grain for themselves instead of starving. The Communists then shot sixteen peasants.

They force us to work on Sundays, although we are Mennonites and don't want to. They won't allow us to have Sunday Schools, or religious magazines. The Russians have lost their religion, but we Germans still stick to ours. A lot of people have gone to America — take us with you! (p. 222-3)

That night their Intourist guide secured train accommodation for them. They left Dnieperstroy for Kharkov, the capital and industrial centre of Ukraine, and from there they took the train to Kiev:

Our hotel was an old one of the most florid Baroque architecture. But we had a piano, a bathroom, and several sentimental statuettes of thwarted and unrequited love, etc. We had a great surprise at the Sports Park where they have a modern restaurant that makes you think you are in Europe, when you get the food you know you guessed wrong.

Kiev is a charming old town, with its many ancient churches and handsome avenues of trees. Jones and I walked through a park, where we saw a fine flower bed with two numbers outlined in flowers — 1,040 and 518. What did they stand for? One thousand and forty machine tractor stations and 518 industrial plants to be opened in 1931. Say it with flowers! (p. 231)

It was the end of Gareth and Heinz's tour. They started for civilisation in the morning, reaching the Russian-Polish frontier station at Shepetorka in the early evening, Heinz wrote:

The Customs were very strict. The officials looked into my small jewelry box and opened every letter, although no one spoke any English! Then we got on

*another train which took us to the Polish-Russian frontier town where we again
went through the Customs. Here they made an awful fuss over Jones's Russian
literature took it away from him and made us lock it up in a sealed suitcase for
shipment to Berlin. (p. 232)*

An International Wagon Lit took them to Warsaw, arriving at 7.00 am the following morning on the 41st day of their trip. Continuing by train, Heinz and Gareth arrived in Berlin 12 hours later and headed for London via Paris. Their six-week round-trip had covered over 5000 miles. In his preface to Heinz's book Gareth wrote:

*With a knowledge of Russia and the Russian language, it was possible to
get off the beaten path, to talk with grimy workers and rough peasants, as well
as such leaders as Lenin's widow and Karl Radek. We visited vast engineering
projects and factories, slept on the bug-infested floors of peasants' huts, shared
black bread and cabbage soup with the villagers — in short, got into direct
touch with the Russian people in their struggle for existence and were thus able
to test their reactions to the Soviet Government's dramatic moves.*

*It was an experience of tremendous interest and value as a study of a land
in the grip of a proletarian revolution.*

Notes on Chapter 12

[1] Gareth Vaughan Jones Papers, National Library of Wales Correspondence Series B6/3. August 2, 1931.

[2] The diaries covering this trip are in the Gareth Vaughan Jones Papers, National Library of Wales Gareth Jones Diary Series B1/11, August 7-15th 1931 and B1/12, August 21-September 4, 1931.

[3] Ibid. p. 19

[4] Ibid. p. 43

[5] Ibid. p. 44

[6] Ibid. p. 69

[7] Ibid. p. 74

[8] Maurice Hindus, Russian American left-wing journalist and author. *The Great Offensive*, 1933

[9] Heinz 1931 p. 83

[10] Ibid. p. 85.

[11] Walter Duranty, *New York Times* Moscow correspondent, referred to in Chapter 23 and 24.

[12] Gareth Jones, 'Lenin's Widow talks to a Welshman'. The *Western Mail. November 7*, 1932, p. 6.

[13] Heinz 1931 p. 99.

[14] Ibid. pp. 108-12

15   Ibid. p. 113.

16   Gareth Jones Diary, 'Russia'. 1931. Also Ivy Ledbetter Lee Papers," Seeley G. Mudd Manuscript Library, Princeton University. (Copy) Series 21 (5). No 7. Karl Radek. interview with Gareth Jones. It can be read on the website: https://www.garethjones.org/soviet_articles/karl_radek_interview.htm

17   Heinz 1931 p. 117.

18   Ibid. p. 133.

19   Ibid. p. 142-3.

20   Ibid. p. 144.

21   Ibid. p. 147-8.

22   Ibid. p. 151.

23   Ibid. p. 153.

24   Ibid. p. 154.

25   Ibid. p. 155.

26   Ibid. p. 174.

27   Ibid. p. 178.

28   Ibid. p. 194.

29   Heinz wrote:

Stretching from bank to bank, the dam was built in a graceful curve, three-quarters of a mile long. At each end were rock-crushing and concrete-mixing plants, through one of which they went; and then down into the power house, which was about two-thirds built, and contains all American equipment, with its nine turbines, each twenty-five feet in diameter, and developing 90,000 h.p. a piece — the largest in the world. They had poured more concrete in three months the previous year than had ever been dumped before anywhere in the world, with an average of about 4,000 cu. yards. per day and 146,000 cu. yards. in one month. Eighteen thousand persons were employed on the job. They went right down inside the turbines and saw how they worked. After much climbing of ladders, they eventually reached the top again and watched the steam derricks lower two-yard buckets down into the fills. Mr M. explained how a dam like this was built by constructing a preliminary coffer-dam and then pumping all the water out of the centre and building right on the bottom. They returned through the centre of the dam, by way of a passage. "This is a secret," said M. M., "but you don't generally build large runways through dams—nor those either" (pointing to small passages running out into the piers). Evidently everything was all set for defence!

The purpose of the dam was two-fold: First, to develop 80,000 h.p. for electric transformation, and second, by backing up the water and having locks at one side it will make the Dnieper navigable from the Black Sea to Kiev. The kilo-watts developed there will light a new industrial city of a million persons that was being built adjacent, and would furnish power for a large steel works, an aluminium smelting plant, and other industrial establishments. The dam was destroyed during the German invasion in World War II.

Chapter 13

A Brief Interlude

After such an intense trip to Russia one might be forgiven for imagining that Gareth would have taken the opportunity to relax before returning to his job in New York with Ivy Lee. Nothing could be further from the truth, and his three weeks' interlude packed with visits to family, friends and colleagues. The voyage back to the USA gave him the chance to write a long letter to his family:[1]

> *An Bord SS Deutschland*
> *Den 4 Oktober, 1931*
> *2.15, Sunday afternoon.*
> *Sitting on my deck-chair with cushions on the promenade deck*
> *Hamburg-Amerika Line*

> *My Dearest All,*

> *Those days in London were a very enjoyable rush, and it was really a great privilege to be invited by Lloyd George to come down to Churt, when the doctor says that he is not to see visitors.*

> *It was splendid that both Mama and Gwyneth could see me off at Cardiff. I took a taxi from Paddington to the Reform Club. One of the pageboys took me to my room, which was very comfortable, overlooking the Carlton Club. Outside an unemployed pianist was playing, and from my window, I could see Conservatives smoking cigars in the Carlton. Whenever I am in London, I want to stay at the Reform. You have a fine room with first class valet and wonderful atmosphere, which reminds you of Cambridge. When I told the valet I had been to Russia, he asked in a P.G. Woodhouse way, "And, Sir, what is the state of affairs in that unfortunate country?" I went down to the dignified library of the Reform and had tea in one of the wonderfully comfortable armchairs.*

Then I dashed across St. James' Park, which was looking fine to Lloyd George's office, where I was given a very warm welcome. They are always glad to see me.

After seeing the office staff, I walked back to the Reform. I saw H. G. Wells there. He does not look very distinguished. Sir George Paish talked to me about the possibility of starvation, should the credit system of the world collapse, as it seems to be collapsing. It seems to me though, that if we didn't starve during the War, in spite of U-boats and credit difficulties, we won't starve now, although there will probably be a shortage unless some world steps are taken. Sir George gave me a message to Mr Lee asking him to use all his influence in the States to bring about a World Economic Conference…

Jack H. [Heinz] came to see me at the Reform on Tuesday evening. Wednesday was a very busy day, getting my articles typed and beginning my last article. Jack. H. came in again to finish his Diary, which he was basing on my notes. At one o'clock, the lunch in my honour was held by a group of mine, which had entertained the PM [Prime Minister] in July. Mr Armitstead was the chairman and the lunch was held in a very tastefully furnished room with a very fine round table and a deep green carpet. There were present Captain Graham White MP (Parliamentary Secretary for something), a Mr Brown and a Mr Green. One of the heads of the Milling Association was there and also Mr Christie, the General Manager of Dean and Dawson's was there with whom I had a very long talk at breakfast on Thursday morning. It is a great string to my bow that Lloyd George asked me to go and see him. I did not give a set speech, but just general conversation about my journey, which seemed to interest them very much indeed. The whole thing was a great success. There were several members of the Reform Club present, including Sir Philip and Lady Gibbs. They all seemed immensely impressed, and Sir Philip said last time that I had enough good material for a book. I made a hit with Mrs Armistead. The cakes were fine and I happened to say, "What lovely cakes you have!" I couldn't have said anything better, because she had made them herself. When I told Sir Philip I had met Radek, (Secretary of the Communist International) he said: "I don't think Radek can be very pleased with me. I put him in a novel and also I don't think he'll like my description of him in Since Then."

I rushed from the lunch in a taxi to 21, Abingdon Street, outside which AJ Sylvester's car was waiting. In a few minutes, he and I were driving down towards Churt. He was boiling about Brown, Hore-Belisha and some others, who were out at all costs for [Ministerial] Office. Jimmy Thomas, he said was out for entirely personal ends and loved money. He was very down on Ramsay

127

[MacDonald] whom he called petty and snobbish. He was very impressed with the lack of great men in politics compared with the time of the War (Balfour, Asquith, Bonar Law, [All former Prime Ministers of Great Britain], etc).

Finally, after some fine Surrey scenery we entered the drive to Bron-y-d⊠. Sylvester said that Lloyd George had seen practically nobody, and that half of his time [Sylvester's] was spent in refusing people who wanted to see the Chief — even close friends.

We arrived and were met by two dogs; went in and were taken through the small library- drawing room into a large room where Lloyd George was reclining on a sofa. He looked very impressive with his absolutely white hair and his smart grey suit. He gave me a wonderfully warm welcome and seemed really delighted to see me. 'Well Gareth', he said, 'You've been wandering over the face of the earth like another very potent figure. I have a large number of questions to ask you.' I told him that everywhere in America, Russia, Germany, France I heard people asking about him. He said. 'Well, I've turned the corner.' He looked bright, well and his eyes flashed as much as ever. Sylvester had told me he was getting on wonderfully. His colour was good and he looked much better and much less tired than he did the day I went to see him from Cambridge two years ago. 'And now tell me about Germany." I described my visit to Germany. "And how is Russia getting on?' I told him that the Communists were much stronger due mainly to the success of collectivisation and the policy of Stalin.

Lloyd George: 'That was a very courageous and statesmanlike speech. I think that Stalin is a really great figure.'

I said that the misery of the peasants was great, and that they hated the collective farms. 'Of course they do. They've got to work now. No peasant likes to work.' He did not seem to have much sympathy for the Russian peasants.

'And now what about America? How many unemployed there?' I said there were probably eight million fully unemployed and about eight million part-time.

Lloyd George: 'Doesn't that lead to bloodshed?' 'Well, Sir. There have been serious riots in Kentucky and a number of people have been shot.'

Lloyd George: 'Do you know we've heard nothing about that. It's that press of ours, which refuses to print anything showing that things are going badly in a protectionist country.'

Just then, Miss Russell, the typist came in with the news she had received over the phone. She read out that MacDonald made no decision about the General Election. Lloyd George's facial expression changed immediately and there was a look of tremendous impatience and anger. 'He's a poor thing!' with absolute

128

scorn. 'He's betrayed his own party and now he's going to betray ours.' Then he almost snarled "neurotic.' And let's come back to Europe. Do you think that Laval and Briand's visit will do any good?'

I said that although the visit of the French to Berlin passed off well you could not change the attitude of France in a weekend.

"Quite right. I quite agree with you," said Lloyd George: 'That's just like the French. They go and make fine speeches with their tongues in their mouths and make great promises. But when they return home, they begin sneering and sniggering."

Just then we heard a car arriving, and in came the maid, who announced Sir Herbert Samuel (Home Secretary), Sir Donald Maclean (Minister for Education) and Sir Archie Sinclair (Secretary for Scotland). I suggested that I should go to the other room, and so Sylvester and I went to the library drawing room and had tea. The historic interview between Lloyd George and the Liberal Ministers in the National Government took place in the next room, and then I could hear raised voices. Lloyd George seemed to be putting vim into them. They had been wavering. Lloyd George was saying, "If there is an election the pound will go down, down, down." You could hear the word 'tariff' being repeated often. Lloyd George is as firm against tariffs as ever.[2]

The arguments about which all the papers made such a fuss next day went on for a long time. Sylvester told me of the trouble they had had in keeping the newspapermen away. He said how pleased Lloyd George was with the way Gwilym [younger son of Lloyd George] was doing in the Government. But it was disgusting how people in Parliament behaved in this crisis; nearly all were working for personal aggrandizement.

I started correcting my copies of The Times' articles then the nurse came worried about Lloyd George's talking so much. She went in, but found it hard to stop the discussion. At 6.45 pm however Lloyd George came out, and told me how sorry he was that we had had such a short talk. 'I want you, Gareth, to keep on informing me as to what is 'happening'. I had a few words with Sir Herbert and the others. We also looked at the Laszlo picture of Lloyd George which made him look old, ill and tired. Then Lloyd George went off to bed. I had no time to show him my Bolshevik posters, which I had left outside so I left one of them as a present to him.

Sylvester and I then left, and on the way home Sylvester told me how he would do anything for Lloyd George because Lloyd George did not care whether he was a University man or not. Sylvester told me how the Conservatives had done him out of a C.B. [Companion of the Bath] and of the opposition he had had because he was not Oxford or Cambridge [graduate]...

Then a busy morning; phoned Sir Bernard [Pares], whom I invited out to lunch. I did not have time to see all those I wanted to. I saw Mr Rowntree in the Reform and had time to tell him how hospitable his friends had been and also to tell him something about Russia. I called in at the Royal Institute of International Affairs, Travel Bureau etc. Then I took a taxi to Sir Bernard Pares, who seemed delighted to see me and hear my views on Russia. He is very fond of me. We had lunch in an Italian Restaurant in Soho and he was my guest.

Taxi again to the Russian Parliamentary Committee Office and to the Communist bookshop. I found myself just a few yards from Tom Jones' Office. Just in front of me going into the Pilgrim Trust was a familiar figure in grey. It was Fred Richards [ARCA Associate of the Royal College of Artists, an artist and etcher, and family friend]... He was astonished when he heard I had been Lloyd George's Foreign Affairs Secretary and that I was working in New York and sailing the next day. He sent his love to you all.

Tom Jones wasn't there; so I went to the Bank Club; then rushed to The Times and saw Barrington-Ward at four pm. It is doubtful whether my articles will be published — stress of election and interest in home crisis. Mama was quite right. He promised to cable me in America. If the Times refuse, I can place the same articles in the States and receive much more for them. I don't mind at all...

I then went off to the Dorchester and saw Jack Heinz and Mrs Heinz in a beautiful green satin suite there. They seemed very grateful to me. I am very glad everything has been such a great success. Jack thinks the trip was wonderful! Although he was pretty bored while he was there...

I caught the 8.31 to Blackheath with one minute to spare and was delighted to see them all. Eirian and Stan gave me such a warm welcome, and I had a fine supper of baked beans, which I enjoyed. John was the most cheerful and happy baby I have ever seen. Stan was as proud of him as Punch...

Friday. Up at 6.30. Before eight o'clock, I had arrived in Waterloo. James Stephen, whom I called to see — he lives near the Armitsteads — and Madame Wolkov were both there to see me off. Mme. W was very moved at receiving her great grandfather's naval clock, and a letter from Moscow, while James was most impressed at my travelling first-class. Then the train left London...

Southampton reached, we got a tender, and saw the Aquitania, Empress of Britain. Before long, in the roads, the huge Bremen the fastest boat in the world loomed. We saw her steaming away. About 11.45 we got alongside the

Deutschland. Hundreds of faces looked down on us and it was impressive to hear the German band play "God Save the King" as we stepped on board... As we got on board, the Leviathan the biggest liner in the world passed about a hundred yards away...

We were not far behind the Bremen in getting to Cherbourg at about 5.30. We were soon under way leaving Europe, leaving Europe behind after a wonderful journey home to Russia, Germany, France and England at the most exciting point of the world crisis...

The boat is very quiet — and unless I had enough to read — dull. The jazz band plays to an empty floor. So, there is a complete lack of gaiety... but there is one great advantage, that I can read and I have already done a terrific amount. I have read a book on economics (nearly 350 pages) by Hartley Withers. I have read Knickerbocker's Five-Year Plan (240 pages), and studied a number of magazines and articles thoroughly...

Thursday night, October 8.

Here we are, nearing Journey's End. The first American lighthouse has been seen. Tomorrow morning early, we'll see the skyline of New York. The voyage has been very quiet, but enjoyable, because for the first time for months I have had a chance to read. Most of the passengers have been old people returning from the German baths, Jewish businessmen...

Gareth wrote a brief final postscript to his letter from 15, Broad Street on the Friday afternoon after his arrival back in New York. 'Here I am again settled down in the office. I shall have intensely interesting work to do following a talk with Mr Lee...'

As a PS he wrote, 'Some people on board have lost 60% of all their money in the last few weeks.'

A second PS, 'I have just had a cable: "Articles accepted. *Times*."'

Notes on Chapter 13

1
  Gareth Vaughan Jones Papers, National Library of Wales Correspondence Series B6/3. October 4, 1931.
2
  The Gold Standard Crisis had occurred a few days previously, on September 21, 1931. Due to the economic depression between 1931 and 1934, the government found it expedient or necessary to abandon the gold standard. This policy was partly motivated by the belief that the exports of the country could be stimulated by devaluating its currency in terms of foreign exchange.

Chapter 14

Back in New York City

On his return to New York Gareth reflected on his recent adventures and his immediate prospects:

> *Another big journey is over — New York — London — HOME [Wales] — Leningrad — Moscow — Nizhny-Novgorod — Samara — Kharkov — Kiev — Warsaw — Berlin — Paris — London — HOME — New York! A fortnight ago it was Sunday night in Eryl. It was a lovely week-end I had. I have not been home for more than a few days for such a long time. Well, perhaps I'll have one next year, because things are looking as black as they could possibly be in America. Mr Lee has lost several clients and is pessimistic about the whole future of society. The banks here seem to be on the verge of collapse. People are hoarding their money. Gold is rushing away from the States. In 20 days over £100,000,000 of gold has left the United States. It is probable that America will go off the gold standard... Many people are holding gold in their homes because the banks are in a shaky position. There have been very numerous failures of banks throughout the country.[1]*

Soon after his return to New York Gareth lunched with Jack Heinz's father, Mr Howard Heinz at the Recess Club — whose members of this exclusive club, according to Gareth, included JP Morgan, the financier, Albert Wiggin of Rockefeller, Ivy Lee, and John W Davis. In his letter home Gareth related that Heinz senior had been exceptionally grateful for him escorting his son in Russia. Heinz junior had written to his father to thank him for choosing a companion who knew the language and the political situation so well and that it had been a privilege to travel with Gareth. Gareth wrote, "I was delighted, particularly as Mr Heinz said he would tell Ivy Lee how pleased he was that the tour had been such a great success."[2] Ivy Lee later showed Gareth the letter from Heinz senior:

I had hoped to see you in New York to personally thank you for the privilege of having Gareth Jones join my son, Jack, in Russia. It was a well worthwhile trip and the results could never have been accomplished had it not been for Jones. My boy paid him a very high compliment, and after my interview with him at the Recess Club on Tuesday, I wish to heartily endorse what my son said about him. I am quite sure the two young men have sized up the Russian situation better than any authorities of whom I know. Sincerely yours, Howard Heinz.[3]

Gareth had already acquired a reputation as a popular public speaker in New York and with his return from, and recent knowledge of, Russia, he was invited to speak on many occasions. He spoke to about 50-60 brokers in the Rothschild's organisation on his experiences, and Mr Rothschild, the head of the firm, was himself present. An organisation called the Mothers' Club asked him, and were most enthusiastic about, "Mr Jones, who was very clever in making the people of whom he speaks come alive". Gareth was intrigued by the invitation to the 'Society for Ethical Culture', whose audience turned out to be twelve to sixteen-year-olds.

At the end of October, Ivy Lee asked Gareth to lecture in Buffalo on his behalf and Gareth wrote in his regular letter home on October 31, 1931:

Here I am in club car of the New York to Chicago train. I have been looking at the Hudson River from the observation car and the Catskill Mountains. The lecture was at the First Presbyterian Church of Buffalo, where I received $1000 as my fee for speaking before 1,200 people. Everything was extremely successful, and the lecture was highly acclaimed. After the talk, I was interviewed by The Buffalo Evening News. I received an appreciative note from the secretary, who wrote that "it was remarkable intimate picture of affairs in Russia."

Gareth was able to speak on a variety of subjects, and on November 22 he told his parents about another successful event.

The great news is now the great success of my address at the Town Hall Club today on 'Whither Germany'. (The title tickles me.) At 12 o'clock this morning young Schröder (of the famous German Banking family) called for me, admired the view from my room and off we went together by subway to West 42nd Street. That is Times Square in the middle of Broadway where the lights are so dazzling. We went in a lift to the Club's Rooms and there in big letters was: 'WHITHER GERMANY?' by Gareth R. V. Jones.'

Then at 1.20 Chairman introduced me, and I got up and held forth. They listened like anything. You would have been amused to see them mopping it up with open mouths. When I had finished, there were questions. A group of ladies (old) just in front of me were wonderfully enthusiastic. They repeated 'Wonderful! Perfect! And Marvellous!' Then when we rose from our chairs there was a rush at me. First the Times representative, then Baron Bothmer, then the old ladies who turned out to be from very distinguished professorial families. One was a German stepmother of the Prime Minister of Prussia. Another, was the widow of Professor Burgess, a formerly well-known international lawyer, another was the wife of Professor Shepherd of Columbia University, an outstanding historian. They swarmed round me until I did not know where I was with some saying 'You must meet my husband!' 'You have a thorough knowledge of Germany!' 'I must congratulate!' 'I must say how much I appreciated it!' And myself saying on all sides, 'Thank you very much.' 'Yes, it has been a great pleasure to meet you'.

Then I was left alone with the New York Times representative. As I left more ladies spoke to me. One said: "What does it matter about bonds when there are spiritual things to think about? How material people are!" So I looked serious and spiritual. So altogether, it was great fun.

Gareth turned to more serious subjects later in his letter.

Monday (23rd November 1931)… about 5 o'clock I went to see Naess of Goldman Sachs and Co. Wall Street who took me to the famous International Bankers firm of Seligman to meet Hohe and talk to him about Germany. He is anxious about a German default on the English banks… The British tariff I think is a great mistake. It effects on the German situation will be serious and that will hit back at our banks. There is sure to be a Hitler govt. in Germany and possibly civil war.[4]

Tuesday night [November 24th] threatened to be very dull but turned out most interesting. The Russian Evening Post asked me urgently to see them at seven Tuesday evening to tell them about Russia. When I got there they had gone and left no message — just like the Russians…

On Wednesday (November 25th) I got up and bought my New York Times as usual. Inside I was surprised to see the space and importance given to my views…[5] When I got to Wall Street (my office) the Town Hall Club rang me up and said how delighted they were with the publicity. (They like it when

their functions are reported in papers like the New York Times.) Before long
the German News Agency rang me up. Might they have a copy of my speech to
cable it to Germany… And I presume it was being tapped over to the German
newspapers before many minutes.

The next step in my sudden awakening to fame was the New York American
(the famous Hearst paper) phoning me. 'We publish every Sunday a page devoted
to the views of distinguished people, and we have been much interested in the
report of your speech. Might we publish it on Sunday together with the speech
of the British Consul-General.' The New York American is the equivalent of
the Daily Mail. So that is coming out tomorrow. I believe it has a circulation
of millions. Its views are the scant opposite of mine. They are anti-European,
anti-British and very hot pro-American. So to get views like mine is very sporting
of them. Still it's all very funny. 'Every penny of War Debts, Reparations must
be paid' says the American, which is also most isolationist.[6]

Gareth also noted that he had lunched with Claud Cockburn [who wrote an
obituary of Gareth] on that day 'an Oxford man who is *Times* correspondent in
N.Y. He is very amusing and we joked a lot.'
On Sunday 29 November 1931:

I went to the Russian Service in the Church this morning and enjoyed
the singing very much indeed. Afterwards, I had lunch at the Russian Club.
The lights in the church were very striking and the mass of colours, but it is
strange, I can get no affection for the Russians as I have for the Germans.
There is too much of the intriguer about them, terribly unbalanced, and you
never have the impression that you can trust them. Friday night, I spoke on
my experiences to a group of Russians in a Russian students' club. It went off
very well, but I had the feeling when I talked to them — they were White
Russians, that they were also hopeless at governing, fanatical and unreliable,
and I prefer the Communists to the White Russians. I hate the atmosphere of
spying and dictatorship that pervades Russian places. It is exciting when one
gets first into such an atmosphere, but when one gets used to it becomes very
underhand and despicable.[7]

During the autumn of 1931, Gareth became increasingly concerned about the
financial situation and sent numerous letters and telegrams to Barry to persuade
his parents to buy a house.

On October 14 Gareth reported again on the dire economic situation. "Events moving rapidly here. It looks like a collapse approaching, perhaps rapidly. I had lunch today with the editor of the Wall St Journal and I talked well. Please let me know about the house. Events may move more rapidly than we think. So buy something tangible immediately. I want you all to buy clothes now. Has Aunty got a warm overcoat? Please buy one and take it from the $440 I sent."[8]

On October 21, 1931, it was clear that there had already been some discussion 'I think the house in Barry sounds fine... and I did not like the idea of coming home to Cardiff, it would not be like home at all. The view must be fine. So I hope you'll buy.' He offered his parents up to £300 towards the cost. 'The world is in for a very bad time indeed and the only safe investment is a house. It is tangible property. I think the £ will drop still further towards the end of the year.'

On the 25th he again pleaded with his family 'Please let me know exactly how you stand financially about the house. I can sell my £100 War Loan and let you have it as well. [9]

On the 27th Gareth wrote 'I am looking forward to news about the house. I see that Dada is hesitating because of distance from school. That is a very small factor compared with the gravity of the world situation and the urgency of having some tangible property.'[10]

The next day Gareth sent a telegram which seemed to imply progress.

PLEASE BUY HOUSE SENDING ANOTHER TWO HUNDRED POUNDS SELLING WAR LOAN DELIGHTED HOUSE WANT HAVE HOME IN BARRY WARMEST LOVE GARETH[11]

He continued in the same vein only three days later.

Don't take too seriously what I say about the crisis, I think everything will come out better, but we had better take no risk and buy a house by all means. We should be happier to have real property than paper or a bank account. Remember what happened in Germany.
So please buy a house.[12]

On November 5, 1931, Gareth sent a telegram to Eryl, Barry: "World situation deeply grave — must buy house within couple of months — Only safe investment. British improvement temporary. Warmest love Gareth." And he wrote a covering letter on the same day:

The new family home, also called Eryl, at Porth y Castell, Barry.

There is a good chance of the present crisis getting worse, resulting in a general banking collapse... This is only a possibility but it is worth taking no risk. A house is real property.[13]

Gareth responded to his family's reply of November 24.

It was splendid to get your cable when I arrived at the office. I think that £1250 is a very reasonable when one consider what a good house it is and what a fine view it has. I am looking forward to my next visit home and to seeing my new room.[14]

He finally received the confirmation he was waiting for and on November 28 wrote:

This has been a really outstanding week. First of all, Tuesday was a great day. When I arrived at the office after the usual crush in the express subway there was the cable waiting for me and I was delighted to get the news about the house...

I think it is a bargain. Such a house would cost £3000 in the United States…
I will send you the other £100 when I think it advisable because every drop of
only 10 cents … means a gain to me of £2-10s-0d when transferring £100. So,
expect £200 from me I should like to send more but I must be prepared in case
in case Mr Lee goes on an economy stunt.[15]

The headlines to Gareth's article published in the *New York American* on November 29, 1931 read "Fascist Dictatorship for Germany Now a Possibility — Development Seems Inevitable in Spring". Gareth's political views, which he considered had been severely edited, were influenced by his profound sympathy for the German nation. The article commenced:

In Germany today we are witnessing the revolt of a great nation. It is, in
the eyes of Germany, a revolt against three betrayals — against the betrayal by
German politicians, against the betrayal by Versailles and against the betrayal
by capitalism.

A great class has been annihilated, the German middle-class. Their savings
swept away by the inflation, educated Germans have been reduced to proletarian
conditions. That is the situation, which we must bear in mind in considering
Germany.

… The moral is, firstly, against Reparations and for the priority of private
debts! Secondly, if tariffs throughout the world shut out German goods, she will
never be able to pay a part of the private debts. The moral is, 'Scrap Tariffs.'

Whatever happens, however, there is a danger that all is too late. A Nazi
dictatorship in the spring seems inevitable. Will this lead to civil war? Will this
lead in the long run to Bolshevism in Germany? Those are problems we may
soon have to face.[16]

Following his lecture at the Town Hall Club, Gareth's opinion was eagerly sought after in the world of finance, and he was called upon to give his advice to the leading bankers of New York. Naess of Goldman, Sachs took to him to meet Sobe, a member of the international bankers' firm of Seligman to discuss the economic crisis:

The banker is anxious about the effect of a German default on the English
banks. And that is why I was always keen on buying a house, although don't
spread it around. We [British] are so involved with German affairs that events
in Germany will affect British banking system gravely… The banks of the world

are creaking and the finances of Central Europe are in a chaotic situation…
The British tariff system, I think is a great mistake. Its effect on the German
situation will hit back at our banks.

There is sure to be a Hitler Government in Germany and possibly a civil war.[17]

Gareth's moderate views were strengthened when he was invited to have tea
with Mr Koznov, of Rothschild's, on November 22. "It was most interesting in the
elegant tea-room of the Plaza. He thinks of nothing but how to make money. When
he thinks of a country, his reaction is, "Can I make money there?" Astonished by
Koznov's remark, Gareth noted in his letter: "To that conception I much prefer
the Communist outlook of work for the Society". He noted with irony that "An
orchestra played light music as we discussed the Depression."

The poverty of the less affluent areas of New York shocked Gareth, and with
his sympathy for the 'underdog', he wished to investigate. he walked up Broadway
and down a road which goes past the quays on the Hudson River he came across
a remarkable sight.

Not many minutes from Wall Street I saw a patch of land covered with bricks
and stones, where a building had been brought to the ground. Suddenly I saw
what looked like huts and there I noticed that there were holes in the ground
and that negro-unemployed had made dug-outs with old boxes and pieces of
wood. They had dug holes in the ground and built walls of cardboard and
wood. There were about a hundred negroes living there. One had made a fine
home for himself and was most proud of it. Walking across to examine these
rough huts, I discovered that I was walking on top of roofs, and that there, sure
enough, were dozens of homes where men had burrowed under the earth. They
were dug-outs, where the hoboes slept.[18]

Gareth continued to explore the seamier side of New York life — the life of the
'down and out'. One evening, after a meal at a restaurant called the *Moskowitz* he
decided to investigate:

I strolled through the poor streets till I got to the North River and there I talked
with a watchman. He told me that in the block of houses where he lived there used
to be, before the prohibition, two saloons, but now there were 27 'speakeasies'…
He said he had never seen the conditions so terrible as they are today. "You go
to the Municipal Lodging House in 26 Street and you'll see for yourself." So I

walked until I came to a large building… It was now nearly 10 o'clock in the evening — and went inside and said I should like to see it. I was met by a very decent man (probably from Tammany Hall, the graft-ridden Democratic machine that governs New York), who took me round to the dining rooms. There, they feed homeless men free of charge. They are given coffee, (very thin and greasy) soup, and as much bread as they want. No man who has more than three dollars (12/-) is allowed to stay. He showed me a list of the wealth of the men who were sleeping there that night and hardly any of them had more than 50 cents in the whole world. When they come in all their clothes are taken from them, and these are fumigated. I was taken downstairs and shown over 2000 dirty suits of clothes which had just come out of tremendous ovens. Then we went to a bedroom where about 400 poor people sleeping in dull rows, a lot were coughing, and were old and white. The next sight was extraordinary. Going outside we went to a pier, where once goods were unloaded. It had been covered in and heated and was very warm. Going in we saw another 2,500 homeless sleeping on quite comfortable beds. The man who accompanied me said: 'Well, you see, New York isn't so cruel and heartless as they make out. Not a cent is charged'…[19]

Gareth could not help being disturbed by events and he described them in a letter to his parents:

I think it is fairly certain I shall be coming back in April, although Mr Lee has not mentioned anything at all… Mr Lee is feeling the Depression very badly — clients have left him; stocks are rushing downhill. US Steel now 52. The dollar is going downhill in an alarming way. German bonds collapsed down to 25 further 5½% yesterday… So he will have to economise… But it does not worry me in the slightest. I am looking forward to it because there is a spice of adventure looking out for new fields of activity.

I shall not mind it in the least because I should like to have a holiday at home and it has been such a wonderful experience for me to come to America. Dudley is afraid that he'll lose his post and he is worried. Poor old Laurie Bunker I am told feels bitterly that he is no longer with JP Morgan.[20]

Do you remember my telling Leland Rex Robinson in May that the Germans were bound to have a moratorium and when he asked my advice about German 5½% and that I said I knew nothing about bonds but that I was certain they would go down? They were then 76 and are now 27. He didn't sell and holds them still.[21]

In one month, 600,000 have lost their jobs in the US. The November 22
Wall Street predictions seem to be coming out correctly, the dollar is down again,
stocks have fallen to all time low. Many teachers have not been paid for months.
People, who had vast fortunes two years ago, are now almost starving.

The banks in America are already shaky. A house is material wealth. I want
you to buy clothes now so buy something tangible immediately! Please order
tinned goods. I am going to write to Heinz and Co. in London to send some
direct to you.[22]

On the evening of December 5, 1931, Ivy Lee left for Europe by the *Bremen*, taking Gareth's research on Russian Gold with him, that he had worked all day on. While Gareth had learnt much about the part that gold played in finance he remarked, "I don't think he will ever write the book on the Soviet Union. It would be much better for him if he had asked me to follow the current situation in Europe." [23]

Gareth's letters, diary and articles show that his time was completely taken up with the financial crisis that was afflicting the world, attending business lunches with men of influence, and the presentation of serious lectures but this was not the case. Every aspect of his life he enjoyed to the full — both in work and in leisure. Anxiety was not a word in his vocabulary, nor was it present in his innermost thoughts. Everything that he undertook was not only a pleasure but also a challenge to him, and he probably pictured his life as one great adventure.

Gareth's diary for 1931 abounded with appointments not only for dinner, but for lunch and breakfast dates. The names he noted were like a *Who's Who* of New York. He met financiers, distinguished professors, the social elite, journalists, and made new friends. People invited him to hear accounts of his experiences in Europe and sought his opinion on world affairs; such was their concern about the world crisis. He was brave enough to profess controversial views on the American policy of Protectionism.

Despite his popularity, he continued to enjoy meeting his old friends. His weekends were occupied with social engagements, invitations to private houses or just exploring the environs of the city. A good friend was an Aberystwyth graduate, Alan Dudley. Gareth described in his letters to his parents how he would spend a day walking along the Hudson River or on Bear Mountain and then return to the Dudleys' home to relax and listen to Haydn quartets and Mozart.

Just before Christmas Gareth mentioned to his parents that he had recently met Heinz, where they had swapped anecdotes about Cambridge. Heinz had told Gareth that as a prank he had been made to recite the whole of the *'Heinz 57'* varieties to the undergraduates in Trinity. They also reminisced about their experiences in Russia and discussed the publication of Heinz's forthcoming book.

Interested in meeting academics and armed with his letters of introduction from Sir Bernard Pares, Gareth spent two days visiting Yale University in the autumn. There he saw his first American football game, a match between Yale and the Army that drew 75,000 spectators. It was the first time he had seen American cheerleaders. He compared the weekend to the May Week in Cambridge, and it reminded him of his days at Trinity College:

> *I wandered through the courts of Yale University and I had visions of New Court. The colourful autumn leaves, very red and yellow, were falling from the trees, the windows were open and I could see undergraduates working with the sound of gramophone and pianos echoing in the quadrangle. I imagined I was back, walking across Great Court to my rooms or dropping in to see Ludovik Stewart, Drury or John Berry or just getting ready to go to Hall. My thoughts were of how lucky I had been to go Cambridge and that I could not have met a nicer lot of friends when there. I am especially grateful to you [his parents] to have been able to afford to send me to the University.*

New York was extremely hospitable to Gareth, and the city's hostesses found him a delightful and entertaining guest. He lunched with Lord Lothian's sister and her husband, the Butler-Thwings who, according to Gareth, had, like many other people, lost a great deal of money.[24]

> *There was present Katherine Mayo[25] who wrote Mother India was invited, and a remarkable Indian lady, Mrs Sorabje, who was a brilliant talker, and gave an account of an interview with Gandhi. 'You are a humbug', she told him. She absolutely twisted him round her finger. 'His greatness', she said, 'was the result of his wonderful publicity board. As for his love for native industry, why, his spinning wheel was one especially constructed in England, which he could fold up like an umbrella. He was self-centred, always thinking of himself and he wanted to be a Dictator of India.*

Gareth was thinking of Christmas at home. It was a time of Aunt Winnie's excellent dinners and the social round of customary visits to very old friends and neighbours. Soon his homesickness was lifted by the warmth of the hospitality bestowed on him by the Bunker family in New England.

He wrote to his family in glowing terms of the sparkling festive season, and the kindness afforded to him in Boston. Not only was he to spend time with his very close friend, Laurie Bunker but also to kindle the memory of the pranks played and the hilarious days enjoyed at Cambridge in the company of Gerald Graham. Gareth vividly described his Christmas vacation as he sailed back from Boston to New York on the SS *George Washington,* once a transatlantic liner in which, as he told his family, President Wilson went to France in 1919.

> *Early on Thursday morning [Christmas Eve] the steamer arrived in Boston Harbor, after skirting the coast from New York going through Cape Cod Canal. A taxi took me through Boston and landed me outside Gerald Graham's small white timber house in the middle of Cambridge. Gerald came down to meet me and gave me a very warm welcome... He was up to his usual tricks. "Pass the matches" he asked. I caught hold of a box but dropped it because it gave [me] a small electric shock! ...Our jokes were very poor and exactly the same jokes as we had in Cambridge but Gerald's laugh is infectious and we roared like idiots. I had my revenge at the tea which Leighton Rollins — distinguished poet and play-promoter — gave in my honour, for there I introduced Gerald to one lady as the well-known writer of that delightful book of free verse, "Faded Flowers".* [26]

After lunch on Christmas Eve Gareth's friend Laurie Bunker took him to his parents' home. Gareth noted that:

> *Wellesley Hills is a very distinguished small residential town about 12 miles from Boston and the country around is very historical. There are numbers of Red Indian names... All the houses are built of timber but look very much like stone houses... The district I was staying is a very proud place all exceedingly keen on descending from people who came three hundred years ago... The New Englanders pride themselves on being the cultural centre of America and look down on foreigners of New York and the rough uncultured people of the West and Middle West. The rest of America regards New England as snobbish and does not like the Boston accent which is said to be too like the English accent.* [27]

In the evening, they drove into Boston to celebrate Christmas Eve and saw Christmas candles burning in the windows and many gardens had Christmas trees with coloured lights. They went to midnight service which was too High Church for Gareth's taste. Christmas dinner was turkey and plum pudding ("but not a patch on Aunty's!") followed by an evening party.

Gareth returned by steamer to New York on December 28th. "It was a wonderful change from the financial atmosphere of Wall Street to the country air of Wellesley and the academic surroundings of Harvard."

From the perspective of a visitor to New York, the plight of the unemployed disheartened Gareth. On most days, Gareth would be fêted by the rich and affluent, and others, he would see how the less fortunate were living in poverty.

His concern for the future was so great that he also arranged for the delivery of emergency tins of Heinz baked beans to his family.

Notes on Chapter 14

1 Gareth Vaughan Jones Papers, National Library of Wales Correspondence Series 1-21 File 12. October 11, 1931.

2 Ibid.

3 Gareth Vaughan Jones Papers, National Library of Wales Correspondence Series B6/3.

4 Ibid. November 22-23, 1931.

5 *New York Times,* 'Declares Germany Can Pay No More'. November 25, 1931, p. 5. "Ex-Aide to Lloyd George Says No Regime Can Continue Payments and Live. Predicts a Dictatorship. Nation's Conviction It Has Been Betrayed Is Dark Omen for 1932, G.R.V. Jones Asserts Here."

6 Gareth Vaughan Jones Papers, National Library of Wales Correspondence Series B6/3. November 28, 1931.

7 Ibid. November 29, 1931.

8 Gareth Vaughan Jones Papers, National Library of Wales Correspondence Series 1-21 File 12. October 14, 1931.

9 Gareth Vaughan Jones Papers, National Library of Wales Correspondence Series B6/3. October 25, 1931.

10 Ibid. October 27, 1931.

11 Ibid. October 28, 1931

12 Ibid. October 31, 1931.

13 Ibid. November 5, 1931.

14 Ibid. November 24, 1931.

15 Ibid. November 28, 1931.

16 Our Correspondent, "Fascist Dictatorship for Germany now Possibility", New York American, November 29, 1931.

17 Gareth Vaughan Jones Papers, National Library of Wales Correspondence Series B6/3. November 25, 1931.

18 Ibid. November 17, 1931

19 Ibid. November 28, 1931

20 Ibid. December 5, 1931.

21 Ibid. December 5, 1931.

22 Ibid. November 25, 1931.

[23] Ibid. December 5, 1931.

[24] Butler-Thwing (Lord Lothian's brother-in-law) who is also deep in debt told me that [Arthur] Claydon was ill from lack of food. Claydon was once a lecturer in economics, an Oxford man, but unfortunately, not possessing an impressive or interesting personality... Butler-Thwing told me that he had sold his furniture... At lunch I proposed lending him $20 but he was terribly embarrassed... Finally I dropped the subject but afterwards put $20 in an envelope and gave it to him with the words written on it "Not to be opened until you are in Grand Central Station".

[25] Dismissed by Gandhi as a "gutter inspector's report", Katherine Mayo's *Mother India* created a storm of controversy when it was first published in the late twenties. Its publication not only facilitated the passage of the Child Marriage Restraint Act in 1929, but also contributed, in the response of Indian women themselves, to the emergence of a so-called "authentic voice of Indian womanhood. Mayo, Katherine. Mother India, NY: Harcourt, 1927.

[26] Gareth Vaughan Jones Papers, National Library of Wales Correspondence Series 1-21 File 12. December 28 ,1931.

[27] Gareth Vaughan Jones Papers, National Library of Wales Correspondence Series B6/7. December 28, 1931.

Chapter 15

Depression Bites America

Spring in 1932

Gareth received many letters after Christmas including the Deed of Assignment for the new house in Barry. "I felt like celebrating my becoming part owner of a house. Luckily who should come in not many minutes later but Larry Bunker so we went out and had coffee."[1]

For a few days after the Christmas vacation, Lee's office was quiet. Then, Ivy Lee returned from Europe and immediately the place came alive; a hive of activity with 'hustle and bustle' and telephones ringing…

On January 15 at 12.30 pm Gareth wrote, "Mr Lee came back from Europe on Wednesday; but he has not written a single line of the book! Has not looked at it hardly I don't suppose he'll ever write it…" On January 20 Gareth confirmed his suspicions. "My work has a completely new orientation now. Mr Lee is sick of Russia and sick of Europe. I don't blame him — and I am working in closer touch with American business and politics! It's exciting! …Mr Lee is not going to write the book about Russia, So all my work will — from his point of view — have been in vain. From my point of view it will have been fine. [2]

This letter semi-confidential. Not to be read to Americans, but may be read to personal friends

What would Nain have said if she knew that her grandson would one day be one of the men behind the scenes in trying to elect a PRESIDENT OF THE UNITED STATES!

We were called into Mr Lee's room… He leaned back in his chair puffing his cigar: "Gentlemen, I have been retained to make Melvin Traylor, President of the United States. Melvin Traylor as you know is President of the First National Bank, Chicago, and a darned fine banker. We have got to make his name known to the Americans and advise him on his problems. There is one big drawback and that he does not want to be President. But a group of friends want me to get him nominated as Democratic Candidate at the Democratic Convention in Chicago on June 27."

So here I am, right in the middle of the most exciting event in American politics. Norton [another employee] told me with a smile: "These men (like Traylor and Rockefeller are our puppets!"³

Mr Lee gets $2,500 per month as a retainer from Traylor's friends and [Lee] is allowed to spend $85,000 a month in expenses. One of our staff is in Texas working on the Traylor stunt. If we can't make him President this time we can succeed in making him Secretary of the Treasury or President in the next election.

That's what they call democracy! It is farcical to call America democratic when a few corrupt city bosses control city politics by bribery and when the Presidential candidates have to spend vast sums of money on publicity."⁴

A week later Gareth commented:

My work in the office has been completely changed. No more foreign affairs! Mr Lee is sick of Russia and of Europe. I don't blame him. He doesn't care if he never sees the place again. He looked terribly ill and tired as he smoked his cigar:

"Good morning Jones. Glad to see you. I want your work to take on a new orientation. Don't waste your time on Russia. It's no use getting out a book on Russia now!!!!" So all the work on the book has been absolutely useless to him. "Europe has also to take a subordinate place. I want you to take part more in the business side of the office — the side which brings in money. I want you to digest everything that comes on my desk. I want you to follow the Washington situation, because we are doing very little publicity now. Our work is mostly consultative and I must be kept informed about everything. Can you type rapidly?"⁵

With this change in his job description Gareth familiarised himself with the business activities undertaken by Ivy Lee and Associates. Despite his scepticism and liberal views, on January 31, 1932, Gareth wrote appreciatively of the firm's achievements:

When one comes to think of it Ivy Lee is a wonderful organisation. I've been trying to reckon the wealth of the firms we work for and who depend largely on Mr Lee for advice on problems of all kinds from international affairs to labour troubles.⁶

With justification, financial concerns (his own and other people's) were never far from Gareth's thoughts:

> *You will be glad to hear my finances are in A1 state. I do no owe a single penny, not a cent. I have £60 in savings and about $850 (£240) in the bank and in cash which means [not] almost starving, some are. In Philadelphia the civil servants have not been paid for some time, including teachers. It looks as if New York were going bankrupt. And there are rumours that the New York teachers will not get their pay next week! The richest town in the world!* [7]

Gareth summed up the American Depression in two letters to Lloyd George, dated January 14, and February 9, 1932, who in turn included them in his book, *The Truth about Reparations and War Debts* [8] as a letter from a, "friend in the United States":

> *There is one word which describes the whole feeling in America to-day and that is disillusionment, disillusionment in the leaders, disillusionment in the businessmen, disillusionment in politics, disillusionment in prohibition — and even the gangsters have lost their glamour. The greatest disillusionment, however, is that of the worker, who only two years ago was getting £8, £10, a week, and now has to stand in the bread line. I had last night a vivid picture of the contrast of the America of yesterday with the America of today, when I strolled down the most dazzling part of Broadway. Piccadilly would be a like a Methodist chapel in the country compared with the electric lights and the movies and the dance places there. But right in the centre I saw hundreds and hundreds of poor fellows in single file, some of them in clothes which once were good, all waiting to be handed out two sandwiches, a doughnut, a cup of coffee and a cigarette. I expect a large percentage of them had their own car a couple of years ago. They now seemed jolly glad to get a bite to eat.* [9]

On February 5, 1932, Gareth's letter tried to disguise some bad news from Lee's office in a cheery letter home:

> *Good news! You will be delighted to hear I hope to be back in Eryl, probably in May and I am looking forward to it immensely.*
> *As I expected Mr Ross just called me in and said that the staff had to*

be cut down and that he regretted very much indeed that I was one of the victims… much of the work they did now was being done on tick… and they had to economise…

It is remarkable how bucked I feel. I am making all kinds of plans — going to Chicago? Going on a lecture tour? Going to Russia? Joining Lloyd George again? writing a book on Hitler? Writing articles so it's fine…

The situation here is just marking time. The unemployment is getting worse and worse and there is great suffering. [10]

Two days later Gareth had more news from the Ivy Lee office:

I find that one-third of Mr Lee's assistants and associates are leaving, there are nine of us. All the others are having their salaries cut by 10%. It will be absolutely impossible for Mr Lee to get on because everybody is overworked already. [11]

On a lighter note he mentioned that on Friday night [February 5] he had gone to the Junior League Ball, invited by Miss Adelaide Hooker, daughter of Elon Hooker, head of the Hooker Electro-Technical Company, one of the greatest companies in America. 'Now that is the very acme of high-hattedness, the top notch of New York Society.' [12]

Gareth's interest in New York City extended well beyond the wealthy people of Wall Street. On February 9, 1932, Gareth recounted a story to his parents, and in his diary which had affected him and was repeated often.

I have just come back from one of the strangest experiences I have had in my life, of a visit to a Negro Spiritualist meeting and I want to set it down before I forget.

I had dinner with Cruikshank and his mother who live on West 119th Street and on my way back about 10'clock I crossed through a part of the negro district. As I passed one house when I heard the strains of 'Nearer my God, to Thee'. Thinking it might be a negro religious meeting I walked up the steps to the door where the sound came from and read on the wall

REV. JOSEPHINE BUFFORD
BECTON
SPRIRITUALIST

*...about 50 Harlem negro women were singing a hymn and took me to a
seat at the back. On a dais was a small altar near which a plump woman stood
clad in white. When they all stopped singing she started: "Yes de Lord have sent
me to give messages to you!" ...she spoke of the Lord and how her religion the
spiritualist one was the only one which proved Christianity "Praise be de Lord.
Oh! So true! So true!" yelled the women. Then she said; "I am going to give you
two demonstrations; I am going to let my spirit move me. Don't be surprised
if it takes on an entirely different voice." Then she stopped, shut her eyes and
started rubbing her stomach. She finally started talking in a low slow voice:
"What would you do if there were a war? I see bombs dropping. I hear shrieks.
What would you do if it came to America?" ...Finally she said: "What would
you do? Pray to the Lord!" She started humming a spiritualist song, "Pray to
the Lord" and all joined in.* [13]

Gareth also returned to the Tammany Club, which he had visited in November
of the previous year. The Seabury investigation[14] had concluded that Tammany
was the most crooked organisation in the world and tainted throughout with
graft [political corruption]. The Democratic Club or Tammany controlled all the
municipal posts, from policemen to teachers and from typists in municipal offices
to tram-conductors. The Tammany sponsored politicians had made vast fortunes.
So Gareth, decided, "I am going to a Tammany Club to see for myself what these
corrupt old rotters are like."[15]

Later, he reported back to his family:

*Here I am back from the Tammany Club (Democratic) where I met the district
boss, a man of great power. ...I found the Democratic club 728 Ninth Avenue,
which is on top of a shop, climbed the stairs and found a big room, looking like
a dance hall, full of working-class people all sitting down and waiting to bring
their troubles to the district boss, who had not yet turned up. I sat next to an
old Irish man who looked as if he were fond of a drop to drink: 'What does the
Tammany club do for you?' I asked.*

*"Oh they're fine, they gets you jobs... all kinds; in the sewerage, in the rail-
ways, in the City Hall or they can get you a job as a bar tender or in a speakeasy.*

"What else does Tammany do for you?"

*"Oh, they pay the gas bills for poor people, they pay burial expenses if poor
people can't afford it, they give food to poor people. They get you out of trouble,
out of jail. They give jobs to people with large families!"*

Tammany is of course the most crooked organisation in the world, shot through with graft. The Tammany politicians have made vast fortunes. The graft was revealed some weeks ago by the Seabury investigation.

What do you think of Seabury? I asked.

A lot of fakers trying to make money. Hoover's behind it. Hoover's no good. It's his fault things are going bad now.

He wouldn't hear a word against Tammany. As a matter of Fact Seabury discovered what terrible corruption was going on. Seabury is a very fine man. [16]

In early February, Gareth lectured on "the Polish Corridor Problem" and "the Revision of the Treaty of Versailles" at Ridgefield, Connecticut. He believed a revision of the Treaty would be the only way to solve the world's financial crisis. Later, Ivy Lee made two speeches on, "the Revision of War Debts" and on "International Cooperation," for which Gareth wrote the memoranda. On February 21, 1932, Ivy Lee gave an address at De Pauw University, Greencastle, Indiana. It was a plea for the realistic treatment of the problem of "War Debts and Reparations."[17] This was a reasoned debate and analysed the conditions under which debts and reparations had developed and their inter-relationship.

Four days after the speech, Ivy Lee called Gareth to his office and said:

"I want to enlarge the speech on War Debts I made at Pittsburgh on Saturday into a book. Will you get that book ready; get all the material."

So I have another book to write! It will be fine — a most interesting subject and a valuable subject. The book is to argue in favour of cancellation of War Debts and Reparations. So I may be doing a bit of work for better conditions and world peace. [18]

Gareth started work immediately on the new book which was to take precedence over the promotion of Mel Traylor as presidential candidate.

Today I started work on the new book and spent some time in the Foreign policy Association and in the British Library of Information where Alan Dudley is. The book will, I presume have to be finished by March 31st!! I shall have to slow down on trying to make Traylor President of the United States! [19]

Gareth was making himself indispensable and three days later he announced another change of timetable.

Mr Lee has been exceedingly charming to me although a lot of members of
the staff say he can be very rude and blustering. He has always been very kind
to me. It looks as if I might stay on with Mr Lee from what he said yesterday,
when he seemed to appreciate the work I had done. So do not expect me in April.
I hope you won't be disappointed. I must say that I shall not jump with joy even
if Mr Lee keeps me on because I had set my mind on sailing on the Mauretania
on April 15th and coming to see you all and the new house.[20]

In a letter on March 1, Gareth tells his parents that while researching the book
at the British Library he received a phone message from Mr Lee to prepare a reply
"to Prof. Kemmerer's[21] speech on the Gold Standard. Kemmerer had said that
the depression was not due to maldistribution of gold and that tariffs had played
little part etc. So off I rushed by subway down to the office and prepared a reply
to Kemmerer's views. (Kemmerer by the way is the leading authority in America
on gold and currency)".[22]

Gareth later commented "Mr Lee wants the book on War Debts and Reparations
to be in the hands of the publishers by April 15th!" [23]

On 20 March Gareth continued to express his doubts, perhaps remembering
the fate of the book on Russia. "He'll have to rush! because he hasn't begun writing
it yet. I have made a plan for the book — 12 chapters and gathered lots of material."[24] He had previously mentioned to his parents that "Mr Lee does not know
what research is. He expects one to skim the surface"[25]

On March 1, Gareth had worn a daffodil to the office to celebrate Saint David's
Day; the national day of Wales. He explained the significance of daffodil and the
leek as a symbol of Wales. Later in the day he found a parcel on his table, containing
a leek — one of Mr Lee's secretaries was responsible.[26] Though a leek was the Welsh
emblem, it was normal to wear a 'less pungent' daffodil to celebrate the date. A few
days later, he attempted to send a cable in Welsh to his family, but the telegraph
office refused to accept it, unless it was translated into English.

On March 4, 1932:
I am delighted with the way everything has turned out. Every one of my
plans has succeeded admirably — to stay on a little longer than my year with
Mr Lee, [and then] to return to Lloyd George... Mr Lee has agreed to every-
thing I proposed. He wanted me to remain. ...I am exceedingly pleased with
the compliment LG has paid me and also M Lee has.[27]
If things improved he would certainly like me to continue on the staff. I was

delighted to get your letters and exceedingly surprised at your lack of appreciation
to be offered a post under someone who was once Dictator of the British Empire
and who moulded the world of today. And you would refuse it! It is the very
thing which has brought me any reputation I may have. I shall have a splendid
summer being able to spend my weekends in Barry or Cambridge. I have saved
up enough money to allow myself the luxury of nice weekends.

Wednesday evening I had a great time. I was invited to have dinner with Mr
Leland Rex Robinson (President of the Second International Securities Trust) at
Bronxville. We went out by train together. Dr Robinson's chauffeur met us at the
station and drove us out in style to his lovely house. Luscius, his four-year-old son,
greeted me warmly. Two Frenchmen had also been invited to dinner. We had a
discussion for many hours in which the British-American point of view clashed
irreconcilably, but friendly with the French. Mr Robinson is afraid of the financial
future. Mrs Robinson is terrified of kidnapping, because they have a fine little boy.

The Lindbergh baby[28] *kidnapping is arousing tremendous interest here.*
Newspaper boys were shouting that the Lindberg baby had been found but it
was a false alarm. New York is a terribly disappointing place if you, in Wales,
imagine there are hundreds of gangsters here. I don't know anyone who has ever
seen a shooting. Everything seems orderly on the surface.[29]

Gareth went to the Community Church to hear the socialist Norman Thomas[30]
speak on 'Liberty', who preached that America was not a land of liberty. There was
little equality in a land where the coal-owners employed thugs with rifles to shoot
strikers. Conditions in the coal areas were terrible in America with starvation and
shootings. He said that, "no civilised country in the world is treating its unemployed
so brutally as we in America."[31]

NT has carried the fighting spirit of Wales into the sordid political battle-
ground of America. He is the champion of honesty and the deadliest enemy of
the gangster and of graft. In his struggles to purify American city life he combines
the fervour of a revivalist with the intellectual keenness of a Welsh philosopher.
He is an enemy of capitalist America. By comparison with Thomas' enemies,
such as ex-Mayor Jimmy Walker and the gangsters, whatever they may say of
him, none deny his charm.

On April 7, 1932, while waiting to hear Governor Roosevelt to speak on the
wireless Gareth wrote:

Roosevelt is probably the Democratic Nominee for presidential candidacy and perhaps the next president. He is weak and wishy-washy man and will most probably make a rotten president. The political public men of America are of poor calibre.[32]

He went on to describe his trip that morning to pay his state taxes at the Empire State Building where he saw a crowd outside the City Hall.

Before long some Ziegfried Follies Girls came down the steps of the City Hall, followed by Mayor Jimmie Walker, Mayor of New York. I have never seen such a horrible, crooked, cunning, smart Alec, overdressed little man in my life.[33]

Jimmy Walker of New York had made millions out of being mayor of the city. Gareth was amused to see a photograph of the mayor in front of his open wardrobe, which contained dozens of pyjamas. Gareth, was later to write in the *Western Mail*, "Jimmy is proud of his collection of 150 silk pyjamas."[34]

Gareth wrote in his diary, "Yesterday I met Al Smith[35], one of the most vulgar, rudest, cheapest men I have ever seen, spitting all the time, horrible voice and is almost as bad as Jimmy Walker." "These American politicians are rotten." Despite this damning assessment, Gareth arranged a further meeting:

Tomorrow morning at 11.30 I shall have an interview in the Empire State Building with AL SMITH, former Governor of New York State. He was Democratic candidate for the Presidency in 1918, and one of the outstanding personalities of America.[36]

Perusing Gareth's diaries it would appear that this was the least successful interview that he ever had, and he remarked:

This week I have met some of the leading Americans, including three presidential candidates, the vulgar Al Smith (who is an East Side Tammany product), John W. Davis, the Democratic Candidate of 1924 and former Ambassador in London, and Norman Thomas, the perennial Socialist candidate. Both the latter impressed me as gentlemen, and I had a good talk with them this afternoon. Norman Thomas is one of the finest men in America an, honourable, idealistic, intelligent, friendly unspoilt man. John W Davis also had a twinkle, white hair etc.[37]

The Democratic Convention is in Chicago in June. Roosevelt is now leading Al Smith, Baker, Governor Ritchie and lastly our candidate, Mel Traylor. I think the American Congress is a set of the most ignorant humbugs and busybodies in the world.

Gareth had visited New England on a number of occasions during the early part of 1932 and was evidently financially better off than his old college friends. He stayed with Gerald Graham who was up to his usual jokes. The universities were badly hit by the Depression. Bunker had no job and had even been to see General Dawes who was unable to assist him in finding one.

Gareth and Gerald Graham [circa winter 1934.]

Gareth spent the first weekend of April in Boston where he went to say "Goodbye" to his friends Laurie Bunker and Gerald Graham. Preferring to travel by ship, he returned to Wall Street on the *George Washington* and with time to spare he sent his parents letter expressing mixed emotions:

This is my last month in America. I shall be on the Atlantic in four weeks'
time. My great American adventure will be over. If I had not come we should
never have been able to buy the house.

Stocks have come down again with a bang and everything is gloom. I had
one and half-hour talk with one of the leading economic authorities of America,
Thomas Woodlock of the Wall Street Journal. He is very black in his views. He
foresaw vast growth in unemployment, railways going bust, revolts and blood-
shed. It is a turning point in world history. Nationalism is a terrible disease.
Depression is nature's backlash to teach men the disease of nationalism resulting
in tariffs and armaments.

On April 15 Gareth visited Philadelphia, the birthplace of the United States, before leaving for Britain. He interviewed some eminent Americans which he believed were going to be of "immense value for the memorandum on the American situation that Gareth intended to write [unfortunately now lost, though recorded in Gareth's diaries] for Lloyd George. He would later show this memorandum to Lord Lothian, Mr Rowntree, and Sir George Paish. In the memorandum, Gareth had gathered together opinions from newspaper journalists, including Walter Lippman, the famous newspaper correspondent, Congressmen, senators, intellectuals, Democratic candidates, businessmen, and industrialists. These he recorded in his diaries. Some of the views were very radical and reactionary. The intellectuals were more sympathetic and considered that the cancellation of War Debts was mandatory.

The viewpoints of these men that Gareth interviewed were diametrically opposed to each other. The American nation on the whole was isolationist, and considered that America's plight was due to the failure of Europe to repay the War Debts, and the fault of the Depression was entirely due the United States having been so generous to the allied countries involved. They feared that if the debts were cancelled, Europe would spend more on rearmaments. The American nation's opinions were coloured by the forthcoming presidential election. The wily politician, Franklin D. Roosevelt did not touch Debts and Reparations in his manifesto but conducted his campaign only on domestic issues. Many answers from these eminent American politicians to Gareth's questions were reasoned but emotionally biased; some men had very radical views, some had sympathy for the British viewpoint, but less so for the French nation and other countries in Europe.

Gareth summarised the US position, "At the bottom of the American insistence upon war debts lie, therefore, not greed and miserliness, but ignorance and mistrust of Europe."[38]

In his last but one letter before Gareth left the United States, he stated:

> *There were riots here yesterday not far from here, at the City Hall where I saw Jimmy Walker, and also riots at Philadelphia also. There is a very bad summer ahead with large scale bankruptcies unless there is an inflation."*[39]
>
> *He [Ivy Lee] wants me to do a little work on Russia and not so much on War Debts." Mr Lee said today "We might want to have you back again. There would be more opportunities for you in normal times than in England, but you have not seen America in normal times."*
>
> *I went to see Mr Lee today in his suite at the Waldorf Astoria and he said he wanted me to consider myself 'on leave' because if the Depression finished he would have me back. He is not going to write the book on War Debts and Reparations, but now he wants me to write the book on Russia. He doesn't know his own mind. I asked him to autograph a photo and his book. On the book he wrote "To my friend and collaborator Gareth Jones with all good wishes and personal regards."*[40]

Six months later Gareth was to write to his parents that while on a bus to St Alban's he read Ivy Lee's *Memorandum on Russia* which was "disappointing. I should have been rather ashamed of writing such a memo!"[41]

And signing off this chapter in his career Gareth says, 'This is my last letter from America where I had a splendid year in every way."[42]

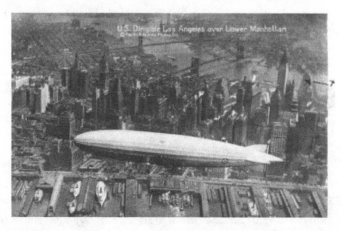

Postcard U.S Dirigible over Lower Manhattan. 1932. Gareth's apartment is marked with X.

Back of the same postcard, sent to the author. New York, Saturday April, 27, [1932],
My dear Siriol, This is the place where I live now at the top of a very high house.
How is John? I am coming home before long. Much love, Uncle Gareth.

On April 28, just under 2 weeks after his original sailing date, Gareth sailed home to Britain on the *Columbus,* Germany's third largest ship arriving in Plymouth. Having met the manager of North German Lloyd Company in New York, Gareth arranged to travel first-class for the price of the tourist fare. In return, Gareth gave him a copy of Lloyd George's book, and a cutting of a favourable speech on Germany.

Gareth was to return to his second term of employment with David Lloyd George with a more profound knowledge and understanding of the American character, world finance, and politics than when he left to join Ivy Lee.[43] Ivy Lee gave him a glowing testimonial to take with him.

> 15, Broad Street,
> NEW YORK.
> 5th May, 1932.

> My dear Jones,
> Now that you are leaving our service on what I hope is only an extended leave of absence, let me state the following:
> When I visited England in the fall of 1930, I had the pleasure of being introduced to you by Sir Bernard Pares who expressed his very high opinion of your qualities. I was so much impressed by them that I asked you to consider the possibility of coming to the United States to assist me in my study of foreign

affairs in the hope that a permanent place might be developed for you in my office. Of course, the study of foreign affairs and any writing I do on that subject is purely a diversion, and not a part of my regular professional activity. I made you a proposition to come to us for one year without commitment beyond that time. Early in the spring of 1931, you accepted my proposition, and, after we were able to overcome the immigration difficulties involved in a foreigner coming to work in the United States, you came to us bravely facing the uncertainties of the situation at the end of the year agreed upon.

You have done most excellent work, having given me in intelligent assistance, all that I could have asked for. During the year you made a trip to Russia at my request in company with the son of Mr H. Heinz of Pittsburgh. You made a splendid impression both upon Mr Heinz and his son. You have shown yourself possessed of unusual ability to make acquaintances and to find connections in the United States. You have made many friends here and effected a deep imprint with your personality and intellectual quality. I regret extremely that the business Depression brought about such a contraction of professional activities that it has not been possible for me to continue spending the money necessary to pursue some of the literary efforts which interested me so much. It has accordingly, not been possible to carry on our arrangement beyond the year agreed upon. I am delighted that you have been able to return to your former connection with Mr Lloyd George.

You are possessed of very great abilities and your conscientious attention to every task committed to you is worthy of praise. You are young, energetic, full of initiative and imagination and I am very certain that whatever niche in the world you find to be ultimately yours you will fill with the greatest credit to yourself and the greatest satisfaction to those with whom may be associated.

I wish you all happiness and success and earnestly hope that opportunity may yet develop for to you to return to the United States and be associated with us.

With kind personal regards,

Sincerely
[Signed] Ivy Lee

Notes on Chapter 15

1   Gareth Vaughan Jones Papers, National Library of Wales. Correspondence Series 1-21, File 13. January 7, 1932.

2   Ibid. January 15, 1932.

3   Ibid. January 20, 1932.

4   Gareth Vaughan Jones Papers, National Library of Wales. Correspondence Series Letter B6/4 February 26, 1932.

5   Gareth Vaughan Jones Papers, National Library of Wales. Correspondence Series 1-21, File 13 January 20, 1932.

6   The total capital of the interests we work for must be at least £300,000,000 ($1,500,000,000) — no surely much more. Take Rockefeller; he must be worth £50,000,000 if not much more. Chilean nitrates had a capital of £75,000,000; Standard oil must be quite as wealthy. Pennsylvania road must be still wealthier; Armour's of Chicago must be very many millions. Then the New York Trust has a capital of probably £60,000,000. Chrysler has a tremendous capital. The Waldorf – Astoria is worth millions of dollars. The world sugar industry too. I think £300,000,000 is much too small and our group of people decides what American public opinion is to think about these firms. Our work touches on almost every aspect of human life.

In International Affairs Mr Lee has represented the Polish and Rumanian Governments and it is rumoured that it was he who arranged the big contract between the Soviet Government and Standard Oil. In Labour Problems it was Mr Lee who settled the oil labour strikes for Rockefeller; and psychologically he absolutely transformed America's conception of Rockefellers. He has been one of Rockefeller's chief advisers on charities and arranged the publicity of the wedding of one of the Rockefeller girls. In politics we are trying to make Traylor, President of the United States and in World Affairs Mr Lee was one of the influences working on Hoover to declare the moratorium. He is Vice-President of the American League of Nations Association. Mr Lee has written a book on Soviet Russia and Communism. In World Trade, Mr Lee was one of the prime movers trying to get all the sugar producers of the world to come to an agreement and in finance our office prepares the economic articles for one of the great banks, the New York Trust and one of the great brokerage houses Dominick and Dominicks. Mr Lee is spreading the fame of Riverside Church built by Rockefeller and in philosophy I had to read Grace in the New Testament for him. We also deal with medicine and promote the study the effect of smoking on the throat. We arranged for the King of Siam to lunch at the Waldorf-Astoria and when doing public relations for Cotton week we stressed the importance and chicness of cotton dresses. Finally we deal with humour and wireless programmes. Gareth Vaughan Jones Papers, National Library of Wales. Correspondence Series B6/4.

7   Gareth Vaughan Jones Papers, National Library of Wales. Correspondence Series 1-21, File 13 January 15, 1932

8   David Lloyd George, *The Truth about Reparations and War Debts*. Garden City, NY Doubleday, Doran & Company 1932. p. 122.

9   Parliamentary Archives, Lloyd George Papers LG/G/26/1

10   Gareth Vaughan Jones Papers, National Library of Wales. Correspondence Series B6/4. February 5, 1932.

11   Ibid. February 9, 1932.

12
  Ibid. February 7, 1932.

13
  Ibid. February 9, 1932.

14
  There was an alarming amount of corruption at all levels of the administration of "Jimmy" Walker, the legendary mayor of New York. This prompted Governor Roosevelt to demand an investigative committee, headed by Judge Samuel Seabury. Ordered by Roosevelt to be more forthcoming, Walker managed to avoid being recalled until after the Democratic Convention held that summer (1932) in Chicago, where he openly supported Al Smith against the Governor Roosevelt. He was forced from office that year when his bribery was exposed. The Tammany Society was the Democratic Party political machine controlling New York City and New York State politics and helping immigrants, most notably the Irish, rise up in American politics from the 1790s to the 1960s. It typically controlled Democratic Party nominations and political patronage in Manhattan. Tammany Hall's influence waned from 1930 to 1945 when it engaged in a losing battle with Franklin D. Roosevelt, the state's governor (1928–33) and the United States president (1933–45). Roosevelt stripped Tammany of federal patronage but it only finally ceased to exist in 1967.

15
  Gareth Vaughan Jones Papers, National Library of Wales. Correspondence Series B6/4. Undated letter, probably February 1932.

16
  Ibid.

17
  The full address delivered by Ivy Lee at De Pauw University can be seen on the website:
  www.colley.co.uk/_garethjones2/american_articles/american_articles.htm

18
  Gareth Vaughan Jones Papers, National Library of Wales. Correspondence Series B6/4. February 25, 1932.

19
  Ibid. February 25, 1932.

20
  Ibid. February 29, 1932.

21
  Prof Kemmerer's speech is summarised in Ivy Lee and Associates Publication, March 4, 1932 and may be seen in full at www.garethjones.org/american_articles/american_articles.htm

22
  Gareth Vaughan Jones Papers, National Library of Wales. Correspondence Series B6/4. March 1, 1932.

23
  Ibid. March 13, 1932.

24
  Ibid. March 20, 1932.

25
  Gareth Vaughan Jones Papers, National Library of Wales. Correspondence Series 1-21, File 13 January 1932.

26
  Gareth Vaughan Jones Papers, National Library of Wales. Correspondence Series B6/4. March 1, 1932.

27
  Gareth Vaughan Jones Papers, National Library of Wales. Correspondence Series 1-21, File 13 March 4, 1932.

28
  On March 1, 1932, the 20-month-old baby son of Charles. A. Lindbergh was kidnapped. A ransom of $50,000 was paid in gold certificates. On May 12, 1932, the child was founded having been murdered.

29
  Gareth Vaughan Jones Papers, National Library of Wales. Correspondence Series 1-21, File 13 March 4, 1932.

30
  Gareth Jones. The *Western Mail* '*Welshman's bid for Presidency*', October 10, 1932. p. 6.

31
  Gareth Vaughan Jones Papers, National Library of Wales. Correspondence Series B6/4. March 1, 1932. In 1932 Wisconsin, a pioneer State, was the only State to have an unemployment insurance scheme.

32
  Gareth Vaughan Jones Papers, National Library of Wales. Correspondence Series B6/4. March 7, 1932.

33
  Ibid.

34
  Gareth Jones. The *Western Mail*. 'Mayor Walker's Secret', 10 September 1932. p. 6.

[35] Al Smith. List Rival with Franklin D Roosevelt for the 1932 Democratic presidential nomination. When FDR won and began pursuing the policies of the New Deal, Smith became even more bitter and disaffected. He became a leader of the Liberty League, a leading opponent of the New Deal, and supported the Republican presidential candidates, Alf Landon in 1936 and Wendell Wilkie in 1940.

[36] Gareth Vaughan Jones Papers, National Library of Wales. Correspondence Series B6/4. April 17, 1932.

[37] Ibid. April 21, 1932.

[38] Gareth Jones, 'How America Sees the Question of War Debts,' The Western Mail, November 29, 1932, p. 6.

[39] Gareth Vaughan Jones Papers, National Library of Wales. Correspondence Series B6/4. April 22, 1932.

[40] Ibid. April 21, 1932.

[41] Ibid. October 2, 1932.

[42] Ibid. April 25, 1932.

[43] Gareth Jones, The *Western Mail*, 'How America Sees the Debt Question,' November 29, 1932. p. 6.

PART 4

Back with Lloyd George
(1932-33)

Chapter 16

Summertime in London

No sooner had Gareth arrived back in London after a few days' break with his family in Barry did Lloyd George invite him to Brynawelon, his Criccieth home in North Wales for the weekend. On May 22, 1932, Gareth posted his Sunday letter from the Lion Hotel:

> *Friday morning at 10.30 am in Euston, I entered my First Class Compartment, and brought a large folder of American documents to read on the way. The journey passed very rapidly and was broken half-way by a good lunch. All expenses paid, of course, by the office...*
>
> *Sylvester met me in Criccieth station and drove me to the Lion Hotel where he... and many of Lloyd George's friends stay...*
>
> *Afterwards, Sylvester, who gave me a very warm welcome — we get on well together — drove me to Brynawelon. Just as we got to the gate, L.G. and Megan came out, L.G. with flowing white hair, hatless with a cloak over his shoulder. He was most exuberant in his welcome, blocked the way of the car, and said with an American accent; 'Well, I guess our American friend is back again. How are you Gareth?' He, Megan and I went for a walk and he asked me questions about personalities in America, which I was able to answer well. L.G. has a fine gift of getting the very best of your knowledge out of you. He is a perfect questioner and gives one complete confidence. On the way we stopped to talk in Welsh with some children who were pretending to fish with a piece of string in a tiny trickle of water.*
>
> *We then returned after a walk of 1¾ miles to the house and I was taken into the drawing room, where Mrs L.G., Tom Carey-Evans and Lady Carey-Evans [Lloyd George's daughter] were. L.G. was in great form, bright, witty, and looking well. The welcome they gave me — especially L.G. himself was tremendously warm, and I had the impression that he was very fond of me.*

165

L.G. said:

'The last election was a sham, but there was all the same a great national impulse. They should have taken dramatic action when the National Government came in. They should have cut down interest rates. The 5% War Loan should have been cut down immediately to 4 or 3½%. They should have cut salaries all round by 10%...'

David Lloyd George relaxing on the golf course (Photograph Gareth Jones).

Megan asked L.G. on what side he would be in the event of a revolution. He replied "I'd be on the side of the revolutionaries. I am a born radical myself."

'Whom would you kill off?' asked Megan.

Lloyd George hesitated and said:

'Well, I wouldn't kill such a worm as Ramsay MacDonald. I wouldn't bother about worms and insects like him. There is nobody I'd like to guillotine. They are all too contemptible. Oh, yes, there's Monty Norman [economist]. I'd certainly like to guillotine him and a lot of people in the City who are responsible for the trouble.'

He went on to speak about unemployment insurance:

'We'd have been Communists here if it weren't for unemployment insurance. But they won't even recognise that for me. They will when I am beneath the soil, but while I am alive they won't admit that I've done anything.' *This was said humorously.*

166

Lloyd George spoke highly of Stalin: 'Stalin is trying an experiment. Of course, he fails but he recognises his failure. He's man enough. I take off my hat to Stalin and to Mussolini. And when Stalin recognises failure or tries a new method they say, "I told you so." Every scientist fails time and time again before he makes a great discovery. People in America are finding that the great business leaders are alright when the car is going along a smooth road, but they are helpless now that the car has broken down. 'not in letter

He thinks that the international situation is desperate. 'The Lausanne Conference will lead to nothing.

It will be just like the Disarmament Conference. [Edouard] Herriot is weak; he's a professor. He's the Ramsay Mair type.

When I said that the Hoover Moratorium might be renewed if there were some measure of disarmament or cutting down of reparations Lloyd George said, "Then it is hopeless."

When I told L.G. of the wave of isolationism in America L.G. gave a look of despair and said, "Well, that's tragic." He began to count up the foods he could get on his farm, to get enough to eat, "Fruit, eggs, chicken and of course, there's honey."

All the news in The Times published Friday and today[predicting large bankruptcies in the United States] have confirmed my pessimistic opinions in the memo I sent L.G. Lloyd George asked me what would happen in a year's time.

I said, logically, I thought I would be lucky to have enough to eat, but that I felt certain all the same I would have plenty to eat. Lloyd George said:

'That's just what I like. I feel that in the long run things will come out alright. I remember just before November 1918 elections, Asquith came to me. He said that society was a huge bluff or it would have collapsed before the war. I never noticed any bitterness or despising with Asquith. Hoover is a surly fellow, but he always managed to get into the limelight. In the war it was the same. He seemed bad tempered and ungracious.

When I talked of Keynes' suggestion in the Atlantic Monthly that raised prices through going off the gold standard might lead to a recovery Lloyd George said, "Keynes always makes a lot of suggestions and when one of them comes out alright, he says it was a prophesy." Not in letter.

After dinner I sat with Mrs L.G, Megan, the Lady Carey-Evans and we talked about rackets in New York. They are all — including L.G. — tremendously interested in the Lindbergh baby.

You must get Gareth to tell you about the Spiritualist meeting in Harlem' said Lloyd George to Megan. Lloyd George was laughing all the time and drawing a plan of the place where Olwen and her husband should go fishing. He put in a drawing of Tom Carey-Evans fishing and a bull in the fields tossing Olwen.

The speech on Wednesday will be sensational. Lloyd George has been working on it for a week...

L.G. is extremely anxious for me to go and see Hitler as soon as possible. So, I may rush off to Germany as soon as an interview can be arranged; perhaps in a few days' time! Won't that be fine! [1]

He wants me to go and see Ludendorff, and many people who were connected with the War for his Memoirs. Isn't that entering into the pages of history with a vengeance! He wants to have a long talk with me before I go. [2]

In a letter from Gareth's Millbank office on May 30, 1932:

The last few days have been among the most enjoyable I have had. I have seen heaps and heaps of old friends and they all seem pleased to see me again. I have had a lot of invitations so I don't know where to begin. London is a great place.

First of all, my weekend in Cambridge. Ludovik met me at the station... Poor Ludo! He has had a quarrel with the headmaster at Uppingham and has now a post at Manchester Grammar School... It was fine to be at Cambridge again. On the way I bought a lot of flowers for Mrs Stuart, and two red carnations for Ludo and me to wear with our evening dress at the dance on Saturday evening...

J R M Butler [3] *asked me to dinner at the High Table and also for breakfast but I had to refuse because I was booked at the Stewarts. Poor Prof. Breul is dead. I am sorry, because I was fond of Professor Breul. I have just written to Mrs Breul, as I only heard on Saturday evening...*

Sunday after breakfast, I went into Cambridge... as I wanted to see Jack Heinz. Jack was so excited to see me. We had a long talk and walk, and we are going to meet in London...

Tea [at the Stewarts'] was amusing. Young Count Sollohub was there. You remember his mother, whom I met in Paris, wanted to learn to speak Welsh. He was a very nice fellow.

I had dinner at the Chapples'. Madeleine Chapple has blossomed forth as the belle of Newnham and had been proposed to seven times. I helped to wash dishes with the Siamese Prince.

Saturday morning, I sent in an application for the Industrial Council Post. Although Lloyd George is very fond of me and thinks very highly of me the financial position is bad. There is now no prospect of a job at the RIIA (I asked [Sir John] Wheeler-Bennett who said he would be delighted to have me there, but that financially... Later, I might have a fine chance.)

Sir John Davis showed my American Memorandum to the President of English "Fords" — a great company — who used my stuff in his speech in the City on Thursday. Sir John wants to know how I should like to join the staff of Fords. They want educated men with knowledge of language for responsible posts. Sir John has put up my salary by £10 as I planned.

Gareth's social calendar was as full as ever and he ended his letter with all the details.

I dined with Barney Janner [later Lord Janner] at the House (who sends his warm greetings); lunched with Ralph Arnold, author of Fortune Favours Fools, novel just out, at the famous Garrick Club... lunching with Paul Scheffer on Wed. lunched John Hood Lincoln's Inn today, Travellers' Club Thursday, dine with Norton at the Turkish Restaurant, lunch with Emlyn-Jones tomorrow, Reform Club. Last night, I went to the Clothworkers' Dinner which was magnificent and really an outstanding experience.

Gareth had evidently taken heed of Lloyd George's advice of the previous week and amongst the social chit chat he slips in a casual remark 'I have written to Hitler's secretary.'[4]

On Thursday, June 2, 1932, Colonel Tweed motored Gareth down to Churt leaving Thames House at 10.45 am It was a beautiful June day and they got to Bron-y-d⊠ at 12.15 pm A smiling Lloyd George welcomed them at the portals. While they sat outside, the maid interrupted and said, "*The Daily Telegraph* is phoning to ask you what comments you have on the book by the daughter of Sir George Buchanan on Russia." Lloyd George said: "I don't want to say anything. Tell them I have nothing to say." He turned to me and said:

They are accusing me of being responsible for the Tsar's death. They say that I should have admitted him to England in 1917. But, at that time, we wanted to keep Russia in the War, and we wanted to have the support of the Russian Liberals. We would have alienated Kerensky had we let the Tsar in. As we did, we kept the Russians in the War until October. That kept a number of German divisions in the East. By the time most of the German troops were sent to the Western Front, the Americans had arrived in France.[5]

Lloyd George, Colonel Tweed and Gareth lunched together with further discussions afterwards. 'Lloyd George spoke for about five hours altogether without stopping!' Gareth remarked, "The metaphors he used were fine. It was a privilege to hear him." [6]

Gareth asked Lloyd George, "How do you define World Collapse?" to which Lloyd George replied:

I don't think there will be complete world collapse. The Titanic is sinking. We shall be water-logged and the Plimsoll line will be well underwater, but will it plunge? I don't think so, unless there is a vast catastrophe. By that I mean a Russian or Japanese War. That would definitely mean an end of civilisation. Supposing Poland took the opportunity to attack Russia. Then suppose Germany wanted to have the Polish Corridor back. That would be the end. I think Russia will be the only country to come out well. That is the only country where the situation has improved.

Lloyd George didn't think the Government should advocate complete cancellation of reparations at the forthcoming Lausanne Conference. Gareth asked him what would he do if he were to attend the Lausanne conference? His response was:

I would play for time. A moratorium is the only way out. Lausanne will end in a moratorium. Herriot is a weak fool. This new International coup will not lead to anything without discussing Tariffs, War Debts, etc.. It's just like Ramsay phoning from Lossiemouth to America in order to be able to say: "'Alone I did it!' Vanity is a terrible thing in a public man."

Hitler should come out and say we will not pay any more reparations. He should tell the French to go to Hell. Laval is a weak creature. He behaved abominably to Briand. Vile fellow. They (Ramsay and co) would rather let the ship sink than let some people in.[7]

Gareth further enquired, "should Great Britain pay Americans in December?" The former Prime Minister considered that "Default would be disastrous. No, we should not default. We have been living beyond our means." Lloyd George was adamant: "I am very opposed to inflation. There is no artificial way out. I do not agree with your American thesis that the crisis is due to too little going into consumption goods."[8]

June 25, 1932 was an important date for the author. It was the day Gareth introduced his niece, Siriol, aged seven, to Lloyd George and to his daughter, Megan, about which Gareth wrote, "it will be something she will be very proud of in later years."[9] It was at a garden party in London. In the annals of the family history Lloyd George said to the author's mother, Eirian that, "Siriol is a pretty little girl and a charming one, too."

Two days later, Lloyd George invited Gareth down to Churt. The former Prime Minister wanted him to go to Italy immediately. On June 29, 1932, he wrote from Folkestone harbour:

> *I had the kind of rush I like this morning and so I had no time to write. I left Victoria at two o'clock. I am crossing to Boulogne-Paris-Rome.*
>
> *I have letters of introduction to the leading people in Rome, ministers, etc., and Mussolini's personal representative in London, Luigi Villari, of the Athenaeum, has done all in his power to help me. Wheeler-Bennett [of the RIIA] has been remarkably kind and has given me fine introductions to people in Lausanne. It will be intensely interesting and a full trip. My regret is that I shall have practically no time for museums etc, because I shall have to write reports to L.G. while I am travelling.*[10]

On his arrival in Rome Gareth wrote to his parents from Le Grand Hotel:

> *This is a wonderful way of beginning July 1932, being in Rome which is a fine city and then going to Geneva, Lausanne, and back to London. I arrived safely this morning at 6.30 after having slept soundly in my sleeper. I woke up outside Rome and had a great view of the Tiber in grey haze. I was greatly impressed by the buildings I saw from the train. On arrival, I came to this first-class hotel which is most comfortable...*
>
> *It was great to wake up in the Alps (near Chambery) yesterday morning. The day passed quickly. The train ride from Genoa-Rapallo-Pisa was magnificent. It was my first glimpse of the Mediterranean. Every inch of the railway track on this journey was electrified, for Mussolini is now carrying out a great programme of railway building.*
>
> *Looking out of the train between the frontier and Rome, one could see that*

every patch of land was cultivated, and that up to the vary fringe of the moun-
tains, the peasants had planted wheat or vegetables. Mussolini is fighting for
the full use of Italian soil, against the crowding of the masses in the great cities.

Mussolini is building roads, bridges, canals, and viaducts in many parts of
Italy. He aims at the re-building of his native country, and it is remarkable that
his programme follows the lines laid down by the Liberal party in Great Britain
and almost identical with Lloyd George's Liberal plans! What irony that the enemy
of Democracy should be carrying out the policy advocated by British Liberals.

And here I am. It will be a rush, because I have heaps of people to interview.
I began by going to the Foreign Office, and then to the Head of Statistical
Department, an interview with Ministry of Corporations, and the Head of
Land Reclamation for Italy, Signor Serpieri.[11]

Isn't Italy a beautiful country? I had no idea it was so fine. And Rome is the
finest city I know. It beats London, Paris, Berlin, Warsaw, Stockholm, Moscow,
Riga — i.e. the capitals I know… The Times' and Reuters' correspondents
and one from Le Temps lunched with me today. They gave me much valuable
information. The latter discussed with me the colonial question concerning the
areas in Africa which the Big Powers would like to acquire. One view was to
divide Africa into three main strips: French in the west, Italy in the centre, and
Britain in south.[12]

I thought Italy was wonderful, and I got masses of things to tell L.G. Mussolini
is carrying out a program which is almost identical with L.G.'s Liberal Plans![13]
At Lausanne, I stayed at the Beau Rivage, and had my dinner Tuesday night
near the table where MacDonald, Chamberlain, and von Papen were dining.
Wednesday morning, I breakfasted just near Sir John Simon whom everyone
heartily loathes, and, at lunch on Wednesday, I was just near the PM, Runciman
and Simon.

In a later letter Gareth comments "Sir John Simon is an awful turncoat and
self-seeker."[14]

From the offices of Lloyd George, Millbank, London, on July 11, 1932:

This had been most exciting day. It began by Paul Scheffer ringing me up to
ask if I had heard of the disgraceful Gentleman's Agreement at Lausanne which
spoils everything. Paul Scheffer thinks MacDonald was duped by Herriot.[15]

The Gentleman's Agreement makes it absolutely impossible for the English to
get special agreement with America without permission from France. If there is no

172

settlement of the American debt the Lausanne Conference will be considered null and void] I sent Lloyd George information about the Gentleman's Agreement, which the French have wrung out of the weak MacDonald, and which makes Lausanne an absolute failure. [16]

It ended by my receiving an invitation from Hitler's Ernst Hanfstaengl, Hitler's Foreign Press Chief private secretary to join Hitler's private aeroplane party on his election tour at the end of July during the coming election tour. He provisionally reserved a seat in the aeroplane and suggested that the most convenient place would be Aachen (Aix la Chapelle) on July 28th. [17]

And, at 7.30, I dine with Paul Scheffer. I saw Lloyd George for just a second, but only time to shake hands because he was hurrying.

Gareth was unable to go home to Barry for the weekend because he had been invited by Lloyd George to visit Churt.

This is a certainly a fine visit. I caught the 3.04 pm from Waterloo after a very busy morning and arrived at Farnham about 4.20 pm. Mr Lloyd George was waiting for me there in his Rolls Royce, and we drove together to Churt. He was in a wonderful mood, bubbling over with jokes and laughter, just like a child. He showed me his roses, and then we had tea…

Lord Beaverbrook came last night, 'Max' as Lloyd George calls him, but I did not see him because he had a talk in the drawing room, and left before dinner. Beaverbrook estimates that about £1,600,000,000 of the War Loan will be converted, and that £400,000,000 will be paid out in cash. Those who receive the cash will invest it in industrial shares, and thus the price of industrials will rise. Beaverbrook said that it was Neville Chamberlain at the Lausanne Conference who did most of the work and not MacDonald, and Beaverbrook is hurt that MacDonald said nothing about his work.

Lloyd George thinks it would have been better for America not to have come into the War; the War would have been a stalemate, and there would have been a better peace.

Lloyd George was very proud of his farm and Gareth noted that he was disappointed that his daughter Megan did not take more interest in the farm and farming. He also mentioned to his parents that "L.G is amused at being a kulak, and he said, 'When I go to Russia — I may go next year. I am going to say to Stalin, 'Well, here's a real Kulak coming to see you."

Notes on Chapter 16

1
    Gareth Vaughan Jones Papers, National Library of Wales. Correspondence Series B6/4. May 22, 1934.

2
    Gareth Vaughan Jones Papers, National Library of Wales. Correspondence Series 1-21, File 18. May 24, 1932.

3
    Son of the late Master Henry Montagu Butler. He was Regius Professor of Modern History, later vice Master of Trinity College.

4
    Gareth Vaughan Jones Papers, National Library of Wales. Correspondence Series B6/4. May 30, 1932.

5
    Ibid. June 5, 1932.

6
    Ibid.

7
    Ibid.

8
    Gareth Vaughan Jones Papers, National Library of Wales. Diary Series B1/8.

9
    Gareth Vaughan Jones Papers, National Library of Wales. Correspondence Series 1-21, File 18 June 26, 1932.

10
    Gareth Vaughan Jones Papers, National Library of Wales. Correspondence Series B6/4 June 29, 1932.

11
    Ibid. July 1, 1932.

12
    Ibid. July 3, 1932.

13
    Ibid. July 10, 1932

14
    Ibid. July 24, 1932.

15
    Eduard Herriot, The French Premier acted to ease Germany's economic crisis by suspending all reparations. The creditor governments cancelled War debts between themselves but made a 'Gentleman's Agreement' that the Lausanne Protocol would not be ratified until they reached a satisfactory agreement about their War debts to the United States. Although never ratified, the Lausanne Protocol, in effect, ended attempts to exact reparations from Germany.

16
    Gareth Vaughan Jones Papers, National Library of Wales. Correspondence Series 1-21, File 18. July 11, 1932.

17
    Ibid. July 10, 1932.

Chapter 17

Will There Be Soup?

After a long summer holiday with his parents in Wales, Gareth returned to his work and a frenetic lifestyle in London. With boundless energy Gareth recorded all of his undertakings and extensive activities in his many diaries and letters. The autumn of 1932 was to be a very decisive period for him. He accompanied Lloyd George in the Rolls Royce to Churt on September 2 for a week. One of his tasks was to help prepare information for Lloyd George's memoirs (which Gareth told his parents not to mention to anyone).[1]

On August 30, 1932, Gareth met his friend Dr Reinhard Haferkorn who had just arrived in Britain for a prolonged stay, and during this visit they saw a great deal of each other. Haferkorn, now Chairman of League of Nations High Commission in Danzig, had been invited to lecture to the RIIA in October, and prior to the presentation Gareth was to entertain the speaker and several dignitaries, including the RIIA Chairman, Sir John Wheeler Bennett to dinner. The frugal Gareth considered it rather an expensive honour, but despite his financial concern decided to entertain them regally.[2]

Gareth portrayed the events of the evening in great detail in a letter to his parents on October 8, 1932. He even included a little sketch of the seating arrangements at the round table: Reinhard, Captain Charley, Mr Hubbard (of the Bank of England), Lord Pentland, Mr MacDonald (Former High Commissioner of Danzig), and the Military Attaché were present.

The dinner party on Thursday evening was a great success on Thursday evening. It was held privately, in a dignified room in the Reform Club with green walls, carpet and an old picture of Charles Dickens. Some good Reform Club's silver, including a fine huge silver candlestick was used, and two waiters, one who looked just like an old waiter on the stage.

There was no difficulty about conversation. Afterwards we all went to

Chatham House, and Reinhard spoke excellently. He was clear and short and the debate which followed was fine. Augur, [pen name for Poliakoff, correspondent for the Manchester Guardian,] G. P. Gooch, [British historian, political scientist, and editor] and many others were there. It was a very full meeting. The RIIA was very pleased, as everything went off excellently, and I was very pleased, as I was responsible.

It was only 11 days later that Gareth was to return to the RIIA to hear Lord Lytton speak about his report following the Lytton Commission and its visit to Manchukuo, which had been published on October 1, 1932. The meeting was packed with eminent people wishing to listen to this prestigious lecture on the political crisis there, and perhaps kindled an interest that Gareth was to pursue three years later that was ultimately to have a tragic bearing on his own life. For the time being Gareth was more than occupied with his enduring concerns with Germany and Russia.

Wolf von Dewall, his wife and a friend.

During his stay in London, Haferkorn introduced Gareth to the von Dewalls, whom Gareth described as a very charming family. Gareth told his parents that Wolf von Dewall was one of the greatest German foreign journalists. He was [previously foreign] editor of the *Frankfurter Zeitung*, the equivalent of the *Manchester Guardian*.

Von Dewall was in the same class as General Kurt von Schleicher in school. He said that Schleicher, was then a nervous timid little harmless fellow at school, and now he is Chancellor of Germany... It has been wonderful today tramping on Box Hill in the sunshine with the Dewalls. They are fine company combining great fun and loud laughter with serious talk. It is fine to get out of London and get some exercise. We laughed a great deal.[3]

During the last few months of 1932, Gareth spent numerous weekends at Churt, researching some of the most 'vital and confidential' Government Wartime documents for Lloyd George's *War Memoirs*. The wartime Prime Minister was a hard taskmaster, and made many demands on Gareth. Before breakfasting with the Lloyd Georges, Gareth would often receive his daily instructions from his employer during a leisurely stroll around the colourful gardens of Bron-y-de.

From Churt he wrote on September 6, 1932:

Yesterday there was an interesting tea here; Lord Beaverbrook, Lloyd George, and your son. I did not like Beaverbrook at all, a bullying type; I thought a rough brute, no finer feelings; intriguer, an absolute nouveau riche.

The work here is most interesting. I am working on some of the most secret documents of the War. The shipping brief I am writing is giving me great pleasure and Lloyd George said the first part was very good. I type all my own stuff. I'm sorry I won't be home next week-end, perhaps the next.[4]

From the Reform Club, September 9, 1932.

Sir George Paish is sitting opposite me, a lovely man, telling me about his food memorandum during the War, which is one of the secret documents I am now studying [for the War Memoirs]... Sir George went on talking and talking about the War — most interesting.[5]

On October 5th Gareth reported that he was going to be the Diplomatic Correspondent for a new newspaper *Y Cymro*[The Welshman].[6]
On October 20, 1932:

I was in the office of The Economist (which I consider one of the greatest periodicals there is) and was talking with Sir Walter Layton [the editor], whom I like very much, a most natural and simple man. He wanted to know whether I could do a little work on tariffs to help him, because he was short-handed. Since Ottawa [the Imperial Conference] is a subject I have to study for Lloyd George, I willingly consented and did some research that day on tariffs in South Africa.

The House met in the afternoon, and L.G. asked me to come and see him in the House of Commons in his private room there. He and Megan greeted me and Lloyd George asked me to prepare a memorandum on, 'The American attitude towards the War in 1916'. He gave me instructions, and I am busy working on that; a most interesting subject.[8]

On October 25, 1932:

Yesterday was most enjoyable for me. I went out to dinner at the Dorchester Hotel with a big Australian industrialist, H. S. Robinson... The conversation was intensely interesting, and I was able to learn a lot which I gave to Lloyd George when he came in this morning... He comes into my room when he comes now and walks up and down. He looks very well, but, in reality, he is very worried and hurt by the Liberals. Lloyd George today talked about; 'When Gareth and I have finished our book.[9]

From the Reform Club on December 12, 1932:

Lloyd George called for me this afternoon and was deeply moved. He had been to Diana Churchill's wedding. "I have never had such a reception in my life." he said: "They mobbed me. Even when I was PM I never got such a welcome. It nearly broke me up."

I was in the House at about 6 o'clock and I met Amery — dull, funny little fellow, not very brainy. Then, Mr Churchill came out of Lloyd George's room. I thought he was charming.[10]

With the dwindling political and financial fortunes of the British Liberal party and with the imminent publication of Lloyd George's memoirs, it became necessary for Gareth to make an important decision as to the direction of his career. Fortunately, he was not short of options.

On December 4, 1932 Gareth spoke at the BBC [the British Broadcasting Company]. His broadcast was the first of a series; 'Wales from Without', entitled, 'A Distant View: From Moscow' He considered, 'The BBC talk is very hard to prepare: the most difficult subject I've had.' He was being modest — his talk was well reviewed.

Mr Gareth Jones's broadcast talk on international affairs last week — which was given in Welsh — was quite remarkably characteristic. The microphone for once preserved every iota of his personality, the enthusiasm and vivacity that mark every speech he makes, and that peculiar impression of intimacy, as of addressing a single listener across the fireside, which is a great part of their attraction. One could almost see his quick, eager gestures, and the changing expressions with which he illustrates every anecdote.

He gave us a little tale which was told among the anti-Nazi Lutherans in Germany, of a staunch Nazi priest who, before commencing a service, ordered that anyone who was a Jew should leave the church. There was a brief pause and then the figure of Christ stepped down from the crucifix on the altar and silently went out of the building.

Yet another was that of an airman who was passing over a lonely lake and saw a man struggling in the water and rescued him. When he had done so he found it was Stalin and immediately considered the advisability of dropping him overboard again: "because of what all the other Russians would say for not letting him drown".

While in Cardiff for his radio broadcast Gareth was invited to speak on the subject, "Behind the Scenes in American Publicity" to the Cardiff Publicity Club. This speech was reported upon in the *Western Mail,* on December 10, 1932. The same day Gareth informed his parents that he was seriously considering a post with the BBC and would be interviewed the following day by the Head of Talks Department.

However, on 21 December 1932, Gareth told his parents:

You will be glad to hear that I have refused the BBC job. Everybody advises against it. … There is the possibility, of course, that they might have had my name in mind as the head of BBC in Cardiff — a job which I would have disliked intensely.[11]

Having declined a post with the fledgling BBC Gareth was able to focus his mind on a career in newspaper journalism. The head of Reuters, the editor of the *Sunday Times* and Wheeler-Bennett of the RIIA advised him that experience with a provincial newspaper would be essential. With this in mind, he secured a post with the *Western Mail,* which would commence on April 1, 1933 and would follow directly after two months' paid leave at the end of his contract with Lloyd George. He had already published a number of articles in that newspaper about the growing problems in the Soviet Union.

During the tumultuous autumn of 1932, reliable though disturbing reports were trickling into London of a severe agricultural crisis in the Soviet Union. He was also aware, from his expert knowledge of the country, of the political problems in Germany which were to culminate in Hitler's rise to power in January 1933. Gareth planned to use his two months' leave after finishing his employment with Lloyd George to make an extensive tour of Europe in order to investigate the situation in these two countries first-hand.

In the course of his confidential talks with many Soviet experts and several 'fellow-travellers' on their return from the workers' paradise, Gareth's prophesy of an ongoing catastrophe was being silently borne out. Gareth had renewed his friendship with Francis Butler-Thwing whom he had met in New York, and they dined at the Marlborough Club (once the club of King Edward VII) with Bruce Hopper, who according to Gareth was a Harvard expert on the Soviet Union. Hopper had given 'a terrible picture of conditions in Russia-famine in Ukraine, hunger throughout. He predicts that millions will starve this winter, terrific discontent. It has never been so bad since 1921, and he has been over 3 years in Russia.'[12]

This meeting prompted Gareth to write to Ivy Lee on September 13, 1932:

Last week, I had a long talk with Bruce Hopper who had returned from Russia very bearish. The Soviet Government is facing the worst crisis since 1921. The harvest is a failure, and there will be millions facing starvation this winter. There is at the present moment a famine in the Ukraine. Collective farms have been a complete failure, and there is now a migration from the farms. There is simply nothing left in many collectives, and numbers of peasants from far South as the Bessarabian frontier have wandered up to Moscow for bread. Even the army is short of food and there is grave discontent in it. Disillusion is spreading through the ranks of the party. There is no open opposition and the silence is dangerous. Russia, says Hopper, is about to enter a period similar to the NEP. The speeches of Molotov, Yakovloev and Krylenko all indicate there are preparations for big changes. Hopper's cook's rations for four months had been bread and water.

The prospect of exporting grain this winter is very slim and butter is wiped out as an export. Hopper is suspicious as to the amount of Soviet gold supply and is afraid that the Soviet Union will not meet its obligations.[13]

In a letter dated October 2, 1932:

> *I entered Butler-Thwing's new house in Montpelier Square Kensington, all dressed up. Before long, Lord Lothian [Under-secretary of State for India] turned up and we had dinner. Lord Lothian has completely changed his views towards Russia. A year ago he thought Socialism would probably be a success, but now he says that Communism is heading for a crash, that Socialism is everywhere a failure, and that there will probably in some time be a violent return in the world to individualism and laissez faire [free market capitalism].*[14]

Gareth further commented in a later letter to his parents that he thought the SCR [unknown acronym] reports 'all baloney!

> *I have got heaps of facts from the Soviet Press which confirm my belief that there is a severe crisis. The harvest is a failure; there is shelter lacking for 1,500,000 head of cattle; potato plans have broken down; in July only 40% of the grain collecting plan was carried out; the peasants are refusing to give up the grain. The Soviet Press at least is honest about the situation. It is the blind people like Mr Worrall [unidentified] who refuse to believe that anything bad there is possible.*[15]

Ivy Lee had sent Gareth a pro-Soviet memorandum to which Gareth wrote a polite, but analytical criticism on October 8, 1932 countering Lee's statement that "This faith in the [Soviet] government and its leaders is unimpaired."[16]

> *My view is that the disillusionment is terrific; it was already last year, and the year before, and it is worse now... I spoke to large numbers of peasants on this subject, and the question I always asked was; 'Did you join the kolkhoz of your own free will, or were you forced?' The reply I always had, with a very significant and forceful gesture, was; 'They forced us to join.' My impression, and it is based on the hundreds of conversations which I pushed into my stays — that 90 percent of the people are opposed to the government, and the large masses of the peasantry would fight against it willingly, if they had arms, an organisation and a leader... I believe that at the present moment, as a result of*

food shortage, and breakdown of grain plans, there are many people starving in many parts of Russia.

As to grain in 1930, their [Soviet] export of grain was only six million tons whereas before the war, the average was ten million tons, and it sometimes reached twelve million or more. Finally, it would be impossible to increase the productivity of the land through collective farms, on account of the great massacre of horses and cattle.

Soviet orders of machinery in England have certainly declined. I heard from one source that they had have been cut down by 60 percent… The question; "is the new machinery to be used, to be German, English or American?" Here is a most valuable contribution for you [Lee] to answer, "will they be able to meet the obligation?" Bruce Hopper doubts it; the Russian expert of the Bank of England with whom I lunched a few days ago, believes that they will not be able to pay and will be forced to have their credits extended. Knickerbocker, with whom I lunched also agreed, and I also think they will have a huge difficulties in paying, in view of the breakdown of the agricultural plans, low prices and tariffs. Moreover, Hopper, the Bank of England expert and Knickerbocker all stated that the Russian gold reserves were pure bluff. The Bank of England's Russian expert said that part of their gold reserve was in certificates for gold still in the ground![17]

Immediately after these communications, Gareth penned two articles which were published in the *Western Mail*, on 15 and 17 October, 1932, entitled 'Will There be Soup?' The first article was headed with the words 'Growing Menace of Communism' and sub-titled 'Russia Dreads the Coming Winter', and the second article was titled 'Russia Famished Under the Five-Year Plan'. In short, they forecast that the last winter of the Five-Year Plan would be one of great famine.[18]

Following his articles in the *Western Mail* there were a number of controversial letters from the readers to the newspaper. Gareth considered the paper was making use of his Russian articles as Tory (Conservative) propaganda.

On October 23rd Gareth wrote with more news of Russia to his parents.

On Friday I had three exceptionally interesting talks on Russia, which fully bear out what I have said. The first was with Prof. Jules Menken (LSE) a very well-known economist. He was appalled with the prospects, what he had seen was the complete failure of Marxism. He dreaded the winter when he thought millions would die of hunger. He had never seen such bungling and such break-downs. What struck him was the unfairness and inequality. He'd seen hungry people one moment and the next moment he had lunched with Soviet Commisars in the Kremlin and seen them gorge themselves with the best caviar, fish, game, and the most luxurious wines. [19]

Menken is the sort of man one would expect to be impressed with Russia. He is the man who wrote the articles in The Economist. …He was so impressed by the failure in Russia that he feared the regime might collapse… Menken said there is already famine in Ukraine. [20]

The *Western Mail* articles triggered a huge response in the readership which Gareth relished:

Do you know I am getting a great tremendous amount of fun out of the letters? It gives me a real kick to be able to set tongues wagging and people buzzing. I haven't had so much enjoyment since the snow-ball fights in school. "Trade Unionist's" letter was jolly good. It is just like a football match. By the way, I am certain Monday's letter was written by a professional journalist in a Conservative Propaganda Office. [21]

…I am not going to be associated with Tories and Catholics of the W[estern].M[ail] type… I should much rather be associated with Disarmament, Free trade and League of Nations than with the Western Mail's readers' views. Moreover it has aroused interest in Communism. And I am writing two articles on the Communist International, which is timely on account of the controversy.

Everybody's views are doubted. Have Lloyd George's views always been accepted? Or anybody's for that matter? And it is rightly so! [22]

On November 8, 1932:

Had lunch today with Kingsley Martin, (editor of the New Statesman) with the Minister of Agriculture (Walter Eliot), and others. I was able to be of great help to Kingsley Martin by translating after lunch passages from Russian newspapers. He went to Russia with Low of the Evening Standard. He spent a month in Russia this year. [23]

His dinner engagements were frequent and varied. In a letter started on December 4 Gareth told his parents of his dinner with Sir Bernard Pares on Thursday December 8 and "enjoyed it exceedingly. He is very fond of me and also of Dada. He always talks of how he was impressed by Dada."

The next evening he dined with his friend Paul Scheffer in Soho after tea with Lawson. "Scheffer's calamitous predictions about Russia are now coming true. Scheffer told me a lot of interesting things. He is regarded as one of the world's greatest correspondents of the 20th century". Gareth also noted that Sir George Paish thought Britain would have to send grain to feed the starving Russians. "Paish forsees the breakdown of the Conservative government either next year of 1934. The younger Conservatives are very liberal in their economics and disarmament views and there will be a break between them and the diehards. 100 young Conservatives are in favour of radical disarmament."[24]

Gareth's interest in Russian affairs did not divert him entirely from Germany. He had mentioned in a letter back in October that 'On Thursday the head of the Nazis in London came and lunched with me in a small restaurant near the office. Ralph Arnold and Lawrence of the RIIA also came and we had a good discussion.'[25] Just before Christmas he decided to make another visit.

> *I shall be taking a long week-end on December 9, after speaking at the lunch on that day... But I have an idea in my head that I shall return to London in the afternoon and leave for Germany that night — Cologne — and come back to London on Monday. I have been to Germany every year since 1923, and I do not want to break the 10-year record. It would be not be good for me as a so-called 'expert'.[26]*

In any event, Gareth appears to have postponed his trip until the weekend before Christmas and reports to his parents on December 18 that he was having 'a weekend crammed with interesting talks 'and that he was 'trying to find out all I can and I have a mass of articles etc to go through' He apologised that he had 'no time to send (m)any Xmas greetings.'[27]

In a brief note written in the Reform Club on December 20, 1932, Gareth stated that his German trip was a great success and that his report on Chancellor Schleicher and Germany (in his opinion) was "first rate".[28]

Gareth penned his first letter of the New Year on January 6, 1933:

> *It was great fun to taking Siriol to the Panto this afternoon and we thoroughly enjoyed it. Tonight, I am going to supper with Jane Evans but I would much rather sit in one of the lovely armchairs in the Reform Club and read.[29]*
> *On Wednesday, I had caviar and a long talk alone for one hour with*

Hitler Speaks to the Students (Berliner Tennishallen 1932). With Hitler are
Goering, Schirach, Goebbels and Hanfstaengl behind Hitler's left shoulder.

the Soviet Ambassador, His Excellency M. Maisky, a funny little chap,
half-Tartar, half-Jew.[30]

Gareth was back in Wales by the weekend of January 13-15, lecturing in
Aberystwyth and, despite his turning down a job at the BBC, had been asked to
give a broadcast lecture on the 18th. He also announced his plans for the future:

> *I am going to write a book, 'Russia and the League of Nations' and am going*
> *to gather material. I shall spend February in Germany and March in Russia.*
> *I saw the Soviet Ambassador and I think he is going to grant me a visa. I may*
> *leave for Germany the end of next week.*[31]

January 17, 1933, he had been David Lloyd George's 70th birthday and, according
to Gareth, he received a thousand congratulatory letters.[32]
On January 19, 1933 Gareth wrote to his parents:

> *I shall look forward ever so much to seeing you next week but I am exceedingly*
> *disappointed that you will be coming at such an awkward time… It will be my*
> *last three days in London and in the office. 'Good byes', work, appointments,*
> *perhaps a visit to Churt. So it will be a whirl…*[33]

185

It turned out that his parents were unable to come to London and Gareth wrote saying he would like to have taken them to dinner and the theatre. [34]

Gareth was full of excitement at the prospect of setting off on his travels once more and on January 23 1933 he wrote, "Hurray! I have got my Soviet visa granted so I shall go there in March — not quite a joy ride, but still most interesting."

On January 25, 1933, Gareth sent details of his travel itinerary to his parents:

I see Lloyd George tomorrow here in London. On Friday morning at 8.30 I leave Waterloo, and travel tourist [class] at 10.30am on the Bremen to Bremerhaven where I arrive on Saturday.

His trip would include Leipzig to see Mr Rudolf Herzog, then his old friend Paul Haferkorn in Waldheim, followed by Dresden, Danzig, then Berlin. "I have to return home for two lectures in February. Then in March 1, I leave for Moscow — Kaluga — Kiev — stay a little longer in the Ukraine, then back home by the end of March."

On Friday morning January 27, 1933, in the Reform Club, Gareth recounted his commitments:

Just called in [at the Reform Club] on my way to Waterloo — before long I shall be on the Bremen.

In the train.

The train is now going along to Southampton exactly the same time and same day, Friday, when I sailed to New York on the Deutschland on Oct 2, 1931…Had a most interesting time yesterday. Lunched with Sir Walter Layton, a splendid and charming man — Crowther, Walter Layton and myself.

Hurray! I have arranged to write a series of articles for The Economist on Russia which is the best periodical in my view in the world.

Also, another honour, I am to address the RIIA on March 30 on Russia. Also writing articles on Germany for the Financial News[35], and three on Russia for The Times.

… I said goodbye to Lloyd George, who was most kind, said he hoped that I would be able to come and see him a lot in the future and wished me good luck etc.[36]

Gareth had met Maisky again who told him to wear warm clothes in Russia and he told his mother that he had "bought all the things you told me to (except spats) i.e. …aspirin, socks etc." and later in the same letter "Yes I got the suit and everything, & handkerchief. Yes I have soap. Thank you for reminding me I would have forgotten."[37]

In a hasty letter written before he left for Southampton en route to Berlin, Gareth noted, "Sir Bernard Pares has received confirmation [of the famine] from many sources". A brief note in Gareth's diary also stated, "The news in the city coincides with Muggeridge's point of view and mine." These notes must have referred to an on-going famine in the Soviet Union as Gareth had discussed his planned trip to the USSR with many of his colleagues before his visit.

On the same date, to Lloyd George from the *SS Bremen*:

> *May I first thank you for the wonderful experience I have had on your staff. I very much regret leaving the office now, and leaving the staff at the end of March. The next month, I shall spend investigating the situation in Germany. …During March, I shall be in Russia visiting Moscow and the Ukraine. I shall send you reports on what I see. In the future, I shall be always be delighted to be of any help, and, since I shall be especially following the Welsh, the industrial, and the foreign situation for the Western Mail; I hope I may be of some service to you.*
>
> *Yesterday I saw the Soviet Ambassador, who has been remarkably kind in obtaining material for you in Moscow. He is looking forward to having you to lunch or dinner and will be glad to hear from you at any time.*
>
> *In preparing me for my visit to Moscow, he said two problems have confronted the Soviet Union, the first — that of construction, that has been solved by the first five year plan, which he claims has been carried out 94%. The second problem remains unsolved — namely the use of machinery. That will be solved by the second Five-Year Plan.*
>
> *Two important decisions have been taken this month: — (he said);*
>
> *The food tax for the peasants. Once the peasant has paid the food tax he is to be free to sell his surplus on the private market.*
>
> *There is to be attached to each Machine Tractor Station a special political section of the party, which will enlighten the peasants on policy work in the collective farm, and combat hostile and kulak elements in the villages.*
>
> *These measures, the Ambassador claims, together with the increased production of the light industries will lead to a brighter, happier life in Russia. "In a year or two, everything will be all right." (Exactly the same words as I was told two years and also a year ago.)*
>
> *The Second Five-Year Plan will aim at quality; at stabilising the situation;*

*not at increasing the sowing area. Its main stress will be laid on consumption
and agriculture. It will be intensive, not extensive.*

*I am not so optimistic as the Ambassador. March will be an interesting month
to judge, and I shall let you know my findings in Russia.*

Notes on Chapter 17

1
  Gareth Vaughan Jones Papers, National Library of Wales. Correspondence Series 1-21, File 18. September 4, 1932.

2
  Gareth Vaughan Jones Papers, National Library of Wales. Correspondence Series B6/4. September 29, 1934.

3
  Gareth Vaughan Jones Papers, National Library of Wales. Correspondence Series 1-21, File 18. December 4, 1932.

4
  Ibid. September 6, 1934.

5
  Gareth Vaughan Jones Papers, National Library of Wales. Correspondence Series B6/4 September 9, 1934.

6
  Y Cymro was a Welsh language newspaper published between 1932 and 2017 and succeeded other newspapers
of the same name that had existed during the 19th and early 20th centuries. Gareth Vaughan Jones Correspondence
Series B6/4 October 5, 1934.

7
  Ottawa Imperial Conference. 21 July-20 August 1932. Representatives from the British Commonwealth met in
Ottawa and negotiated seven bilateral agreements which provided limited imperial preference to Commonwealth
goods. These agreements led to the resignation of Free Trade Liberals from the British cabinet, who joined the opposition, including Lothian and Sinclair. The British government gave Dominion raw materials a preference of about 10
percent of the British market and the British government imposed preferential tariffs on foreign meat, butter, cheese,
fruit, and eggs. The British offered to remove restrictions on Canadian live cattle and reached new tariff arrangements
on Canadian cooper, timber, fish, asbestos, zinc, and lead. In return, the Canadians extended concessions on British
manufactured goods. The conference led to new trade relationships between Australia, Britain, Canada, the Irish Free
State, New Zealand, Rhodesia, and South Africa. The most important of all the conversions of the British debt was
effected by Mr Goschen in 1888 the year David Lloyd George entered Parliament. It applied to the whole of the 3%
1888 stocks, amounting to a total of £558,000,000.

8
  Gareth Vaughan Jones Papers, National Library of Wales. Correspondence Series B6/4. October 20, 1932.

9
  The first volume was published in the spring of 1933. *War Memoirs of David Lloyd George*, Vol 1. Bron-y-de, Churt:
Oldham Press Ltd 1933-34. Correspondence Series 1-21 File 18. October 25, 1932.

10
  Gareth Vaughan Jones Papers, National Library of Wales. Correspondence Series B6/4. December 12, 1932.

11
  Ibid. December 21, 1932.

12
  Ibid. September 9, 1932.

13
  Letter from Gareth to Ivy Lee. Ivy Lee September 15, 1932. Ivy Ledbetter Lee Papers', Seeley G. Mudd Manuscript
Library, Princeton. Box 2 Folder 27.

14
  Gareth Vaughan Jones Papers, National Library of Wales. Correspondence Series B6/4. October 2, 1932.

15
Ibid. October 5, 1932.

16
The Lee memorandum is not in the Ivy Lee archive.

17
Letter from Gareth to Ivy Lee. Ivy Lee October 8, 1932. Ivy Ledbetter Lee Papers', Seeley G. Mudd Manuscript Library, Princeton. Box 2 Folder 27.

18
'Will there be Soup' articles in the *Western Mail* (October 7, 1932) based on Gareth's diaries notes of the Soviet Union with Heinz in 1931 and his frequent reading of Izvestia.

19
Gareth Vaughan Jones Papers, National Library of Wales. Correspondence Series B6/4. October 23, 1932.

20
Ibid.

21
Gareth Vaughan Jones Papers, National Library of Wales. Correspondence Series B6/7. October 25, 1932.

22
Ibid.

23
Low's *Russian Sketch Book* with Text by Kingsley Martin, Victor Gollancz Ltd. Publication. Date Friday 25, November 1932. Letter 8/11/32 B6/4)

24
Gareth Vaughan Jones Papers, National Library of Wales. Correspondence Series 1-21, File 18. Letter started December 4, 1932.

25
Gareth Vaughan Jones Papers, National Library of Wales. Correspondence Series B6/4. October 23, 1932.

26
Ibid. November 28, 1932.

27
Ibid, December 18, 1932.

28
Gareth's December 1932 report on Germany and Chancellor Schleicher may be seen at: http://www.garethjones.org/german_articles/impressions1932.htm

29
Gareth went to Strasbourg University with Jane Evans and was said within the family to be 'unofficially' engaged to her.

30
Gareth Vaughan Jones Papers, National Library of Wales. Correspondence Series B6/5. January 6, 1932.

31
Ibid. January 17, 1932.

32
Ibid. January 23, 1932.

33
Ibid. January 19, 1932.

34
Ibid. January 25, 1932.

35
The *Financial News* was a daily newspaper founded in 1884 by Harry Marks and published in London. It was set up to fight against fraudulent investments. It went into a slow decline after Marks' death in 1916. Bought by publisher Eyre & Spottiswoode in 1928 it was eventually merged with its great rival the Financial Times.

36
Ibid. January 27, 1933.

37
Ibid.

PART 5

A Welshman Looks at Europe
(1933)

Chapter 18

Wales Bonds with the Continent

Gareth set sail for Europe on Friday January 27, 1933 Jones and was to write a series of articles for the *Western Mail* called 'A Welshman Looks at Europe' which were published between February 7 and March 2, 1933. He began writing even before he embarked ship:

> *Near the Isle of Wight the fastest liner in the world, the steamship SS Bremen, having arrived from New York, is waiting, and before long I shall be on board sailing to the Europe of 1933. A journey of 6,000 miles lies before me through a continent, which is torn by national passions and class hatreds.*
>
> *This turbulent Europe of 1933 is more closely linked with Wales than one would imagine. … To find out what is happening in Europe is the object of this journey which will take me across the North Sea to Bremen, down to Saxony, into the new State of Czecho-Slovakia to Prussian Berlin, to the danger zone of the Polish Corridor and Danzig, through the vast area of the new Poland, across the Soviet frontier into Moscow, into Red villages and towns and then back home to Wales…*
>
> *Stewards seize our luggage and march down endless corridors. "You've just come from New York. What's it like there?" I ask my steward.*
>
> *"Terrible," he replies. "There are more beggars on the street than in Germany. The poor fellows have no unemployment insurance. And there's over million out of work in New York.*
>
> *…Poetry of the leading nations of the world is carved into the wooden panels, and the first quotation I see is from Dafydd ap Gwilym, poem [Y Gwynt- The Wind] and begins:*
>
> *Yr wybrynt helynt hylaw*
> *A gwrdd drwst a gerdda draw…*
> *[The wind from heaven – an imminent calamity,*
> *A mighty uproar – is in motion over there…]*

Underneath there is carved another Welsh poem:

Gwawr! Gwawr!
Geinwawr ei grudd
Mae'r haul yn dod ar donnau'r wawr
Fel llong o'r tragwyddoldeb mawr.
[With gorgeous cheeks
The sun arrives on the wave of the dawn
Like a ship from far eternity.]

"The songs of Welsh bards now decorate the swiftest vessel ever built" writes Gareth.

But the vessel is almost empty. A few lonely people stroll about, and the very silence on board is symbolic of the crash in world shipping. A talk on the bridge with the captain and other officers gives a clear picture of the distress of seafaring folk.

The boat is only 25 per cent occupied. Out of a possible complement of 2,500 passengers there were only 600 on board from New York. Some of the officers curse the tariffs of the world, and one of them says: "…Every nation is trying to save itself and basing its policy on a nationalism of a hundred years ago. Only a new outlook can rescue us."

Will the Europe of 1933 have this new outlook?

A crowd has gathered in one of Bremen's chief streets and is staring at a group of pictures in a shop window. Two or three youngsters look with flashing eyes at the scenes depicted.

The first photograph is of Mussolini — stern, with firm jaw. The German boys look at one another, nod, and say, "That's the kind of man we want here."

The second photograph shows thousands upon thousands of Nazis meeting in Danzig in their khaki uniform, carrying red banners with the swastika upon a white circle in the middle. 'Danzig shall remain German' run the words underneath. 'Thirteen years ago Danzig was torn from the Fatherland by the brutal Treaty of Versailles.' The youngsters, I can see, are burning with indignation when they look upon that scene.

The third photograph depicts French soldiers dragging a German policeman through the streets of a German town. French cavalrymen are riding alongside, some of them smiling scornfully. Underneath the photograph are the words: 'The attack on the Rühr ten years ago. A despicable blot on France's honour. Germany, awake!'

Postcard depicting Frederick the Great, Otto von Bismarck, President Hindenburg and Adolf Hitler. Caption, "What the King conquered, the Prince shaped, the Field Marshall defended, the soldier saved and united."

The German youngsters look at each other, and one says, 'to think that we Germans have stood that disgrace for thirteen years! But we will stand it no longer. Hitler will bring us honour again.' This sentence gave me a clue to the feeling in Germany today. Frederick the Great, the Prussian King who struggled against almost all the powers of Europe in the eighteenth century and built the military system of Prussia, is now the hero of Germany.

The Germans feel that when they are surrounded by the French, the Poles, and the Czechs, and have their army reduced to 100,000 men, their honour and self-respect have disappeared. They bear no personal rancour against Britain, but their feeling against France, Poland, and also America, is often violent.

That is what national-minded German men are thinking. ...I was soon to learn one widely-spread point of view, for the train had come into Hanover and I had to change for the Leipzig train.

Gareth arrived in Leipzig on an historic day, January 30, 1933, when Hitler was elected Chancellor of Germany. He penned an article entitled, "Hitler is there, but will he stay?":

My Saxon host came rushing into my room, slammed the door and shouted: 'Hitler is Chancellor!' Even the Alsatian wolfhound in the corner barked with excitement.

*Chancellor Hitler and President von Hindenburg on their way
to a youth rally in the Berlin Lustgarten.*

*The Saxon continued, "Hindenburg has appointed Hitler Prime Minister.
It's a coalition between the National-Socialists and the German Nationalist
party. Papen is Vice-Chancellor. At last Germany has a National Government
such as you have in Britain."*

*Nevertheless, the advent of Hitler may well open a new chapter in German
post-war history. It makes the class-struggle in Germany more violent than it
has been before. The Nazis have now co-operated with the most capitalistic
sections of Germany. In the Cabinet, led by Hitler, there are Nationalist
industrialists and great landowners. The German workers will be more bitter
in their opposition to the Government than they were to Schleicher. Therefore,
many people fear that Hitler, in spite of his desire to unite all classes and all
creeds, will only succeed in making Germany more divided into master and
worker than ever.*

*…Hitler promises to overcome Bolshevism in Germany and to crush the
followers of Marx. But it is misery and hunger, and not agitation, that have
made 6,000,000 Germans vote for the Communist Party. If Hitler fails to
banish misery and hunger many more millions will vote for the Communist
Party, and the already nerve-stricken Germany will again be on the verge
of civil war.*

In German politics, however, nothing can be prophesied. There are to be elections on March 5th, and what will happen then no one knows. Perhaps there will be a National Dictatorship. Perhaps... but no one can tell.

The personality of Hitler arouses no confidence in the calm observer. It is hard to reconcile his shrieking hatred of the Jews with any balanced judgment. It is hard to think that a telegram he sent congratulating certain Nazis who had brutally murdered a Communist before the eyes of the murdered man's family reveals any spirit of justice. Nor have Hitler's scornful hints about the old age of Hindenburg and his reminder to the President that he could wait, while a man of over 80 years could not have earned the Nazi leader the respect of certain observers. Hitler's neurotic behaviour in a December meeting of Nazis, when he burst into tears and wept without control, was not that of a Bismarck.

Hitler is Chancellor. The former Austrian lance-corporal, with his thirteen million followers, has reached his goal at the very moment when his fortunes seemed to be turning and when defeat was staring him in the face. He has begun quietly and legally. The strong whisky of the Nazi speeches has so far, in practice, been milk-and-water. He has not destroyed the Republic. He promises merely a Four-Year Plan to give employment. His is a tremendous task.

If he fails to bring Work and Bread in Germany, far more blood will flow in the streets of Berlin than has ever flowed before.[1]

From Leipzig, Gareth travelled to a valley in Bohemia, an area that formed the northern part of the new State of Czechoslovakia. As quiet as it seemed, however, in reality, the valley was a virtual battlefield. Two civilisations were struggling against one another — the German and the Slav — a centuries-old problem of minorities. Just as in Wales where two cultures and two languages, Welsh and English, were striving for mastery, the two cultures of Germany and Czechoslovakia, came into conflict. That fight was a hundred times more bitter, and the consequences for the peace of the world a hundred times graver that that between the Welsh and English cultures, though basically the problem was the same.[2]

Gareth outlined the reasons for this clash in his article published on February 13:[3]

The State of Czechoslovakia, set up by the Treaty of Versailles, out of fourteen million inhabitants only about seven million belong to the dominant race, the Czechs. Three-and-a-half million are Germans, while the others are Slovaks, Ruthenians, and Hungarians. The seven million Czechs, one half of the population, now the masters, are seeking to spread their power as rapidly as possible. One weapon is the law. In police courts, it is sometimes difficult for Germans to obtain justice.

...By other methods, such as education and favouritism for non-Germans, by ejecting landowners and settling the land of the Germans by Czech or, in Poland, by Polish labourers, the dominant Slavonic races are attempting to crush their Teutonic subjects. The tables are turned. Formerly, the Germans were ruthless in destroying the Slavonic cultures. Now, the hour of revenge for the Slavs has come.

The fine veteran statesman, Masaryk, the President of the Czechoslovak Republic, had tried his best to reconcile the races, and was respected by all. Many Czech officials did their best to help the Germans but still the petty oppression went on.[4] [Czechoslovakia was eventually invaded by Germany in 1938.]

Gareth considered that oppression in the new States would be a serious danger for Europe. He wrote to his parents on February 9, "Yesterday I came through Berlin. I went to see *The Times* correspondent who, like myself, has little faith in Hitler... *The Times* correspondent is most pessimistic."[5]

It aroused passionate emotions in Germany with the desire for the nation's lost territories to be won back, and this was causing misery, injustice, and terror in Europe.

Sunday February 19 1933 Berlin. I went to see the Nazis on Friday at the Kaiserhof. I had 2 ¼ hours with Hitler's secretary — one of the funniest interviews I have ever had — he played marches on the piano and I sang nearly all the time.

Continuing his investigations in Bohemia, Gareth wrote of the "Spectre of the Machine," and that of Tariffs in Europe and worldwide. Millions of men in Europe were unemployed.

On February 22, 1933, Gareth wrote an article on another danger zone in Europe entitled, 'Storm over the Polish Corridor'. He had travelled from Dresden via Berlin and across part of Poland to the Free State of Danzig, which had been annexed from Germany by the Treaty of Versailles. The article described a most hazardous flight from Danzig, where he had visited Haferkorn, to Tempelhofer Aerodrome in Berlin passing over a most disputed area of Europe:

At last we are off. After rushing across the aerodrome field, and then bumping slightly, the aeroplane has left the ground, and beneath us we see the fields, roads houses, shores, and woods of one of the most fateful regions in all Europe.

A strong wind is blowing. The Moscow-Berlin plane is now rocking over the Baltic coast. The Baltic is looking bright blue, although from the west black storm-clouds come. If I look around I can see the city of Danzig, which is about as large as Cardiff.

A small steamer is entering Danzig harbour, about which diplomats have been fighting since 1919. That streak [river] is the Vistula. Now exactly underneath is the Monte Carlo of the North, Zoppot. The casino and the pier can be clearly seen. Near the sea, one has a glimpse of the two pre-war villas of the Crown Prince, and one recalls that he was most popular with the Danzigers.

It is getting difficult to write, for the wind seems to be growing stronger. Underneath is the railway which links Danzig with the Fatherland. We are now flying over woods. The plane has several times dropped suddenly and then rocked.

We are leaving the Baltic, but one moment. There is a port — one only gets a slight view of it — does not look a natural harbour at all. It is Gdynia, and was recently built by Poland.

Now we are flying over the Polish Corridor. There are more woods underneath and a lake here and there. We must have crossed the frontier between the Danzig Free State and Poland. How that German pilot must boil with rage when he thinks that his East Prussia is separated from the rest of Prussia by that narrow stretch of territory belonging to Poland and extending to the sea!

The land is very flat underneath. We are flying about 1,000 to 1,500 feet high, and can see the peasants' huts, some with straw roofs, some with tiled roofs. Over there is a brick factory-the only factory to be seen. The rest of the land is farming land, with a village here and there, lakes, and many small pine forests. Some of those villages are inhabited by a tribe called Kashubes. So, that is the Polish Corridor.

The aeroplane is rattling and shaking. There are more storm-clouds in front. I am beginning to regret the excellent meal I took of pork cutlets and pancakes. The aeroplane has just recovered from a drop in the worst air-pocket I have ever experienced.

By a lake which is frozen over there is some timber. It is difficult to realise that that stretch of land which has only a few villages and woods and fields, is one of the danger spots of Europe, and that millions of Germans would willingly die to win it back.

The aeroplane is tossing still more violently. This article will have to be finished elsewhere…

A few hours ago I had never heard of Stolp [Pomerania]. But now we are forced to spend the night here. I saw the passengers get alarmed as the wings of the aeroplane seemed to go up still higher and down. At last we saw a town to the north. The pilot flew for it, and before long we made our forced landing smoothly.

A man came rushing up, opened the door, and said: 'There's another colossal storm coming.' The pilot came out. 'Impossible to fly further. It's dangerous', he said. 'We've taken an hour and a quarter to do 55 miles. The force of the wind against us was terrific.'

Thus we find ourselves in this typical Prussian town, which has as its hero Blücher, is proud of its soldiers, and considers itself a bulwark of Germanism near the Polish Corridor.

To-morrow we fly on to Berlin-when the storm has died down.

One day a far more violent storm may break over the Polish Corridor. The names Danzig, Gdynia, East Prussia will be on the lips of all. When that storm of national passions will break no one knows, but the dark clouds are rapidly gathering. [6]

On February 23, 1933, some hours after landing at the Tempelhofer Aerodrome, Gareth was again on the tarmac and contemplating a most momentous event in his journalistic career. He and another newspaper correspondent (Sefton Delmer)[7] were the first foreign journalists, and the only two non-Nazis, who were to fly with the newly appointed Chancellor, Adolf Hitler. Gareth was to write a most noteworthy article. 'With Hitler Across Germany' which appeared in the *Western Mail*.

In Hitler's Aeroplane,
Three o'clock Thursday Afternoon,
February 23, 1933.

If this aeroplane should crash, the whole history of Europe would be changed. For a few feet away, sits Adolf Hitler, Chancellor of Germany and leader of the most volcanic nationalist awakening which the world has seen.

Six thousand feet beneath us, hidden by a sea of rolling white clouds, is the land which he has roused to a frenzy. We are rushing along at a speed of 142 miles per hour from Berlin to Frankfurt-on-Main, where Hitler is to begin his lightning election campaign.

The occupants of the aeroplane are, indeed, a mass of human dynamite. I can see Hitler studying the map and then reading a number of blue reports. He does not look impressive. When his car arrived on the airfield about half an hour ago, and he stepped out, a slight figure in a shapeless black hat, wearing a light mackintosh, and when he raised his arm flabbily to greet those who had assembled to see him, I was mystified.

How had this ordinary-looking man succeeded in becoming deified by fourteen million people? He was more natural and less of a poseur than I had expected; there was something boyish about him as he saw a new motor-car and immediately displayed a great interest in it. He shook hands with the Nazi chiefs and with those others of us who were to fly with him in the famous 'Richthofen', the fastest and most powerful three-motored aeroplane in Germany.

His handshake was firm, but his large, outstanding eyes seemed emotionless as he greeted me. Standing around in the snow were members of his bodyguard in their black uniform with silver brocade. On their hats there is a silver skull and crossbones, the cavities of the eyes in the skull being bright red.

I was introduced to these, the elite of the Nazi troops and then to a plump, laughing man, Captain Bauer, Hitler's pilot, the war-time hero. We then entered the plane and we sit above the clouds.

Behind Hitler sits a little man who laughs all the time. He has a narrow Iberian head and brown eyes which twinkle with wit and intelligence. He looks like the dark, small, narrow-headed, sharp Welsh type which is so often found in the Glamorgan valleys. This is Dr Goebbels, a Rhinelander, the brain of the National-Socialist Party and, after Hitler, its most emotional speaker. His is a name to remember, for he will play a big part in the future. ...I look at the vivacious little man and see that he is reading Wilson's Fourteen Points. His smile has disappeared, and his chin is determined, he looks as if he were burning to avenge what the Nazis call the betrayal of 1918. I recall the Nazi slogan: 'Retribution.'

We are now descending, however. Frankfurt is beneath us. A crowd is gathered below. Thousands of faces look up at us. We make a smooth landing. Nazi leaders, some in brown, some in black and silver, all with a red swastika arm-band, await their chief. Hitler steps out of the aeroplane. But he is now a man spiritually transformed. His eyes have a certain fixed purpose. Here is a different Hitler.

There are two Hitlers — the natural boyish Hitler, and the Hitler who is inspired by tremendous national force, a great Hitler. It is the second Hitler who has stirred Germany to an awakening.[8]

The only known newsreel showing Gareth records this event when Hitler greets the newsmen on the airstrip.

On arrival in Frankfurt-on-Main, Hitler's party retired for a short rest in a hotel. There, "the cream of his followers were gathered preparing for the vast meeting which was to stir the population of Frankfurt." Gareth spent several hours with the "Herr Doktor," as Goebbels was called. It was apparent to Gareth that before long, the dictator of public opinion, Goebbels, the head of a new Ministry, would have control of the press, of the wireless, of art, and he was determined to educate the whole of Germany along National Socialist lines. Accordingly, Goebbels was responsible for German newspapers being banned for criticising the new regimes.[9]

Gareth was not to meet Goering, but described him as perhaps the most determined of Hitler's followers:

> He has already dismissed hundreds of non-Nazi police, presidents, officials, and Civil Servants in Prussia and replaced them with keen Nazis... Goering's actions have amounted to a coup d'état without violence. He had already dismissed hundreds of non-Nazi police, presidents, officials, and Civil Servant in Prussia and replaced them with keen Nazis. Germany is going full speed towards a Fascist Dictatorship.[10]

Gareth described the scene in the auditorium in his article, the "Primitive Worship of Hitler" in the *Western Mail* and he compared the emotion at a Nazi Rally with that of the National Eisteddfod (seated gathering)]:

> For eight hours the biggest hall in Germany has been packed with 25,000 people for whom Hitler is the saviour of his nation. They have waited, tense with national fervour. Five cars rush towards the hall. In the first sits Hitler; in the next two open cars are the stalwart, bemedaled bodyguards; then comes our car with Hitler's secretary [Dr Meissner]. The hall is surrounded by Brown Shirts. Wherever we go resounds the shout, "Heil, Hitler!" and hundreds of outstretched hands greet us as we entered the auditorium. We dash up the steps after Hitler and enter the ante-chamber.
>
> From within we hear roar upon roar of applause and the thumping, and the blare of a military band and the thud of marching feet. The door leading to the platform opens, and two of us [Gareth and Meissner] step on to the platform. I have never seen such a mass of people; such a display of flags, up to the top of the high roof; such deafening roars. It is primitive, mass worship.
>
> Through the broad gangway, Nazi troops are marching with banners, and as each new banner comes there is another round of shouting. Steel Helmets now

march in with the old Imperial and regimental flags, symbolic of the rebirth of militarism.

Then, Hitler comes. Pandemonium! Twenty-five thousand people jump to their feet. Twenty-five thousand hands are outstretched. The 'Heil, Hitler', shout is overwhelming. The people are drunk with nationalism. It is hysteria. Hitler steps forward. Two adjutants take off his brown coat. There is a hush.

Adolf Hitler, photographed by Gareth, speaking at the 1933 Frankfurt Rally.

Hitler begins in a calm, deep voice, which gets louder and louder, higher and higher. He loses his calmness and trembles in his excitement. In the beginning of his speech, his arms are folded and he seems hunched up, but when he is carried away he stretches out his arms and he seems to grow in stature. He attacks the rulers of Germany in the past fourteen years. The applause is tremendous. He accuses them of corruption

Another round of enthusiasm. He whips the Socialists for having vilified German culture. He appeals for the union of Nationalism with Socialism. He calls for the end of class warfare. When he shouts, 'The future belongs to the young Germany which has arisen', the 25,000 hearers leap to their feet, stretch out their right hands and roar: 'Heil, Hitler!'

It is the emotion of the National Eisteddfod exaggerated multi-fold. Imagine the Welsh national feeling responding to Mr Lloyd George, and add to bitterness of defeat, the depth of humiliation which Germany has gone through; the painful poverty of the middle class, the sufferings through inflation, the rankling injustice of the War Guilt Clause and savage political hatred, and a picture of the Hitler crowd is there.

Imagine a speech of Mr Lloyd George. Take away the wit, take away the intellectual play, the gift of colour, the literary and Biblical allusions of the Welsh statesman. Add a louder voice, less varied in tone, a more unbroken stretch of emotional appeal, more demagogy, and you have Hitler. Hitler has less light and shade than Mr Lloyd George. He has less variety of gesture. Hitler's main motion is to point out his right hand, which trembles. He is without the smile and the sharp glance of Mr Lloyd George without his hush and sudden drop of the voice.

Mr Lloyd George is more of an artist and knows that life is not all emotion or all tragedy. He lightens a grave speech with humour, as Shakespeare brings in the comedy of life in the Porters' Scene in Macbeth. Hitler is pure tragedy or heightened melodrama, and reminds one of Schiller's "Robbers". His only comic relief is bitter irony. Mr Lloyd George has a wider scale and as in a Beethoven symphony, makes lighter mood follow or precede a tragic part. Hitler is the Wagner of oratory, a master in repeating the leitmotiv in many varied forms, and the leitmotiv is, 'The Republican régime in Germany has betrayed you. Our day of retribution has come.' His use of the brass instruments of oratory is Wagnerian, and he thunders out his resounding blows against Bolshevism and against democracy.

Whereas Mr Lloyd George is more complex and more subtle and a speech of his is kaleidoscopic, changing in tone and colour from one moment to another, Hitler is more uniform, and his oratory is in colour one blazing red which makes the people mad.

But, both orators know their audiences, and Hitler's speech is the speech for nationalist German. He has now ended with the words:

I shall complete the work which I began fourteen years ago as an unknown soldier, for which I have struggled as leader of the party and for which I stand to-day as Chancellor of Germany. We shall do our duty.'

Again the hall resounds. He marches out and we follow into the ante-chamber. He is wet with perspiration. From the hall we hear 25,000 voices singing, "Deutschland Uber Alles."

We rush to the car. As we step out of the hall we see thousands of blazing torches, and we drive through an avenue of Brown Storm Troops, each man of which holds his torch in the left hand, and stretches out his right hand in adoration to the leader, Adolf Hitler.

Such was the manifestation of Fascism in Germany. With the shouts of 'Heil;'

Hitler', resounding in my ears I prepare to leave Germany, the land where dictatorship has just begun, and to go to the land of the dictatorship of the working class. From the country of Fascism, I now go to the home of Bolshevism. In a few days' time I shall be on my way to Berlin across the Polish Corridor, East Prussia, Lithuania, Latvia, until I enter the territory of Soviet Russia.

The Europe of 1933 has seen the birth the Hitler dictatorship in Germany. What will it see in the Soviet Union? [11]

The Frankfurt Rally from Gareth's papers.

After the Frankfurt rally, Hitler's State Secretary, Dr Meissner entertained Gareth for two and a half hours, by singing and playing the piano, before Gareth caught the night-train for London to fulfil two prior lecture engagements.

Back in London, Gareth's letter home was a mixture of exuberance and the mundane:

My trip in Germany was wonderful. What a coup it was to be invited to fly with Hitler! I thoroughly enjoyed that. Please don't worry. I am innoculated against typhus (in Berlin). I have a very warm fur. (I don't want a rug. The trains are too hot.)...

The Hitler meeting was the most thrilling thing I have seen in my life, absolutely primitive.

There won't be any trouble at all in Russia. Now I have to write some articles for the Financial News.

Cariad cynsaf,

Gareth

Don't send the Hitler articles to Russia."

Notes on Chapter 18

[1] The *Western Mail,* "Hitler is there, but Will He Stay", 9 February 1933, p. 11.

[2] Ibid., "German and the Slav- Century old Problem of the Minorities", February 13, 1933, p. 6.

[3] Ibid.

[4] Ibid.

[5] Gareth Vaughan Jones Papers, National Library of Wales. Correspondence Series 1-21, File 14 February 9, 1932.

[6] , The *Western Mail,* "Storm over the Polish Corridor", 22 February 1933, p. 6.

[7] Sefton Delmer – *Daily Express* Berlin correspondent – Present with Hitler and Goebbels in reviewing the damage of the Reichstag fire, two days after flying with Hitler and Gareth. In WWII, he was the Special Operations Executive 'dirty tricks' radio controller broadcasting British 'black propaganda' to German troops about the infidelities of their womenfolk back home with foreign workers (and to the moral disgust of Churchill). Suspected of being Soviet spy after the war.

[8] The *Western Mail,* 'With Hitler Across Germany', 28 February 1933. p. 6.

[9] Ibid., 'Beginning of German Fascism', March 1, 1933, p. 8.

[10] Ibid.

[11] Ibid., "Primitive Worship of Hitler". 1 March 1933, p. 8.

Chapter 19

Witnessing Famine

Russia if taken in general is better stored with tame Cattel and Wild beasts than any of the Counterey in Europe… The Rivers and standing Lakes are stored with fish of all kinds which are throughout the whole land incredibly cheap; in sum Moscovia has whatsoever is necessary for food and Rayment as good and as easy rates, as any other Land in the World, none excluded Moscow.[1]

Before setting off on his carefully planned visit to the Soviet Union to investigate conditions in a country torn by strife, Gareth sent a hasty letter home from the Liverpool Street Station Hotel:

I am waiting here for Paul Scheffer[now the London correspondent of the Berliner Tageblatt] to dine together. Then I leave at 8.30. What luck that the articles [in The Financial News] coincided with events in Germany… The German Embassy was very impressed with my article. It was read to the German Ambassador and considered, "very balanced and reasonable and unbiased".[2]

On March 3, 1933 he stayed in Berlin with a colleague, Eric Schuler. Schuler was to collaborate on a book that Gareth intended to write on 'Russia and the League of Nations.' Gareth had first met him and his wife in New York in 1931, during the height of the Depression and had had Russian lessons from him. Schuler had lived for some time in Moscow and it is quite possible that it was he who introduced Gareth to Scheffer in the United States.

Gareth arrived at the Hotel Metropole in Moscow on March 5, 1933. Though he was still technically in the employ of Lloyd George until the end of March, he paid for his own expenses.

This hotel is far more up to date than the North Western Hotel Liverpool
which had
   No telephone!
   No running water!
   No bathroom!
   No central heating!
   Although it was about the best hotel in Liverpool.[3]

The following day, he visited the British Embassy and at nine o'clock that evening, Gareth met Malcolm Muggeridge in Moscow.[4] Gareth may have been introduced to Muggeridge by Kingsley Martin, who had been a close colleague when he worked at The Manchester Guardian. Gareth made brief notes of their conversation in his diary. Muggeridge forecast the collapse of Bolshevism and believed that the end of the Communist party was absolutely inevitable.

[He had] returned from the villages — terrible — dying. No seed for sowing. Practically no winter sowing. Stalin hated by party but party cannot do anything. 95% of Party opposed to Stalin's policy but there is no discussion [among the party members]. Any opposition & man is removed. The outlook for next year was disastrous.[5]

Having heard of the dire conditions in the north Caucasus from Eugene Lyons in early February, William Stoneman of the Chicago Daily News and Ralph Barnes of the New York Herald Tribune decided to go south, and visit Kuban, Rostov-on-Don and its environs, but they were soon arrested by the Soviet secret police and sent back to Moscow.[6]

On February 23, 1933, a travel ban that prevented journalists from travelling within the USSR was confirmed. According to the Manchester Guardian archives, Muggeridge left for his own visit to Kuban on February 5 and had returned to Moscow before the ban was effected, though in later years he was to claim otherwise. Nevertheless, after meeting Muggeridge, Gareth, undeterred by the newly imposed travel restrictions, set off for Kharkov in Ukraine. He initially took a 'local' train to Kaluga, 90km south of Moscow, for which he wouldn't have needed a permit, and from where he was able to travel onwards without arousing undue suspicion. It is then apparent that he alighted from his train and followed the railway track on foot, because according to his diary: "I crossed the border from Greater Russia into the Ukraine."[7]

During his trip, Gareth made comprehensive notes in his small pocket diary of the conditions he had observed in both the Black Earth District and also in Kharkov.

The first news from Gareth following his return from Ukraine was on March 17, 1933, when from the Hotel Metropole in Moscow, he wrote a hasty, but guarded, letter to his parents. In order to pass the censor, he made no reference to what he had seen, though he mentioned where he had been:

> I have arrived from Kharkoff after a most interesting journey. I was delighted to get your letter... In Kharkoff the people in the German Consulate were most kind to me. Tonight I am dining with the German Ambassador [von Dierksen]. This afternoon I had a talk with our Ambassador, Sir Esmond Ovey. On Thursday 23rd I leave for Danzig where I shall spend the weekend with Reinhard... On Monday night 27th I shall arrive in Berlin. I leave Berlin on Wed. 29 and arrive 30th in London where I shall speak at the Royal Institute. Home 31st. I shall spend the night of the 30th at the Reform Club, London.[8]

Gareth wrote a further letter from the Hotel Metropole on March 19, 1933, when he reported:

> ...I am continuing to have an exceedingly interesting time. On my return from Kharkoff I went to see our Ambassador (Sir Esmond Ovey) and had a talk with him. ... This afternoon I am going to a Foreign Office reception, where M. Litvinov will be present. My conversations have been exceedingly instructive, and I have been received with the utmost kindness. The Foreign Office (Narkomindel) has spared no trouble to make my visit a success.[9]

Gareth had used his credentials as private secretary to Lloyd George to arrange a much-coveted interview with Maxim Litvinov. Litvinov was People's Commissar of Foreign Affairs, the top-ranking diplomatic position in the Soviet state, based at the People's Commissariat for Foreign Affairs, as it was known from 1930-1939. The Ministry was one of the most powerful in the regime, being responsible for handling diplomatic treaties,[10] and also controlled the issue of travel visas. They met on March 23, 1933, shortly before Gareth's departure from the Soviet Union, when he gave Gareth a comprehensive and wide-ranging interview which covered many current international problems. Litvinov expressed concern about the Japanese expansion into China, the rise of Hitler and the possibility of conflict with Poland as well as the more immediate concerns surrounding the arrest of the British Metrovick engineers (see Chapter 23). He also made a point of saying:

Respects & regards to Mr L[loyd] G[eorge]. Always enjoyed being with him. Always admired. Followed with great interest LGs activities when in London as [an] émigré. Remember writing article with gr[ea]t enthusiasm about the Insurance Scheme [of] 1909. Always studied his speeches, admired his boldness. What politicians lack now is boldness? Diplomacy has been vegetating. No bold step on the p[ar]t of any statesman. Read articles. Don't mind [his] criticism of Conservatives.[11]

Leaving Moscow on March 25, 1933, Gareth arrived at the Haferkorns' home in Danzig on the following day, relieved to be in 'civilisation' at last. Letters were awaiting him from his family and his reply to them was more revealing than those he had written from within the Soviet Union:

The Russian situation is absolutely terrible, famine almost everywhere, and millions are dying of starvation. I tramped for several days through villages in the Ukraine, and there was no bread, many children had swollen stomachs, nearly all the horses and cows had died and the people themselves were dying. The terror has increased tremendously and the GPU has almost full control. It was a disgrace to arrest the 6 engineers, two of whom I know. I saw Monkhouse [a British engineer and referred to in a later chapter] a few days ago at our Embassy, a splendid man.[12]

Gareth also sent a letter from Berlin, on March 27, 1933 to Sylvester in the office addressing him warmly as, "My Dear A J" and signed-off with the valediction, "With best greetings. Gareth." Enclosed with that letter was one for the 'Chief' [Lloyd George], for whom he, "had first class information."

The situation [in the Soviet Union] is so much worse than in 1921 that I am amazed at your admiration for Stalin I discussed the situation with almost every British, German and American expert. I had interviews with the following:
Litvinoff; Karl Radek; The Commissar for Finance, [GT] Grinko; The Vice-Commissar for Light Industry; The Vice-Commissar for Education; The President of the Atheists (who has given me a special message to you as a Baptist!); the British and the German Ambassadors ...I had a long conversation with Goebbels and other Nazis, with Breitscheid, von Schleicher and others.
Therefore I have much material on which you may want to question me. In the meantime I enclose my conversation with Litvinoff.[13]

When Gareth left Moscow for Danzig, most of the world was unaware of the extent of the on-going famine raging in the villages of the USSR. Immediately on his return to Berlin on March 29, 1933, Gareth contacted H. R. Knickerbocker, the German correspondent for New York Evening Post. In 1931, Knickerbocker had won the Pulitzer Prize for his articles describing and analysing the Soviet Five-Year Plan and knew of the conditions in the USSR. It is most likely that it was with his assistance that Gareth held a press interview in Berlin attended by the international press, where he exposed the terrible agricultural food crisis brought about by Stalin's policy of Collectivisation and Industrialisation.

Knickerbocker cabled Gareth's press interview to New York a summary of "Mr Jones' first-hand observations".

> *Mr Jones, who spoke Russian fluently was the first foreigner to visit the Russian countryside since the Moscow authorities forbade foreign correspondents to leave the city. Famine on a colossal scale, impending death of millions from hunger, murderous terror and the beginnings of serious unemployment in a land that had hitherto prided itself on the fact that every man had a job.*

It appeared as a front page exclusive on the same evening, in the New York Evening Post entitled, "Famine Grips Russia".

New York Evening Post, 'Famine Grips Russia", 29th March 1933.

211

BERLIN, March. 29. — Russia today is in the grip of a famine which is proving as disastrous as the catastrophe of 1921 when millions died, reported Gareth Jones of Great Britain, who arrived in Berlin this morning en route to London after a long walking tour through the Ukraine and other districts in the Soviet Union.

The arrest of the British engineers in Moscow is a symbol of panic in consequence of conditions worse than in 1921. Millions are dying of hunger. The trial, beginning Saturday, of the British engineers is merely a pendant to the recent shooting of thirty-five prominent workers in agriculture, including the Vice-Commissar of the Ministry of Agriculture, and is an attempt to check the popular wrath at the famine which haunts every district of the Soviet Union.

Everywhere was the cry, 'There is no bread. We are dying.' This cry came from every part of Russia, from the Volga, Siberia, White Russia, the North Caucasus, Central Asia. I tramped through the Black Earth region because that was once the richest farmland in Russia and because the correspondents have been forbidden to go there to see for themselves what is happening.

In the train a Communist denied to me that there was a famine. I flung a crust of bread which I had been eating from my own supply into a spittoon. A peasant fellow-passenger fished it out and ravenously ate it. I threw an orange peel into the spittoon and the peasant again grabbed it and devoured it. The Communist subsided. I stayed overnight in a village where there used to be 200 oxen and where there now are six. The peasants were eating the cattle fodder and had only a month's supply left. They told me that many had already died of hunger. Two soldiers came to arrest a thief. They warned me against travel by night, as there were too many 'starving' desperate men.

'We are waiting for death' was my welcome, but see; we still, have our cattle fodder. Go farther south. There they have nothing. Many houses are empty of people already dead', they cried.

A foreign expert returning from Kazakhstan told me that 1,000,000 out of 5,000,000 there have died of hunger.[14] I can believe it. After Stalin, the most hated man in Russia is Bernard Shaw among those who read his glowing descriptions of plentiful food in their starving land. The future is blacker than the present. There is insufficient seed. Many peasants are too weak physically to work on the land. The new taxation policy, promising to take only a fixed amount of grain from the peasants, will fail to encourage production because the peasants refuse to trust the Government."

In short, Mr Jones concluded, the Collectivization policy of the Government *and the resistance of the peasants to it has brought Russia to the worst catastrophe since the famine of 1921 and has swept away the population of whole districts.*

Coupled with this, the prime reason for the breakdown, he added, is the terror, lack of skill and collapse of transport and finance. Unemployment is rapidly increasing, he declared, because of the lack of raw materials. The lack of food and the wrecking of the currency and credit system have forced many of the factories to close or to dismiss great numbers of workers.[15]

Similar statements were syndicated in many British newspapers, both in London and in the provinces, including the then Soviet-sympathetic, but highly respected Manchester Guardian on the following day.

With Gareth's usual energy, by the next day he was in London and on that evening of March 30, 1933, he gave a speech to the Royal Institute of International Affairs entitled "Soviet Russia", repeating much of his press release, but he added:

The noose is getting tighter and tighter around the neck of the Russian peasants and exile, starvation and serfdom hover round him. May I say as a Liberal in this regard, how disgusted I am by liberal opinion in this country. The attitude of the Liberal press has been cowardly and hypocritical. The Manchester Guardian gets red in the face when there are disgraceful events in Eastern Galicia, but when a hundred million peasants are condemned to hunger and serfdom the Manchester Guardian is quiet. The Eastern Galicia oppression is a fleabite compared with the events in Russia. There is no excuse, for the Manchester Guardian has an excellent correspondent in Moscow [Malcolm Muggeridge]. I hold that that paper has betrayed the reliance upon which liberal people in the world have in it. The News Chronicle is not much better. It has an admirable source of information, but it has remained cowardly in its attitude of tolerating any kind of tyranny in Russia, while getting violent about any form of oppression in Germany or Italy.

Typical of the Liberal opinion is the letter to the Manchester Guardian of March 2nd [from Bernard Shaw]. I read a translation of it in Izvestia when I was in Moscow and it appeared farcical to me. Viewed from Moscow it was a mixture of hypocrisy, of gullibility and of such crass ignorance of the situation that the signatories should be ashamed of venturing to express an opinion on something about which they know so little.[16]

In 1933, neither Knickerbocker nor Scheffer were in a position to be able to write about the agricultural situation in the USSR from first-hand knowledge, but they were in a position to influence Gareth. Gareth's decision to give his press interview in Berlin may have been due the advice of these men. Scheffer had been the very last person to see Gareth on leaving London and Knickerbocker, the first person on his return to Berlin. Gareth on his arrival in London met Scheffer again, who immediately telephoned the story to his paper, which first broke in Germany on Saturday April 1.[17]

At this stage in his career, Gareth was endowed with supreme confidence in his own abilities. He had seen the distressing situation in Ukraine and had heard about it in the Soviet Union from many of the foreign residents in Moscow. He was prepared to put his head above the parapet and to speak out, perhaps encouraged by others who either did not have the bravery or the will, or the insecurity of their own personal circumstances prevented them from doing so.

Notes on Chapter 19

1   *The perillous and most unhappy voyages of John Struys* (1683) English translation from the Dutch (published 1676). A travelogue covering 25 years of adventures on three seafaring trips. His third journey took him to 'Muscovy' (mainly the area around the Caspian Sea). Gareth quotes this passage in his diary while on the train from Kharkiv back to Moscow (Gareth Jones 2015, 197; Diary 2 p. 33). He also quoted the passage in his talk to the RIIA on his return to England at the end of March 1933. Gareth Vaughan Jones Papers, National Library of Wales Series A/4.

2   March 1, 1933.

3   Gareth Vaughan Jones Papers, National Library of Wales. Correspondence Series 1-21, File 14. March 5, 1933.

4   Gareth Jones 2015, *Tell them we Are Starving*. p. 100 (Diary 1 p. 2) transcript of the diaries held at the National Library of Wales. Gareth Vaughan Jones Papers Diary Series B1/15.

5   Ibid. p. 106 (Diary 1 p. 21).

6   Modernization from the other Shore; American Observers and the Cost of Soviet Development', American Historical Review, April 2000 p. 66,67, 97, 98, nn. 34, 36.

7   Gareth Jones 2015, *Tell them we Are Starving*. p.131 (Diary 1 p.92) transcript of the diaries held at the National Library of Wales. Gareth Vaughan Jones Papers Diary Series B1/15.

8   Gareth Vaughan Jones Papers, National Library of Wales. Correspondence Series 1-21, File 14. March 17, 1933.

9   Ibid. March 19, 1933.

10   Litvinov was instrumental in winning formal diplomatic recognition of the Soviet government by the United States in November of 1933.

11   Gareth Jones 2015, *Tell them we Are Starving*.p.261 (Diary 3 p.30-31). Transcript of the diaries held at the National Library of Wales. Gareth Vaughan Jones Papers Diary Series B1/15.

12   Ibid. March 27, 1933.

13

Letter to Sylvester

14

Otto Schiller is most likely to be the foreign expert as Gareth mentions this in his diary. (Gareth Jones 2015, p.262 Diary 3 p.34). The same figure quoted of 5,000,000 Kazakhstanis is referred to in *The Foreign Office and The Famine*, p. li., n 2.

15

H. R. Knickerbocker, 'Famine Grips Russia', *New York Evening Post*, March 29, 1933, p.1.

16

Transcript of Gareth Jones' lecture to the RIIA. Gareth Vaughan Jones Papers, National Library of Wales Series A/4 March 1933.

17

Paul Scheffer, 'Hungersnot in Russland?' *Berliner Tageblatt*, April 1, 1933.

Chapter 20

Reporting a Famine

"You see that field. It was all gold, but now look at the weeds." The weeds were peeping up through the snow. "Before the War we could have boots, meat and butter ... We had horses and cows and pigs and chickens. Now we are ruined. We are doomed. We were the richest country in the world. We fed the world. Now they had taken all away from us."[1]

Until his new employment with the *Western Mail* began on 1 April, whether by accident or design, Gareth was still a 'freelancer' and would therefore not yet have been contracted to write exclusively for them.

Gareth wasted no time in getting a total of 21 articles published in three newspapers within the first three weeks of April 1933, beginning with an exclusive in the London *Evening Standard* on March 31, the day after his talk to the RIIA. Directly after the *Evening Standard* scoop, there followed a series of seven articles in Lord Beaverbrook's more 'sensationalist' sister paper, *The Daily Express*, which at that time was the world's largest selling daily newspaper.[2] These were more graphic in their description of his personal observations.

Before his foray into the Soviet countryside, Gareth had been warned, in no uncertain terms, by William Strang,[3] the First Secretary at the British Embassy in Moscow, against making an investigative visit into the villages of Ukraine and furthermore the embassy staff told him, "The peasants are starving, and will steal anything they can get hold of."[4]

April 5th 1933
Disregarding this warning I piled my rucksack with many loaves of white bread, with butter, cheese, meat and chocolate which I had bought with foreign currency at the Torgsin stores. I arrived at the local station in Moscow from which the trains leave for the south, picked my way through the dirty peasants

Genuine non-Soviet authorised slide of street beggars in Gareth's collection - year unknown, possibly 1931 by Jack Heinz or Gareth, but as yet without provenance.

lying sleeping on the floor and in a few minutes I found myself in the hard-class compartment of the slowest train which left Moscow for Kharkov.

To see Russia one must travel 'hard-class', and go by a slow train. Those tourists who travel "soft class" and by express trains, get only an impression, and do not see the real Russia. The compartment filled slowly. Peasants with sacks full of bread came in. An energetic man, who looked well nourished, and wore a leather cap and a leather jacket, came and sat opposite me. Then the train gave a jolt, and we set off on our day's journey towards the Ukraine. The types in that train throw light on the Russia of 1933. There is first the Communist Party member, who sits opposite me, and who maintains that in England every Communist is starving to death as a prisoner in the Tower of London. He thinks that Scotland Yard has as firm a grip over English life as the OGPU has in Russia.

…Not far away sits a peasant, who stares with glassy eyes at the floor. He has a small sack to which he clings. He mutters to me: "I went to the town for bread and bought bread, but they took my bread away from me." He repeats several times: "They took my bread away from me, and I shall not have bread for my family in the village where they are expecting bread. I have only a few potatoes."

217

That is one of the many little tragedies so frequent in Russia. In a village in the Ukraine they are waiting for the peasant to return from the town-but he will come breadless.

Another type in the train is the disillusioned young Communist. We stand alone in the corridor and look out at the vast expanse of snow covering the Russian countryside. "A lot of us young Communists," he says, "are getting dissatisfied, because we have no bread. I have had none for a week, although I work in a town — only potatoes. I only get sixty roubles a month, but by the time they have taken a lot away I only get about forty to fifty. How can I live?" "What do you mean when you say they take part of your wages away from you?" I ask him. He gets angry, "Don't you know that we are forced to give up part of our wages for loans? What do I want to subscribe to the Five Year Plan at four per cent? Loans for what? But they take it away at the source."

The young Communist looks worried, and goes on: "When I left my mother and two sisters a couple of days ago they only had two glasses of flour left. My brother died of hunger. No wonder we young Communists cannot help feeling sick at things."

As I stand in the corridor and look out at the wooden huts covered with snow amid at the silvery birches, a swarthy man, a Jew or Armenian, enters into conversation with me. He has a row of gold teeth. "Going to the Ukraine?" he asks. I nod assent. "So am I. I have been thrown out of Leningrad. And now they'll throw me out of Kharkov, I expect. It's a dog's life."

"Why were you thrown out?" I ask. "Well they would not give me a passport in Leningrad. They said I was one of the scum, and the sooner I got out the better. You see, I am a private trader. I sell thing in the streets and because of that they deprived me of all my rights"

A domineering man in a khaki coat then talks with me. At the first glance one can tell that he is a party member, for most Communists in Russia have a stamp of vigour and ruthlessness which marks them as the ruling class. He tells me that he is a member of the Politodel (the Political Department), and I prick up my ears, for the Political Department is that detachment of many thousands of Communists, who have been sent to the villages to make a violent drive to force the peasants to work. He looks ruthless and cruel. "We are semi-military," he- says: "We'll smash the kulak (the peasant who was formerly better off) and we'll smash all opposition." He clenches his fist. "We are practically all men, who served in the civil war. I was in the cavalry in the finest Red regiment."

"We who are now going into the villages are the chosen ones, the strongest, and we are all workers, mainly from the factories. We shall show the peasants what

218

strict control means." This man is typical of the spirit in which the villages are to be tackled. He will not hesitate at shooting. He is filled with the doctrine of class warfare in the villages, and he is determined to carry on what he considers to be a holy war against all those, who are against the Communist collective farms.

In every little station the train stops, and during one of these halts a man comes up to me, and whispers to me in German, "Tell them in England that we are starving, and that we are getting swollen."

A little later I decide to leave the train and make my way into the villages. I pull my rucksack over my back. The young Communist says to me: "Be careful. The Ukrainians are desperate." But I get out of the train, which rattles on to Kharkov, leaving me alone in the snow.[5]

My tramp through the villages was about to begin. My feet crunched through the snow as I made my way to a group of huts. A white expanse stretched for many miles. My first encounter was ominous, for the words I heard in the countryside were the same as those I had heard from peasant-beggars. A woman with bowed head walking along the railway track turned to me and said: "There is no bread. We have not had bread for over two months, and many are dying here."

I was to hear these same words in the same tone from hundreds peasants in that region, the Central Black Earth district, which was once one of the most fertile of all Russia. There was another sentence which was repeated to me time and time again: "Vse pukhli." "All are swollen."

"What then do you eat, if you have no bread?" I asked one raw lad. "Up to now we have had some potatoes, but our store has run out, and we only have cattle fodder left." He showed me what he had to eat. It was a kind of coarse beet which is given to cows. "How long will this last?" "Only a month. But many families have neither potatoes nor beet, and they are dying."

In every village the bread had run out about two months earlier. Finally, sunset came, and I talked to two men. One said, "You had better not go further, for hooligans will rob you of your coat, and your food and all." The other added: "Yes, it is dangerous. They might jump out at you when it is dark. Come and stay with us in our village." They took me to the village Soviet, a hut which was full of peasants. There were two children there, one of which had a large swollen stomach.

When the news spread that there was a foreigner in the village, the young men came to ask questions. Their knowledge of events in the world was remarkable and showed that they had been well drilled in the reading of newspapers. Their enthusiasm for learning, impressed me, and I thought they must have been through a good school.

My stay in that village threw much light on what the peasants thought. There was only one Communist among the whole population. The hut in which I stayed became a Mecca to which came all those who wished to see and wonder. They all laid their griefs before me openly. They had no fear in telling me that never had it been so bad, and that it was much worse than in 1921. The cattle decrease, they told me, was disastrous. "We used to have two hundred oxen, but now, alas there are only six," they said. "Our horses and our cows have perished and we only have about one-tenth left." The horses looked scraggy and diseased, as do all the horses in the countryside. Many peasants in the village had died of hunger.

Bewilderment reigned there as it did over the twelve to fourteen collective farms through which I tramped [in Ukraine]. The peasants nodded their heads at the continuous changing of policy. "We do not know where we are," one peasant said. "If only Lenin had lived we would be living splendidly. We could foresee what was going to happen. But now they have been chopping, and changing their policy, and we do not know what is going to happen next. Lenin would not have done something violently, and then suddenly have turned round, and said it was a mistake."

One evening two soldiers came into the hut, and I found that they had come to arrest a peasant thief, who was guilty of murder. The thief had gone to steal potatoes from the hut of the other. The owner hearing the noise had come out to seize the intruder, and the thief had stabbed him in the heart. The soldiers told me that theft had increased rapidly, and another Red Army soldier who came next morning warned me: "Do not travel by night. There are too many wild, uncultured men who want food and to steal." My tramp took me further through several villages until I came to the Ukraine. On the way I entered a school, where there was a notice, "The Soviet school is foremost among all the schools in the world."

The peasants had eaten horseflesh in the next collective farm which I visited. This is significant, for the Russian peasant never ate horseflesh. It was only the Tartars who ate horses, and for this they were despised by the Russians. Along the route that I took going south I noticed frequently patches where the dry skeletons of last year's weeds were peeping above the snow. One old peasant stopped me and pointed sadly to the fields. "In the old times," he bewailed, "that was one pure mass of gold. Now it is all weeds." The old Ukrainian went on moaning, "In the old times we had horses and cows and pigs and chickens. Now we are dying of hunger. In the old days we fed the world. Now they have taken all we had away from us and we have nothing. In the old days I should have bade you *welcome and given you as my guest chickens and eggs and milk and fine, white bread. Now we have no bread in the house. They are killing us."*

In one of the peasant's cottages in which I stayed we slept nine in the room. It was pitiful to see that two out of the three children had swollen stomachs. All there was to eat in the hut was a very dirty watery soup, with a slice or two of potato, which all the family and in the family I included myself ate from a common bowl with wooden spoons.

Fear of death loomed over the cottage, for they had not enough potatoes to last until the next crop. When I shared my white bread and butter and cheese one of the peasant women said, "Now I have eaten such wonderful things I can die happy." I set forth again further towards the south, and heard the villagers say, "We are waiting for death."

Many also said: "It is terrible here and many are dying, but further south it is much worse. Go down to the Poltava region, and you will see hundreds of empty cottages. In a village of three hundred huts, only about a hundred will have people living, in them, for the others will have died or have fled, but mainly died." Before long I set foot in the city of Kharkov, the capital of the Ukraine.

What I had seen in one small part of vast Russia was typical of conditions throughout the country, from the borders of Poland to the distant parts of Siberia.

How the men and women in the towns were faring I was soon to learn.[6]

I splashed my way through the streets [of Kharkov]. The early Russian thaw had suddenly come, and streams of water from the snow of yesterday poured along the gutters, and formed pools in the middle of the road ... On the opposite side of the road a church had been blown up and men were busy shovelling the masonry and carting it away. I heard later that for a long time the workers had refused to work on the site of the destroyed church. "It is haunted," they said. Peasant children seated on doorsteps shouted at me as I passed, "Uncle, give me some kopeks (or bread)."

Near-by a little gipsy girl, about eight years of age, is singing a tzigane song with all the dramatic emotion of an operatic contralto. After each song she bows. "Uncle, give me a ruble." I see another long queue, with its incessant bickering. At least a thousand people stand for bread, which is being sold at a high price.

Numbers of OGPU soldiers with their green lapels passed by. They are the land OGPU, who control the countryside, and are hated like the plague by the peasants. Before long, I heard people shout and quarrel and turning the corner I saw what was happening. Outside a bread shop the windows of which had been battered in, and were now boarded with planks, a hundred ragged people were crying, "We want bread." Two Soviet policemen were keeping the people away front the doors, and replying, "There is no bread, and there will be no bread to-day." There was an outburst of anger. The queue lost its form, and the mass of women and peasants and workers surrounded the policemen. "But citizens, there is no bread. Do not blame me," he cried in despair. I went up to a man in the queue. "How long have you been standing here?" "This is the second day", he replied. The crowd would not disperse. There always remained a forlorn hope that a wagon of bread might suddenly turn up from the blue.

Some of the bread queues in Kharkov number from four thousand to seven thousand people. They begin to assemble at about three or four o'clock in the afternoon and stand all night in the bitter Russian frost for opening of the shop at seven o'clock in the morning.

No wonder, I thought as I made my way to market that this bitterness expresses itself in those biting witticisms with which the Russians try to laugh away their sorrows. In Kharkov, I heard the following: "A louse and a pig meet on the frontier of the Soviet Union. The louse is going into Russia, while the pig is leaving."

"Why are you coming into Russia?" the pig asks. "I am coming, because in Germany people are so clean that I cannot find a single place to rest, my head so I am entering the Soviet Union. But why are you leaving Russia?" replies the louse. The pig answers: "In Russia to-day people are eating what we pigs used to eat. So, there is nothing left for me, and I'm saying good-bye."

The market provides me with a proof of the truth of this allegory. Ragged and diseased people loiter about, the booths. A boy is selling two slices of doughy black bread, which he holds in his hand. "One ruble each," he says. That means nominally two shillings for a slice of bread.

But the feature of the market which strikes me most is the number of ragged, homeless boys, in so-called 'bezprizorny.' With the foulest of rags and the most depraved of faces, they hover about … In the station waiting-room three hundred of them were herded to be taken away. I peeped through the window. One of them near the window lay on the floor, his face red with fever and breathing heavily, with his mouth open. "Typhus," said another man, who was looking at them. Another lay in rags stretched on the ground, with part of his body uncovered, revealing dried up flesh and thin arms.

I turned away and entered the train for Moscow. In the corridor stood little girl — she was well dressed. Her cheeks were rosy. She held a toy in one hand and a piece of cake in the other. She was probably the daughter of a Communist Party member or of an engineer. The train rolled on to Moscow.[7]

CHILD BEGGARS IN MOSCOW

there was famine in several great regions, but in most parts the peasants could live. It was a localised famine, which had many millions of victims, especially along the Volga. But to-day the famine is everywhere, in the formerly rich Ukraine, in West Russia, in Central Asia, in North Caucasia—

Child Beggars in Moscow - Library photo accompanying Evening Standard, March 31, 1933, article.

In Moscow, Gareth had been impressed by the warm clothes of most of those people who frequented the centre of the city and by the health of the children. After a reception at the Soviet Foreign Office he decided to explore the homes of the workers:

I had learned that the children were given good meals in school. I had talked to skilled workers who were well paid, and received plenty to eat in their factories, and I knew that some shops were moderately well stocked, although entrance was limited to privileged persons. The number of fine motor-cars rushing through the streets had struck me as a great improvement over 1930 and 1931… If it were not therefore for begging peasants, I would have drawn the conclusion that all was well with Moscow. But would my visits to Soviet workers' homes confirm that impression.

I left the centre of the town and found myself alone in a dark side street. I entered a courtyard littered with rubbish. To the left stood a wooden house with an. open door, through which I went. It led me into a semi-lit corridor with doors on each side leading into rooms. A working woman came out. "What do you want?" "I want to see how workers live," was my reply. Her husband invited me in. "We'll show you how they make us workers live," he said bitterly. There was one small room with a bed which occupied almost the whole of the space. "Three of us live here," said the woman.

"Come and visit the next family." The next room was still smaller. An ikon was hanging in the corner. On the bed an old woman was lying, pale and ill.

"Three live here," she said, "but when my sons came back on leave from the Red Army we were five." I wondered how five could possibly sleep in the small space of the room. In some of the rooms in the house there were six, seven, and even eight in each room.

As I talked to the old woman a girl of about twelve years of age, with a large red necktie, entered. Her face around her eyes was swollen with crying. Her mother followed her, and her pale face was also swollen with tears. "What is the matter?" I asked. The mother replied: "We have been refused passports, and we have to leave Moscow by March 30. We know no one in the world except in Moscow, but we have to go beyond sixty-five miles from Moscow. Where can we go? How will we have food there?"

"But surely they will leave you your bread card?" I asked. "Not even a bread card, and we have no money." The old woman said also that she was refused a visa and would have to leave Moscow, but she was quiet, and seemed resigned, although she knew well what her fate would be. These people were the victims of passportisation.

No wonder I got angry next day when a Communist, who seemed to know every statistic there was to be known, told me: "We hope that by our system of passportisation we shall be able to remove the surplus labour from the towns. About 700,000 will leave Moscow. But I can assure you that only crooks, speculators, kulaks, private traders, and ex-officers will have to go."

Passportisation, labour discipline and unemployment; those were the three spectres which haunted the Russian worker.[8]

Gareth wrote another series of three articles in the more high-brow broadsheet, *The Financial News*, that were published at the same time as the articles in the *Daily Express* which contained a more detailed and considered overall appraisal of the first Five-Year Plan. Though more sombre in style, the last article in this series, was no less damning in its indictment of the Stalinist regime, repeating much of what had been stated in his Berlin press release.

The words that echoed throughout all of Gareth's famine articles were "There is no bread. We are waiting for death."

Notes on Chapter 20

1
  Gareth Jones 2015, *Tell Them we Are Starving*.p.131 (Diary 1 p. 93) transcript of the diaries held at the National Library of Wales. Gareth Vaughan Jones Papers Diary Series B1/15.

2
  The circulation of *The Daily Express* in 1936 was 2.5 million.

3
  The Foreign Office and the Famine, 1988 p.215. Gareth's diary records that he had an appointment to see Strang on March 4, 1933.

4
  Daily Express, 'Soviets Confiscate Part of Workers Wages', April 5, 1933, p. 8.

5
  Ibid.

6
  Ibid. 'Nine to a Room in the Slums of Russia', April 6, 1933, p. 8.

7
  Ibid. 'People in Bread Queue — 15 Hours Wait for Food,' April 7, 1933, p. 11.

8
  Ibid. 'Pitiful Life of Soviet factory Slaves', April 8, 1933, p. 7.

Chapter 21

Goodbye Russia

*Alas! You will be very amused to hear that the inoffensive little 'Joneski' has
achieved the dignity of being a marked man on the black list of the OGPU and is
barred from entering the Soviet Union. I hear that there is a long list of crimes which
I have committed under my name in the secret police file in Moscow and funnily
enough espionage is said to be among them. As a matter of fact Litvinoff sent a
special cable from Moscow to the Soviet Embassy in London to tell them to make the
strongest of complaints to Mr Lloyd George about me.*[1]

On the evening of March 8, 1933, Gareth met someone by the name of Lidin
(possibly VG Lidin, a Soviet writer) and discussed the new-found relaxation of
censorship for Soviet playwrights. Lidin volunteered that they were free to write
about any subject, including 'Artistic Realism':

> [Lidin]: *"Give us books for new readers. True books with living truth."*
> GJ [Gareth]: *Would [you] describe famine in villages?"*
> [Lidin]: *"Well, there is no famine… You must take a longer view. The present
> hunger is temporary. In writing books you must have a longer view. It would
> be difficult to describe hunger.*[2]

Privately noting his disdain for this reply, Gareth summed up his views at the
bottom of this page in the diary in single word, 'Prevarication'.[3]

This personal denial (from such an influential politician in the Soviet Union) may
well have been remembered when three weeks later Gareth exposed the famine to
the world. It may have had some bearing on Maxim Litvinov's personal intervention
in making, "the strongest of complaints to Mr Lloyd George," for what he would
have regarded as unforgivable behaviour by Gareth.

Gareth was well aware that the coterie of Moscow correspondents, with whom he had extensively discussed the agricultural situation in confidence, feared losing their jobs if they displeased the Soviet press censors. Gareth's colleague Paul Scheffer was the first Moscow-based journalist to have had the courage to severely criticise the Five-Year Plan in 1929. At that time he was banned from returning to the Soviet Union simply by not issuing his re-entry visa.[4]

Gareth never named any of the correspondents as a source of his information but he was to refer to their predicament in his third article for *The Financial News*:

> *The Soviet Government tries its best to conceal the situation, but the grim facts will out. Under the conditions of censorship existing in Moscow, foreign journalists have to tone down their messages and have become masters at the art of understatement. The existence of the general famine is none the less true, in spite of the fact that Moscow still has bread.*[5]

Gareth had no fear of the Soviet censors since, unlike the Moscow correspondents, he was not beholden to them for his employment, but after his private interview with Litvinov, but he must have realised that his revealing articles on the famine would be considered by Litvinov as a personal affront to his hospitality and a challenge to Soviet authority in general. Furthermore, by exploiting his connections with David Lloyd George in order to gain access to Litvinov, he must have known he would also be offending his erstwhile employer, who was sympathetic to the Soviet regime. In any event, this did not sway Gareth in his decision to publish and be damned, so affected was he by what he had seen. On his return to Berlin, Gareth wrote to Lloyd George "The situation is so grave, so much worse than in 1921, that I am amazed at your admiration for Stalin."[6] Lloyd George was a man who did not accept criticism lightly and their previous close relationship cooled markedly from that point onwards.

With his Soviet ban assured, Gareth fittingly concluded his series of articles in *The Daily Express* with a measured valedictory entitled, "Goodbye Russia". It was based on his observations from three Soviet visits and was a personal analysis of the fortunes and failures of the first Five-Year plan and was published on April 11, 1933:

> *For years young men in Britain have been bewildered. The capitalist system seems to be on the brink of a precipice. Nationalists have run rampant in all countries, waving their banners of cheap patriotism.*
>
> *Everywhere the cry has been: "Put up more tariffs," and the world became tariff mad. 'Pile up your armaments' shriek others and the armies of the world mount in size and attacking power.*

Men have lost their jobs in every town and village in Britain. Seeing this many young men have said: "There is something radically wrong. Perhaps we can learn from the Soviet Union." I was myself one of those millions who thought that Russia might have a lesson to offer.

Being a Liberal, I had no patience with the Diehards, and was not bound by traditional ways of conservative thinking.

The idealism of the Bolsheviks impressed me before I went to Russia in 1930. Here was a country where the rulers sought to build an industry for the benefit of the workers. Equality was in time to rule and classes were to disappear. The injustice of capitalism was to be no more. Education was to be spread to the humblest peasant, and everything was to exist for the good of the masses.

The courage of the Bolsheviks impressed me. They tackled their difficulties like men. They sought to build vast cities where once there were bare steppes. They planned the great factories in the world. They wished to do things and not stand idle without a plan, as in England.

The internationalism of the Bolsheviks impressed me. They set aside all petty prejudices between races. They abhorred pogrom. They gave rights to the smaller nations to speak their own languages. They were not guilty of the narrow nationalisms of post-war days.

Then I went to Russia.

There I had every chance to see the real situation, for I travelled alone, walked through villages and towns, and slept in peasant homes. ...I liked personally most of the Bolsheviks I knew. Lenin's widow, for example, was one of the finest women I have met, and she commands my deep respect. I was able to go about freely without hindrance.

What did I find? All was not black. Much work was being done to care for the working class children in the towns. Many new houses for working class people had been built in Moscow. The problem of the homeless boy had in 1930 and 1931 been tackled with vigour. The art galleries and the museums were among the finest that exist.

In industry, also the Russians were building rapidly. I saw the torrents pouring through the Dnieperstroy dam. The motorcar factory in Nizhny-Novgorod went up with a speed of which even the British Ministry of Munitions during the war would have been proud.

The Kharkov tractor factory was also an achievement about which the Bolsheviks might rightly boast.

On the human side, the Bolsheviks had some admirable features. Many of them showed in 1930 and 1931 great enthusiasm and heroic self-sacrifice. In foreign affairs I was and still am impressed by the policy of peace which the Soviet Government is carrying on. Soviet Russia will never attack.

Such is the credit side. What of the debit side?

There is first the rapid way in which the standard of living has fallen; 1930 was a bad year, but now it seems even prosperous compared with the spring of 1933. Famine stalks the land. Surely the building of vast factories is no compensation for hunger.

There is the savage class warfare, which is no literary slogan, but a real programme of terror.

Class warfare has led to the crushing of millions of innocent people whose only sin was that they were not of working class parentage. It has led to domination by the OGPU and to visitations of torture.

It has led to justice, which should be above class, becoming a weapon of the Communist Party to crush those who are not of working-class origin. 'Art is a weapon of class warfare' was the notice over an art gallery in Moscow. Everything is subordinated to class warfare. The oppression of religion, which is no myth but a definite fact, is another black mark to be put against the Soviet régime.

Hypocrisy has been bred to a greater extent than ever. Communists dare not criticise the policy of the party, and, though they know that famine is there, and that the Five-Year Plan has wrecked the country, they still speak of its glorious achievement, and of the way in which they have raised the standard of living. But the idealism of 1930 and 1931 has disappeared.

Fear has become the dominant motive of action. The party member fears that he will be turned out of the party. The peasant fears that he will die of hunger. The worker fears that he will lose his bread card. The professor fears that he will be accused of counter-revolutionary propaganda in his lectures. The town dweller fears that he will be refused a passport. The engineer fears that he will be accused of sabotage.

But the greatest crime of which the Soviet régime is guilty is the destruction of the peasantry. Six or seven millions of the better-off peasants have been sent away from their homes to exile. The treatment of the other peasants is has been equally cruel. Their land and livestock taken away from them, they have been condemned to the status of landless serfs.

The noose is getting tighter and tighter round the neck of the Russian peasant, and exile and starvation hover round him. But by destroying the Russian peasant the Bolsheviks are destroying Russia and this mad policy will be their nemesis.

What then is the lesson of Soviet Russia? It is that a State cannot live upon the doctrine of class warfare, and that the ideas we have in Britain of personal freedom and of the rights of each individual man are not so far wrong and must be defended at all costs.[7]

In Gareth's last ever article in the British press on the USSR he considered the prospects for the next Soviet harvest in an article for the Financial News published on April 13, 1933 entitled 'Ruin of Russian Agriculture':

One of the most decisive Spring sowing campaigns in Russia's history is in progress. To try and gauge the result of this campaign, I asked these questions in March in each village I visited:

1. *Have you seed?*
2. *What will the spring sowing be like?*
3. *What were the winter sowing and the winter ploughing like?*
4. *What do you think of the new tax?*

On the question of seed, several villages were provided with seed, but many lacked seed. Experts are confident that the Government has far greater reserves of grain than in 1921, but evidence points to a lack of seed in certain areas.

Peasants were emphatic in stating that the spring sowing would be bad. They stated that they were too weak and swollen to sow, that there would be little cattle fodder left for them to eat in a month's time, that there were few horses left to plough, that the remaining horses were weak, that the tractors, when they had any, stopped all the time, and, finally, that weeds might destroy the crops.

... The outlook for the next harvest is, therefore, black. It is dangerous to make any prophecy, for the miracle of perfect climatic conditions can always make good a part of the 'unfavourable factors'.

The chief fact remains, however, that in building up industry the Soviet Government has destroyed its greatest source of wealth — its agriculture.

Notes on Chapter 21

1

    Excerpt from a personal letter from Gareth addressed to his friend Margaret, who was at Girton College Cambridge University (surname unknown), who was about to visit the Soviet Union, written from the *Western Mail* Offices, May 28, 1934. National Library of Wales, Gareth Vaughan Jones Papers Series C1/1.

2

    Gareth Jones 2015, *Tell Them we Are Starving*. p. 115 (Diary 1 p. 48) transcript of the diaries held at the National Library of Wales. Gareth Vaughan Jones Papers Diary Series B1/15.

3

    Ibid. See Gamache's assessment of the significance of this reference perhaps to Hamlet's soliloquy 'To be or not to be' *Gareth Jones, Eyewitness to the Holodomor* 2013, p. 132-3.

4

    If Scheffer thought that was be the end of the story, he was to be sorely mistaken. In testimony at the Third Bukarin Moscow show trial in 1938, he was quite ludicrously accused of being the head of a Nazi spy ring involved with the sabotage of Soviet grain. The only person who would believe this specific accusation was to be J. Edgar Hoover, who had Scheffer interned after Pearl Harbor, even though he was at the time working personally for General Bill Donovan, the head of the OSS.

5

    Gareth Jones, The Financial News, April 13, 1933, p. 6.

6

    Parliamentary Archives, The Lloyd George Paper ,LG/G/26/1/2

7

    Gareth Jones, 'Good-bye Russia', *Daily Express,* April 11, 1933, p. 12.

Chapter 22

The Metrovick Affair

"I explain it thus, Stalin and his assistants know the real situation in Russia, and they want, by a terrible increase of terror, to frighten the growing opposition within the party." – Kerensky[1]

The spread of terror by the OGPU was now manifest in the Soviet Union and would increase in the succeeding years. Even Gareth was subjected to their intimidation and related his own story about being apprehended by the OGPU on his way to Kharkov:

> *I had narrowly escaped being arrested myself not long before, at a small railway station in the Ukraine, where I had entered into conversation with some peasants. These were bewailing their hunger to me, and were gathering a crowd, all murmuring, "There is no bread," when a man had appeared. "Stop that growling," he had shouted to the peasants; while to me he said, "Come along; where are your documents?"*
>
> *A civilian (an OGPU man) appeared from nowhere, and they both submitted me to a thorough gruelling of questions. They discussed among themselves what they should do with me, and finally the OGPU man decided to accompany me on the train to the big city of Kharkov, where at last he left me in peace. There was to be no arrest.*[2]

In the same week as Gareth's brush with the secret police, six British engineers were arrested on March 12, 1933, and until after their trial a month later, this event was to take precedence over any news of an on-going famine. Large sections of the British newspapers were filled with reports of their detention. For example, *The Times* in their 'Parliamentary Procedures' and 'Overseas News' sections devoted whole columns to the arrests and subsequent trial, but never made a single reference to the disastrous agricultural conditions in the USSR during this crisis. Those involved were six employees of Metropolitan-Vickers, who were accused of, "wilfully wrecking the Soviet electrical industry and of plotting against the Soviet Government, of military espionage, and bribery". Gareth explained:

> When I heard the news of the arrests I was seated at tea with a group of diplomats in a house in Kharkov, 400 miles south of Moscow. A silence fell over the party when a servant entered with the news. "It is incredible," said one of those present... Next morning, however, I looked at the 'Izvestia', the official organ of the Soviet Government, and there the news stood in black and white.
>
> I ran my eye down the list and suddenly fixed on one name: "Alan Monkhouse!" I had known Alan [Allan] Monkhouse on a previous visit to Moscow. I had seen him at work in the office of Metropolitan there... I knew the deep respect in which the British colony in Moscow held him. It seemed incredible that he should be at that moment in the Lubyanka, the headquarters of the OGPU in Moscow.
>
> I did not really accept the news to be true until three days later when I arrived in Moscow, and there shook hands with Alan Monkhouse. He was standing in the entrance hall of the British Embassy, a tall figure approaching middle-age, with a dignified bearing. He looked older than the previous time I had seen him when I was in Moscow in 1931. He was nervous after the mental torture of continual questioning [19 hours], but he smiled courageously.[3]

The British Ambassador intervened on behalf of the prisoners:

> There is no doubt that Sir Esmond Ovey has placed the facts about the whole situation before the Government. His testimony is all the more to be believed on account of his former sympathy for the Soviet Government... He has recently, however, become fully aware of the catastrophic conditions in Russia, as I gathered a fortnight ago in the Embassy in Moscow... but in his firm handling of the present case he has earned the praise of the most critical journalists in Moscow.[4]

In Gareth's interview with Litvinov on March 23, 1933, he enquired about the fate of the six arrested engineers. Litvinov specifically asked Gareth to consider that his reply should remain strictly confidential (and for the ears of Lloyd George alone):

> [The] greater the pressure the less chance [there is of helping] because we cannot give way to pressure. ... The men will not be shot. There will be a trial...[5]

233

Maxim Litvinov was less than complimentary about Sir Esmond:

Sir Esmond Ovey has been too tactless, and too bullying. He is seeking a quarrel, and has as [his] aim the breaking off of diplomatic relations… We cannot have his bullying, tactless way. He is a very unfortunate representative. [6]

Soon after Gareth's meeting with Litvinov, Sir Esmond Ovey was withdrawn from his position as British Ambassador in Moscow.

In his newspaper articles Gareth considered in some detail the reasons for the engineers' arrest:

What could there be to explain it? Then I looked across the river to the Kremlin, whose golden domes and red ramparts face the Embassy. Within that citadel, the Kremlin, lives Stalin. There the whole policy has been framed which has changed the life of every man, woman, and child in Russia in the last five years.

The Kremlin gave me one clue to the arrest. Half an hour later I walked past another building. It was of ugly grey and yellow brick and was formerly an insurance office. Outside, on the pavement, a few Red sentries marched up and down with fixed bayonets. This building gave me another clue. It was the Lubyanka, the headquarters of the OGPU. Then I realised that the cause for the arrests was to be found in the Kremlin and in the OGPU… It was to divert attention from the famine and find blame elsewhere.

The Kremlin is now panic-stricken, for a catastrophe has come over that rich country of Russia. The people are seething with discontent. Among the ranks of the young Communists there is an ominous rumble of wrath at the crashing of their ideals… The worker, having been promised a paradise, has had his fine dream shattered.

…Fear, which had so often gripped the Kremlin in centuries past, had returned to haunt its dwellers. Now the Bolshevists dread the wrath of a starving peasantry. Seized with panic, they sought to find the foreigner on whom to put the blame when their promises fail.[7]

…When I was in Russia in 1931 a period of toleration had begun. The OGPU had had some of its fangs extracted and was under the control of Akuloff, a moderate man and an economist. The dangerous Yagoda had been removed. Stalin had preached the doctrine of fair play to non-Communists and the whole country breathed a sigh of relief that the terror was over.

But now, in 1933, the terror has returned, and in a form multiplied a hundredfold. Yagoda is back again at his work, slashing out left and right at all those suspected of opposition to the regime. The drive is now against all kinds of opposition. Formerly there would have been a drive against the Right Wing opposition, then against the Trotskyists, then against the former bourgeois.

But now the attack is on all fronts — on party members, of whom numbers have been shot; on the intelligentsia, of whom there are countless representatives in Solovki; on the peasants for merely having wished to till their soil for themselves, and on the Ukrainian, Georgian, and Central Asian nationalists who have struggled for the rights of small countries. More and more power is being put into the hands of the OGPU and a small clique dominates the rest of the party, the members of which, although in their heart recognizing the colossal failure of the Five-Year Plan policy, do not dare to raise even one small voice in contradiction to the general line of Stalin.

Symptomatic too, of this collapse of Russian agriculture was the shooting of thirty-five prominent workers in the Commissariat of Agriculture and in the Commissariat of State Farms, including the Vice-Commissar of Agriculture, and Mr Wolff, whose name is well known to foreign agricultural experts.

These agriculturists confessed themselves guilty or rather were forced by torture to confess themselves guilty of such actions as the smashing of tractors, the burning of tractor stations and of flax factories, the stealing of grain reserves, the disorganisation of sowing, and the destroying of cattle. This was surely a formidable task for thirty-five men to carry out in a country which stretched 6,000 miles. 'Pravda' (March 5) stated that, "the activities of the arrested men had as their aim the ruining of agriculture, and the creation of famine in the country". The announcement added, "The sentences were carried into execution."[8]

The engineers were eventually tried on April 12, 1933, and four were released at the end of the trial on April 19. Of the two men who made elaborate confessions of guilt, MacDonald adhered to his confession and was given two years in prison; Leslie Thornton attempted to repudiate his, and received three years. Gregory was acquitted. Allan Monkhouse, Cushny and Nordwall were expelled from the country.[9] Thornton and MacDonald were later released in July. Their co-arrested Russian colleagues were imprisoned.

After the trial, those who were reprieved returned to Britain and *The News Chronicle* on April 24 reported their rapturous homecoming:

London gave the four engineers from Moscow a heroes' welcome yesterday. A few thousand people, cheers, the National Anthem, "For he's a jolly good fellow", bouquets, handshakes, slaps on the back, tears of thankfulness. But not overdone. Quite English.

The reception at Liverpool Station to the four British engineers on their arrival from Moscow. Mr Monkhouse was met by his wife, son and daughter. The News Chronicle, April 24, 1933.

Gareth's thoughtful account of the affair dwelt more on the causes:

In spite of the heralding of this achievement throughout the world as a super-triumph for Socialist construction, the tramways within the very area of the Dnieperstroy stopped, because there was no electric current. The great cities of Kharkov and Kiev, the leading cities of the Ukraine, were often plunged for hours on end into darkness, and men and women and children had to huddle in black-ened rooms, because it was difficult to buy candles and lamp oil. In the theatres, in Kharkov, the lights would suddenly go out, and hundreds of people would sit there, dreading the crush and the fight in the dark for the way out. At the same time as the people not many miles away from the Dnieperstroy sat in darkness, resounding slogans of the triumph of the Soviet electrical industry were drummed into the imagination of the world's proletariat by impressive statistics, and by skilfully taken photographs of electric works and of workers wreathed in smiles.[10]

Just as the 35 agriculturists were arrested, because of the tragic ruin of agriculture, so the British engineers were arrested, because the electrical plans failed. Gareth had also foreseen another potential consequence of the trial for the Soviets, which was the barrier it put in the way of American recognition.

> *…A great triumph for Soviet diplomacy was in the offing. The United States, which had refused to recognise the Soviet Union and which has never had an Ambassador nor a Consul in Moscow, was seriously considering taking the step which Britain took in 1924.*[11]

The OGPU perhaps did not anticipate the world-wide political and economic consequences following the arrest of the British engineers in Moscow. With the world in a state of severe Depression, world prices had declined drastically and the deleterious effects of Five-Year Plan on Russia's agriculture meant the Soviet Government would have great difficulties in meeting obligations abroad. "An embargo on Soviet goods would be another factor damaging their exports."[12]

President Roosevelt had seemed in favour of entering upon diplomatic relations with the Soviet Union, but the Moscow trial alarmed the American, and American recognition was now "farther away than ever".

Notes on Chapter 22

1
  Gareth Jones, 'We are Starving', *Western Mail & South Wales News*, April 3, 1933, p. 7.
2
  Gareth Jones, 'The Real Truth About Russia', *The Daily Express,* April 3, 1933, p. 1-2.
3
  Ibid.
4
  Gareth Jones, 'Majority for Russian Imports Bill', *Western Mail & South Wales News*, April 6, 1933, p. 8.
5
  Gareth Jones 2015, *Tell Them we Are Starving.* p.261 (Diary 3 p. 29 and 33) transcript of the diaries held at the National Library of Wales. Gareth Vaughan Jones Papers Diary Series B1/15.
6
  Ibid. Diary 3, p.32.
7
  Gareth Jones, 'The Real Truth About Russia at Last; Secrets of the Kremlin', *Daily Express*, April 3, 1933, p. 1-2.
8
  Gareth Jones, 'OGPU'S Reign of Terror in Russia'. *Western Mail & South Wales News.* April 5, 1933, P.8.
9
  Eugene Lyons, *Assignment in Utopia.* Harcourt Brace, New York, 1937.
10
  Gareth Jones, 'Ruin of Russian Agriculture'. No. III, The Financial News, Thursday, April, 13, 1933, p. 6.
11
  'OGPU Blow to Russian Trade', *Western Mail & South Wales News* April 20, 1933, p. 12.
12
  Gareth Jones, 'Russian Exports' *The Western Mail'* April 6, 1933, p. 8.

PART 6

The Other Famine Witnesses
'The Good, the Bad and the Ugly'

This section of the book deviates from using Gareth's own diaries, letters and newspaper articles. It investigates the aftermath of Gareth's famine reporting from the words and actions of others whose lives and fate were also inextricably entwined in their reporting of the Holodomor.

Chapter 23

Dare to be a Daniel

Dare to be a Daniel,
Dare to stand alone,
Dare to have a purpose firm,
Dare to make it known.

"To bring this hymn up-to-date one would have to add a 'Don't' at the beginning of each line... 'Daring to stand alone' is ideologically criminal as well as practically dangerous..." – George Orwell

After George Bernard Shaw's letter to the editor published in the Manchester Guardian on March 2 1933, and attacking the paper's apparent anti-Soviet reporting, Gareth might have anticipated some similar spiteful correspondence in other pages of the British press. But there was not one single pro-Soviet article or letter (known to the authors) contradicting reports of a Soviet famine published in the UK during the whole of April 1933.

However, just a day after the publication of his first article on the famine, Gareth was to receive an unexpected personal bombshell. Across the Atlantic, a storm was brewing and from an unexpected source. To his shock and amazement Walter Duranty had penned a denial of Gareth's Berlin press statement (a story which Duranty's newspaper had not even covered). Duranty's article was sent by special cable from Moscow on March 30 and published in the *New York Times* on March 31, 1933. Duranty, who had won the 1932 Pulitzer Prize for journalism, was at the time the most influential journalist in Moscow and the highest paid international correspondent in the USA. The damning article was entitled, 'Russians Hungry, but not Starving' and is a rebuttal considered by some to be a classic example of Orwellian 'doublespeak'.

Duranty began by belittling Gareth's observations stating that "there appears from a British source a big scare story in the American press about famine in the

241

Soviet Union, with 'thousands already dead and millions menaced by death and starvation.'" (It should be noted that at the time of Duranty's dispatch, Gareth's story had actually only made the pages of the *New York Evening Post*, which one would hardly describe as representing the "majority" of the American press.)

The offending article went on to undermine Gareth's story, claiming that it was founded merely on a three-week Soviet trip (which by inference could not match Duranty's much longer acquaintance with Russia). His article questioned the dependability of Gareth's Soviet credentials by spelling out four historical instances where other foreigners had been proven wrong in their predictions of Soviet "doom".

Having put some serious doubt into his readers' minds regarding Gareth's relative lack of Soviet expertise, Duranty continued:

> *But to return to Mr. Jones. He told me there was virtually no bread in the villages he had visited and that the adults were haggard, gaunt and discouraged, but that he had seen no dead or dying animals or human beings.*
>
> *I believed him because I knew it to be correct in not only of some parts of the Ukraine but of sections of the North Caucasus and lower Volga regions and, for that matter, Kazakhstan…*

Duranty then blamed the "deplorable" harvest on the inability to drag ancient nomadic lifestyles into the modern practices of twentieth century collective grain farming, on hapless mismanagement and down-right sabotage. Duranty alluded to the Bolshevik's leaders' resolve in their "drive towards Socialization," with that of a First-World War' General's "costly" disregard for human life, culminating in his much used stock-phrase, "But — to put it brutally — you can't make an omelette without breaking eggs."

Finally, Duranty turned on Gareth again, claiming that he had, "made exhaustive enquiries" with Soviet departments; foreign embassies, their outlying consuls; British specialists and his own "personal connections." Compared to Gareth's, "hasty study," he was therefore in a better position to, "present the whole picture…":

> *There is a serious shortage food shortage throughout the country, with occasional cases of well-managed State or collective farms. The big cities and the army are adequately supplied with food. There is no actual starvation or deaths from starvation, but there is widespread mortality from diseases due to malnutrition.*
>
> *In short, conditions are definitely bad in certain sections — the Ukraine, North Caucasus and Lower Volga. The rest of the country is on short rations but nothing worse. These conditions are bad, but there is no famine…*[2]

Gareth had met and talked with Duranty on at least three occasions — in 1931 with Jack Heinz, again in 1933 prior to his journey to Ukraine, and a few days later before leaving Moscow for Berlin. At their final meeting on March 19, 1933, Gareth wrote in his diary, "I don't trust Duranty — He still believes in Collectivisation."[3]

Perturbed more by Duranty's dishonesty than the insinuation that he was a liar, Gareth wrote a stinging reply on May 1, 1933. To allow Duranty's lies to stand without redress would have been the antithesis of Gareth's highly moral Welsh up-bringing. If this meant he had to speak with a lone voice and fly in the face of arguably the world's most 'eminent' foreign correspondent, then so be it.

Gareth's letter to the editor of the *New York Times* was eventually published on May 13, 1933, in which he, "…stood by his statement that the Soviet Union was suffering from a severe famine":

> …*While partially agreeing with my statement, he [Duranty] implied that my report was a "scare story" and compared it with certain fantastic prophecies of Soviet downfall. He also made the strange suggestion that I was forecasting the doom of the Soviet régime, a forecast I have never ventured.*
>
> *Journalists… are allowed to write, but the censorship has turned them into masters of euphemism and understatement. Hence they give "famine" the polite name of "food shortage" and "starving to death" is softened down to read as "widespread mortality from diseases due to malnutrition."*
>
> *May I in conclusion congratulate the Soviet Foreign Office on its skill in concealing the true situation in the USSR? Moscow is not Russia, and the sight of well-fed people there tends to hide the real Russia.*[4]

In 1937, two years after Gareth's death, Eugene Lyons published his book *Assignment in Utopia*, where he sheds some light on the background to Duranty's article. His account of life as an American correspondent in Moscow between 1928 and 1934 included a chapter entitled, "The Press Corps Conceals a Famine". In it he describes Gareth's betrayal at the hands of his fellow journalists.

> *Jones had a conscientious streak in his make-up which took him on a secret journey into the Ukraine and a brief walking tour through its countryside. That same streak was to take him a few years later into the interior of China during political disturbances, and was to cost him his life at the hands of Chinese military bandits. An earnest and meticulous little man, Gareth Jones was the*

sort who carries a note-book and unashamedly records your words as you talk. Patiently he went from one correspondent to the next, asking questions and writing down the answers.

… To protect us, and perhaps with some idea of heightening the authenticity of his reports, he emphasized his Ukrainian foray rather than our conversation as the chief source of his information.

Throwing down Jones was as unpleasant a chore as fell to any of us in years of juggling facts to please dictatorial regimes — but throw him down we did, unanimously and in almost identical formulas of equivocation. Poor Gareth Jones must have been the most surprised human being alive when the facts he so painstakingly garnered from our mouths were snowed under by our denials.

The scene in which the American press corps combined to repudiate Jones is fresh in my mind. It was in the evening and Comrade Umansky [Soviet Press Censor], the soul of graciousness, consented to meet us in the hotel room of a correspondent. He knew that he had a strategic advantage over us because of the Metro-Vickers story. He could afford to be gracious. Forced by competitive journalism to jockey for the inside track with officials, it would have been professional suicide to make an issue of the famine at this particular time. There was much bargaining in a spirit of gentlemanly give-and-take, under the effulgence of Umansky's gilded smile, before a formula of denial was worked out.

We admitted enough to soothe our consciences, but in roundabout phrases that damned Jones as a liar. The filthy business having been disposed of, someone ordered vodka and zakuski, Umansky joined the celebration, and the party did not break up until the early morning hours.[5]

In 1977, James Crowl interviewed Lyons about this occasion, but:

…he remembered little about the meeting with Oumansky [other] than the description of it in Assignment in Utopia. It was not a "general session" of the foreign correspondents, he recalls, nor did Oumansky have to do more than "hint" as to what should be done. Lyons cannot remember who attended or even more specifically where the meeting was held. He adds however, that "presumably" Duranty was there.[6]

This obduracy on the part of Lyons could at first sight be put down to the passing of time or even the onset of old age, but if one were to revise the above "Vodka and Zakuski" passage, noting the careful usage of the words, "we," "us" and "our," then perhaps it becomes plausible that Duranty's article might well have been composed by a "committee" of American journalists, before their drunken party began. The stated "formula of denial" would in this instance refer to the American press corps "collectively" agreeing to allow Duranty's respected column in the *New York Times* to be the messenger to espouse Gareth's public humiliation. So far as the authors are aware from research at newspaper archives on both sides of the Atlantic, neither Lyons nor any of his Moscow-based American colleagues had any of their own stories published repudiating Gareth, as that task appears to have been left for Duranty alone to fulfil[7].

Furthermore, the Lyons famine chapter, although its opening words quoted quoting Duranty's article, "There is no actual starvation...", did not attribute the quote to Duranty, but merely cited the *New York Times* as the source:

> *This amazing sophistry, culled from a New York Times Moscow dispatch on March 30, 1933, has become among foreign reporters the classic example of journalistic understatement. It characterizes sufficiently the whole shabby episode of our failure to report honestly the gruesome Russian famine of 1932-33.*[8]

If collusion did occur, then it is quite understandable why Lyons might have appeared later in life to have had selective amnesia on the subject of the Moscow party, so as to avoid admitting to his own culpability in the whole sorry saga, thereby leaving the then late Duranty to shoulder the blame single-handedly. This does not mean that Duranty was any the less guilty for allowing his Pulitzer reputation to be used to attack Gareth's reputation, but quite probably he was not alone...

To add to this vilification by Duranty, another character slur followed, but unbeknown to Gareth at the time, nor probably to the world outside Colorado. Louis Fischer, whom Gareth had met in 1931 in Moscow, was on a lecture tour of the United States. Fischer, was quoted in the Denver Post on Gareth's claim that a million[9] had died in Kazakhstan:

> *Who counted them? How could anyone march through a country and count a million people? Of course people are hungry there — desperately hungry. Russia is turning over from agriculture to industrialism. It's like a man going into business on small capital.*[10]

For his honest reporting of the plight that Stalin had imposed on the proletariat of the USSR, Gareth was thus condemned by his journalist colleagues. Had Gareth, in his haste to tell the world of the terrible plight of the peasant population in the Soviet Union, appreciated the personal consequences that would ensue? Though he obviously had his suspicions about Duranty, would he have expected to have been privately humiliated by his fellow colleagues who on the one hand had encouraged him to expose the famine, on the other were evidently quite prepared, for professional reasons, to condemn him? One person who Gareth might have felt he could rely on to counter Duranty's damning article was Muggeridge, but he too, from his new home in Switzerland in April 1933, remained publicly silent on the famine in Gareth's hour of need.

Gareth had had the courage to stand up and face the world. But did he realise that he would have to face his ordeal alone?

Notes on Chapter 23

1
Revivalist hymn. – from Orwell's 1945 essay, "The Prevention of Literature."
2
New York Times. Walter Duranty. 'Russians Hungry, but not Starving'. March 31, 1933.
3
Gareth Jones 2015, *Tell Them we Are Starving*. p. 203 (Diary 2 p. 47) transcript of the diaries held at the National Library of Wales. Gareth Vaughan Jones Papers Diary Series B1/15.
4
New York Times, 'Gareth Jones Replies', May 13, 1933.
5
Eugene Lyons, *Assignment in Utopia*, Harcourt Brace, New York, 1937, p. 576.
6
James Crowl, *Angels in Stalin's Paradise*. Lanham, Maryland: The University Press of America, 1982, p. 160.
7
The New York Herald Tribune, during first week in April 1933, contained Soviet articles by their own correspondent, Ralph Barnes, Eugene Lyons of the United Press and Stanley Richardson from Associated Press – each of these correspondents only filed reports on the forthcoming trial of the Metrovick Engineers, and nothing was printed about a possible famine, let alone any mention of Gareth's name.
8
Lyons p. 574
9
Gareth Jones 2015, *Tell Them we Are Starving*.p.262 (Diary 3 p. 34) transcript of the diaries held at the National Library of Wales. Gareth Vaughan Jones Papers Diary Series B1/15

"Central Asia [Quote from a] German [Otto Schiller] from Central Asia: Corpses in Kazakstan. Terrible conditions. One Million at least out of 5 million Kirghyz have died of hunger. Their herds have died. No hope; they will probably nearly all died. They are nomadic & collectivisation tried to tie them to the soil. In cotton-growing areas it is better. National feeling is terribly strong, hatred immense, but the peoples are too weak. Diseases spreading everywhere. Bread: 20 rubles a kilo in Tashkent. 'I am afraid that they may arrest me for sabotage.' Horrible conditions in Central Asia."
10
"'New Deal' Need for Entire World, Says Visiting Author," *Denver Post*, April 1, 1933, p. 3. Cited in Crowl, p. 157.

Chapter 24

Walter Duranty

"Oh! What a tangled web we weave when first we practise to deceive.[1]

During the summer of 1933, the Associated Press confirmed Chamberlin's report in the *Manchester Guardian* that Gareth and other journalists were still banned from visiting Ukraine and the North Caucasus, although the Commissariat for Foreign Affairs was already claiming a bumper crop. On August 21, William Henry Chamberlin announced in the *Guardian* that he and his colleagues had been ordered not to leave the capital without submitting a detailed itinerary and obtaining authorization from the Commissariat for Foreign Affairs.[2] However, in September of that year, Duranty and a colleague, Stanley Richardson, the Moscow correspondent of the Associated Press, were allowed to visit the surrounding area of Kharkov. Duranty reported on their trip in the *New York Times*:

> *Kharkov. I have just completed a 200-mile auto trip through the heart of the Ukraine and can say positively that the harvest is splendid and all talk of famine now is ridiculous. ...Babies to the old folks look healthy and well nourished — the peasants have accepted Collectivization. ...I sum up my impressions from this trip and from conversations with scores of peasants and local officials — the Collectivization policy was not generally popular, there was much passive resistance last year, and those who resisted suffered bitterly... The Kremlin has won the battle with the peasants.*

According to Duranty, everyone, from communists and officials to local peasants, had told him the same story:

> *Now we will be all right, now we are assured for the winter, now we have more grain than can easily be harvested. This "now" is significant. It contrasts with "then"*

— last winter — which, they tell you, was hard… Hard it was and I saw empty houses that bore witness — people ran away to find work and food elsewhere.[3]

Alexander Asatkin, the chief of the Ukrainian Communist section of the tractor stations, declared, when asked by Duranty whether the death rate had been as high as 10 per cent, "No, nothing like it. There was certainly distress in some sections, but the reports were greatly exaggerated."[4] He avowed to Duranty that the autumn had surpassed the highest expectations but that the average elsewhere was lower.

There was little or no authentic documentary evidence in the months following Gareth's visit to Ukraine relating to the famine so it was difficult to verify Duranty's account of the good summer harvest. It would appear that Gareth had sent this September article by Duranty to Muggeridge and from the tone of his reply from Geneva on September 29, 1933, Muggeridge questioned the veracity of Duranty's article:

> *Thank you for your letter, and for the Durranty [sic] cutting. He just writes what they tell him to. At the same time, since his message refers to the new harvest, I can't challenge him on first-hand knowledge. That is to say, I know and you know that his description of things in the Caucasus is untrue; but he can always retort, "You haven't seen and I have."*
>
> *One idea I had, however. If I could get hold of specimens of his messages during, say, the last year, I believe I could write an amusing article on Durranty as a foreign correspondent that a paper like TRUTH might publish, and that might do some good. I'd want about fifteen to twenty specimens spread over the year; even going back earlier. Do you happen to have, or know how I might get hold of, such specimens of his messages?*[5]

The Soviet Union craved diplomatic recognition by the USA and it is generally accepted that Duranty's articles in the *New York Times* following his visit to Ukraine in September 1933 were published with this aim in view in order to smooth the passage of a formal agreement. This diplomatic recognition had been an issue of importance during the 1932 presidential election when President Roosevelt was elected and Duranty saw himself at centre stage in the proceedings:

> *When he was grooming for the Presidency, sagacious Governor Roosevelt called to Albany's Executive Mansion a small, calm, wooden-legged Englishman from Moscow. For hours they talked about Russia. "I turned the tables on Walter*

Duranty!" laughed Candidate Roosevelt afterward. "I asked all the questions. It was fascinating!"[6]

Gareth at Cold Knap, Barry.

When interviewed by Gareth on March 23 1933, Maxim Litvinov told him that the position in Europe could only be changed by a change in American policy and that he was not optimistic:

> *Some want Roosevelt to have prelim[inary] negotiations which may put off recognition for a long time. The conditions put before us by the US years ago were not accepted. We are still less inclined to accept conditions [today].*[7]

Diplomatic recognition was eventually granted by the United States to the Soviet Union in the autumn of 1933. Duranty accompanied Commissar Litvinov to the United States for the formal recognition where he was acclaimed for his contribution in the outcome. At a dinner given in honour of Litvinov in New York's

Waldorf-Astoria Hotel, when it came time to pay tribute to Duranty, the cheers and applause were so loud that American critic and bon-vivant Alexander Woolcott wrote, "Indeed, one quite got the impression that America, in a spasm of discernment, was recognizing both Russia and Walter Duranty." Following his triumphal return to the Soviet Union in December 1933, Duranty wrote from Moscow:

This result [of a bumper harvest] fully justifies the optimism expressed to me by local authorities during my September trip through the Ukraine and North Caucasus — optimism that contrasted so strikingly with the famine stories then current in Berlin, Riga, Vienna, and other places, where elements hostile to the Soviet Union were making an eleventh-hour attempt to avert American recognition by picturing the Soviet Union as a land of ruin and despair.[8]

Duranty never openly admitted the devastating extent of the famine of 1932 and 1933 in Ukraine, the Caucasus, the Volga area and other areas of the USSR caused by Stalin's Five-Year Plan in his articles. The closest he came to acknowledge the problem was in an article published in the *New York Times*:

Moscow, November 24, 1932 — The Soviet programme of socialisation and Industrialisation, known as the Five-Year Plan, has run against an unexpected obstacle — the great and growing food shortage in town and country alike. It is as if a huge machine, constructed with incredible effort, had begun to function, not perhaps with full efficiency, but far better than any save the most optimistic of its builders expected, only to confront the danger that the fuel supply that drove it suddenly had begun to fail.

Two-thirds of the Soviet population will be lucky if it gets more than bread, potatoes, and cabbage this winter as a regular diet, with fish three times a week, say, and meat perhaps once a week. And that in quantities below the people's wants and probably below their needs. There is no famine or actual starvation, nor is there likely to be.[9] *And, for the most part, all will share alike in the various localities. But it is a gloomy picture, and as far as the writer can see, there is small sign or hope of improvement in the near future... On the face of things to-day, the first plan has done well.*[10]

Although Walter Duranty was the 1932 Pulitzer Prize winner for Correspondence, he should perhaps have also been awarded the 1933 accolade for duplicity. His articles were certainly a masterpiece of misinformation, as privately, he was fully aware of the presence of the famine in Ukraine. On October 31, 1932, William Strang, the First Secretary at the British Embassy in Moscow, reported to the Foreign Office in London a conversation with him:

> Mr Duranty came to-day to exchange views… He has at last awakened to the agricultural situation. He has been talking to Maurice Hindus and others who have been travelling about the country, and he says that the true position is only just being realised… The root cause of the present breakdown in agriculture in his view is the shortage of labour and of draught-power." [11]

On December 6, 1932, William Strang sent a further communication to London:

> A few days ago, however, he [Duranty] sent an article to the New York Times by safe hands to Paris … The New York Times made a great feature of it. Shortly afterwards Duranty was "visited by emissaries from governing circles here (not from the Censorship Department of the People's Commissariat for Foreign Affairs but from higher spheres) who reproached him with unfaithfulness. How could he, who had been so fair for ten years, choose this moment to stab them in the back, when critical negotiations were taking place and when the prospects of recognition by the USA was brightening? What did he mean by it, and did he not realise that the consequences for himself might be serious. Let him take this warning. [12]

On December 6, 1932 Sir Laurence Collier, head of the British Foreign Office, Northern Department, commented on the British Embassy dispatch from Moscow about Duranty stating "Mr Duranty is a somewhat shady individual, who has been accused (though not on convincing evidence, as far as I can tell) of being in the pay of the Soviet Government." [13]

This suspicion was also alluded to in *Time Magazine* on April 10, 1933, in a commentary about the public spat between Gareth and Duranty, "A rebuttal was promptly presented by Walter Duranty, a US correspondent long in Soviet good graces…" However the most damming evidence for his Soviet credentials came from Duranty, himself. In 2003, Dr James Mace whilst at Harvard University's Ukrainian Research Institute wrote in the Ukrainian newspaper, *The Day*:

> In the 1980s during the course of my own research on the Ukrainian Holodomor I came across a most interesting document in the US National

Archives, a memorandum from one A W Kliefoth of the US Embassy in Berlin dated June 4, 1931. Duranty dropped in to renew his passport. Mr Kliefoth thought it might be of possible interest to the State Department that this journalist, in whose reporting so much credence was placed, had told him that, 'in agreement with the New York Times and the Soviet authorities,' his official dispatches always reflect the official opinion of the Soviet government and not his own. [14]

Back in December 1932, according to Foreign Office records, Duranty even put off a departure to Paris for fear that he would not be allowed back into the Soviet Union. "He affects to think it possible that like Paul Scheffer he may not be able to return." [15]

Duranty's Russian mistress was already heavily pregnant, and with the anticipated arrival of his offspring in April 1933, this may have been a factor in his agreeing to continue his favourable reporting of conditions in the Soviet Union. Whether to placate his conscience, or purposely to muddy the waters for future historians, Duranty called at the British Embassy on September 26, 1933, before he travelled with Litvinov to the USA, and gave a more honest account of the impressions he had gathered following his recent visit to Ukraine to a member of the staff:

> *According to Mr Duranty, the population of the North Caucasus and the Lower Volga has decreased in the past year by three million, and the population of the Ukraine by four — five million. Estimates that he had heard from other foreigners living in the Ukraine were that approximately half the population had moved either into the towns or into more prosperous districts... Mr Duranty estimated that about 30 per cent of the harvest would be lost as a result of pilferage and weather conditions... The Ukraine had been bled white... Mr Duranty thinks it quite possible that as many as 10 million people may have died directly or indirectly from lack of food in the Soviet Union during the past year.* [16]

In retirement Duranty rationalised to himself what he considered was a plausible explanation for his failure to recognise the famine and its disastrous consequences. After the Mukden Incident of 1931 in Manchuria, Stalin feared a war in Siberia against the militaristic nation, Japan. In the early thirties while General Araki was War Minister, Japan planned to expand northwards and to invade the Soviet Far Eastern territory. Food and equipment were needed by the Bolsheviks in the east to counter this threat. The Soviet Union was bled dry of food to finance defences and thus to give the appearance military strength in Siberia north of the Manchukuo border. It was important that the Japanese believed the Soviets "awaited their attack without anxiety." Thus Stalin allowed the food and fuel shortages to be attributed to difficulties accompanying the first Five-Year Plan. "It worked," wrote Duranty. "The Japanese moved south instead of north, and China bore the brunt of Japanese Imperialism." Thus Duranty justified his guilty secret in the latter years of his life.[17]

Duranty was not the first person to express this point of view. Whiting Williams had published an article on March 3, 1934 where he stated that an intelligent, educated informant had said to him; "Machines are more important than men. ...Even if we don't export any of it [wheat], I expect that there will be some of it wanted for the War Chest." He went on to explain that the situation in the Far East was so grave that the Government had no choice but to build up reserves of food and essential stores for use in the event of emergency.[18]

There is a curious correlation between Duranty's final justification for the famine and Gareth's interview with Maxim Litvinov. Litvinov said:

> Up to advent of Hitler I believed it possible that... [the] only danger of war lies in [the] East. There, Manchukuo is a Japanese province and Japan wants to go further. Expansion may lead to conflict with United States on one hand and with the USSR on the other hand, if expansion [is] towards our frontier.
>
> Refusal of Japan to sign the pact of non-aggression with us means that war with USSR is within [the] practical plans of Japan. In this respect we must admire the sincerity of Japan. They don't veil it. [They] say: "We don't want to tie our hands. We may attack you."
>
> That's how I regarded it few months ago. But now I'm not so sure something may not happen in the West. I wonder whether Hitler is in position.[19]

Litvinov's analysis may well have been the catalyst for Gareth's desire to investigate the situation in the Far East for himself. (Japan eventually moved south following the strategies of the War Minister, General Hayashi and the 'strike South Faction', but this was never attributed to Stalin's diversion of food from the breadbaskets of the Soviet Union to finance a possible war zone.) It is the author's belief that this change of plans by Japan had a direct bearing on the Gareth's death.

Notes on Chapter 24

1
Walter Scott, *Marmion*, Canto vi, stanza 17. (Sometimes attributed to Robert Burns.)

2
"Journalists In Russia" *Manchester Guardian*, August 21, 1933. Also Chamberlin 1934 *Russia's Iron Age*, p. 148-151; *Ukrainian Weekly*, September 11, 1983, No. 37, Vol. LI; Carynnyk *et al.* 1988.

3
New York Times September 17, 1933.

4
Ibid.

5
National Library of Wales. Gareth Vaughan Jones Papers Correspondence Series B6/8.September 29, 1933

6
Time Magazine, Foreign News, "Stalin to Duranty," January 8, 1934.

7
Gareth Jones 2015, *Tell Them we Are Starving*. p. 260 (Diary 3 p.27-8) transcript of the diaries held at the National Library of Wales. Gareth Vaughan Jones Papers Diary Series B1/15.

8
Walter Duranty, 1934 *Russia Reported*.,. Moscow, Gollancz December 16, 1933, p. 359.

9
These are the exact same words used by Duranty in his *New York Times* article of March 31, 1933.

10
Duranty, *Russia Reported* 1934. p. 313.

11
Carrynyk et al. 1988. *The Foreign Office and the Famine*, p. 202.

12
Ibid. p. 204.

13
Ibid. p. 204.

14
James Mace, "A Tale of Two Journalists" in Luciuk (ed.) 2003.

15
Carrynyk et al. 1988, p. 202.

16
Ibid., p. 309-313.

17
Walter Duranty, U.S.S.R.: The Story of Soviet Russia. (New York), J.B. Lippincott, 1940 p. 192. Quoting S.J. Taylor, Stalin's Apologist, p.239.

18
William Whiting. Answers, 'Why Russia is Hungry', March 3, 1934, p. 3.

19
Gareth Jones 2015, *Tell them we Are Starving*. p. 131 (Diary 3 p.25) transcript of the diaries held at the National Library of Wales. Gareth Vaughan Jones Papers Diary Series B1/15.

Chapter 25

Malcolm Muggeridge

"The first article he [Muggeridge] wrote about me after I had gone to Moscow was reasonably friendly. But other people were doing the same, so he thought it an opportune time to take the opposite stance. I foresaw years ago he would end up in the Catholic church. But he was great company and I still feel a genuine affection for him. If you see him say: 'Hello, you old rascal' for me." – Kim Philby[1]

When Gareth was attacked by Duranty he wrote to Malcolm Muggeridge in search of moral support, as the *Manchester Guardian* had published a series of his (unsigned) famine articles published in earlier in the same week. Muggeridge replied to Gareth on April 17, 1933, from Switzerland, where he was now working for the League of Nations International Labour Office:[2]

Thank you for your letter. I am glad you liked the M.G. articles. They were villainously cut. Duranty is, of course, a plain crook, though an amusing little man in his way. I broke finally with the M.G. over the Metrovick affair... As I wrote (in effect) to Crozier [the editor]: "You don't want to know what is going on in Russia and you don't want your readers to know either; if the Metrovick people had been Jews or Negroes, your righteous indignation would have been unbounded. You'd have published photographs of their lacerated backsides. They being just Englishmen, you refuse to publish the truth about their treatment or the general facts which make that truth significant — and this when the M.G. is packed with stories of what the Nazis are doing to the Jews and the Poles to Ukranian [sic] and Silesian minorities."

Also it appears that the M.G. refused permission to the Ukranian Bureau to republish my articles as a pamphlet, so they've [the Ukranian Bureau] asked me to write a 3,000 word pamphlet for them. I'd very much like to see your articles on the agricultural situation before I do this because it would strengthen the thing for me to be able to quote someone else. Would you send them to me, or any sort of rough draft of them, from which I could quote? If you send me a cutting of Duranty's piece, I'll gladly write to the New York Times a letter of protest. I am afraid I won't be in England for some time because I've got to get on with a book and I am hard-up. When I am in England, I'll be delighted to come to Cardiff and lecture.

Gareth evidently obliged and sent his copy of Duranty's *New York Times* article of March 31 to Muggeridge in Switzerland following his request for 'a cutting of Duranty's piece,' since it is now missing from Gareth's cuttings book. Richard Ingrams included Duranty's derogatory article about Gareth in his book, *Muggeridge: The Biography*. Ingrams remarked, "If not actually contradicting the Muggeridge/Jones account, Duranty and the *New York Times* had succeeded in creating a smokescreen of doubt."[3]

Duranty had been open in his attempt to destroy Gareth's reputation, but Muggeridge on the other hand, went on in later life to build part of his reputation on having personally exposed the Ukraine famine, but for whatever reason, never publicly wrote about Gareth on any occasion.

In the autumn of 1932, when Muggeridge arrived in Moscow as the temporary relief correspondent for the *Manchester Guardian,* he was a fully committed 'fellow-travelling' Marxist, having sold all his bourgeois possessions in anticipation of his future life in the workers' paradise. Concurrently, Gareth was either in Churt assisting David Lloyd George writing his *War Memoirs* or in London meeting friends, journalists and people of influence from whom Gareth was gaining first-hand information. High on the list of topics discussed was the Soviet Union and news of a desperate agricultural crisis was seeping into London through various informed channels, one of which arrived from Muggeridge in early October 1932; within a month of his arrival in Moscow.

According to Eugene Lyons, Muggeridge was still a committed "Fellow Traveller," on the foreign journalists' chaperoned visit to the opening of the Dniepstroy Dam in November 1932:

Muggeridge, himself, was among the most gullible on this journey, having only arrived from London, with all the preconceptions about Russia fostered by the paper he represented and other well-meaning liberal publications. I remember how he and another young Londoner defended their dream against the doubts and cynicisms of the more seasoned correspondents.[4]

Muggeridge's political awakening seems to have occurred by the time he wrote a critical article in January 1933 entitled, "Virtual Breakdown of Agriculture."[5] This used information which was readily available from translations of official speeches (as Muggeridge spoke next to no Russian, nor read it) possibly supplemented by some rogue provincial Soviet newspapers — thereby managing to pass the Soviet censor's pencil. Anything published in the USSR must, by virtue of being in black and white newsprint, be "the truth" and was out of the censor's remit. W P Crozier, the editor of the *Manchester Guardian*, published Bernard Shaw's pro-Soviet letter on March 2, 1933.[6] Shaw found, "Particularly offensive and ridiculous is the revival of the old attempts to represent the condition of Russian workers as one of slavery and starvation, the Five-Year Plan as a failure, the new enterprises as bankrupt and the Communist regime as tottering to its fall."

On January 14, the day after his article was published, Muggeridge wrote to Crozier requesting a £30 advance to make an unaccompanied journey to investigate the famine.

> *It is becoming increasingly obvious to me that the only way to write properly about the existing situation in Russia is to visit the provinces — especially North Caucasus, Kuban and if possible, West Siberia."*

On February 5, 1933, Muggeridge set off for the south, three weeks before the official travel ban on journalists was enforced. It is somewhat doubtful whether his itinerary actually included Ukraine, as he claimed in the course of his later famine articles and on February 26, he wrote again to Crozier:

> *Actually, I didn't get as far as I had hoped because it's difficult in Russia in the winter, especially now when there's no food at all outside the towns. Also, I haven't been very fit lately. But I think, in fact I know, I saw and heard enough to grasp the general situation.[7]*

On his return to Moscow, Muggeridge sent five articles in a diplomatic bag to his editor, which were not immediately published. Crozier in reply to Muggeridge on March 8, 1933 wrote that he found his articles were extraordinarily interesting, but that he had not yet published them because they were not factual enough and he proposed to leave out some of the comment, feeling that this method of presentation would be stronger. Crozier added that in view of public opinion various factions when reading them might make use of the inferences one way or another.[8]

On the same day, March 8, (their letters would have crossed) Muggeridge wrote to Crozier that his time working for the *Manchester Guardian* was coming to an end in Moscow because their regular correspondent, Chamberlin, would soon be back. In a circuitous manner he implied that he considered the *Manchester Guardian's* support of the regime was a mistake and that in his [Muggeridge's] opinion the Bolshevik system was bound within a year or so to be utterly discredited, but that it was not for him to advise on the policy of the newspaper. He would not trouble Crozier again except for sending him the occasional article. He ended the letter by saying, "I have an uneasy feeling on the whole I've been a nuisance to you since you became editor of the M.G. In any case the nuisance is at an end. Please give my kindest to your family."[9]

In later years Muggeridge claimed that he had lost his job through his famine articles, though clearly it was the fact that his time in Moscow had come to a natural end.[10] In fact, three unsigned articles by Muggeridge entitled, "The Soviet and the Peasantry," did eventually appear in *The Manchester Guardian* on 25, 27 and 28 March, 1933. The articles, according to Muggeridge,[11] had been held up to follow a series by their correspondent, Voigt, on the terror in the Polish Ukraine, and were run side by side with another series by him on the rise of Nazism.[12] Muggeridge tried to describe the whole grim situation, "To say that there is famine in some of the most fertile parts of Russia is to say much less than the truth; there is not only famine, but a state of war, a military occupation." He wrote about the abandoned villages, the absence of livestock, neglected fields; everywhere there were famished, frightened people and intimations of coercion, soldiers about the place, and hard-faced men in long overcoats. One particularly remarkable scene he stumbled on by chance at a railway station in the grey early morning was the sight of peasants with their hands tied behind them being loaded into cattle trucks at gun-point.

In his second article, despite his poor health, Muggeridge apparently managed to visit a farm on the outskirts of Kiev, where he interviewed a Ukrainian peasant, which is surprising in itself as he spoke virtually no Russian and had no interpreter with him:

In a village about 25 kilometres from Kiev (old capital of the Ukraine; enchanting town! Now Kharkov is the capital). I visited a collective farm worker, or kolhoznik.

[Muggeridge asked]… "What about the winter sowing?"

"Very bad."

"Why?"

"Again bad organisation. People lost heart and stopped working. Weeds everywhere, and, with the cattle dead, no manure; no horses to transport fertiliser even if it was available." He hushed his voice. *"There are enemies even on the Council of the collective farm. Now they wouldn't elect me on to the Council."*

"Some grain must have been produced. What happened to it?"

"All taken by the Government."

"It'll be better in that respect this year. You'll only have to pay a tax in kind — so much per hectare — and not deliver a quota for the whole district. When you've paid the tax in kind you'll have about two-thirds of the crop left for yourselves."

"If we get as big a crop as they estimate. But we shan't — not with the land in such bad condition and with no horses. They'll take everything again." He showed me his time-book. His pay was seventy-five kopeks a day. At open market prices seventy-five kopeks would buy half a slice of bread. He said that for the most part he spent the money on fuel. Sometimes he bought a little tobacco. Nothing else. No clothes, of course, or boots or anything like that.

"What about the future?" I asked. He put on a characteristic peasant look; half resignation and half cunning. *"We shall see."*[13]

Gareth wrote a letter of support to the *Manchester Guardian* to confirm Muggeridge's tragic description of conditions in the Soviet Union. Gareth's letter was published by Crozier on May 8, 1933, entitled, "*The Peasants in Russia, Exhausted Supplies*":

> *Sir,*
>
> *In a series of articles published in the 'Manchester Guardian' on March 25, 27 and 28, your correspondent described his visit to the North Caucasus and the Ukraine and summed up his impressions as follows:*
>
> *To say that there is famine is to say much less than the truth. The fields are neglected and full of weeds; no cattle are to be seen anywhere; and few horses; only the military and the GPU are well fed, the rest of the population obviously starving, obviously terrorised. Attempts have been made in your columns to discredit the views of your correspondent. The 'Moscow Daily News' has written on him an article entitled 'When is a Lie not a Lie?'*
>
> *…In each village I received the same information — namely that many were dying of the famine and that about four-fifths of the cattle and the horses had perished. One phrase was repeated until it had a sad monotony in my mind, and that was: "Vse Pukhili" (all are swollen, i.e. from hunger), and one word*

was drummed into my memory by every talk. That word was 'golod' — i.e.,
'hunger' or 'famine'. Nor shall I forget the swollen stomachs of the children in
the cottages in which I slept

...As a liberal and a pacifist, I wish that something could be done to relieve
the suffering of the peasants in Russia, which, according to foreign observers
and to the peasants themselves, is worse than in 1921. Already efforts are being
made to succour many of the German colonists, whose letters to their fellow
countrymen are tragic. These letters, some of which I have seen, contain such
passages as the following: 'We have not had for one and a half weeks anything
except salt and water in our stomachs, and our family consists of nine souls.'
From the Volga district we read: 'I went out to seek him and I went out to feed
him, but I couldn't find him. One cannot get lost on the road. It is marked by
human bodies. There is nobody left among all our friends who has anything
left ... Our brother's four children died of hunger.' The Evangelical Church
in Germany is helping, and those who wish to assist are advised to write to the
committee, 'Bruder in Not' (Brothers in Need), Berlin.

I hope that fellow liberals who boil at any injustices in Germany or Italy or
Poland will express just one word of sympathy with the millions of peasants who
are victims of persecution and famine in the Soviet Union.[14]

The day after Gareth's letter appeared in *The Manchester Guardian* there appeared
a critical reply by E. H. Brown, from the National Committee of the Friends of
the Soviet Union, an organisation now believed to have been funded in part by
Amtorg, a trading front for OGPU espionage operations in the USA (and coincidentally emanating from the same address as Shaw's letter of two months before).[15]
Brown countered Muggeridge's March articles in seven lengthy observational points
containing the usual pro-Soviet rhetoric. On the subject of kulaks Brown quoted
Russia Today:

One woman delegate, Tkacheva, from the North Caucasus, recounted how
the Poltava staniza "said they had no grain, and didn't carry but the grain collec-
tion plans. We deported this village. I helped to deport them. After they went
grain was dug out of the graves. You find pits under the beds, under the stoves.
The same at Slavinsk. There in the neighbouring collective farm they have got
nothing, but you find grain in the pits". Why did the kulaks succeed in persuading
whole villages, in some cases, to conceal their grain? Your correspondent thinks
it was because people feared they would have nothing to eat.[16]

In April 1933, Muggeridge left the Soviet Union to join his wife Kitty in Switzerland. It was apparent that he had become increasingly hostile towards the Soviet régime despite having being a protégé of his in-laws, Sidney and Beatrice Webb. Muggeridge remained on good terms with the Webbs and never appears to have been banned by the Soviets for his own defamatory famine articles, as he was allowed to visit the USSR on another occasion in 1958, accompanying British Prime Minister Harold Macmillan.

His book *Winter in Moscow* was published in February 1934, and in the preface he states, "The characters and events are real people and real events (those with a taste for the sport may even amuse themselves by trying to spot the originals); but no particular character or particular event is necessarily real." In one chapter he describes an ash-blond, bearded, pipe-smoking, wine-drinking elderly, Mr Wilfred Pye.'[17] Gareth, a young man, was none of these, but the description in every other respect suggests that Muggeridge may have had him in mind.

While on a train journey three peasants watch Pye eat an orange and then throw the peel into a spittoon. A young man (a Communist) on the train denied there was any food shortage, at which the peasant: "leant forwards, his hand went nearer the spittoon; suddenly made a dart and clutched the orange peel. He ate it up ravenously, giving none to his two companions." This passage is identical to Gareth's published words describing the ravenous peasant on his own train journey to Ukraine in his Berlin press interview. There are many other passages which can only relate to Gareth — Pye was "making more notes"[18] and Gareth regularly acquired "letters of introduction [that] took him from place to place". Before leaving London, Gareth had met the Soviet Ambassador, and was well versed with the political situation in India, both incidents are alluded to in Muggeridge's book. One highly imaginary passage in the same chapter refers to a "great English newspaper," which might be the *Manchester Guardian* and Muggeridge's own editor, Crozier and:

> *Pye's articles in the great English Liberal newspaper were widely read and widely quoted. Now at last, readers of the articles thought, we know what really is going on in Russia. It's a great comfort to think that there's at least one newspaper left that gives a balanced, objective, unprejudiced account of things; at least one journalist left who can be relied on not to lose his head; to give us the facts, truth, and leave us to form our own conclusions.*

A later chapter describes an imminent trip to the Soviet Union by Lloyd George, which would have coincided with Gareth's own visit in March 1933. On this occasion,

Muggeridge may have had Gareth thinly disguised as Lloyd George. Muggeridge undoubtedly portrays himself as the character Wraithby — and is probably the most faithful published account of his actual Soviet experiences. During Wraithby's (February 1933) trip to Kuban, he was engaged in conversation with a group of Communists and described one person in particular.[19]

After 1934, Muggeridge became almost silent on the famine for quarter of a century. Though he came close in his celebrated 1940 book, *The Thirties*, where he relied upon Lyons' *Assignment in Utopia* for a parody of Bernard Shaw's 1931 visit to Moscow referring to, "food shortage," and for some reason related none of his own experiences of the famine.

It was not until 1958 did Muggeridge publicly mention for the first time since 1933 his part in exposing the famine (as arguably he never actually mentioned his own contribution to its exposure in his book *Winter in Moscow*):

> *The articles I wrote describing the suffering and privations of the peasants, and the monstrous brutality of their treatment, were dispatched to the Guardian by diplomatic bag to avoid the censorship, and I knew that when they were published my position would be untenable. The articles duly appeared, heavily sub-edited, but even so caused some stir. In both the Guardian and the New Statesman letters were published calling me a liar. For confirmation of the truth of my report I had to wait for Khrushchev's speech at the 20th Party Conference in 1956, in which he gave his account of the 1933 famine and its consequences, showing mine to have been, if anything, an under-statement. While in Switzerland I wrote my book, Winter In Moscow, about my time in the USSR.*[20]

Muggeridge curiously omits the whole period relating to his February 1933 trip to Kuban and Kiev in his edited diaries published in 1962. His last Soviet entry is dated 29 January and his public dairies do not resume until his arrival in Switzerland. He was more forthcoming in his autobiography published in 1972 in which he recalled that "his journey to Rostov remained in his mind as a nightmare memory." Despite the cold, he broke his train journey several times, and what he saw made a deep, lasting impression of famine, which he would never forget. The famine was planned and deliberate: "not due to any natural catastrophe like failure of rain, or cyclone, or flooding. It was an administrative famine brought about by the forced Collectivisation of agriculture".

Notes on Chapter 25

1
  Knightley 1988. p. 253-54.

2
  National Library of Wales. Gareth Vaughan Jones Papers Correspondence Series 35-47 File 47.

3
  Muggeridge, The Biography, Richard Ingrams, Harper Collins 1995, p. 69.

4
  Eugene Lyons *Assignment in Utopia* 1937, p. 545.

5
  "Virtual Breakdown of Agriculture", *Manchester Guardian,* January 13, 1933, p. 13.

6
  Bernard Shaw *et al.*, *The Manchester Guardian,* letter to the editor. March 2, 1933.

7
  Manchester Guardian archives *(B/M463A/30)*

8
  Manchester Guardian archives

9
  Manchester Guardian. archives

10
  Ian Hunter. *Malcolm Muggeridge: A Life*, Nashville, Thomas Nelson Publishers, 1980.

11
  A Correspondent in Russia. (Malcolm Muggeridge) 'The Soviet and the Peasantry', *The Manchester Guardian.*
March 25, 27, 28, 1933 p. 9,10,10.

12
  Malcolm Muggeridge 1972 *Chronicles of Wasted Time. Volume I: The Green Stick.* London, William Collins &
Son Ltd., p. 211.

13
  Ibid.; "Hunger in The Ukraine" *The Manchester Guardian.* Monday 27 March 1933 p. 9-10

14
  Manchester Guardian: 'The Peasants in Russia, Exhausted Supplies', May 8, 1933. Letters to the Editor

15
  Manchester Guardian: 'Agriculture in Russia. Breakdown Denied', May 9, 1933. Letters to the Editor

16
  Ibid.

17
  Malcolm Muggeridge, *Winter in Moscow*, Eyre and Spottiswoode, London, 1934, p. 125.

18
  Lyons also refers to Gareth carrying a notebook. *Assignment in Utopia,* p. 576

19
  Malcolm Muggeridge, *Winter in Moscow*, Eyre and Spottiswoode, London, 1934, p. 248.

20
  Malcolm Muggeridge 1958 "Many Winters Ago in Moscow"

PART 7

A Year in the Wilderness (1933-34)

Chapter 26

Revolution which Sprang from Poverty

"I have for my leader," said one leading Nazi to me, *"a love which is as deep as my love for my country, and I have in him a faith than which no faith, even faith in religion, could be deeper. Hitler can never be wrong, and his orders I shall carry out to the death."*[1]

Gareth started his job as a staff journalist with the Cardiff *Western Mail* on April 1, 1933. He lived at home with his parents until October 1934 in the newly purchased house, once again called Eryl. He had a small bedroom at the top of the house which was always known as Master Gareth's room, and it was in this room over fifty years later the posters he had brought back from the Soviet Union in 1931 were discovered under his bed. Each day he caught the bus from Barry to Cardiff to his offices at the *Western Mail*.

Gareth at Cold Knap, Barry.

267

For the second time in that year, and barely a month into his new job, Gareth visited Germany in May 1933 to report on the new political situation. He had been to the country every year since 1921, at which time the mark had become worthless due to rampant inflation, and the savings of millions of families disappeared. Even when Germany had enjoyed a period of sham prosperity from 1925 to 1929 on borrowed money,[2] there were a steady million or two out of work, but when the cloud of Depression broke over the world in 1929 the figure sprang up to six million with a speed that terrified politician and workman alike. The Great War had destroyed a whole generation leaving no men of middle age. Gareth described these changes:

> *I have seen Germany in the depths of poverty and in growing prosperity, under democracy and under dictatorship, in a time of national despair and in a time of national awakening. When I first went there ten years ago, so chaotic were conditions that I paid 1,750,000 marks for a railway journey of 350 miles — and these 1,750.000 marks cost me in English money exactly 1s.10d. ... Then, gradually, I saw Germany recover. And I saw her change in other ways as well.[3]*

Gareth went on to comment on the new regime:

> *The German National Revolution, although possessing a far narrower economic, and philosophical foundation than that brought about by Lenin, has certainly been more rapid than its Russian counterpart. ... The lightning pace of the National Socialist triumph makes the French Revolution appear almost like prolonged slow motion.*
>
> *... The Brownshirts have put one party, and one party only, into control, and that is the National Socialist party, which has become as all-powerful as the Communists in Russia, and the Fascists in Italy. The Nazis have put themselves into the position of leaders in the universities, in all committees, in factories, on boards of directors, in schools, in public offices.*
>
> *... They have started a ruthless campaign against the Jews. Distinguished scholars and great men, whom we in Britain would be honoured to consider as our citizens, are not allowed to enrich German scholarship or law courts or hospitals. They have abolished two powerful parties, the Social Democrats, who numbered about 8,000,000 voters and the Communists, who numbered almost 6,000,000, and have seized their funds, the private property of those parties. They have imprisoned many tens of thousands of men and women for their political views and hold them now captive in prisons and concentration*

268

camps. They have swept away the liberty of the press, and they come down with a heavy hand upon any editor, who dares criticise the leader or his policy. They have created a secret police which will make still more nebulous any freedom of expression which may remain. ... They have re-organised education on lines of narrow nationalism and intolerance. They have had midnight bonfires of some of Germany's most valuable Socialistic books.

...Moreover, the German democracy of 1918-1933 was, in the eyes of young Germany, a régime of old men. 'Make way for youth', became the slogan of young people, and they were determined to overthrow the republic which had so little room for them. Young Germans not only felt themselves enslaved by their system at home, but also longed to break the shackles of the Treaty of Versailles. They were not willing to admit that they had been defeated in the war but attributed their debacle to a Socialist "stab in the back" in November 1918.

The War Guilt Clause, the sending of troops into the Rhineland by the French, the refusal to admit Germany into the League of Nations until 1926, the inferiority in armaments, the need to pay £100,000,000 a year in reparations — all these forces mounted up resulting in revolution in 1933.

What rankled most in the German mind was the taking away from Germany of lands inhabited by Germans, and placing them under peoples like the Poles, whom they despised. Millions grew up with the conviction that they would willingly die on the battlefield, to win back for Germany the Polish Corridor, and other parts which they longed to see re-united to the Fatherland.[4]

Perturbed at the rise of militarism as a result of the humiliation wrought on the nation following the Versailles Peace Treaty, Gareth wrote about the worship of the soldier under the Nazi Regime:

If you listen to the wireless in Germany today, you will hear in the intervals four notes being played time and again, and you find that it is the tune, "People to Arms! People to Arms!" which is being drummed into the ears and the minds of listeners.

... The worship of the soldier is again being implanted in the minds of young Germans, and no nobler death is presented to them than death on the battlefield. There is an urge, shared by almost all Germans, even by Socialists, to have a powerful army again, and this reverence for an army is typically described by Hitler in his autobiography when he writes: 'What the German people owes to the Army can be summed-up in one word, namely, Everything.

Towards the East! That is his policy, and to carry out that policy which means in the long run a war with Poland, he is determined to have a powerful army, a strong air force, and a modern Baltic fleet. Germany must expand and carry out the policy of conquering Eastern Europe which was the Prussian policy of six centuries ago.[5]

Gareth was so taken aback by the medieval terms applied to the Jews by the Nazis that he decided to consult *Mein Kampf* to try to understand the origin of this behaviour.

This is what he [Hitler] said of England. In this country of 'free democracy' the Jew is almost the unlimited dictator through the devious method of controlling public opinion!"

It was not the British, in Hitler's opinion, but the Jews who wished the destruction of Germany in 1914-18. Now the Jews, he says, are aiming at the destruction of Japan, for Japan is the barrier to a Jewish world dictatorship. Therefore, the Jews are now rousing the peoples of the world against Japan.[6]

He quoted directly from *Mein Kampf.* 'Everything which we see in human civilisation, in achievements of art, science, and engineering, is almost exclusively the creative production of the Aryan.' Gareth then remarked:

With one sentence Hitler swept the Japanese art, Chinese philosophy, and Jewish science, the achievements of an Einstein or the healing of Jewish doctors, into the wastepaper basket. The worship of the Germanic past led to an orgy of inventions about the history of Germany. The fact that the Germans are a people of mixed origin, and that the Slav element in the Prussian is exceedingly strong, were brushed aside scornfully, for Hitler had spoken, and Hitler was always right.

…Nazis launched a campaign against the Jews, because they believed that Jews were largely responsible for the decline in morals, and for the corruption in public life. They stated that the influx of Polish Jews had been damaging to Germany. The Jews were accused of the nefarious purpose of desiring the triumph of Parliamentarism.

…But the greatest loss to Germany, in my opinion, will be the loss in brains, in initiative, and in economic genius through which Jews enrich the countries where they live.

...Before me I have a German book called Christianity in National-Socialism, which attempts to proclaim and prove the following doctrines. First, that 'the philosophy of the Nazis is in accordance with God's creative will, and with the teaching of Christianity'. Secondly, that the principles and the deeds of the Nazis are practical applications of the doctrines of Christ, and finally, that the Nazis are the only true defenders of Christianity.

... The vast majority of German pastors have courageously refused to be dictated to by the Nazis and have kept their belief pure. They elected a non-Nazi, Pastor von Bodelschwingh, as first Evangelical bishop of the Reich, with control over 40,000,000 [Sic] members.

The German Protestants, in doing this, have been the first body in Germany to stand up against the dictates of Hitler, and have shown courage and determination. ... Christ has not yet conquered over the gentler, nobler idea which inspires better Christians than the Nazis, and which is summed up in the teaching, 'Love thy neighbour as thyself.'

The Catholics were no less happy under Hitler. While numbers of them were Nazis, there were millions who feared an attack on their institutions.[7]

Even more unsettling was that Gareth found much of what he saw, and heard, was strangely familiar:

Where had I experienced before a similar atmosphere of idealism combined with fear, of unbounded hope on one side, and of whispered despair on the other? Then I realised that it was in Soviet Russia and in Fascist Italy that the same atmosphere had encircled me.

The first point of contact was the idealism of many of the leaders. The Hitlerites expect a new heaven on earth, just as the Bolsheviks are convinced that they will build up in Russia a paradise. This idealism has led to an admirable feeling of self-sacrifice, courage, and selflessness, and the Brownshirt, who in Germany is willing to lay down his life for his leader, has his counterpart in the Russian Young Communist, who will work twenty hours voluntarily for the sake of the Five Year Plan. But the idealism of the Nazis and of the Bolsheviks has its dark side of intolerance, and their faith is that of the fanatic who, driven by deep emotion, keeps his mind completely closed to another point of view.

You cannot argue with a Nazi, or with a Bolshevik, any more than you could convince a fundamentalist believer in the Bible of the validity of Darwin's theories. 'Germany' has become a religion for the followers of Hitler, in the same way as Communism has become a religion for Bolsheviks. As in Soviet Russia and in Fascist Italy, art is to become a tool of the Government. The theatre has been put under the guidance of Nazis, who are turning it into a propaganda machine for the Nazification of Germany. The cinema is to be a weapon of the Government to make Germany into a Nazi paradise, and the result of this policy can already be seen in the nationalistic and military films which are now the vogue. The use of the cinema, of the stage, the staging, of vast demonstrations to arouse public enthusiasm, the booming of Nazi speeches through loud-speakers as one goes through the streets, the thousands of 'gay' flags — all these methods are similar to the propaganda methods of the Soviet Union.

Even the worship of Hitler makes one think of the worship of Lenin in Russia, and of Mussolini in Italy. In each office his photo hangs, just as Lenin's and Stalin's adorn the Bolshevik office. The cult of the leader is the feature of every dictatorship. However much the methods of the Nazis and the Bolsheviks may be similar, they differ profoundly in aims, for the Nazis believe in maintaining private property, whereas the Bolsheviks hold private property to be the root cause of human ills.[8]

Gareth continued to enquire of people from all walks of life about the situation in Germany. He found families who were hungry, that bread was scarce, and it was this hardship that had nurtured the seeds of the Nazi revolution. It was apparent from his writings that Gareth had great sympathy for the Germans people, but he was fearful of the new régime under Hitler.

The only political article that Gareth wrote about Germany after this series in June 1933 was on October 16, 1933, on her withdrawal from the League of Nations.[9] The League of Nations was synonymous in the German mind with surrender, compromise, and disgrace. However, the failure of the League of Nations to further the cause of disarmament was the main reason for Germany's outburst. Germany felt she was fooled by the promise of the Allies at Versailles to disarm and resented the position of inferiority to which she was condemned by her inequality in armaments. Gareth questioned whether this gesture of scorn in the face of Europe would lead to war?

It was not until June 1934 that Gareth was to visit Germany again to investigate the situation in Germany after Hitler had been in power for 16 months.

Notes on Chapter 26

1
Western Mail, 'Germany under the Rule of Hitler,' June 5, 1933, p. 9.

2
America and Britain lent money to the Weimar Republic and demanded high interest further impoverishing the nation.

3
Western Mail, 'Germany under the Rule of Hitler,' June 5, 1933, p. 9

4
Ibid., 'Germany was not Ready for Democracy', June 6, 1933, p. 9.

5
Ibid., Worship of the Soldier Under the Nazi Regime, June 8, 1933, p. 6.

6
Ibid., Campaign of Hatred against the Jews', June 7, 1933. p. 9.

7
Ibid., 'Nazis' Interpretation of Christianity', June 9, 1933, p. 11.

8
Ibid., 'Methods of the Nazis, Fascists and Bolsheviks', June 10, 1933, p. 11.

9
Ibid., Herr Hitler's Breakaway', October 16, 1933., p. 11.

Chapter 27

The World Economic Conference: Gold in the Coffers of the Banks

The poverty that Germany was experiencing was not unique, and Gareth was to review this problem against a global background in an effort to explain the causes of the Depression. Gareth was to compare the plight of countries he visited in the following year with situation he had observed in the USSR:

> *When I arrived in London [from the Soviet Union], and saw the placard "The Land Without Unemployment," the pathos and the hypocrisy of the state of affairs struck me. In Moscow, in Kharkhoff, in every city, thousands are being turned out of the factories. They receive no bread card, as I was told by numerous workers, or in some cases a bread-card for a fortnight. They receive no unemployment insurance. They are deprived of passports and are sent away from the towns into the countryside, where there is no bread and where they often know no one.[1]*

The problem of unemployment was universal and, returning to his home to assume his new post with the *Western Mail*, Gareth found that Wales was also in the depths of a deep Depression. The desperate plight of the colliers in the Rhondda, the mining district of South Wales, dominated the thoughts of all those concerned, and it took the nation's priority over current world events. Gareth was assigned the task of writing a series of articles from first-hand knowledge about the problem of tackling unemployment and poverty, not only at home, but abroad. It was his wish to stimulate thought, impart solutions and create action to solve the despair of the miners. Gareth wanted to stir consciences, as he believed that the politicians had no answer to the situation. He described the upsetting effects of Welsh unemployment:

> *In every mining village and town in South Wales there are men idle… Everywhere there are brains idle, intellects lying fallow and degenerating. The keenness is disappearing, and the discussions are getting threadbare. Apathy is*

growing, and disgust at life, and at the economic system is taking the place of the love of labour and pride at skill. Deterioration of the use of the hands has led to deterioration of the whole moral outlook.[2]

Gareth believed that by recounting his experiences in Europe and America he would make Wales aware of how other countries were coping with the scourge of unemployment. It would be an excellent opportunity for the Principality to study how Germany was tackling unemployment, as she appeared to be years ahead of Wales in the matter. The German miners had the same sorrows as the Welsh miners, but their suffering was far deeper and published an article in the *Western Mail:*

To carry out their aims the German Government encouraged a Voluntary Labour Service and set up thousands of labour camps throughout Germany. Germany led the way in unemployment and health insurance and was hopeful that these labour camps were a method of rescuing the youth of Europe from the demoralising effects of unemployment.[3]

He sent a copy of this article to David Lloyd George who replied:

May 3, Bron y de, Churt

My dear Gareth,

Thank you so much for your interesting article. Whether you are right or wrong about my speaking, it is a first-class piece of writing. The notes from the Unemployed Camps are valuable. The papers here do not fully report Hitler's speech. What is it he definitely proposes to do, and how? I am particularly anxious to know what his intentions are about the Land Settlement.

Best wishes, Ever sincerely,

D. Lloyd George[4]

During Gareth's travels across Europe in February 1933, he had visited North Czechoslovakia and noted that the workers there were also suffering, hit by tariffs and the machine age. Gareth pitied the people who received no unemployment pay at all, though a few of the jobless were given a bread card, which was worth only a meagre 1s.3d. per week.

In the previous July, Lloyd George had assigned Gareth the task of investigating the conditions in Italy and, armed with letters of introduction, Gareth journeyed to Rome. He reported:

Fascist Italy was suffering as much as most countries from the effects of unemployment… Mussolini waged his war on unemployment with great rigour. He set thousands of men to battle against the Pontine marshes which for centuries have spread the curse of malaria in many regions of Italy and was determined to reclaim for cultivation, land which was lying idle.

Mussolini fought unemployment with large schemes of public works, similar to those, which have been advocated by Mr Lloyd George and Mr Keynes. Roads and bridges were built. Rome was transformed, a task employing about 6,000 men in that city. Even so, Mussolini's schemes left untouched four-fifths of the unemployed.[4]

In the same article he turned his attention to the state of unemployment in America:

America is now following the example of Italy and Germany. President Roosevelt, the United States' new dictator, is forming a labour army. Unemployed men who enrol take an oath to remain in service for six months unless released earlier. After being examined medically, instructed in their work, and clothed in the Regular Army uniform, they go in bands of one or two hundred to work camps in the national forests, when they work for a dollar (4s. 2d.) per day and their food.[6]

Continuing his concern for the troubles of the poor in Wales, Gareth wrote about the problem of the slums, so near to his home and closely allied to the problems of unemployment. More than one million men, women, and children lived in slums in Great Britain. Gareth was appalled by the state of affairs in the town of Merthyr in the Rhondda Valley and in Dowlais, the birthplace of his mother. In the Rhondda Valley, the density of the population was as much as 23,650 persons per square mile.

I visited a house where the husband had been ill in bed with silicosis for twelve months, and where the whole family of seven lived in two rooms. The wife explained to me, 'The children have to sleep in a temporary bed in the kitchen at night.'

There were back-to-back houses, dampness, lack of through ventilation, bad windows which were smashed in or which were difficult to open and overcrowding. …Merthyr's task of clearing these slums was made especially difficult by lack of funds, due to the economic stress, which had hit Merthyr almost more than any other town in Wales.

... Though Britain had the highest standard of living in the world, about two hundred thousand families still lived in stuffy, overcrowded and dilapidated rooms in narrow, sunless streets. A big drive to destroy the slums has been launched and, clearing the slums would give jobs to builders. It would save the country unemployment benefit, lessen tuberculosis, and lower the amounts spent on fighting disease, and reduce expenses on crime treatment and prisons.[8]

Throughout the world there were 30 million unemployed.[9] Both David Lloyd George and Ivy Lee were deeply concerned about the worldwide economic malaise, and were aware that the origins of the Depression were largely the outcome of the acrimonious decisions taken at the Treaty of Versailles. Gareth's letter with its "harrowing account" of conditions in the United States was quoted in Lloyd George's book, *The Truth about the Reparations and War Debts*,[10] and he had researched material for a lecture by Ivy Lee on 'War Debts and the Gold Crisis'.[11]

Watching the political developments in the United States with interest, Gareth had closely monitored the 1932 election of Franklin D. Roosevelt who, on the strength of his New Deal, was elected President. Roosevelt abandoned his commitment to the League of Nations, in order to appease isolationists such a William Randolph Hearst, and thus was able to swing the Californian delegation's support in his campaign for the Presidency. The new President found "14,000,000 people out of work, miners starving in the Kentucky coalfields, hunger even in New York, panic in the financial centre of Wall Street, and the American banking system wrecked".[12]

The critical American situation was covered in Gareth's article published on May 5, 1933, in the *Western Mail*:

The Inflation Bill had been passed and there is thus an inflation of the dollar... This week Roosevelt went still further along the path of Financial dictatorship, and the dollar began a new chapter in its history. For on Wednesday, the House of Representatives gave the President power to issue $3,000,000,000 (£600,000,000) of new currency, and to reduce the gold content of the dollar up to 50%. There is thus an inflation of the dollar.

America's planning was going towards lines of economic self-sufficiency. She was bringing in an Industrial Recovery Bill with the danger of even greater quotas, tariffs and embargoes.[13]

He returned to America's problems a month later:

...America's revolution has been almost ignored in this country, for it coin-cided with the far more spectacular advent of Hitlerism in Germany. But it is nonetheless true that Roosevelt is moving rapidly towards State planning and State control of industry. [14]

Gareth was still riding on the crest of a wave following his successful series of articles covering Germany and the Soviet Union, when he was asked to cover the World Economic Conference convened on June 12, 1933, at the Geological Museum in London. Representatives from sixty-six nations gathered there and included on the agenda were prices, the Gold Standard, tariffs, quotas, subsidies and loans.

Despite the fact that King George V appealed for international co-operation, Gareth was to be disappointed. He hoped he would hear solutions to the world economic problems from the eminent politicians present but none were offered and Gareth found the most absorbing topic at the conference was entitled, "The great question mark is America." Gareth addressed the issue in his article on the Conference and suggested that the "spirits," the "forces" that dominated the conference were those of a desperate country seething with discontent and misery. America was a rich country with the two-thirds of the world's gold in the vaults of its banks, but where at the same time there was tragedy, hunger, starvation and sweated labour[15].

There were level-headed Americans delegates present at the Conference, including Norman Davies and the Secretary of State, Cordell Hull, but these delegates were answerable to the US Congress on their return home. Hull spoke on economic nationalism but did not mention war debts. Gareth wondered if just as President Wilson had worked on the Treaty of Versailles, but failed to have it ratified, would Congress vote down the motions passed at the London Conference? There was a danger that whatever the American delegates might do, their plans would be wrecked when they returned to their native land. Though the American delegates were sincere in their support of international co-operation, their ideals would be swept away at home by a wave of isolationism.

Gareth then questioned:

Would the Americans consent to cancel war debts? Will the Americans lower tariffs? Will they co-operate or not? Cordell Hull, Secretary of State, has been admirable in advocating the lowering of tariffs, and is the friend of a reasonable

internationalist policy. … These decisions, these forces from America would affect
the lives of South Wales' miners; of Argentine farmers, Glamorgan tin plate
workers and the New York engine-drivers.

What are those forces hovering invisibly over the delegates? The first is the
American home-town man, or Middle West farmer — honest and brave, but
who is now in misery. He thinks that the international bankers are to blame for
everything. … 'Why should we Americans pay for the war?' The second group
of spirits haunting the Conference are those of vested interests, who will fight
bitterly rather than lower tariffs. … The last set of spirits who fill the minds of
delegates is that of the American politicians, unscrupulous, pandering to public
prejudices. The American delegates will never forget these American politicians,
for it was they who wrecked Wilson.[16]

An American journalist introduced Gareth to Jimmy Walker, the ex-Mayor of
New York, who had been assigned to write a report of the Conference for the Hearst
Press. "'You're lucky to be out of Russia', Walker said with a smile."

After talking to this representative of New York politics, Gareth went to listen to
one who had diametrically opposite political views, namely the Soviet representative, Maxim Litvinov. Gareth who had interviewed this man in Moscow just 10
weeks before was eager to see and listen to his views. Seated in the auditorium he
made his notes of Litvinov's speech:

The Soviet Foreign Minister is liked and admired in all international gath-
erings, for he is frank and witty, and tells the world exactly what he thinks of
it. The hall was crowded, and all expected "fireworks," but none came, for M.
Litvinoff was mild and guarded. He made no open reference to the British
embargo on Soviet goods.

If the Soviet Union were given markets, for their exports and credits, he
promised about £250,000,000 of orders to the world, but this offer was received
with scepticism. The bright picture he painted of the Soviet Union was based
on Soviet statistics, which are unreliable, and intended to serve as propaganda
rather than a real contribution to the Conference.[17]

On the third day, David Lloyd George addressed the Conference on the British
position, but as he was no longer in office, he had no power to influence the revision
of the Treaty of Versailles.[18] Gareth reported on the 'Chief's' speech:

Had the [British] Government any plans for unemployment? Had anyone heard what were the plans or proposals the Government were going to submit on those vital issues upon which the future of the world might depend, not merely for ten years, but for generations?" "No, there are no plans; I regret it" said Mr Lloyd George.

'Tariffs', said Mr Lloyd George, 'were not a plan. We [the British] were undertaking the leadership of the World Conference.' He supposed that the questions of war debts, tariffs, restrictions, and quotas would be dealt with by the Conference. He presumed the question of the effect of mechanisation upon labour would also be a vital issue. Speaking to the delegates, he denounced the treatment of the Germans by the Allies. He could see the problem clearly. The answer was simply to cancel the Reparations and War debts.

The events of the Conference clearly highlighted the old rivalries in the world; the struggle between Austria and Germany behind Dollfuss's speech; the Anglo-American differences over dollars and debts, behind the speeches of Mr Chamberlain and Secretary Hull; and behind M. Litvinov's words, the antagonism between two systems — Capitalism and Communism.

Notes on Chapter 27

1
Gareth Jones, *The Daily Express*, 'Pitiful Lives of Soviet Factory Slaves', April 8, 1933, p. 9.

2
Gareth Jones, *The Western Mail and South Wales News*. 'Social Services War on Unemployment in Wales'. April 25, 1933, p. 14.

3
Ibid, 'How Germany Tackles Unemployment', April 27, 1933, p. 11

4
Ibid., 'Productive Work in Italy and USA Friday April 28, 1933, p. 11.

6
Ibid.

7
Ibid, 'Five-year Assault on the Slums, May 9, 1933. p. 6.

8
Ibid., The Slums of Merthyr and Dowlais', May 11, 1933. p. 11.

9
Ibid., *e Western Mail*, 'Invisible Forces at the Conference', June 13, 1933, p. 7.

10
David Lloyd George, The *Truth about the Reparations and War Debts*, 1932. p. 126.

11
An address delivered at De Pauw University, Greencastle, Indiana, February 21, 1932 by Ivy Lee.

12
Ibid.

13
Western Mail, The Dollar Inflation, May 5, 1933. p. 11.

14
Ibid. 'Greater Tariff', June 14, 1933. p. 5.

15
Ibid., 'Invisible Forces at the Conference,' June 13, 1933. p. 7.

16 Ibid.

17 Ibid., 'Britain's Policy before the World Economic Conference', June 15, 1933. p. 5

18 Telegram from Sir Ronald Lindsay to Sir John Simon.(Newspaper cutting. Source unknown.)

WASHINGTON, June 10, 1933.

Following Note received from United States Government, dated June 9 (begins):

"I am requested by Secretary of the Treasury to notify you that 75,960,000 dollars interest is due and payable on June 15, 1933, on account of your Government to, United States, pursuant to debt agreement of June 19, 1923. The debt agreement of June 19, 1923, requires 30 days advance notice in case your Government desires to make payment in obligations of United States issued since April 9, 1917, but I am requested by Secretary of the Treasury to advise you that be will be glad to waive the requirement of 30 days advance notice if your Government wishes to pay in that manner."

Telegram from Sir John Simon to Sir R. Lindsay, Washington.

Foreign Office, June 13, 1933.

Following is text of note, which you should communicate to-day to U.S Government... Juncture would inevitably be judged to mean that no progress whatever had been made towards such a settlement, and would, therefore, deal a damaging blow at the confidence of the delegates.

"In the circumstances, and in view of their action last December, his Majesty's Government had hoped that the United States Government would have been able to accede to the request of his Majesty's Government to postpone the payment of the June instalment pending the discussion of war debts as a whole since, however, this does not appear to have been found possible, his Majesty's Government are obliged to decide upon their course of action. Such a decision must, in any case, be of an extremely difficult character; and in considering it, his Majesty's Government have felt, their deep responsibility not only to -their own people, but to whole world, which is awaiting the deliberations and recommendations of Conference with the utmost anxiety."

Chapter 28

Stalin's Scapegoat

"And the Goat shall bear upon him all their iniquities unto a Land not inhabited."

(*Leviticus 16:22*)[1]

Whether the London Economic Conference marked the beginning of a forced period in the 'Wilderness' for Gareth, we may never know. His career to date had been quite meteoric, but now his star was to briefly glimmer, before waning into obscurity for almost a year. His articles describing the Conference and, in particular, the one that referred to Maxim Litvinov were stark and uninformative. Perhaps Litvinov, an admirer of the former Prime Minister's liberal policies, criticised Lloyd George directly for Gareth's outrageous behaviour in his condemnation of the Five-Year Plan. Gareth very rarely mentions Lloyd George again, the man who had praised his work when assisting him in writing his *War Memoirs,* and affectionately called him "My Dear Boy". One wonders whether the former Prime Minister shunned him on this occasion in the presence of Maxim Litvinov, and that he was belittled by his childhood idol, whom he admired as a leader of the Liberal Party. Was it on this occasion that Gareth learnt he was on the blacklist of the OGPU? Had Gareth suffered a further insult to add to the previously damning treatment he had encountered in his endeavour to tell the truth about the plight of the suppressed minorities in the Soviet Union?

Gareth had been brave enough to stand up and be counted and he must have been devastated by the way he was treated by politicians and his journalist colleagues. Did Gareth appreciate when he undertook to expose the inhumane deeds of Stalin that the personal repercussions were to be so great? It would take a strong character to stand-up to the rebuffs he had experienced by telling the truth about the famine in Ukraine, Russia and elsewhere in the Soviet Union, and it is no wonder that he was to be silenced by the faint-hearted. He may have considered that for his actions, he would merely be banned by the Soviet Union and face the verbal wrath of the left-wing intelligentsia. He may have thought that one day he would be able to return to Russia and Ukraine, if the Stalinist regime collapsed, as he firmly believed the prophecy of Paul Scheffer who predicted in 1929-1930 that: "the Collectivisation of agriculture would be the nemesis of Communism"[2].

It would have been a bitter disappointment to Gareth when he eventually realised that he might never return to Soviet Russia and Ukraine. He had spent his academic career studying Russian culture, history, and language which he spoke fluently. He was arguably as knowledgeable about the USSR as any contemporary colleague in Britain. He had written a treatise on the Soviet agricultural policies; he had assisted Dr Ivy Lee in writing a book on Russia, though it was never published, and written briefs for David Lloyd George on Soviet policy. Had he not been demonised because of his honest reporting, he might have been able to contribute much of his learning to the important debates of the day.

No longer in the exciting milieu of London, he was trampled on by his political acquaintances. The establishment had ostracised him for its own political ends, and his journalist colleagues shunned him, perhaps jealous of his international 'scoop' in exposing the Soviet famine. It was his German friends, Reinhard Haferkorn and Wolf von Dewall, that remained true. Another staunch friend was Paul Scheffer, who was to become editor-in-chief of the *Berliner Tageblatt* in the spring of 1934.

Though many of those who knew Gareth had decried his exposure of the famine, he felt vindicated following a visit to his friends, the Haferkorns, in Danzig. There, he met a diplomat who privately corroborated Gareth's Soviet observations and he informed his parents on Sunday May 28, 1933.

...The German Consul in Kharkov and his wife thought that my Russian articles gave a wonderful picture, but that it was really much worse than I described it. Since March it has got so much worse that it is horrible to be in Kharkov. So many die, ill and [are] beggars. They are dying off in the villages, he said, and the spring sowing campaign is catastrophic. The peasants have been eating the seed. To talk of a bumper crop, as Molotoff did, was a tragic farce, and he only said that to keep their spirits up, but nobody believed Molotoff. Many villages are empty. The fate of the German colonists is terrible, in some villages 25% have died off and there will be more dying off until August. In August, he said there would be an epidemic of deaths because hungry peasants would suddenly eat so much as to kill themselves.[3]

Just after returning from the USSR, Gareth had interviewed the exiled Soviet politician, Alexander Kerensky.[4] Kerensky, who preceded Lenin, became Prime Minister of the Russian Provisional Government in July 1917. According to Gareth, Kerensky was "one of the most dangerous enemies of the Tsarist Government and had played a great part in the overthrow of the Monarchy in March 1917".[5] He was receptive to Gareth's opinions of the changes that had come over his country since the Bolsheviks overthrew him in the October revolution of 1917 and shared his perception of Joseph Stalin:

> *Before his death in 1924, Lenin — in his famous political testament — wrote that certain features of Stalin's character were dangerous to the Communist party. Lenin had in mind the stubbornness of Stalin (Stalin's will power is stronger than his reason), and also the absence in Stalin of the feeling of personal fear. When Stalin is convinced of something, or wishes to obtain something, he pushes straight on regardless of the consequences. These two characteristics combined — stubbornness and an absence of personal fear — have made Stalin into the gravedigger of the Bolshevik dictatorship.[6]*

Gareth's last article on the Soviet Union was published in the *Western Mail* on April 20, 1933,[7] and though he expected further articles on the subject to be published in the major London newspapers, by the summer of 1933 none were forthcoming. Why was this the case and, for that matter, why was there so little reference to the famine in most British newspapers? In the spring of 1933 precedence had been given to news of the arrest of the six Metrovick engineers. *The Times*, in its parliamentary editorial and leader columns, covered the fate of these men comprehensively, but never once mentioned the plight of the starving peasants in the Soviet Union. The paper had published Gareth's Soviet articles covering his previous Soviet trips in 1930 and 1931 but did not do so again in 1933.

The last British references to Gareth's famine exposure for almost fifty years appeared were published anonymously in the *Daily Telegraph*.[8] Schiller, the German Agricultural Attaché in Moscow, declared that "the famine was not so much the result of last year's failure of crops as the brutal campaign of State Grain Collection."[9]

The *Western Mail* obtained an edited version of Dr Otto Schiller's article and published three articles in which it was stated that Schiller's report fully bore out the tragic conclusions of "Dr Ammende[10] and of Mr Gareth Jones".[11]

A possible explanation for this selectivity in news reporting may lie with the ownership of the paper or governmental pressure. At this time, the editor of the

Times was Geoffrey Dawson, and the owner was John Jacob Astor, the brother of Waldorf Astor. Astor was the husband of Lady Astor, who went with George Bernard Shaw to Moscow in 1931, and owned *The Observer* newspaper.[12] It was known that Dawson suppressed all negative news from Germany and Italy during the 'Appeasement' government of Neville Chamberlain [May 1937-May 1940]. It is therefore not beyond the bounds of possibility that the paper was influenced by government policies towards the Soviet Union. Sir Laurence Collier, head of the Foreign Office Northern Department, furnished a reply to Sir Waldron Smithers MP [a life-long anti-Communist] on July 2, 1934 who had enquired about the economic situation and the famine in the Soviet Union:

> *The truth of the matter is, of course, that we have a certain amount of information about famine conditions in the south of Russia similar to what has appeared in the press, and that there is no obligation on us not to make it public. We do not want to make it public, however, because the Soviet Government would resent it and our relations with them would be prejudiced… We cannot give this explanation in public.*[13]

Some years later George Orwell was to observe:

> *The sinister fact about literary censorship in England is that it is largely voluntary. The British press is extremely centralised, and wealthy men, who have every motive to be dishonest on certain important topics, own most of it.*[14]

The fact that Sir Walter Layton, editor of *The Economist*, and more to the left of the political spectrum than *The Times*, did not accept any of Gareth's articles, as promised, is also nonetheless understandable, albeit regrettable. In the summer of 1932 Jules Menken, a British journalist sympathetic to the Soviets, toured the USSR after which an account of his trip, "Russian Impressions", was published in a series of articles in the *Economist* in October 1932.[15] Following these articles, William Strang, in Moscow wrote a 'Confidential' memo to Laurence Collier at the Foreign Office, on 6 December 1932, (which also included a mild castigation of Duranty for his negative Soviet reporting):

> *I learn from Cairns that the Soviet Ambassador — whether Sokolnikov or Maiskj he does not say — recently had Sir Walter Layton and Jules Menken on the mat for some articles in the Economist on the Soviet Union written by*

the latter, after his visit here last summer, on the ground that they were not up to the Economist's usual 'objective' standard and painted too black a picture. "[16]

In the May, 1933, Layton published two very bland and non-committal articles signed as 'Our Correspondent' entitled 'Russia Revisited', which were certainly not written by Gareth.

When Ambassador Esmond Ovey was removed from his post in the British Embassy in Moscow, at the end of March, 1933, William Strang assumed the position of 'acting-Ambassador'. Ovey had been recalled to London to make a personal report on the arrest of the Metrovick engineers and according to Eugene Lyons on "reaching London he proceeded to lambast the Soviet Union... Sir Esmond's flaming indignation was particularly distasteful to the Moscow government. "[17]

The British Government was thus clearly aware of the famine in the USSR. Strang continued to enlighten the British Foreign Office about the agricultural crisis in the dispatches sent in the diplomatic bag and in telegrams. These were to fall on deaf ears in London and the British Government chose to keep silent about the tragic situation. Sir Robert Vansittart, permanent Under-Secretary of State for Foreign Affairs, and Sir Laurence Collier, Head of the Foreign Office, Northern Department advocated better relations with the Soviets. By July 1933, Vansittart, who was wary of the Germans and leant favourably towards the French, had made up his mind that Nazism was more dangerous for Britain than Communism. "It does not help us". he wrote to Simon, "to compare the internal excesses of Hitlerism with those of Bolshevism.[18]

Gareth's articles may have been too sensitive an issue for the British government to allow further publication. It was possible that a government, frightened of war with a military dictatorship, suppressed further reporting by Gareth fearing to give offence to the Soviet Union a country with whom they wished to remain on friendly terms for political reasons?

When probably at his lowest ebb, Gareth, fortunately returned to the safe haven of his family and his beloved Wales, where, while in the employment of the *Western Mail*, he was to write arguably some of his finest articles. The editor, Sir Robert Webber, assigned him the task of writing stories about the principality. The question is why Gareth, who was so knowledgeable about world affairs, was confined to writing about Wales and later to Ireland? Nonetheless, these articles

SIR ESMOND OVEY, the British Ambassador to Moscow, with Lady Ovey, at Liverpool-street Station yesterday.

Sir Esmond Ovey and his wife, Lady Ovey, on their return from the Soviet Union. March 1933.

about rural Wales gave great delight in their power and vitality of description, and were undoubtedly an antidote in anxious times, not only for Gareth, but also for their readers.

Gareth recorded for posterity the work of the dying trades of Welsh craftsmen and of home industries which were fast disappearing and have now gone forever; some even forgotten. Who would think that there was an oil industry in Wales when oaks were brought to the village of Brecha to produce a light oil and a residue of charcoal? Where does one find a coracle-maker today, a trade which went back to pre-Roman times? Gareth wrote of the wood-turner, who made spoons, ladles, platters, axe-handles and stools, and the hammer mill that had that had lain idle after turning for 300 years; the basket maker, the cooper-philosopher, and not least the poet in the clog-makers' shop of Tanygroes, who told him why the sycamore is the sacred wood of the craft. There was the tweed-maker of Talybont still producing Welsh tweed and flannel from the sheep which flocked on the mountain sides; all woven into his stories about the crafts of yesteryear. He wrote a series entitled "Horse and Hound" in which he described the character of colourful huntsmen and their Welsh hounds, ready for the chase, following the scent of the fox. Today these articles are a pleasure to read, and a record of past home industries.[19]

But some of his best articles were in the series, "Tramping in Three Welsh Counties". The first article, "Over the Edge of the Black Mountains" commences with a quote from Francis Bacon written more than three centuries previously: "If a man be gracious and courteous to strangers it shows that he is a citizen of the world".[20] The articles closest to his heart were those that he wrote about the farm at Blaenau where his forbearers had reared their sheep in the Black Mountains of Breconshire for ten generations.[21]

In another article in the same series Gareth recalls a mining town, which was brimming over with music, where he "listened to cornets and trombones vying with each other in a Niagara of melody," Gareth told an unnerving story, in view of his future fate:

I went on to a little town which delighted me — Cwmllynfell. It was so thoroughly Welsh, and so thoroughly alive. The children played on the heath in Welsh language and shouted greetings to strangers. It was here that I was for the first time in my life taken prisoner by bandits and ransomed. They were Welsh bandits, varying in age from seven to thirteen years, who seized me and took me to their tent. I have no complaints to make about my treatment by these outlaws, and they speedily released me from my captivity, when a supply of chocolate was forthcoming as ransom.[22]

In these pieces one can hear the sound of the tumbling water in the waterfall, savour the smells of the farmyard, see Gareth grope through the mist following the course of a mountain stream or experience the laughter of his jolly companions. His colourful mode of writing was an art now long dead in today's materialistic society. He wrote with emotion and with subtle pulpit humour, typical of Wales, perhaps forgotten with advent of time. He was able to evoke the senses of the reader, a descriptive talent which has too tragically, been lost today.

Gareth at the Wrexham Eisteddfod, holding a copy of the Western Mail, 1933.

Gareth wrote with passion of the Welsh Eisteddfod, where poets and authors keeping the Welsh language alive, gather for the accolades of the crown or the prestigious chair and where when the bard is chaired the hall echoes three times with the call "Ar Oes Heddwych?" (Is there Peace?) to which the answer is "Oes Heddwych". (There is Peace).[23]

Present at the August 1933 Eisteddfod in Wrexham, Gareth was to meet and hear David Lloyd George and perhaps attempt to mend the rift between the two men after an interlude of some 6 months. Gareth again, in his description of the event published in the *Western Mail* compared the oratory of the former Prime Minister to that of Adolf Hitler:

> *Where Hitler had trumpeted political accusations, Mr Lloyd George gave a word picture, with the mines closed, the workless lining the streets, but [where] the Eisteddfod pavilion was packed. Where Hitler would have been humourless, Lloyd George was delightful in his light witty speeches, as when he spoke of England having built Offa's Dyke to keep out the Welsh, "but some of us got through'. ...Lloyd George rejoiced that Offa's Dyke had gone and hoped that the dykes separating other nations would disappear.*[24]

When the ovation had died down after the Lloyd George speech and when the male voice choirs from the Rhondda, to which the great man had listened appreciatively, had faded away, Gareth took the opportunity to speak to his former "Chief". Proudly dressed in Bardic robes, Gareth asked him: "What do you think, Mr Lloyd George of the place of crafts in the country?"

His reply was like a flash: "Crafts are essential. You can't do without the crafts and rural industries if we are to restore Wales. ... Take my village, Llanystumdwy. It used to be self-supporting. Our boots were made from leather made in the tannery from our own cattle. Our clothes were home spun, and the wool was from our own sheep."[25]

Soon after the Eisteddfod meeting Gareth received a cordial letter from Frances Stevenson. Dated August 25 it was from Bron-y-de, Churt, Surrey:

Mr Lloyd George asked me to thank you for sending him cuttings of your very interesting articles. He has read them with the greatest of enjoyment and he congratulates you on having collected such an interesting series. When you are in this neighbourhood, do look us up. Mr Lloyd George would, I know be delighted to see you. With kindest regards, F. L. Stevenson.[26]

Gareth's poster promoting his lecture tour.

290

The rift seemed mended though there is no record of Gareth having visited the great man again.

Although no further articles were published by Gareth on the Soviet Union or Germany in the British national press, Gareth undertook a lecture tour throughout Britain and Ireland during the winter of 1933-34, including Cardiff, Newcastle, Manchester, Birmingham, Dublin and many other cities. This was entitled *The Enigma of Bolshevik Russia* with the aim to make public the failures of the Soviet régime. These were reported in provincial newspapers, though little mention was made of famine in the reports.

Even in the memorial book dedicated to Gareth, *In Search of News,* containing a selection of articles written by him, and published by the *Western Mail* in 1936, there is not a single reference to any of his famine articles, which they themselves had published in 1933. With the healing power of his touching stories, Gareth slowly emerged from the wilderness, and once again took on commitments beyond Wales.

Notes on Chapter 28

1
    William Holman Hunt's painting *The Scapegoat* is framed with the quotation beneath: "Surely he hath borne our Griefs and carried our Sorrows; Yet we did esteem him stricken, smitten of GOD, and afflicted." (Isaiah 53:4).

2
    Gareth Jones, *The Financial News* 'Balance Sheet of the Five-Year Plan, III — The Ruin of Russian Agriculture' April 13, 1933.

3
    Gareth Vaughan Jones Papers, National Library of Wales. Correspondence Series 1-21, File 14. May 28, 1933.

4
    Western Mail, 'We are Starving', April 3, 1933. p. 7.

5
    Ibid.

6
    Ibid.

7
    Ibid., 'OGPU's Blow to Soviet Union', p. 12.

8
    Otto Schiller had accompanied Andrew Cairns in Western Siberia, and Kazakhstan in early 1933 and in July of that year he went to Ukraine.

9
    The Daily Telegraph by An Expert Observer (Otto Schiller), 'Famine returns to Russia, August 25, 1933', p. 10.

10
    Dr Ammende, Secretary General of the European Nationalities Congress. To quote, John Vyvyan of the British Foreign Office 'Muggeridge, has no doubt that Dr Ammende, whose protégé is Dr Dietloff, is financed as an agitator by the German Ministry of Propaganda'. *The Foreign Office and the Famine,* p. 409.

11
    Western Mail, 'Russia's Starving Peasants August 28, 1933', p. 8; 'Famine's Aftermath in Russia. Corn Growing in Fields Where All the People Have Perished', August 30, 1933, p. 10.

12
    During the 1930s, Lady Astor entertained the great and the powerful of the time at her home, Cliveden. She

numbered among her close friends, Lord Lothian who later became known as the second arch-appeaser and George Bernard Shaw. She entertained others who were kindly disposed to Hitler and the Nazis whom Gareth knew including Dr Thomas Jones. Like many at that time she disliked the French and though not herself known as an appeaser, many whom she entertained were known to be so.

13
    Marco Carynnyk et al. 1988 *The Foreign Office and the Famine British Documents on Ukraine and the Great Famine of 1932-1933*, p. xix.

14
    George Orwell, *Animal Farm,* Penguin Books, 1951, p. 99.

15
    By a Correspondent, (Jules Menken), Russian Impression' *The Economist,* October 1, 8, 15, 1932 p . 584-5, 629-30, 676-677.

16
    Foreign Office and the Famine. p. xxix.

17
    Eugene Lyons, *Assignment in Utopia,* George G. Harrap and Co, London, 1937, p. 563.

18
    The Foreign Office and the Famine, p. xiv.

19
    Gareth Jones 1935. *In Search of News. A Selection of Articles from the Western Mail.* Cardiff, *Western Mail* & Echo Ltd.

20
    Gareth Jones *Western Mail* "Tramping in Three Welsh Counties: Over the Edge of the Black Mountains" September 14, 1933.

21
    Ibid.

22
    Gareth Jones *Western Mail* "Tramping in Three Welsh Counties: Mining Town Brimming over with Music". September 13, 1933.

23
    Gareth Jones, 'The Eisteddfod', *Western Mail*, August 8, 1933.

24
    Ibid.

25
    Ibid.

26
    Gareth Vaughan Jones Papers, National Library of Wales. Correspondence Series 1-21, File 20. August 25, 1933.

Chapter 29

"The Enigma of Ireland"[1]

Malone: *"Me father died of starvation in Ireland in the Black '47. Maybe you have heard of it."*
Violet: *"The Famine?"*
Malone: *[with smouldering passion] "No, the starvation,. When a country is full of food, and exporting it, there can be no famine. Me father starved to death; and I was starved to America in me mother's arms..."*[2]

Unable to stay in the wilderness forever, and with his self-esteem now recovering, Gareth reached out for new pastures. On a visit to London, he met people with conflicting opinions about the state of Ireland, both north and south, and Gareth was inspired to investigate the problems of the 'Emerald Isle', which many British governments had (and have) failed to solve. When the Anglo-Irish Treaty was signed in December 1921, twenty-six southern counties became the Irish Free State, a dominion within the British Commonwealth of Nations. Of the many memoranda that Gareth produced for Lloyd George, Ireland was not one of them, so Gareth took it upon himself to visit the country. As he had stated in an early diary on January 6, 1930 when referring to a newspaper article: "I was surprised Lloyd George did not bring in Ireland, since something on Ireland would suggest to the British public that since Lloyd George solved Ireland he would solve India."[3] He became determined to investigate the cause of the factions in Ireland, visiting the country in November, 1933, and again in March 1934, partly because his intended interview with Eamon de Valera had to be postponed because of illness.[4]

The Irish, like the Welsh, felt that they had been dominated by the English; the Celt was subservient to the Anglo-Saxon. The culture of Britain in the inter-War period was dominated by the Establishment, the men who had received a public (private) school education, and who were primarily Oxford and Cambridge graduates. Gareth was a grammar school (state) boy with a 'regional', Welsh accent. The

English had always ruled the Welsh and so Gareth was sensitive to the rights of the minorities. Ireland was another country suppressed by the English, a Celtic country with whom Gareth as a Welshman, felt a great bond and sympathy towards its people. The Irish had a catastrophic famine in the 1840s; a further reason to dislike the British, and why they wished to strive for independence from Britain.

"Mark my words, Ireland is heading full-speed towards the blood and terror of a civil war" a white-haired old gentleman rapped out as Gareth and he sipped their coffee in the Reform Club.

Startled at this remark Gareth contacted a friend who retorted: "Civil war! Nonsense! De Valera has the whole country at his command and is building up a stronger, finer Ireland, and winning the economic battle against England."

Intrigued, Gareth contacted an expert on the Irish Free State, who declared: "De Valera, that half-Mexican dictator, is sending the country to wrack and ruin. Ireland is doomed. O'Duffy's Blue Shirts[5] are the only ones who can rescue the country."[6] Gareth wrote of his bewilderment in the *Western Mail:*

> *What a medley of clashing views! The more I asked the more I was puzzled by the varying analyses of those, on one hand, who described a sinister Irish Republican Army, drilling in secret with smuggled rifles and machine-guns, and of those on the other — especially Welsh Nationalist friends of mine — whose picture of Ireland was a land blossoming under de Valera into a paradise of prosperous peasant proprietors; of those who bade me hasten there lest I should be too late to see de Valera declare a republic; and of those who said a republic was never to come.*
>
> *These conflicting opinions made my urge to go to that land of dissension almost irrepressible, and thus I found myself on the Belfast boat watching the lights of Liverpool twinkle good-night, and wondering whether I should ever glean the slightest information about that most fascinating and yet most tragic of enigmas — the enigma of Ireland.*[7]

A political organiser whom Gareth had met in the north described the political and religious strife, and declared with passion, undying loyalty to Britain:

> *We in the North are British to the core. The Protestants are made more British by their antagonism to the Catholics, who usually become more Nationalistic against Protestant domination. The Protestant versus Catholic fight becomes a British versus Irish struggle and the Protestant section (nearly two-thirds of*

the population) do all in their power to keep the upper hand over the Catholic minority. We are two nations, North and South.[8]

On his arrival in Belfast, finding that the dissension was so bad, Gareth asked his hostess why it was so, and she replied by telling him a story of an English family, who had come to live in Ulster, and who laughed at the tradition that Catholic and Protestant servants could not be mixed:

They engaged a Catholic cook — fat and forty — and a little wisp of a Protestant kitchen maid. The experiment was a great success, and the atmosphere in the kitchen was as amicable as it could be, until the family went away for, a holiday, leaving the pair behind. One day the English people received a telegram, "Come back immediately. House wrecked." They took the first train home, entered the house, and found shattered furniture, broken pictures, and a litter of smashed crockery. After a bout of questioning, they got at the cause of the destruction. The Catholic cook and the Protestant maid had been seated happily before the fire when the cook said, 'I wonder what William of Orange is now doing in hell?' 'Having a chat with the Pope, probably', replied the Orange girl — and the furies of centuries of religious strife entered their souls, gave power to their arms, and they did not rest until they lay weary amid the wreckage their fight had caused.[9]

In Belfast, Gareth interviewed the Lord Craigavon, Prime Minister of Northern Ireland, who in character, as Gareth was to describe later, was the very reverse of President de Valera, his counterpart in the Free State of Ireland. Craigavon had a few ideas firmly embedded in his mind, and from these he would not move one inch. One of the main causes for the quiet and solidity in Northern Ireland was that Craigavon, who carried on the tradition of Edward Carson was a man devoted to Ulster. He had dominated the affairs of the country since taking over the reins of office in 1920 and he reaffirmed his stance: "Ulster stands as firm as a rock for Britain, and for the Empire. But under no circumstance could the people of Northern Ireland consent to come under a Free State or Republican Government."[10] Gareth left the interview listening to him booming a criticism of the new militia in Southern Ireland.

Travelling to southern Ireland, the background of the Irish problem as the Nationalist Irishman saw it, was illustrated vividly to Gareth as he explored Dublin with a jovial, energetic Irishman who had fought in the 1916 Rising, had been sought by the British, captured and imprisoned, and later reached a high position in the Free State Government. He was Professor Michael Hayes, who had been Speaker in the Cosgrave Parliament. He pointed out a building to Gareth:

> *That building, brings back memories of the shot and shell in 1916, when, on Easter Monday, we rose against the British and occupied the building. For almost a week this street — one of the finest in Europe — was a shambles. You could hear the thud of the British bombarding us from the river a few hundred yards away. We stuck out until the Saturday, a grim feat of determination. Just think of it, a small band of men defying an empire for the sake of freedom.*
>
> *'There', Prof. Hayes pointed to a bare wall in an ugly patch of ground, 'That is where a number of Irishmen were shot down. That is Mountjoy Prison', he said. 'That is where the battle for freedom was won, for behind those walls the young leaders of the Easter Week Rising were executed.' I myself spent some time behind prison-bars here', and he smiled.*
>
> *'This is where Dick Mulcahy, who was Chief of Staff, hid in my rooms for many months in 1919, when he was on the run and when the British had a hue and cry after him. We had a narrow escape one night, when a British officer and a policeman came to raid us, but Dick just got out in time over the roof!'[11]*

Walking on further, Gareth was shown the streets and canal banks where the conflicts with the Black and Tans in 1920 occurred — and he wrote:

> *Events which make young Irish people clench their fists. To the British these are vague happenings in a distant age, but to the Irish they are ever present, for in Irish politics, memory of the past is the most important factor.*
>
> *The Irish pass these spots every day; they still mourn friends executed in the times of trouble; they can see the bullet marks on the Bank of Ireland columns; every stone speaks of the struggle against the British. To the British, 1916 is many years ago, and the Irish War of 1920 is stuff for memoirs, not for emotions; but to the Irish they both happened yesterday, and for them Cromwell lived only the day before. As a result, hatred of Britain still is the greatest rallying-cry to whip up Irish feelings.[12]*

Gareth then visited the house of the late Kevin O'Higgins who had devoted himself to stamping out the rule of the gun in Ireland, though in the end the gun had triumphed over him — an Irish gun. The shot which killed him brought an echo of the days when in 1922 'Free Staters' scoured the country for rebelling Republicans, and when ambushes by Irishmen took toll of Irish lives. Gareth met the widow of this stern former Minister of Justice, who was a statesman, and even had the makings, it was said, of a dictator, but who was so hated by his opponents that in 1927, he was shot down on his way to Mass not long after he had declared: "The South of Ireland is quite safe now, (even for him!)"[13] Gareth wrote to his parents "I found Mrs O'Higgins one of the most striking personalities and most brilliant conversationalist I have ever met."[14]

Gareth described the current situation as seen through the eyes of contemporary Irish politicians that he interviewed:

> *Although the "Cease Fire" of 1923 ended the internecine bloodshed, memories of Civil War are green. Republicans still recall their fellow-fighters being blown to pieces by Free State bombs, and Free Staters cannot forget the ambushes which destroyed some of their finest soldiers, such as Michael Collins. Desire for revenge, lives on from the Civil War.*[15]

Gareth drove to a meeting at Kilkenny, at which, the leaders of the Blue Shirts, Gen. O'Duffy and Mr Cosgrave; de Valera's greatest opponents, spoke. He returned by car to Dublin with Mr Cosgrave, the first President of the Irish Free State. Cosgrave had been condemned to death after fighting in Easter Week, 1916, but later the sentence was commuted to penal servitude for life. He had supported Arthur Griffith and Michael Collins in fighting for the treaty with Britain. As President, Cosgrave built up a new State after the foundations of law and order had been swept away in Ireland, and when bands of Republicans were seeking to overthrow the Government by force and denounce the treaty with Britain. Cosgrave believed that de Valera was undermining the strong economic structure which he had founded. Cosgrave's comment on the economic war between the Free State and the United Kingdom was that he doubted if in the circumstances any two Governments in the world desiring — as these two Governments assured each other they did — amity and concord would have allowed a situation to develop so harmful to both countries.[16]

The United Ireland Party in opposition, with their youth organisation the Blue Shirts, represented Mr Cosgrave's party and they were battling against de Valera for the maintenance of the treaty with Britain and for the end of the economic war. The leader, O'Duffy believed that de Valera's policy had brought disaster upon the farmers of the country caused by the economic war, and the tariff put on the goods going to Britain. Gareth reported on the meeting to his parents:

> *On Sunday I went to the United Ireland Party meeting and saw all the fun there. The IRA tried to interfere with the meeting and there were scuffles with the police. The soldiers (in steel helmets and gas masks) were called out. I had a splendid view from the platform…* [17]

Having met the leaders of the United Ireland Party Gareth decided to interview a member of the force in armed opposition to the Free State — the Irish Republican Army (IRA):

> *One morning I set out to find "Mr Gallagher" (that is not his real name), who, I was told was an IRA officer. …He attacked the Blue Shirts as tools of England and O'Duffy as an Imperialist … We want freedom. We cannot discuss economics until we have freedom," but he stated, "that an economic structure could not be built unless it had its foundations in nationality".*

This reply pointed out one of the greatest weaknesses in Irish politicians of Republican hue, namely, an emotion which bids them cast aside practical problems of bread and butter as something unworthy compared with a vague ideal of freedom. Their answers to questions on trade or exports or finance were usually of the utmost ignorance, and were couched in terms of nationalistic sentiment or of dramatic allegory which have no reference to the question asked:

> *… 'We are an independent body and are independent of Mr de Valera. We differ from the Fianna Fáil (Mr de Valera's party) in that Mr de Valera and his followers have thought that by working through the Free State Parliament, and eventually by obtaining a majority in Parliament, they could by constitutional means restore the Republic'.* [18]

Gareth later found that: "I had come to the right source for a judgment of the character of IRA leaders, for when I told an Irishman that I had met 'Mr Gallagher', he was surprised and said, 'He **is** the IRA'" [19]

Gareth returned to Dublin in March 1934. After listening to an attack on the Irish Government in the distinguished hall of the Dáil [Éireann], the Free State Parliament, by Mr James Dillon, son of the Irish Nationalist, John Dillon, of Westminster fame, Gareth left for an appointment with de Valera (who had been unable to see him in the previous October). He was not as Gareth had imagined him:

This curious personality, who still has a great hold over the uneducated masses, and almost dictatorial powers over members of his Cabinet, who hesitates to declare a Republic and yet has destroyed some of the links between Ireland and the United Kingdom.[20]

I expected a grim, fierce, rigid type, but I found a man whose face lit up from time to time with a subtle, charming smile. After shaking hands, he bade me sit by him at the desk, and began discussing the respective positions of the native language in Wales and in Ireland.

…Welsh has been preserved as a spoken tongue and has been used and is being used in life and literature to a far greater extent than Irish is being used in Ireland, but we are making headway in preserving Irish as a community language and extending its use throughout the country.

He then described an historic talk between himself and Mr Lloyd George in 1921 in which the Prime Minister asked him: 'Have you a word for 'Republic' in Irish?' Mr de Valera replied that there was a word, 'Poblacht', but that some doubt had been expressed by purists as to whether that was a good chosen Irish word, and the word 'Saorstat' was chosen instead.

'What does that word mean?' asked Mr Lloyd George. Mr de Valera said it was a compound word — 'Saor' free, and 'Stat', state, 'Free State'.

Contrasting nationalism in Wales with that in Ireland, Lloyd George said that the Welsh people had paid more regard to linguistic and cultural nationalism than the Irish people, and that for a considerable period the idea of political independence had overshadowed the cultural aspects of nationality in Ireland. The more the people of Wales and other countries with their own distinctive cultures retained their national individuality the richer would be the variety of thought and achievement in the world.[21]

Gareth portrayed De Valera as: "a dreamer with vague thoughts that wandered over the face of the globe"[22], who aimed at making Ireland self-sufficient and embarked on an economic war with Britain. Gareth was informed that de Valera's Government had squandered the reserves built up by Mr Cosgrave, and that the country was living on its capital.[23] In 1932, de Valera refused to pay land annuities to England, following which both England and Ireland set up barriers against each other's goods. Prices of industrial commodities rose on account of the tariffs placed upon the import of British products. The greatest loss, however, had been among the farmers, who were called "the crippled soldiers of the economic war." The cattle situation was a disaster. Prices had fallen so steeply that it no longer paid either to breed or to graze cattle.[24]

The tariffs had not only brought about the smuggling of cattle across the border to Ulster, and thus to England to avoid duty, but also to a store of jokes, one of which Gareth described on his first visit to Ireland:

A road outside a Customs house, along which was rushing a motor-car containing a farmer-smuggler at the wheel, and as its only passenger [was] a cow with a muffler around her neck. The farmer shouted to the Customs officer: 'Don't stop me, officer. My cow's got a very bad cold, and I'm taking her to the vet!'[25]

Before leaving Dublin in March 1934, Gareth spoke at the Dublin Rotary Club meeting on 'The Russia of Today'. He gave a wide-ranging lecture on the régime but made no mention of 'famine' or 'death from starvation', merely using the phrase 'sheer hunger', possibly for diplomatic reasons not wishing to refer to the Irish famine of 1845-9. The crushing of religion and the worship of the machine rated high in his talk. The vote of thanks praised Gareth, describing him the most eloquent speaker they had had for some time, and placed him alongside the finest orators known in the [19th century] English Parliament — Parnell, Sexton, Healey and Dillon (Irish Nationalists) to name but a few famous Irish men.[26]

Gareth's affection for Ireland was clear and his visits to the country were sufficient to lift his spirits and restore his confidence away from the hostility of the 'wilderness'. His sense of fun had returned. Slowly he had risen from the depths of dejection, and he started to make plans for the future.

Irish hospitality knows no national boundary, and to individuals it is gay, unselfish, and sincere. Irish friends are of unlimited kindness to visitors, whether they be Welsh or English. Their humour is spontaneous and so irrepressible that even the President is not spared its shafts.

Notes on Chapter 29

1
Western Mail. 'The Enigma of Ireland', November 6, 1933, p. 11.

2
Man and Superman by George Bernard Shaw, Constable & Co Ltd, first published 1903. 18th impression 1926 p.150. In 2003, on looking through this book which had belonged to Gareth, his great nephew, Nigel Colley found that it naturally opened up at this page, perhaps for the first time since Gareth had used the book.

3
Gareth Vaughan Jones Papers, National Library of Wales. Diary Series B1/3.

4
Gareth Vaughan Jones Papers, National Library of Wales. Correspondence Series 1-21 File 19. October 29, 1933.

5
Blue Shirts. A fascist organisation led by General O'Duffy.

6
Western Mail. 'The Enigma of Ireland', November 6, 1933, p. 11.

7
Ibid.

8
Ibid.

9
Western Mail. 'The Enigma of Ireland', Ulster a Centre of Uneasiness and Strife, November 6, 1933, p. 11.

10
Western Mail, 'Ulster More British Than the British', March 10, 1934, p. 7.

11
Ibid., 'Hatred of the British and Internal Dissension', November 7, 1933 p. 11.

12
Ibid.

13
Ibid.

14
Gareth Vaughan Jones Papers, National Library of Wales. Correspondence Series 1-21 File 19. October 20, 1933.

15
Western Mail, 'Hatred of the British and Internal Dissension', November 7, 1933, p. 11.

16
Ibid., 'Mr Cosgrave's Fight for the Treaty', November 8, 1933, p. 7.

17
Gareth Vaughan Jones Papers, National Library of Wales. Correspondence Series 1-21 File 19. October 26, 1933.

18
Western Mail, 'Policy of the Irish Republican Army', November 9, 1933, p. 7.

19
Ibid..

20
Ibid., 'Ulster More British Than the British', March 10, 1934, p. 7.

21
Ibid., 'De Valera Praises Wales', March 12, 1934, p. 9.

22
Ibid.

23
Ibid., 'Why de Valera Hesitates to Declare a Republic'. November 10, 1933. p. 8.

24
Ibid. .

25
Ibid., 'How Long Can Free State Maintain Economic War', November 11, 1933, p. 11.

26
The Irish Times, 'The Russia of Today', March 6, 1934.

PART 8

Germany Calling

Chapter 30

New Directions

Encouraged by his successful trip to Ireland, Gareth was now ready to return to his first love of reporting political events. During this quiet period in his life he had listened to the legends of the past, that dwelt in the folklore of Wales, and was inspired by hearing them in his native Welsh. He was welcomed with such kindness by the inhabitants in the land of his forbears that its very nature healed his wounds, and it appeared to leave no signs of personal bitterness. His visits to Ireland, where he received "hospitality which is so warm that it melts at once even the freezing national antagonism, and humour which is so sparkling that it even lightens the strife" and uplifted his spirits. Always convinced that he was correct in his evaluation of international situations, his self-confidence returned, and he had recovered from the ordeal so cruelly dealt to him in the previous twelve months.

Before taking his first step back into the politics of mainland Europe, Gareth decided to make a private visit to Berlin with two friends and in his Sunday letter of June 3, 1934, he told his family:

> *This afternoon Eric, Idris Morgan and I are going to the great [Berlin] Flying Gala where we shall hear Goering speak. It will be a great occasion; thousands of balloons and aeroplanes will fly; the aeroplane storm troopers will march and will be received by Goering in his capacity of Air Minister. The aeroplane Stormtroopers look fine in a blue-grey Uniform.*[1]

Though Gareth wrote an article about this event at the time, his paper decided for reasons unknown, not to publish it until August 1934. It was entitled '10,000 planes on German Frontiers', in which Gareth warned his readers:

> *As I stepped out of Berlin's main station some days ago I saw stretched high across the street a brilliantly blue banner with these words written large upon it.*

'Germany Must Become a Nation of Aviators!' It was a declaration of Germany's greatest ambition of the moment — to lead the world in civil and military aviation.

The Germans are air-mad; their passion for flying is being fostered by the leaders of the National Socialist Party. Hitler, when he visits a town, swoops down upon it from the air.

… The real force behind the German air plans is not Hitler, however, but Goering, who probably cares nought about the economic visions of the National Socialist Party as long as he has power to blacken the European sky with a host of German squadrons. Goering was the inspirer of the air display which I visited in Berlin, and which not only impressed, but startled me. Through the Berlin aerodrome ground marched thousands upon thousands of strapping young men clad in the new grey-blue uniform of the German aviators. As I watched their keen, determined faces, their fine physique, and the perfection of their marching, I thought that Germany had in them the germ of a magnificent air force.

It is not only ambition, but fear which is leading to the training of these thousands of young men. "More than 10,000 aeroplanes are now standing on the German frontiers ready to start." This is one of the slogans driven into the minds of the German people by pamphlet, cinema, and radio. "In one hour every German city can be attacked by foreign bombers."

And there were young women, too, clad in that grey-blue uniform which is becoming as much the darling of the Prussian crowd as was the most resplendent of Guards' uniforms in 1914. Will it be as ominous for Europe? I wonder?[2]

Leaving Berlin, Gareth travelled to Prague with a letter of introduction from Sir Bernard Pares, hoping to have an audience with President Jan Masaryk. He spent a long time waiting in the Presidential Palace waiting room; only to be told that the President had received no one for a fortnight and had been ordered to rest in the country. He further commented in the same letter that "Hitler is in rather a bad way in Germany. Heaps of grumbling and a severe crisis (economic) about to break. There's great disillusion. But I have practically no new material because the English papers are far better informed than are the German." So, he spent the afternoon sightseeing; visiting the Wallenstein exhibition, the castle and the cathedral, dining by the river and enjoying the lights over the city.[3]

He returned to Leipzig the next day and sat opposite a Stormtrooper on the train. Never slow to engage in conversation, Gareth asked him: "What of the future?" The young man pointed to his black, white and red swastika armband and shouted:

Ten thousand planes are standing on the German frontiers (Western Mail).

That swastika is going to be the symbol of Socialism as well as of nationalism. The future lies with us people of the Left, and the day will come when we shall sweep away the accursed remnants of the capitalists, who are still ruling Germany. The revolution is not yet at an end. The money makers, the big bankers, the manufacturers who live by crushing the poor have to be mercilessly crushed. And we shall do it![4]

In Gareth's opinion, this Stormtroop leader was typical of many hundreds of thousands of Nazis throughout the country, who realised that the goal of Socialism was as distant as ever:

Indignant at the capitalist domination in Germany, these Nazis of the Left Wing or National Bolsheviks, as they were sometimes called were revolting against the Right Wing. …If there is discontent among the left wing Germans there is fear among the moderates. This fear is mainly economic, and during my visit this month I was surprised at the frankness with which people expressed their forebodings of evil days to come. Everywhere the drying up of foreign currency resources was accepted as the proof that a grave economic storm was threatening and might break very soon. The German crisis is grave, and popular disillusion is considerable.

Nevertheless, Hitler has recognised many factors on his side which should not be under-estimated… It is recognised that he has restored order to public life… He has in the view of millions of Germans — banished the spectre of Bolshevism. He has, through the German Youth, the Labour Camps, and the Stormtroops contributed to the health, sturdiness, and discipline of the nation.

Moreover, even the discontented Germans realise that the only alternatives to Hitlerism are a dictatorship based upon the bayonets of Reichswehr or a civil war.[5]

On his return to Wales Gareth undertook a prestigious assignment that would change the whole direction of his life, ultimately with tragic consequences. He went to interview William Randolph Hearst, the great American newspaper magnate, at his Welsh retreat St Donat's Castle, in Llantwit Major only a few miles from Cardiff.

Gareth with Randolph Hearst at Llantwit Major.

His interview, entitled 'World Peace in Hands of Anglo-Saxons', was published in the *Western Mail* on June 27, 1934. It was conspicuous that Gareth did not refer to the Soviet Union or Germany in his article. Hearst, "the biggest figure in the American newspaper world" proclaimed his faith in the Anglo-Saxon people:

If the British Empire and the United States had the greatest sea and air forces in the world, they could probably (if they had the sense and unselfishness) work together to make sure that peace, and security of the world be maintained.

308

Gareth asked Hearst: "Is not the continuation of the war debts question a barrier to this union?"

Hearst: "Unfortunately, the repudiation of the debts has to a degree destroyed mutual confidence and esteem. I wish it could be settled fairly."

Gareth: "Was not America's contribution to the War millions of dollars, whilst that of Britain and France was millions of men?"

Hearst: "It was their war, not ours. The Allies said, 'Our backs are to the wall, and if you do not come in we shall be destroyed.' But now they have their obligation to us."

Gareth: "We in Wales were amused at your statement that England had 'welshed on her debt.' Now that you have lived in Wales do you think that 'welshing' is a Welsh characteristic?"

Mr Hearst definitely had a sense of humour. He twinkled in the first part of his reply, and then grew serious: "'Welshing on a debt' is a phrase devised by Englishmen to gratify the vanities and prejudices of Englishmen."

Hearst: "But I said on Sunday, in an interview, that since England had defaulted on its debt it would be more proper and more accurate, and more definitely descriptive to say that a man who had repudiated his obligations had 'Englished' on his debt. I do not know any occasion, public or private, when the Welsh have repudiated obligations. Certainly there has never been in all history such a conspicuous example of national default of honourable obligations voluntarily incurred, and advantageously employed as the repudiation of England's debt to America."

Gareth: "Do you believe that the League of Nations can preserve peace?"

Hearst: "I do not believe that peace is to be established in a League of Nations, the majority of whose members are warlike. ...For this reason I have urged that America should keep free from all entanglements with the present League of Nations, which is controlled — and selfishly controlled — by the European Powers.

Gareth: "What do you think of President Roosevelt's naval plans, in view of the Japanese menace?"

Hearst: "I think the President's idea is that the world should disarm in the interests of peace and civilisation, ...I don't think that any civilised nation can really afford to spend in armaments the money which should be devoted to developing the arts of peace, but the United States will surely not allow the forces of Japanese aggression to surpass our forces for defence. Japan is a warlike nation. The United States is a peaceful nation.

Gareth: "What do you think of President Roosevelt's influence?"

Hearst: "Roosevelt's cheerfulness has been a fine factor in his work for the American people. Wilson said that a Depression was largely psychological. It helps to end the Depression if the public can be kept from being depressed. Mr Roosevelt exercises a heartening and inspiring influence."[6]

Gareth stayed for tea with Hearst and his companion, the film star, Miss Marion Davies. He must have impressed Hearst, as he was invited to stay at San Simeon, Hearst's ranch, when in the United States. Gareth had already announced to his family that he was planning his 'Round the World Fact Finding Tour' after he had left his employment with the *Western Mail* in the autumn.

On July 16, 1934, three weeks after the Hearst interview, Gareth conveyed the following exciting and personal news to his parents from the Reform Club in London:

> *It is funny. Jobs seem to be showering down on me.*
>
> *International News suggest I become Berlin Correspondent. What terms I asked Connolly in the train? 'Oh, our correspondents get a couple of hundred dollars a week'. (About £2000 a year)*
>
> *International News suggest, also, articles on the Far East. (£40 an Article).*
>
> *Paul Block, a big American newspaper man, who has been staying at St Donat's, and travels up to London says he doesn't want to take a good man from Hearst, but if I refuse Hearst, 'I can offer you something good in Europe.'*
>
> *Paul Block offers me £100 and expenses if I accompany him over Europe for a fortnight. I don't think it is possible — it's Eisteddfod time.*
>
> *I saw Pulvermacher of The [Daily] Telegraph. He suggested (not a definite offer) that I go round the world for The [Daily] Telegraph writing descriptive and political articles.*
>
> *So there you are! I think I may be able to combine Telegraph and International News with Round-the-World trip; although Germany at about £2000 a year seems also tempting.*

Notes on Chapter 30

1

Gareth Vaughan Jones Papers, National Library of Wales. Correspondence Series 1-21 File 15. June 3, 1934.

2

Western Mail, '10,000 Planes on the German Frontiers', August 1934 (date uncertain).

3

Gareth Vaughan Jones Papers, National Library of Wales. Correspondence Series 1-21 File 15. June 6, 1934.

4

Ibid., 'Fear of an Economic Storm in Germany', June 25, 1934. p. 7.

5

Ibid.

6

Western Mail, World Peace in Hands of Anglo-Saxons', June 27, 1934, p. 9.

Chapter 31

Night of the Long Knives

The *Western Mail* was again to become reliant on Gareth's undoubted expertise in German Foreign Affairs, which he must have seen as confirmation of his rehabilitation. From his profound knowledge he was able to write with authority about the momentous events that were taking place in Europe. He had an article published on June 25, 1934, entitled, 'Fear of an Economic Storm in Germany'. However, a storm of a different nature was about to break — dark clouds were gathering and on June 30, the lightning of the predicted crisis finally struck. The Nazi revolution, until now, had progressed without the stain of political murders, but for three days there was a bloody purge of the SA leaders in a coup which was to become known as the Night of the Long Knives.[1]

Hitler had taken the advice of his War Minister, General von Blomberg, one of the old brigade of politicians, to put an end to the plans of the Brownshirts and their leader, Ernst Roehm, and to reduce the number of adherents. The Brownshirts were the three and half million army of Hitler's supporters clothed in brown uniforms and were mainly political in their aims.[2]

In his article 'Behind the Drama of Germany', Gareth described the appalling situation that had arisen in a nation whose people he had held in such high regard:

> *These Stormtroopers (Brownshirts), known also as the "SA" men (not for their "Sex Appeal". but because SA stood for "Storm Department") were composed of the lower middle-class and unemployed supporters of Hitler.*
>
> *Recently, there has been a wave of discontent among their ranks, because the Socialist era to which they had looked forward has seemed farther away than ever, and because the big capitalists, the financiers, the proprietors of the large stores, and the aristocratic landowners are as firmly in the saddle as they were before Hitler came. The Communistically inclined Brownshirts well deserved their nickname of "Beefsteaks" (brown outside but red within).*

... The event began with Hitler entering Roehm's house early on Saturday morning and arresting the startled plotter. Capt. Roehm was a military adventurer of low moral standard, but a brilliant organiser. He and a number of other Brownshirt leaders were shot on June 30. Roehm had allied himself with left wing men, including General Schleicher, who was murdered with his wife at the same time in the coup.

This General Schleicher, Chancellor prior to Hitler, was not the reactionary he is sometimes reputed to have been. He was definitely a Left Wing man, who during his Chancellorship flirted with the trade unions, had a vision of a "socially ruled" empire, and was preparing to deal a smashing blow at the big landowners when he was cast out of power.

Such were probably the three ingredients in the plot which has failed the baulked ambitions of Stormtroop leaders, the bitter disillusion of the 'National Bolsheviks' and the Left Wing intrigue of the 'Socialist General.'

The plotters are dead. Roehm's place has been taken by Victor Lutze, a man, with whom I lunched a year ago in the train between Berlin and Hanover. I have rarely met a man who impressed me so much by his ruthlessness, grimness, lack of humour and fanaticism.[3]

Following the purge of the SA leaders on June 30th, the storm over Europe continued to gather strength and less than a month later, on July 25, 1934, the Austrian Chancellor Engelbert Dollfuss was assassinated.[4] Gareth had heard Dollfuss speak at the World Economic Conference the previous year and wrote in an article for *the Western Mail*, published on June 15, 1933: "The plucky little Austrian Chancellor, Herr Dollfuss had a sympathetic audience for his fight against Herr Hitler, and the blows of the German Nazis against Austria. He quoted prophetically a poem. 'The best man cannot live in Peace, if his neighbours cannot live with him in Peace.'"

Possibly as a consequence of these momentous events, Gareth took up the offer to accompany Paul Block, the American newspaper magnate, on a tour of the continent, gathering information for the *Western Mail*. It was not to be one of his most enjoyable assignments.

As he travelled on the train through France to meet Block, Gareth had time to contemplate the grave state of affairs in Austria. A French companion who joined him in his compartment said: "The murder of Dollfuss is the most tense moment in European history since the shot rang out at Sarajevo in July 1914."[5] Two decades had elapsed since the day that the Great War had been declared, and as the express locomotive sped through the countryside, looking out of the windows, Gareth viewed the same fields and same towns which were once battle sites. He reflected on that fateful epoch, and pondered upon the news, which dominated the present: "Would there soon be war?" He had received conflicting replies to this enquiry in France from shopkeepers, officials and the diplomats.

The conversation with the Frenchman inspired Gareth to write the article 'France Does not Expect War at Present' published by the *Western Mail* on August 3. 1934.

> *The French, with their usual logic and reason, reply that Hitler is in too weak a position internationally. He is isolated, and has the armed forces of France, Poland, and Czechoslovakia encasing him like a steel strait-jacket... The spectre of a German-Italian alliance had fleeted away with Hitler's hatred of Italy. ... This calmness is re-assuring, but it is only the calmness of the man who fears no storm to-morrow, but dreads an earthquake in a few years' time. ... Thus, grave as are the events of Austria, they have their compensations to politically-minded Frenchmen. But these compensations — such as the friendship of Italy are still not enough, and France will not rest until she has built up a collective system based on armed force, which will secure her against war.*[6]

Block was ill during their trip which led to unexpected delays and personal disappointment. On July 31, 1934, Gareth told his family that he was "so very sorry I shall not be at the Eisteddfod. Mr Block is anxious I stay with him and go to a number of capitals... it is a wonderful opportunity both for me and the *Western Mail.*" Gareth's opinion of him however, was not exactly flattering. "It's not much fun travelling about with a poor fellow whose colossal conceit at his brain power is as astounding as his real ignorance and who at the same time is cringing and subservient."[7]

From Berlin, Gareth sent a perceptive article to the *Western Mail* on the immediate future of Germany, entitled "Three Catastrophes in a Month", and published on August 2, 1934:

> *Hitler Regarded as Successor to Hindenburg*
> *The President, Field-Marshal von Hindenburg is gravely ill. Herr Hitler is on his way to the President's estate in Neudeck, East Prussia, and we are fearing the worst.*"
> *To them [the Germans] it was the latest of three catastrophes which have shaken Germany within the short space of a month.*

314

Out of the blue on June 30, had come the ruthless stamping out of the Roehm revolt which destroyed not only the bodies of men, but also the soul of a movement, and which has left rancour in the hearts of thousands of Stormtroopers.

On July 25, the greatest ambition of the National Socialists in foreign affairs was to regain the soil of Austria — sacred to them not only for the Germanic race of its countrymen, but for having brought to the world, the Leader, Hitler — was dashed to the ground, and converted into a crushing defeat which has humiliated them before the world.

Now comes the third catastrophe, the fear of the disappearance of the strongest link with the German past, and of the most reasonable and restraining force in German politics — Hindenburg.

With Hindenburg's death there will probably be a renewed struggle for power, more bitter, I believe, than before in the history of National Socialism in Germany. It was due to Hindenburg's personal influence that many posts in certain Ministries, such as the Foreign Office and the War Ministry, were in the hands of Nationalists — conservative men who have been revolted by the excesses of the revolutionaries in the national Socialist party.

It has been largely due to Hindenburg's influence that many of the Ministers have not been National Socialists, although they have paid lip service to its ideals and to its leaders. With Hindenburg's passing the fight for these posts will begin. Young Nazis, feeling themselves deprived of power and pay by the continuance of the Conservatives in privileged places, will seek to capture those prizes of authoritative posts which are now withheld from them.

… What of Hindenburg's successor? It is possible that the great old man has been the last President; that there will not again be a Presidential election, and that Hitler will make himself "Leader".[8]

In a later article, 'Germany Asking', Gareth posed the question, "Can he [Hitler] last?"[9]

Hindenburg's funeral had taken place. Herr Von Papen had been appointed as German Ambassador to Austria. There were many forces against Hitler — there was the fear of food shortage, the revolt of the intellectual class, the oppressed Roman Catholics, the Protestants and the working class who had supported the Brown Shirts and the Communists. His foreign policy was catastrophic — the hatred of Italy, the murder of Dollfuss, the strengthening of Soviet Russia's diplomatic position, and the alienation of the sympathies of civilised peoples, all because of the barbarities of National Socialism. All were against his favour but Gareth considered these bodies would not have the courage to revolt against the Nazi regime. Hitler had the power of the Reichswehr on his side, backed by the Minister of Defence General von Blomberg, as well as the support of those with right wing policies, the industrialists and the landowners.

Gareth questioned the future political situation in Germany:

> It seems that the forces fighting for Hitler are more powerful, more united and better armed than the forces against Hitler. Unless he falls a victim to the mediæval wave of political assassinations that has swept across Europe, he will probably be the figurehead of a military dictatorship.[10]

Thus, Gareth's verdict was that Hitler would survive the current crisis but would still be subservient to the power of Blomberg's army.

Notes on Chapter 31

[1] The purge of the SA was kept secret until it was announced by Hitler at a rally in the Reichstag on 13th July. It was during this speech that Hitler gave the purge its name: Night of the Long Knives (a phrase from a popular Nazi song). Hitler claimed that 61 had been executed while 13 had been shot resisting arrest and three had committed suicide. Others have argued that as many as 400 people were killed during the purge.

[2] The *Sturmabteilung*. The SA men were often known as Brownshirts from the colour of their uniform and to distinguish them from the SS who were known as Blackshirts. The SA played a key role in Hitler's rise to power in the early 1930s.

[3] *Western Mail*, 'Behind the Drama of Germany', July 2, 1934, p. 8.

[4] Chancellor Dollfuss was shot by members of the Austrian Nazi party.

[5] *Western Mail*, 'France Does not expect War at Present', August 3, 1934, p. 11

[6] Ibid.

[7] Gareth Vaughan Jones Papers, National Library of Wales. Correspondence Series 1-21 File 15. August , 1934.

[8] *Western Mail*, 'Three Catastrophes in a Month', August 2, 1934, p. 9.

[9] Ibid., 'The Forces that are Menacing Hitler', August 8, 1934, p. 9.

[10] Ibid.

Chapter 32

Austria and Germany: Dissension and Hatred

"Two souls, alas, are dwelling in my breast,
And one is striving to forsake its brother."[1]

Block had recovered sufficiently for them to continue their travels and by August 3, 1934, they were in Vienna. Gareth could not resist further comments on his travelling companion.

> *We went to the Schönbrunn yesterday. I got absolutely furious but I said nothing. Mr Block saw a picture (a very charming one) of Marie Antoinette as a child. He turned to the guide and said: 'Can I buy that?' !!!!"*[2]
>
> *…He asked, 'Was Maria Theresa [Archduchess and ruler of Austria, from 1740-1780] the wife of Franz Joseph' [Emperor of Austria, 1848-1916, and of the Austro-Hungarian Empire, 1867-1916]? The guide winced. He has insulted every Viennese he has met by his tactlessness. 'What's the use of you bringing me here to see this river?', he asked when the guide took us to look at the Danube. 'It's just like any other river.*[3]

> *Gareth and Block parted company in Vienna on August 5 when Block left for Venice and Cannes. "He says he may want to work with me when he goes to Rome in about a week or two but I do not think I shall go. He is too terrible, vulgar, cheap, objectionable, with no respect for tradition or feeling… He has insulted every Viennese he has met by his tactlessness… Still it has been a fine trip and for the 11 days I have worked for him I have had £77 plus all expenses…*
>
> *…I discover to my amazement that here in Vienna I am famous!!, because of my Russian articles and also because the Cardinal [Innitizer[4]] referred to me. So I am in clover and I am meeting most interesting people."*[5]

Despite having bade farewell to Block, Mr Sandbrook of the *Western Mail* sent a telegram telling Gareth he could remain longer in Europe, so he decided to stay on in Vienna for a few days before taking a tour through southern Austria and into northern Italy before returning to Munich.

On August 8, before he left Vienna, and protected by his British passport, Gareth roamed through the deserted streets patrolled by police and soldiers and he portrayed the scene to his *Western Mail* readers:

> *In this forbidden zone is the prison where the Nazis, who entered the Chancellery and took part in the murder of Dollfuss, are now being carefully guarded... Troops march past the hotel window; Heimwehr lads, with bunches of feathers in their grey-green caps, parade before the Opera House; and the purple shirts of the Catholic troops (Ostmärkische Sturmscharen) add colour to the Viennese streets. These troops gave a superficial impression of strength and loyalty to the Dollfuss régime, but beneath the surface there is no land so tragically torn by dissension and so flaming with hatred and with the longing for revenge as Austria today.*
>
> *...In spite of the deep human feeling which has been felt for Dollfuss, there is strong opposition within the country to the policy which his Government has pursued and which Herr Schuschnigg, the new Chancellor, is pursuing. ... The Socialists, who once ruled over all Vienna... have not forgiven the Government for the brutal bombardment of the Karl Marx-Hof in February; for the torture of many prisoners; for the breaking of promises to some of those captured; for the imprisonment of men without trial, and for the introduction of a dictatorial régime... and the imprisonment of thousands of workers in concentration camps throughout Austria.*[6]

Hatred of their government had persuaded many Austrian Socialists to join the National Socialists. Students and intellectuals supported the Nazis, and in the south where anti-Italian feeling was highest, the peasants longed for a closer union with Germany. Gareth was advised to go south to Carinthia where the animosity of the Austrians towards the Italians, whom they fought in the last war, was great. Here, soon after Dollfuss' death there had been an uprising, suppressed by the artillery leaving 40-50 dead.[7] Gareth felt the 'savage' murder and that the failure of the uprising by the secret Nazi Stormtroopers was merely a temporary setback to an Anschluss.[8]

Gareth took the night train from Vienna, travelling south-west to the provincial capital of Klagenfurt. It was an uncomfortable journey and Gareth experienced a sleepless night on hard-class benches, before arriving at dawn. There he found a state of martial law, the young men were in prison, and the soldiers and police had been instructed to make immediate use of the rifle if necessary. Questioning the local mayor as to why the uprising had failed in Carinthia, "Machine guns" was the answer given to Gareth. But the mayor considered there would be a day when it would not be easy to crush the Austrian Nazis. The mayor revealed that nearly all the peasants were in favour of Union in Germany — the Anschluss.

South Tyrol is the dotted area south of the Italian border with Austria.

A further cause of Austrian anger was that the Italians were endeavouring to suppress the German language in South Tyrol. Gareth, in his article 'Austria "Enslaved" by Italy', sympathised with a minority people, the Germans:

> *Imagine a land where you would not be allowed to carve a word of your native language upon the tomb stones of your dead relatives; where you might be fined £25 for teaching your tongue to schoolchildren, where you might be persecuted by the police, if you formed a choir... It is South Tyrol, which was taken away from Austria after the Great War and placed under the rule of Italy. ...It is these people that the Italian government is trying to convert into thorough Italians by the method which has failed almost everywhere by the forceful uprooting of national language and customs. In this area there are no German*

319

schools, no German societies and the German theatre has been abolished. It is only through the mother tongue the children can learn moral teachings, and it is only with the mother tongue that they can truly understand the lessons of the Bible. Why is this question important for Europe? It plays a part because the South Tyrolese are growing violently Nazi and will be a source of internal weakness for Italy should Italian troops ever decide to cross the Brenner into Austria. ... These Austrians [in Italy] are growing to hate Italy more bitterly than ever, and to despise Schuschnigg, their Chancellor, for being the minion of Mussolini. The feeling that fellow Austrians are being enslaved by the Italians will fan the flames of another Nazi rebellion in Austria.[9]

Such was the bitterness in the area that Gareth observed, "If Austria becomes united with Germany will not the Italians march into this very region, and will that not lead to a European War? South Tyrol was such a lovely place it was difficult to imagine that its peace might be disturbed."[10]

A calm, elderly man, the head of a travel agency, predicted that if Klagenfurt became a seat of war, Yugoslavia might send in her troops. Appreciating this would be a strategic point, Gareth decided to investigate the situation further and crossed over briefly into Slovenia, Yugoslavia. To enter Austria, the Italians would have to cross the Brenner Pass via the frontier town of Tarvis, leaving the Yugoslavs at their mercy, and cutting them off from North Europe. So tense was the situation that several regiments had been stationed on the frontier.

Gareth noted some wonderful waterfalls as his train crossed the pass from Austria into Italy and arrived at the frontier station of Tarvis. His first impressions were of many troops. From the train, alongside the Italian railway track, there were of hundreds of brightly-coloured camouflage tents to be seen, and from these Italians soldiers waved to the passing train. An excitable Italian entered his compartment, and spoke with great passion to Gareth about how the Italians hated Germany; they hated Hitler, and were shocked at the murder of Dollfuss. "The moment Austria joins Nazi Germany our troops will enter Austria. France must be our ally". declared the Italian. The Italians feared the Germans were casting a longing eye at the Adriatic port of Trieste:

An independent little Austria is no danger to Trieste. Therefore, the Italians by recent agreement have allowed Austria a free harbour in Trieste, where the Austrians pay no custom duties, and have extra-territorial rights. Italy's fight for the independence of Austria is therefore Italy's fight for Trieste... Trieste is

Italy's spearhead for expansion throughout Africa. There are, for example, four
Italian shipping lines from Trieste which sail round Africa, and because Trieste
means [Italy's] mastery of the Adriatic, Mussolini is not likely, without a grim
struggle, to allow Austria to join with Germany.[11]

As he approached the city of Trieste, Gareth looked towards the blue crystal-clear
Adriatic Sea. In this area 20 years previously the Austro-Hungarian and Italian
armies had battled against each other for two years over such positions as Gorizia,
Monfalcone, Monte san Michele, Doberdo and the River Timavo.

Gareth had heard on good authority that there would be a fierce doctrinal struggle
between the Vatican and Mussolini, between the church and state in Italy. In Trieste,
he was aware of the suppression of minorities, and was concerned for the plight of one
million Slovenes, who were living in the area bordering Yugoslavia and spoke a Slavic
language. Italians were doing all they could to suppress it. The Bishop of Trieste, who
believed that all people had the right to worship in their own language, was combating
the Italianising influence and was fighting for the rights of the Slovene minority. He
had, however, been forbidden to publish a Prayer Book in the Slovene language.

Before Gareth left Trieste, he called on a fellow journalist who was bitter that he
was not able to write freely and that his newspaper was restricted to being published
three times a week. He was anxious that Gareth did not report their conversation:

There will be four people waiting outside my office, while you are here. They
will have noticed you coming in, and they will know who you are. 'How?' When
you came through the frontier, they will have looked at your passport, and seen you
were a journalist. They will have followed you. In a few days' time, I shall be politely
asked to come to the police, and they will ask what you wanted and what I told you.

The Italians are very cunning in their secret police methods. The English and
the Americans are too naïve, and always fall in the trap. Of course, nothing will
happen to you if you write something, but I shall get it in the neck.

When we read that Mussolini sent troops, and saw them in the houses, thou-
sands of them, and on the Brenner Pass, we laughed. They'll never march. The
Italians are too cowardly. It's all bluff. Why, during the war they never got an
inch of our soil here. They are trying to destroy our culture, but they are making
the young people all the more Nazi.

I don't think there'll be any real trouble on the frontier. Austria will not
have her Anschluss for a long time, and then it will come quietly and gradually
like Danzig.[12]

After his whirlwind visit to Italy, Yugoslavia and Austria, Gareth planned to stay in Munich for a day or two, before returning to Berlin. It was his birthday on August 13 and he was in reflective mood when he wrote to his parents "It was splendid to have your letters this morning and to be able to read them on the steps of the Residence Theatre [Munich]. I am lucky to have such wonderful parents who have always looked after me splendidly and let me travel everywhere and given me such a fine education and I am deeply grateful to you… Tonight I am going to hear Goering speak. I have a press ticket. So I'll have a good view."[13] Birthday or no birthday, Gareth was at work and he described the dramatically staged event in his *Western Mail* article as a "priest surrounded by the chorus in a Greek play":

> *A cruel, fleshy fist, ever moving, ever threatening fascinates me, and I can hardly take my eyes away from it. Sometimes clenched with the strength of a powerful man it shakes back and fro in a gesture of warning, sometimes it crashes down as if ascending ruthlessly upon a victim. It is a fist with personality, but a brutal, mailed fist. It is the fist of Goering.*
>
> *He stands elevated on a stage a few yards away from me before a mass of Brownshirts, of Hitler youths, and of German middle-class citizens. He is the centre of the most magnificently staged drama I have seen.*
>
> *Behind him rise the lofty pillars of a classic temple, from which the red, black and white swastika banners are flowing. Illuminated so that the red brilliance of the Nazi colour may stand out against the blackness of the sky and crowned with a dazzling swastika electric sign, this temple looks over a grassy square, now filled with National-Socialists, who read between the centre pillars the slogan, "With Adolf Hitler for Germany."*
>
> *Not long ago, this crowd was waiting for Goering in the darkness. Then, with a suddenness which made one's eyes blink, searchlights flashed, a military band blared out a Nazi march, and hundreds upon hundreds of banners were seen approaching from the distance down the avenue towards the temple. The Storm troopers, with their leaders, marched past.*
>
> *There was silence for a few minutes, while the crowd waited. Then a faint cheer came, and rapidly down the avenue drove a car, with a fat man in a brown uniform standing up and giving the Fascist salute. Goering had arrived to speak in the campaign for Hitler's election on Sunday.*
>
> *The crowd stood with outstretched arms — I must have been the only one in that vast multitude whose right arm remained obstinately unraised.*

322

Like a priest surrounded by the chorus in a Greek play, Goering stood motionless beneath the Ionic columns of the temple, while the Storm Troop flag bearers carried their brilliant banners with the silver crests glittering beneath the searchlights.

His features, rendered hard by his high cheekbones, and by the grim expression of his mouth, were deepened by the light which shone down upon him.

His musical voice boomed out a greeting to the German people. It had a touch of rich harmony about it, but soon I felt a note of hardness. He had not spoken long before there rang out in those clipped tones of the German officer, a jarring sound of cruelty, impatience, and intolerance, which contrasted with the studied harmony, and pleasing volume of the opening sentences. There was, in some high points of Goering's speech, the same note of hysteria and unbridled passion which I had heard in Hitler's speeches, a note which inspires one with fear that the speaker will suddenly break down, or lose absolute control of his mental powers.

But that Goering is a tragic actor of the first rank there can be no doubt. I myself will on Sunday and on many days in the future be thinking not so much of the ballot box, and of the vote to be counted by 100 per cent National Socialists, but of something far more powerful — that iron fist of Goering which I saw clenched and threatening as the lights shone down upon it in temple at Munich.[14]

Gareth was back in Berlin where he stayed until after the Referendum of August 19 when the people of Germany were being asked to approve the merging of the posts of President and Chancellor, under the strengthened leadership of Hitler.

According to Gareth, the election result would be a foregone conclusion and he wrote in his next article 'Hitler's Trump Card' that "Germany feared it would cease to be a unified country if the electorate did not vote for the Dictator."[15]

The election poster that most drew Gareth's attention was, 'Hitler has fulfilled these prophetic words of Bismarck. Vote for him on August 19. 'We Germans, placed in the centre of Europe, must hold together more than other nations. We must be united if we are not to perish. — Bismarck'.

The unification of the German nation was Bismarck's creation of 1871 and she was but a 'child among nations'. 'Deutschland Uber Alles' (Germany above all) meant 'Germany before Saxony, before Prussia, before Württemberg.' It was an invocation: 'O God, give us unity.' But to the Germans, who had only recently become a nation, unity meant the very breath of life. …It had been a stupendous task to make a nation out of this medley of different races, lands, traditions, and creeds!"

This longing for unity is the subconscious cause of Hitler's fanatical desire to mould the country into one single form. It explains his ruthlessness in stamping out differences of opinion, differences of uniforms, differences in political parties, and differences in religious beliefs. Hitler's revolution is a violent swing of the pendulum away from the ramshackle discordant medley which was Germany, to a super-regimented, forcefully cemented people, who are to speak with one voice, think with one brain, and march at a single command.

The fear that Germany might crumble to pieces is Hitler's trump card, and he will use it skilfully. He will, when bread and potatoes and fats run short, paint a picture of the world threatening Germany. He will implore his fellow-countrymen to tighten their belts for the sake of German unity. He will depict himself as the keystone of the structure of a united nation.

And men who hate his methods will rally to his side because they fear that if he falls chaos and conflict will rend the country and there will be farewell to the dream and prayer of "Deutschland Uber Alles!"[16]

A week later Hitler stood at the window of the Chancellery greeting his worshippers, who crowded the street before the Palace. He had had a triumphant victory:

The awe-filled eyes of the children were fixed upon their leader as upon some bright comet flashing through the sky. 'I saw their lips move as if they were chanting, not a national anthem, but a fervent prayer, an exhortation to Heaven — 'Germany above Everything!'

There was a look of quiet confidence on Hitler's face when I saw him saluting the enthusiastic crowd outside the Chancellery… That confidence will be shaken far more by the economic tasks of the winter than by the votes of four million men. Who were the 38,000,000 who voted for Hitler and who were the 4,000,000 who had the courage to say "No"? …But what are votes, after all, to men of strong will who have energy ruthlessness, and the determination to stay in power — and machine-guns?[17]

On the night of the referendum Gareth wrote to his parents to tell them he had met up with his former employer Ivy Lee and had lunched with Paul Scheffer who had asked him to write articles for the *Berliner Tageblatt*.[18] In his diary, Gareth also noted that he had met Hans Otto Meissner, a friend from his Cambridge days, in Berlin. Hitler had appointed Meissner's father, Dr Otto Meissner, as the First Secretary of State, and previously, he had acted in the same capacity for President

Hindenburg. [19]A further entry in this diary, headed "M" (and from the context this was undoubtedly Meissner Junior, by then a known Nazi sympathiser) discussed the "Night of the Long Knives":

["M"] *was present at the shooting that night of 19 [men] and saw Ernst*[20] *shot. [M said,] 'My friend was the man who gave the command.'*

'Were they really guilty?' I [Gareth] asked.

'Definitely', he [M] said. 'He's the man who would not hurt a fly.' [Presumably the friend who fired.]

[M] 'The prisoners were not told of their sentence. They were brought before Goering and others, and asked questions, and then led out. Ernst did not die well. He did not know he was going to be shot when he came out of the court. I was there. He looked up and saw the SS (black uniformed elite of the Stormtroopers) men with rifles. He was dragged before the lights of motorcars. He shouted. 'You can't shoot me. You can't shoot me.' One SA man said for himself, 'I'll give my command.' He said, 'Shoot'.

'They should have been given a trial, but it was right to shoot them. I spent nearly three weeks waiting for an SA attack. The hatred between the SA and the SS is terrible. They call us the Schwarz Schweinhunde. When we captured the SA men, I myself saw that there was FN (Fabrique Nationale)[21] *[carved] in their rifles. One man, just before we shot him, shouted out: 'Just one more day and you'll have stood where we stood'. Isn't that proof that they were guilty?'*

'Why Klauser? Yes, that was a mistake. Klauser was on Roehm's minister list and he did not know about it. He was Minister of Traffic so he was shot. One Dr Schmidt[22] *was shot by mistake for another man. The SS went into the office, and he was dragged out and shot. He turned out to be the wrong man.'*

[Gareth remarked:] 'Typical of the Germans was that a flower garden was in the spot where the men were to be shot. The SS men in the cars were anxious not to drive over the flowers and took the utmost care that not a single flower should be trampled on. Then they shot 19 men. [23]

With an air of despondency, he left a country he loved, a country which had lost its soul, and its freedom. 'What a stupendous task it is to make a nation out of this medley of different races, lands, traditions, and creeds!' Goethe's Faust exclaimed, 'There dwell, alas! Two souls within this breast!' But within the breast of Germany there dwell thousands of souls struggling for supremacy.[24]

Gareth never again wrote any articles about Germany, but in October of the same year he returned one last time, to the country for which he had had so much affection, to bid farewell to his friends, before embarking on what was to be his final adventure, a 'Round the World Fact Finding Tour'.

Notes on Chapter 32

1
   von Goethe, Johann Wolfgang, Peter Salm (translator) 1988 *Faust Part* One, Bantam Classics.

2
   Gareth Vaughan Jones Papers, National Library of Wales. Correspondence Series 1-21 File 15. August 3, 1934.

3
   Ibid. August 5, 1934.

4
   In the *New York Times* of August 20, 1933. a striking appeal for the Russian famine victims was made by Cardinal Innitzer, Archbishop of Vienna who declared deaths were likely to be numbered once more by the million: "The appeal was addressed before all to the International Red Cross, but it was made also to all those who were today negotiating for the enlargement of economic relations with Soviet Russia in order to make those negotiations dependent on the comprehension of the necessity for help in the stricken districts of that country.;"

5
   Gareth Vaughan Jones Papers, National Library of Wales. Correspondence Series 1-21, File 15. August 5, 1934.

6
   Western Mail, 'Austria Torn by Dissension and Flaming With Hatred', August 10, 1934, p. 8.

7
   Ibid., 'Sacred Crusade" to Unite Austria with Germany', August 16, 1934, p. 11.

8
   Ibid., 'Austria Torn by Dissension and Flaming with Rage', August 10, 1934. p. 8.

9
   Ibid., 'Austrians "Enslaved" by Italy', August 23, 1934, p. 9.

10
   Ibid., 'Sacred Crusade to unite Austria with Germany', August 14, 1934, p. 11.

11
   Ibid., 'Italy's Big Guns Point Towards Austria', August 16, 1934, p. 9.

12
   Gareth Vaughan Jones Papers, National Library of Wales. Series 35-42.

13
   Gareth Vaughan Jones Papers, National Library of Wales. Correspondence Series 1-21 File 15. August 13, 1934.

14
   Ibid., 'Hysteria of Goering', August 18, 1934, p. 9.

15
   Ibid., 'Hitler's Trump Card', August 22, 1934, p. 11.

16
   Ibid.

17
   Ibid., 'Who are the 'Yeses 'and the 'No' in the German Plebiscite', August 21, 1934. p.11.

18
   Gareth Vaughan Jones Papers, National Library of Wales. Correspondence Series 1-21 File 15. August 19, 1934.

19
   Hans Otto Meissner's father was made First Secretary of State to Hitler and had acted in this capacity to President Hindenburg. Meissner described Adolph Hitler as having "some attractive qualities. He only smiles with children. He can make all classes of people at home. One evening he telephoned us at home to come over. My mother is a society lady and was very amazed when she went to Hitler's place and Hitler's chauffeur invited her to dance. Hitler's chauffeur can say 'Adolf, I'd like a glass of beer.' Hitler thinks corruption is terrible. There was Mutschman in Saxony who was going to give a dinner party. He bought 2000 marks worth of porcelain, and the table was laid. Suddenly

Hitler arrived, took hold of the tablecloth, pulled it and upset all the dishes. He said: 'You pay for that out of your private money and went.'"

20
   Karl Ernst was shot at the SS army college at Botanical gardens at Richtefelde in Berlin.

21
   Fabrique Nationale Nationale de Herstal, more often known as Fabrique Nationale and abbreviated simply as FN, is a well-known arms manufacturer that originated in the Belgian city of Herstal in Liege.

22
   Dr Willi Schmidt, music critic for a Munich newspaper, was mistaken for another Willi Schmidt on the list. Dr Schmidt was assassinated and his body later returned to his family in a sealed coffin with orders from the Gestapo that it should not be opened.

23
   Gareth Vaughan Jones Papers, National Library of Wales. Series 35-42.

24
   Western Mail, 'Hitler's Trump Card', August 22, 1934, p. 11.

PART 9

Gareth's World Tour:
St Simeon and Beyond the Rising Sun
(1934-1935)

Chapter 33

Farewell Europe

On October 1, 1934, Gareth's diary entry read:

> *[I am] a free man; belong to no organisation; at the whim of nobody, but myself; have about £1000, made my will on Friday and I am now off to Germany, Farewell at home; au revoir to Ianto [Gareth's dog]. Hall Williams takes me in his car and we go through Cadoxton [near Barry]. He points out the old Traveller's Arms, now a white-washed cottage where once travellers used to call. Told me a story of how an old man went out of the cottage one day and was never seen again. It was noticed that the grass grew greener in on spot in the field. 20 years later digging this area up a skeleton was found.*[1]

Gareth said his 'goodbyes' at the *Western Mail* office before taking the train to London. He learnt that Lord Davies was going to see Hitler in Germany where Davies had succeeded in founding a branch of the New Commonwealth Society, an organisation created in 1932 to promote disarmament.

There were more farewells in London. Gareth went to see Prof. Jules Menken; then to Sir Bernard Pares whom he described as looking "pale, wizened and ill. He was wearing old clothes, and was serious with his, "D'you see what I mean?" He looked a lonely tragic figure, full of the best ideals and had a remarkable affection for his friends but he had too much faith in human nature — a real idealist and a liberal with tolerance — a true gentleman." Sir Bernard gave Gareth a number of letters of introduction to University dons in the United States.[2] Later Gareth dined with Wolf von Dewall, the London correspondent of *Die Frankfurter Zeitung* and a non-Nazi who had just been to Poland with a delegation to discuss the necessity of an understanding between Germany and Poland, but not a military expansion.

Gareth also went to see the writer and journalist Hugh Hessell Tiltman who had worked in China. He said he would be interested in Gareth researching following subjects including, "Life in Manchuria today", "Japan today with particular reference to factories working conditions" and "Russian back-door — truth about the troubled frontier life in Eastern Siberia" and would pay 20 guineas for the information. He had already been commissioned by the *Manchester Guardian* to write a series of eight articles during his trip, two on America and six on the Far East.[3]

By October 3, 1934, Gareth was in Germany to bid goodbye to the people for whom he had such high regard, to a country he had visited so many times over the past twelve years. Following a few days walking in the Harz Mountains with a friend, Lydia, he called on his old friends in Berlin. There he found the political situation had deteriorated even further and recorded in his diary such remarks which he had heard: "There is going to be a number of arrests. There is a [ethnic] cleansing going on. There is a lot going on under the surface." "There is discontent — number of arrests — concentration camps are full of SA men." No personal freedom was left according to one shop keeper: "One morning a few weeks ago at 6 am criminal police came to fetch me — accused of me of writing to SA man, but I had never done so. I was put in prison for a fortnight." ... "Moral terror is strong because bishops are afraid the Nazis will send them to prison. 90% of priests are against Hitler but prefer the status quo."[4]

He lunched with Paul Scheffer who discussed the political situation in Germany with Gareth. "There seem to be many deaths of violence", according to Scheffer.

> *The leaders have too many rights. There are a large number of cases of injustice. The daughter of Minister Kerrl ran over and killed two men in car — nothing happened and she got off free. Spies are everywhere. The place is full of SA men who will report and denounce you. There are two kinds of justice; one for SA men or SS and one for ordinary citizen who can hardly hope to get a hearing. They'll believe the SA men every time.*

Gareth dined with his friends, Johann and Melita, who told him the story of the terrible fate of a beautiful blond girl, Fraulein Sommer. She had been found dead in the apartment of Hitler's Adjutant Brückner. The criminal police telephoned the parents long afterwards to say, "Your daughter has been found dead. 'Alles ist erledigt.' There was no medical examination. The police seemed to be afraid of those who had a lot of power. ...The police said it was poisoning. The parents who were almost demented wrote to Brückner. He replied he was too busy and had to go to Munich but he would reply to them on his return. He never wrote to them." When Gareth told Otto Meissner, Bruckner's reply had disgusted him.

Gareth went briefly to see his close friends in Danzig, Bridgit and Reinhard Haferkorn to say goodbye after which he returned to London before leaving for the United States, and the first stage of his 'Round the World Fact Finding Tour.'

Early on the morning of October 26, 1934, Gareth's liner, the *SS Manhattan*, steamed out of Southampton harbour bound for the city of New York on the first leg of his tour. His final destination was to be the Far East. The evening before, his father, Major Edgar Jones, his sister, Eirian, his niece Siriol (the author), and his close friends, the von Dewalls, said goodbye to him, on the boat train at Waterloo station, London. He jotted in his diary, "Dada was moved, Eirian shed a tear and Siriol bent forward for another kiss". As the train left, Wolf von Dewall gave him the Chinese name of Yo Nien Sse (which translates as lofty mountains, studying and reflecting).

Gareth's voyage on the *SS Manhattan* passed quickly. Telegrams and letters awaited him in his cabin, and his company on board was lively and cheerful. On October 28 he had his last glimpse of England with Land's End in the distance. Gareth was disappointed when the journey was over. The skyscrapers of New York appeared on the horizon early on the morning of November 2, and soon the liner berthed in the docks. Gareth stayed for a few days with his old friends, the Dudleys, and spent a weekend with Leland Rex Robinson in Westchester County before getting down to work.[5]

Gareth wrote a bumper letter to his parents with several days' news as he had been kept very busy with the Congressional Elections that took place on November 6, 1934, and he had not written for 10 days. He started with sad family reminiscences. His Great Aunt Modryb had died on her 97th birthday.

> *I have just heard of Modryb's death. The memory of spending school holidays and the link with Pennorth have gone and Modryb's blackberry tart and the excitement of chasing the pigs, John Willy and Willy John, and the visits to Brecon which seem so very far away...*
>
> *And now for all my news. I had a letter from Matsudaira, the Japanese Ambassador in London to whom I had written last week saying, 'I am glad to learn that you are going to visit my country in the near future for the purpose of writing articles on Japan for various English newspapers.' He enclosed a letter to Mr Amau, (sic) Chief of the Information Bureau in the Foreign Office in Tokyo. 'I sincerely hope that your stay in Japan will be enjoyable and profitable one.' Yours Faithfully, T. Matsudaira...[6]*

Gareth then set out in some detail his itinerary for the proposed trip to the Far East with gossip about his friends before telling his story of the election night:

Tuesday was the day of all days. It was the day of the election and the day (or the night rather) when I sent my first cable to the Berliner Tageblatt. The day began in gloom. I had promised Paul Scheffer in Berlin to send him a 1000-word cable (to be paid for in Berlin, that's what they call a collect cable) on the election results. I telephoned Commercial Cables and they said, 'No. Collect cables to Berlin have been abolished. We are exceedingly sorry. You will have to pay seven cents (3½d) a word!!' That would mean $70 for a cable or £14! It would be impossible for me to pay. So, I was rather disappointed at being unable to send a cable.

Now the election results do not begin to come in until 10 or 11 o'clock at night. I came to an arrangement with the New York Herald Tribune that I could cover the election in their office, because the Berliner Tageblatt (my paper) and the H-T help each other out. But I was fed up, because I could not cable.

I planned to write an article instead of cabling and to send it by The Manhattan which was sailing early next morning. But I was fed up because I could not send my cable.

The Herald Tribune newsroom was packed with people and excitement. A tremendous Democratic victory! Dozens of reporters were hard at work and the copy-readers and headlings (i.e. sub-editors) were busy as anything. And I sat mournful in a huge armchair, because all I could do was to write an article which would be stale by the time it got to Berlin.

Suddenly at midnight I saw a man come in, and he looked familiar. I wondered where I had met him. I asked the office boy who he was; 'It's Mr Barnes, our Moscow correspondent.' I had met him in Moscow. I went up and he gave me a wonderful welcome. He introduced me to all the political editors as a leading journalistic figure. (It's funny newspapermen know me here because I 'scooped' the world on the Russian famine, and because all my stuff was confirmed by the most responsible American journalists later.)

I happened to tell Barnes about my cable fix. 'That'll be O.K.' he said. 'We'll arrange that. Come and meet Mr Callahan of the Western Union.' Great news! Mr Callahan said; 'That's O.K. We'll send the cable.' Hurray! I was delighted. I was given a room to myself away from the bustle of the vast newsroom. Messenger boys (and editors also) rushed to bring me the latest news. By 3 o'clock in the morning Mr Callahan had tapped most of my message, and it was being received in Berlin in time for the first editions of the evening papers.

It was one of the most exciting and enjoyable nights I've had. There is nothing like the thrill of sending the latest news from New York to Berlin, and you see that Paul Scheffer was very pleased with my cable...

On Thursday I went for my talk with the President of the International News Service, Mr Connolly who immediately arranged for a series of articles on the Far East...[7]

Three days after the election Gareth set off for Worcester, Massachusetts to visit friends and give a lecture to the Worcester Women's Club on November 12, 1934, hosted by Mrs Herbert Bagley who, expecting a much older man, declared "I feel I want to mother you!"

The flower of Worcester assembled to dine with me [at Mrs Bagley's house], and afterwards we motored to the lecture hall where literally hundreds of cars were assembled and I saw a huge building into which men and women in evening dress were pouring. I was to address the whole elegance of Worcester which is a city of about 600,000, or more than three times the size of Cardiff.

The president took me behind the scenes and led me up a high iron staircase and brought me on to a stage. I found 700 people in front all dressed to kill, and I was looking down. Anyway I began and I described graphically my flight with Hitler, and they listened with open mouths. After I finished and had disappeared behind the curtain I heard applause continuing for a long time. Afterwards I was like the Prince of Wales, trying to bow and shake hands graciously to the high-hats of the city. It was very funny.

Suddenly I saw Larry and his brother Ray. Larry was tremendously amused at everything, and... thought it a great joke that they were making such a fuss...

Tuesday [November 13th] I lunched with Gerald Graham who is a proud father. I saw some of the leading Professors in Harvard, thanks to Sir Bernard's letters [of introduction] and they were exceedingly kind. On Wednesday Stackpole had tea with Larry and me...

Oh, Wednesday morning I was talking with a Professor and there was another man in the room waiting to talk to the Prof. The Prof asked me "Are you Welsh?" and suddenly the other man said in a foreign accent "Diolih yn fawr!" [thank you very much] I recognised it to be a Russian accent so I spoke to him in Russian "It's remarkable" said the Prof. to find a Russian who can speak Welsh at the same time as a Welshman who can speak Russian!"...[8]

On November 14 Gareth set sail from Boston for New York. Where he was to stay with the Robinsons. "Poor Ivy Lee is dead. I saw it in the paper in Worcester. I am very sorry, because he was most kind to me. I called at his office the day after I arrived, but did not know he was so ill. I wrote from New England to Mrs Lee and Jim Lee. I think that Mr Lee had great worries in the last few years."[9]

On November 22 1934, Gareth was off on his travels again, this time for Washington. From there he continued to Wales, Wisconsin staying in Chicago and Milwaukee en route.

On Sunday December 2, 1934, he wrote from Taliesin, Spring Green, Wisconsin:

> *This is the most remarkable day I have spent. I am here with the world-known architect Frank Lloyd Wright, a Welshman, and he has a group of apprentices here in a superb house whom he teaches a philosophy all his own combined with architecture and painting. He is an outstanding personality — one of the greatest I have met. I am just about to read his autobiography. He has a magnificent theatre here right in the heart of the country. It has curtains of a strange design and riotous colours. His pupils are devoted to him.*[10]

Gareth amidst farm vehicles. Unknown location in the USA.

The *Western Mail* published an article about his visit to Taliesin on the 8, February 1935:

Frank Lloyd Wright! When you mention his name, note the expression on the faces of those with whom you talk in America. There is hatred, there is shock, there is disapproval, there is jealousy, there is respect, worship, adoration, but one expression you will never find, and that is indifference. He wrestled with fire, and insanity, and a hostile public opinion with an indomitable will, and his story is a saga of experience, was the verdict of an American writer.

Of Frank Lloyd Wright as an architect I can say little. I can only repeat what artists say, and that is that by bursting the fetters of architecture in the nineties, he freed it from its unnatural, imitative character, and from its imprisonment in a fortress far removed from life, and that he is more responsible than any other individual for the beauty of new buildings in Europe and America.

But of Frank Lloyd Wright the man I can say much. With his piercing, witty sparkling twinkle which is ever playing around his lips, with the deep sincerity of his musical voice, with the force and faith of his views, and with the charm which he radiates, he has fascinated me more than any man with the exception of Mr Lloyd George.[11]

Frank Lloyd Wright and his wife, Olgivanna, at Taliesin.

Gareth with Olgivanna Lloyd Wright at Taliesin.

The following day, Gareth was in the Park Hotel, Madison:

> *Back again through the snow from Taliesin to Madison. I have just had*
> *an interview with Governor La Follette, a great political personality in the*
> *country. I'll send you Lloyd Wright's books when I've finished them. Then you*
> *can see what a wonderful time I had at Taliesin. He was the forerunner of the*
> *New Architecture.*
>
> *The Welsh have given me a great time. ... There'll be a series of articles. The*
> *Welsh here impress me very much. And in Wales [Wisconsin]! What a time I*
> *had! I had to make heaps of speeches and was hailed as a distinguished visitor*
> *from the old country. I had to give two sermons. I talked about 'Freedom to*
> *Worship' and 'Persecution of Religion'. I was a great favourite. I had to talk to*
> *the... children in Bethesda Chapel. ...I must get down to work... I am keeping*
> *my diary active with conversations.* [12]

A more restrained account of Gareth's visit to Wales, Wisconsin was published
a few months later in the *Western Mail*:

> *From the whirl, the crash and the glaring lights of Chicago and Milwaukee I*
> *descended upon the calm and the dignity of the Welsh community of Waukesha*
> *County. To illustrate the contrast between the two worlds I shall tell the tale*

of the eve of my departure for the Welsh district, when I spent a night in a Milwaukee hotel. It was at the time when 'Baby Face' Nelson had been shot down by the police; the old gangsterdom seemed on the verge of doom and the remaining gangsters were concentrating on the racket of kidnapping. ... Within twenty-four hours I slept in the quiet house of the Rev. and Mrs John Pugh Jones. There was a Bible by the bedside, a religious picture on the wall, a library of philosophical works and of Welsh poetry not far away. No thought of locking a door, no thought of gangsterdom! I was in Wales, and I was in a Welsh atmosphere. Within a day I had escaped from the America of the great cities, and I was back with my own countrymen.[13]

Gareth's visit to Madison was most enjoyable, and he found the city was calm and dignified. He was not impressed by Chicago which was lit up with dazzling lights, and where he said he had not seen so many tough hard-boiled thugs in his life.[14]

December 9, 1934, saw Gareth on the train, 'The Grand Canyon Limited' on the way to Santa Fe:

Here I am in the observation car of the great train 'The Grand Canyon Limited'. For half an hour I have been standing outside on the platform right at the back of the train watching the dreary bare cornfields of Kansas (and when I say 'corn' I don't mean corn but 'maize'; corn is not wheat or barley or oats here); they are half covered with snow. The scene is monotonous, with just a few trees here and there and a big river, the Missouri, frozen over in parts reminding me of Uncle Tom's cabin.[15]

The train made a brief stop in Newton, Kansas where he went for a walk, before continuing on to Santa Fe to meet his friends the Samuelsons. He was not there for long and the next day Gareth continued his journey to Los Angeles, across the Arizona Desert.[16]

Gareth wrote a 20-page Christmas letter to his parents which he said took him three hours to write:

What a week! I have been chased by a Red Indian woman with a poker, have travelled 2000 miles, have come from the snow to palms trees and June weather, have galloped on the swiftest horses I have ever been on, and had a collision with another horse, have lived in a house made of mud and have crossed a desert and have addressed the most famous and elegant audience in the West of America on a subject for which I only had 24 hours' notice, have seen oranges and lemons and strawberries ripening in December, have broadcast to 11 States of America at five minutes notice, have been in tropical floods, have talked with a man, an Indian, 109 years old and arrived in the film city of the world...

... Thursday morning, December 13, on Dada's birthday I woke up, lifted the blinds and saw torrents of rain pouring down on California's desert. Cactuses, desert plants, rocks everywhere; dark clouds covering the mountains, and after breakfast we stopped at San Bernardino. Here I was to change for Riverside where I was to lecture at the Institute of World Affairs...

Finally I got to the Mission Inn... The place was packed with earnest Americans thirsting for knowledge and the finest experts on foreign affairs in the West were there. My heart sank and I was fed up for the first time in ages and rather afraid that my show next day would be a flop.

Then something worthy of a satire on America happened. Just as I was going into lunch one of the dozens of Professors there an excitable man dashed up to me and muttered, "Radio! Radio! Put on your coat at once and come with me." ... [In a later letter Gareth revealed that this was a Dr Carruthers of the University of Pasadena]. He dragged me into a car and we sped along beautiful roads along avenues of palm trees; but tropical rains swept across our paths. Every now and then we cross a road which came down from the mountains and that would be a real rushing stream. The car would splash through and the windows were drenched with showers

Suddenly we stuck; right in the middle of such a stream. The mysterious man swore: 'I've got to be at the radio station at 1.45 pm to announce.' He pushed and tugged. Luckily the car went and after half an hour we came into Pomona.

Just before coming in he said, 'You're going to speak to the people of eleven States. You're going to meet the famous aviatrix Thea Rascher who flew from London to Melbourne. Quick, tell me something about yourself. I've got to sell you to the people of the West. I've got to describe you as one sent by Heaven to tell the people of California about Russia or whatever you know about. I want to tell them you are the finest greatest, swellest authority God ever created on foreign affairs. Then you will be followed in the programme by the 'flyer'. 'But you don't mean to say I've got to speak on the radio now' I said.

'Sure. It doesn't matter what you say. Anything will do as long as you say it. Now the programme is on 'Aviation and World Peace' and you've got to say something about aviation in Russia.'

We were in Pomona. 'We've got 6 minutes in which to have lunch', he shouted. We leaped into to a drug store, swallowed a sandwich and coffee; flew out and

340

got to a little house at 1.41 (4 minutes before the programme was to begin). It was a branch of the radio station.

A very charming woman of 40 was there. 'Meet Miss Thea Rascher. Mr Gareth Jones'.

We rushed into a----- bedroom! and there in the bedroom was the microphone. A little boy was playing.. Then my driver (the mysterious man) spoke into the mike. 'We have some of Europe's greatest personalities here with us and they are going to talk about 'Aviation and World Peace'. First I'm going to ask Mr Gareth Jones a question. What do you think about aviation in Russia?'

...I said into the microphone that aviation was going forward rapidly in Russia and that the Soviet Government was carrying out a policy of peace, that they would never risk a war because of the discontent of the peasants. Therefore the aeroplanes were for defence.

'Thank you very much for your views Mr Jones and now the charming German lady who flew all the way from London to Melbourne will speak...

... 'Now we will have to scurry', said my companion and off we rushed in the car. I had to give my speech in Riverside 30 miles away. Through the torrents, past the orange groves. Oh! What a ride and I found that the man [i.e. Dr Carruthers] was the secretary to the president of the Institute of World Affairs.

Back at the Mission Inn Gareth was not happy "especially after having left the thrills of New Mexico for a depressing conference in pouring rain. I attended lecture after lecture and they were all so thorough and solid and earnest that I was afraid my lecture would be an anti-climax." He need not have worried. "Hurray! It went off splendidly and the audience clapped so much that the chairman told me to get up and bow (just like an actor). I was very relieved. I brought in Russia, Hitler's foreign policy and the New Commonwealth."[17]

Writing from Hollywood on December 23 he wrote "I have never seen in such a wonderful and beautiful place as this. It's Christmas Eve tomorrow and it's like June... I am being fêted and entertained and motored around. I have never known such kindness.[18]

Following an entertainment-filled Christmas, Gareth found it difficult to work. On Boxing Day he was taken around a number of Hollywood studios "including Fox Films, RKO etc. The woman journalist Dr Cross is taking Dr Polyzoides (the Greek edition from New York) and myself around. I believe we are to be entertained to lunch at one of the studios"[19] He also visited the Metropolitan Goldwyn Mayer studio and seeing most of the stars, being entertained to the preview of 'David Copperfield' at which the leading lights of the film and press world were present."[20]

In his last letter of 1934 Gareth noted with excitement:

I went round the MGM studios, lunching there in the same room as two of the Marx Brothers... It has been a grand year and coming to an end in a lovely place. But what a rush. I have just had a telegram from Hearst, 'Glad to see you any time. Let me know when you will come. W. R. Hearst.'

Notes on Chapter 33

1
  Gareth Vaughan Jones Papers, National Library of Wales, Diary Series 35-42, 42.
2
  Sir Bernard was shocked at Lloyd George's *Memoirs*: Volume III about the Tsar's return. "It was not Sir George Buchanan's fault but Lloyd George," said Sir Bernard. "Lloyd George was a twister about it and stopped the Tsar coming for inner political reasons"
3
  Gareth Vaughan Jones Papers, National Library of Wales. Correspondence Series 1-21 File 15. September 18, 1934. See also diary entry Series 35-42, 42.
4
  Gareth Vaughan Jones Papers, National Library of Wales. Diary Series 35-42, 42
5
  Gareth Vaughan Jones Papers, National Library of Wales. Correspondence Series B6/5 November 2, 1934.
6
  Gareth Vaughan Jones Papers, National Library of Wales. Correspondence Series B6/5 November 16, 1934.
7
  Ibid.
8
  Ibid.
9
  Ibid.
10
  Gareth Vaughan Jones Papers, National Library of Wales. Correspondence Series 1-21 File 15 December 2, 1934.
11
  Western Mail, 'Wales Invades America', February 8, 1935, p. 8.
12
  Gareth Vaughan Jones Papers, National Library of Wales. Correspondence Series 1-21 File 15. December 2, 1934.
13
  Western Mail. 'Wales-Wisconsin', March 29, 1935, p.8.
14
  Gareth Vaughan Jones Papers, National Library of Wales. Correspondence Series B6/5 December 5, 1934.
15
  Ibid. December 9, 1934.
16
  Ibid. December 12, 1934.
17
  Ibid. December 16, 1934.
18
  Ibid. December 23, 1934.
19
  Gareth Vaughan Jones Papers, National Library of Wales. Correspondence Series 1-21 File 15. December 26, 1934.
20
  Ibid.

Chapter 34

Will-o' the-Wisp

The Will o' the Wisp is the most common name given to the mysterious lights that were said to lead travellers from the well-trodden paths into treacherous marshes.[1]

On New Year's Eve Gareth boarded a train to San Luis Obispo, where he alighted in the early hours of the next morning. A group of New Year's revellers, mostly Hollywood stars, including Harpo Marx, arrived from Hearst's party at the station in one of Hearst's cars, to catch their homeward bound trains. After their departure Gareth returned in the car to San Simeon, Hearst's palatial ranch:

> *It was a clear starry night. There were 52 miles to the ranch, of winding roads with mountains here and there. I saw a ship and on the shore of the Pacific; the ranch runs 36 miles along the sea. Then lights appeared at the top — Mr Hearst's ranch. Underneath was a series of bright red and white lights with a light tower flashing. That was Mr Hearst's aerodrome.*
>
> *There was a notice, which said, "Danger Wild Animals". Beside the road were buffaloes, bears, and white antelopes. We drove through a series of gates, which separated the animals from the house. Then what looked like a great Spanish cathedral came into view — huge and magnificent. We drove round the house and came to the bottom of some marble stairs. ... There was a cathedral like entrance with marble statues and orange trees everywhere. I was taken to my room, which had an exquisite Persian carpet above the bed, a ceiling of strange gold and dark red design, and a mirror with gilt oak leaf surround. Over the mantelpiece was a medieval bible scene in wood and two angels, and below a great fireplace decorated with angels — an ancient chest of drawers, a great gold covered Madonna, a Persian design around the windows, armchairs covered with Persian tapestry completed the scene in the room.*
>
> *Soon I was asleep and I was called at 8.30 am. Looking out of the window*

I saw a beautiful view of the Pacific stretching away, and to the right the blue waters of a new swimming pool with classical columns and Cypress trees, slender white statues of goddesses around it.

I dressed and crossed to the main building where there were masses of scented red and white flowers, oranges palm and lemon trees. Entering the first room there were huge Christmas trees, and on the walls hung grand tapestries. Next was the dining room, which was like the interior of a church with choir stalls taken from a Spanish church. The wooden ceiling had carvings of St George and the Dragon. The whole hall had been built around the ceiling from Italy. Six big Christmas trees with silver tinsel and candles stood in the room.

The Pacific stretches towards the horizon from my windows; and from other windows I look out on a vast swimming pool with classical colonnades around and spotlessly white statues. There is a scent of dozens of different kinds of flowers within a hundred yards there are tigers, bears, an elephant, apes, Irish wolf hounds, antelopes, buffaloes, leopards, jaguars and lions. I ventured this morning into the cage of two Royal Bengal man-eating tigers. Luckily the trainer stood by my side with a pitch-fork and would not let me go more than a couple of feet beyond the threshold. The tigers were extremely savage and bared huge teeth at me. I managed to take photos. I hope they'll come out. Funnily enough I wasn't a scrap nervous…

Next, I explored the swimming pool with its beautiful clear blue water, lined with gold and blue mosaic and surrounded by white classical statues. I wandered about and everywhere there were Babylonian, Greek, Roman, Persian and Egyptian statues and treasures. Lunch was very late and eventually Marion Davies came in wearing brown slacks and a red jumper. Later her sister in breeches and a riding habit joined the company. I got hungry waiting for Mr Hearst who eventually came at 2.45 pm for lunch. The conversation at lunch was light-hearted. The telephone rang all the time and the news service kept coming in. Hearst kept an eye on the news all the time.[2]

While Gareth notes that Hearst is keeping his eye on the news there is no record of any political content in their conversations either in his diaries or his letters home. We will also never know whether their summer meeting at St Donat's had any bearing on Hearst's anti-Soviet views. What is in no doubt is that following Hearst's autumn return to the US his publications became profoundly anti-Communist. He sent his editors and reporters on a surreptitious witch-hunt to investigate the Communist activities of university staff, and he endeavoured to expose offending academics. In

Gareth's bedroom at San Simeon.

contrast, he commissioned articles by Goering and several Nazi sympathisers within his newspapers. Hearst had already planned to visit Adolph Hitler, before leaving New York for Europe, and they did meet briefly that August.[3] His bias towards the German régime stirred American pro-Communists into accusing Hearst of being influenced by Goebbels and the Gestapo. They deemed that his pro-fascist views had been fuelled by Nazi propaganda.

Concurrent with Gareth and Hearst's St Donat's meeting, Dr Ewald Ammende, General Secretary of the Nationalities Congress, arrived in the United States to plead, somewhat belatedly, for Soviet famine aid.[4] The *New York Times'* editor asked their new day-to-day Moscow correspondent, Harold Denny (Duranty had been elevated to the status of their occasional special correspondent), to report on the veracity of this charity appeal.

After two visits to Ukraine in July and October, 1934, Denny, another "Stalin protagonist" wrote, "The hunt for famine in Russia … was like chasing a Will-o'-the-Wisp. It was always somewhere further on."[5] Curiously, Duranty had also used the expression, "Will o'-the-Wisp" in 1933,[6] and Gareth was to use it in one of his 1935 *Manchester Guardian* articles describing President Roosevelt and 'The New Deal'. It was a term which Gareth had never previously used. Had Gareth read, and then copied, the expression from either Denny's or Duranty's articles? It is possible that he had been shown Denny's article, either while braving the lions' den of the *New York Times* offices in November 1934 or, alternatively, by Ralph

Barnes at the *New York Herald Tribune;* where Barnes commendably congratulated Gareth as having, "scooped" the news about the Soviet famine.

His article describes Gareth's impressions of the changes that had taken place across America since his last visit in 1931, where businessmen were accusing President Roosevelt of, "State Socialism".

> *It is none the less true that a more formidable opposition to the "New Deal" exists in all parts of the country than is realised... He [Roosevelt] is regarded as a 'will-o'-the-wisp' who flits lightly from one fundamental decision to another... How much more reactionary the United States is in this respect [to the labour unions] than the so-called 'conservative' Britain! 'No labour unionist shall stay in my town.' ... Then he [the traveller] begins to reflect, and slowly he realises that, while the business men are reactionary and optical, there is among the mass of the people a new faith and a new confidence in the future, that the whole outlook is brighter than it was in 1932, that in spite of conservative antagonism, President Roosevelt has achieved in less than two years the task of saving the banks, of abolishing child labour and the sweat shops, of giving to the workers the right to organise which they have had for many years in Great Britain, of saving many hundred thousands of farmers from foreclosure, of increasing the price of farm produces, and of introducing a new philosophy of security through social insurance for the worker which was conspicuously absent from the nomadic, unsettled United States of pre-Roosevelt days.*[7]

These views were diametrically opposed to Hearst's, who had spent the summer reviewing the European political situation, following which he had become fearful of Roosevelt and his New Deal, the National Recovery Act, and loss of the "rugged individualism" of the conservative American. Hearst saw these as threats to the foundations of American democracy, capitalism and the free press.

On January 5, shortly after Gareth's visit to San Simeon, Hearst made his annual New Year's radio broadcast at the NBC studios in San Francisco. On this occasion, instead of focusing on American politics and prosperity, he devoted his entire address to Soviet Communism describing the atrocities of the Bolshevik regime.

The following day Gareth informed his parents that he had, "been commissioned to write three short articles on Russia for 225 dollars," through syndicated publication within Hearst's empire, including the flagship, *New York American.* This

Gareth in California.

opportunity would certainly have renewed Gareth's self-confidence and provided him with a wide platform for his Soviet expertise; which had been absent in Britain since April 1933.

Gareth's graphic Soviet experiences from two years earlier (and originally published in the British press) appeared in the *New York American* on three consecutive days in January 1935. Before he left California for the Orient, he managed to catch sight of his articles in the *Los Angeles Examiner.* They were also syndicated in at least two other Hearst newspapers.

The first of these articles was entitled:

'Russia's Starvation: What Lies Behind the Official Murders that Followed the Assassination of Kirov. Grim hunger of Peasants witnessed by Former Foreign Affairs Adviser to Lloyd George.'

The very voice of the secret police agent, the crack of the firing squad and the thud of the falling victim have been heard more in the last few weeks in Russia than for many years. For 1935 has dawned upon a period of terror following the assassination of Stalin's friend Kirov [Leningrad Party leader] on December 1, 1934.

But no-one has yet told the true story of the wave of shootings which is terrifying Moscow. What is behind the rifle shots? Why is Stalin descending with such ruthless slaughter upon Soviet citizens at a time when he claims to have brought happiness and prosperity into their lives?

... There is throughout the country a feeling of revolt and hatred of the Communists that Stalin can only crush by terror and more terror.[8]

The question remains as to why the issue of the famine allegations had been raised anew? Why did Gareth write a further series of famine-related articles for Hearst, after nearly two years of silence, based on his testimony of 1933? Had Hearst simply used Gareth to promote his own newfound, anti-Communist opinions? Did Stalin's new reign of terror motivate Hearst to re-issue the articles on the 1933 famine, or was it more likely that Hearst simply wished to mount a side swipe against President Roosevelt's New Deal policies and the problem of current trade debts with the Soviets?

Unbeknown to Gareth, the Hearst media empire continued to publish further anti-Communist articles, including the "scoop" of fresh allegations of a 1934 Ukrainian famine. On February 18, 1935, the Hearst press published a series of five articles by their correspondent, 'Thomas Walker'. The February 25, 1935 headline in the *Chicago American* read, "Six Million Perish in Soviet Famine: Peasants' Crops Seized, They and Their Animals Starve." In the middle of the page, a sub-heading read, "Reporter Risks Life to Get Photographs Showing Starvation" and at the bottom of the page, "Famine — Crime Against Humanity."[9]

Following Walker's articles, *The Nation* published a letter from Louis Fischer on March 13 (dated March 4), entitled, "Hearst's Russian Famine," which pointed out that Walker's articles were a fabrication and a fraud. Fischer, who was living at the time in New York, must have been aware of Gareth's work for Hearst, just as he was of Walker's later articles. Fischer was certainly aware of Gareth's 1933 Berlin press statement exposing the famine in the Soviet Union, which he (Fischer) had discredited at the time (see Chapter 23 above). Fischer researched Walker's background by consulting the Soviet authorities in Moscow (or was he conveniently supplied with the evidence by the Soviets themselves?) namely Walker's exact entry and exit dates in the Soviet Union. He was able to show that Walker; had never been to Ukraine; having spent only five days in total in Moscow in 1934, and his so-called investigation had placed the height of the Soviet famine in 1934 and not in 1933. Fischer asked: "Why then does the Hearst Press publish these 'revelations'? ...These Walker articles are part of the Hearst's anti-red campaign."[10]

Thomas Walker turned out to be the *nom de plume* of a convicted forger whose real name was Robert Green. After the publication of his 1935 articles, he was arrested for passport fraud and simultaneously discovered to have been on the run from the American police, having escaped from Colorado prison in 1921.[11]

The exposure of Walker's criminal past, as reported, and possibly first exposed, by the *New York Times* on July 13 1935, the Soviet propaganda machine would not only have had the pleasure of duping Hearst through publicly discrediting his anti-Soviet rhetoric, but they also 'literally' buried any credibility afforded in the western press to allegations of famine within the USSR, either past, present or future.

In response to Fischer's revelations, William Chamberlin, having recently arrived in Japan, also wrote to *The Nation*, recalling his own observations after the travel ban had been lifted in September 1933, reminding Fischer that he could scarcely have been unaware of the famine that resulted from the State's grain requisitions. Chamberlin's letter was dated March 31 — written a fortnight after Gareth had left Tokyo on his final journey. (According to Gareth's diary, he had, "Dined with Mr & Mrs Chamberlin on Tues 26th February 1935" in Tokyo and they had agreed that, "We should form a 'We cannot go to Russia' club.") To quote Chamberlin who was able to respond in Gareth's absence:

> *[Walker's] irresponsible reporting, whether it takes the form of inventing famine, or concealing them, is certainly subject to condemnation. It seems to me that Mr Fischer's article would have some balance if it had included reference to the fact that Russia, during the winter of 1932-33 and the spring of 1933 experienced one of the worst famines in its history.*[12]

While this stormy debate was at its peak, a protest against Hearst was organised by pro-Stalin activists, and on February 26, 1935 some 15,000 people gathered in Madison Square Gardens in New York to protest with the Friends of the Soviet Union against the collapse of debt negotiations between USSR and the United States. Randolph Hearst was assailed for the damning editorial attitude of his newspapers against the Soviet cause. Frank Palmer of the *Federated Press* wrote, "We know the man who had the utmost influence in causing the collapse of the negotiations."[13]

The American Communists continued to condemn Hearst, and William F. Dunne[14] wrote three open and vitriolic letters, addressing them to Hearst, 'At Your Fortress Castle' and entitled, "Why Hearst Lies about Communism."[15] Despite adverse criticism, Hearst persisted with his anti-Communist campaign through the spring, commissioning further anti-Soviet articles.

Gareth would doubtless have been truly flattered by the powerful newspaper magnate's patronage, but back in Moscow, would his anti-Soviet articles have gone unnoticed? While Gareth understood that he was on the blacklist of the OGPU, perhaps he underestimated the potential dangers of allowing himself to be placed in the spotlight. Letters to his parents clearly demonstrate that an already self-assured Gareth was overwhelmed by the enthusiastic reception given to him by the Americans, a factor which may have contributed to him to becoming over-confident and oblivious to impending danger.

Notes on Chapter 34

1
   There are various explanations for the Will o' the Wisps, the most general being that they are malevolent spirits who have a mischievous and often malevolent nature, luring unwary travellers into dangerous situations.

2
   Gareth Vaughan Jones Papers, National Library of Wales. Correspondence Series 1-21 File 15. January 2, 1935.

3
   David Nasaw, *The Chief, The Life of Randolph Hearst*, Gibson Square Books London, 2003, p. 502.

4
   Marco Carynnyk, '*The New York Times* and the Great Famine', *The Ukrainian Weekly* October., 1983. No. 40, Vol. L1.

5
   Harold Denny, *The New York Times*, 'No Famine found in North Ukraine', October 17, 1934, p. 7

6
   Marco Carynnyk, 1983 'Making the News Fit to Print: Walter Duranty, the *New York Times* and the Ukrainian Famine of 1933', p. 95. n. 70. "Duranty used the will-o'-the-wisp line in April 1933, but two years later forgot that he had claimed to have had the experience himself and attributed it to a Pravda correspondent who accompanied Soviet President Kalinin on a tour of the Volga region during the famine of 1921. The journalist expressed surprise that there was no evidence of famine in the towns and villages they visited, although in each they were told that in the next village people were dying like flies. 'None of the appalling stories which have reached Moscow… have yet been substantiated by facts', concluded the journalist." See also Walter Duranty, 1935. *I Write as I Please*. New York, Simon & Schuster p. 124-125.

7
   Manchester Guardian, "United States under Roosevelt", January 24, 1935, p. 9-10.

8
   Gareth Jones, *New York American*, 'Russia – Land of Starvation, January 12, 1935 p. 2; Two further articles followed in the same publication " 'There is no bread'", January 13, 1935, p. 8.; "Reds Let peasants Starve" January 14, 1935, p. 8.

9
   Collectivization and the 'Ukrainian Holocaust' http://www.plp.org/books/Stalin/node68.html

10
   According to Louis Fischer, Walker was in the Soviet Union October 13-18, 1934. "His train did not pass within several hundred miles of the Black Soil and Ukrainian districts which he "toured" and "saw" and "walked over" and

"photographed". Louis Fischer, *The Nation,* Vol. No. 140, No. 3636, March 13, 1935, p. 567.

11
'Passport Fraud Charged', *New York Times,* July 13, 1935 p. 4. 'Indicted Writer Also Accused as Escaped Convict'..

"Robert Green, a writer of newspaper articles describing famine conditions in the Ukraine, was indicted yesterday and held without bail pending an arraignment on Monday on the charge that he had made false statements obtaining in a passport. George Pfann, Assistant United States Attorney, alleged that Green, who wrote under the pen name, Thomas Walker, was a fugitive from Colorado prison where he escaped in 1921 while serving a sentence for forgery. After escaping from Prison Mr Pfann said, Green went to Canada, learned chemical engineering and got a job with an exporting Company as its German representative...

12
Ibid. William Henry Chamberlin, 'The Ukrainian Famine', *The Nation,* CXL, No. 3647 (May, 29, 1935), p. 629.

13
New York Times, '15,000 Here Object to Rift With Reds', February 26, 1935, p. 8.

14
William Francis Dunne was a union organiser, politician, editor, and Communist Party activist for most of his life.

15
W. F. Dunne, 1935 *Why Hearst Lies about Communism. Three open Letters to William Randolph Hearst.* New York. Workers Library Publishers p. 35

Chapter 35

"The King of Kalgan"

Gareth's three months in the United States had been a great success and despite an extremely busy schedule Gareth managed to keep his family up to date. On January 13, 1935 wrote:

> *A week today I shall be on the Pacific on my way to Honolulu where I shall arrive on Friday January 25th. On Wednesday January 30, I sail to Yokohama where I arrive on Friday, February 8th [1935].*
>
> *I have just finished doing two interviews for the Manchester Guardian: one with Upton Sinclair[1] and one with Governor La Follette, two leaders of the radical movements in America. I hope the Manchester Guardian will take them. Last week I sent an article on the 'New Deal' to them… Today the Los Angeles Examiner splashes my second article in great form. I presume it splashed my 1st article yesterday but I did not see it. Tomorrow night I broadcast from Los Angeles and on Thursday from San Francisco.*
>
> *I really don't know where to begin describing everything and besides I've got to rehearse my radio talk, rehearse my speech on the Commonwealth and the International Police Force at the farewell luncheon, which the University Club of Los Angeles is giving in my honour tomorrow…[2]*

With great reluctance Gareth left the hospitable Los Angeles and took the overnight sleeper to San Francisco, where on January 18, 1935 he embarked on the *SS Munroe* bound for Hawaii. From there he would travel to Japan, with an eventual destination of the newly named Manchukuo. This was the colonial province of Japan in China, bordering the sensitive area of Siberia.

He had a miserable voyage. The sea was extremely rough — the old boat pitched and tossed and rolled continually; it constantly poured with rain. The company was very dull — so dull that he spent most of his time reading. The best-selling book which especially excited his imagination was *One's Company* by Peter Fleming,[3] an account of the author's adventurous journey through Chinese bandit country in the previous year. This thrilling story subsequently inspired Gareth's choice of route from Hong Kong to Manchukuo where he intended to stay four weeks.

He wrote to his family: "I would give anything to be at home in front of a good fire or to go for a walk with Dada and Ianto [his dog] on the beach. I am homesick, but not seasick." He hoped that when he reached port he would have more enthusiasm for Japan and China.[4] After a terrible journey through a storm lasting 6 days the sun shone again and to his great relief the ship berthed in Honolulu on January 25, 1935.

In Hawaii, Gareth was introduced to a local family who showed him the beaches, the newly built airfield and the naval base, Pearl Harbour. "Here I am on the famous Waikiki Beach but entre nous Barry island is a thousand times better for bathing because of the coral here which sometimes cuts the feet."[5]

He published two articles on the Pacific situation in relation to Hawaii. An article published in the *Western Mail* on June 25, 1935, entitled "America's "Great Hawaiian Problem", was uncannily prophetic in predicting the circumstances that would bring the USA into the Second World War.

> *The problem in a few words, is this: A few miles from the town lies the powerful United States naval base, Pearl Harbour, which is to America what Gibraltar and Singapore are to us [British]. … What is the important strategic point in the Pacific for the defence of the United States? Hawaii. No enemy could land in California unless they first capture Hawaii. … There are 140,000 Japanese, nearly one half of the population. Are they loyal to the Stars and Stripes, or do they still worship the Son of Heaven? Have they among their number a percentage of spies who report the secrets of America to Tokyo? Will they be able to blow up parts of the naval base in a time of war? Will they be able to ignite the petrol tanks?"[6]*

After a few days in Hawaii, Gareth arrived in Japan after another stormy trip on February 9, 1935. Disembarking at Yokohama, Gareth made his way to the Imperial Hotel in Tokyo, built by Frank Lloyd Wright in 1922, where he spent his first few days, and which Gareth described as having the appearance of a "railway station." But he did not stay there long and in his news home a week later he reported "I am having a great time and am most happy. I found a journalist friend, Günther Stein, whom I knew in London, Jew, formerly of the *Berliner Tageblatt,* and we are living in the same apartment house. He's good company."[7]

Stein was now a newspaper correspondent for the London *News Chronicle* (a known hotbed of NKVD spies, including David Crook, who was later involved with the kidnapping of POUM Trotskyist leaders during the Spanish Civil War, and also admitted to spying on Orwell in Spain). Gareth may have first met Stein in Moscow in March 1933, as he was then working for the *Berliner Tageblatt*. Stein, a German by birth, who had become a naturalised British citizen, arrived in Tokyo very shortly before Gareth in early 1935. In Tokyo, the frugal Gareth gladly accepted the invitation to share his Bunka apartment — the same apartment which, from early 1936, was used by Richard Sorge, arguably the 20th century's greatest spy, for secret radio communications with Moscow. According to F. W. Deakin and G. R. Storry, Sorge asked his Moscow paymasters accredit Stein as a member of his spy ring, but was refused, which they attributed to Stein being on other unknown work for the Soviet secret police.[8]

In Tokyo, Gareth regularly attended the news conferences of Eiji Amau, the Japanese Foreign Office press officer. After the first press conference Gareth discussed Outer Mongolia with the Russian correspondent for Tass and, "then a man of about forty-five who introduced himself as 'Mr Cox' [Jimmy Cox], the Reuters' correspondent.[9] Either through his acquaintance with Cox or because he had previously worked for Lloyd George, Gareth had an entrée to interviews with Japanese politicians who were making world news. Gareth was instrumental in introducing Stein to several eminent Japanese figures. He would have readily related accounts of these interviews to Stein and may unwittingly have been a most valuable colleague to Stein in his role as an undercover Soviet agent.

In his letter home dated February 20 he wrote, "By the way I think that it is going to be a terribly quiet summer in the Far East. Japan is making friends with Russia. So a war is practically unthinkable. I'm afraid I'm in for a calm time. It looks as if Japan and China will be out of the news."[10]

Coincidentally, on February 24, 1935, soon after Gareth's arrival in Japan, Walter Duranty sent an article by cable from Moscow to the *New York Times* reporting a period of rapprochement in Soviet-Japanese relations:

> … *Temporarily the Soviet relations with Japan are somewhat improved by the virtual settlement of negotiations for the sale of the Chinese Eastern Railway. … Irritation was caused here, however, by the Japanese [claiming] that the Soviet Government was planning or had already begun to build a railroad from China to Urga, capital of Outer Mongolia — which was promptly denied. Irritation was caused too, by the occupation by a mixed Japanese-Manchukuoan force of border territory that had always been recognized as Outer Mongolian.*[11]

The ill-defined frontier between Manchukuo and Siberia was a potential war zone on the sensitive border of Soviet Russia, an area where there were many skirmishes between the opposing forces. In this region of territorial conflict, according to Eiji Amau, 200,000 Soviet troops were stationed prepared to attack Japanese forces. Stalin, fearing an attack from the Japanese, had built up an impressive force at the expense of the starving peasants elsewhere in the Soviet Union.

Group in Tokyo. Gareth is second right holding the hand of a Geisha girl.

On March 7 Gareth noted:

This is going to be an exceedingly interesting week, because I am going to have interviews with four of the outstanding personalities in Japanese life: Matsuoka, who took Japan out of the League of Nations at Geneva,[12] General Araki, the firebrand who was Minister of War, General Hayashi, who is now Minister of War and Admiral Osumi, who is the Minister of the Navy. These politicians are the men who play such a big part in modern Japan. [13]

After spending five weeks in Japan, Gareth left Tokyo informing both his colleagues and the Japanese to whom he had been introduced of his travel plans.

…I sail for the Philippines via Shanghai and Hong Kong. A year ago I was in Ireland interviewing De Valera. Don't you think I have an interesting life? I like Japan immensely. The people are courteous and kind. They seem to grin

and laugh without stopping. Everybody giggles! It is most clean here — spotless.
People seem to spend their time having baths. When I go to visit Matsuoka or
Shidehara I always take my shoes off at the threshold. Nobody dreams that there
will be a war here — out of the question for a long time — if ever.[14]

On that last day Gareth lunched with Iwanaga (formerly station master on the
South Manchurian railway) and sat next to Tanaka Tokichi[15], formerly Japanese
Ambassador to the Soviet Union (1925-30) [Hirohito's highest representative in
Manchukuo and involved in a coup to assassinate Prime Minister, Inukia Ki in 1931].
He attended Amau's press conference for the last time where he met a Hungarian,
Metzge, who took him to see Kozo Yamada, the head of a commercial information
bureau. Metzge said Mr Yamada had a great influence behind the scenes. Gareth
was to send a telegram to Mr Yamada when he arrived in Manchukuo. He was given
a visiting card to see Mr Tsutsui, the First Secretary of the Japanese Embassy in the
capital of Manchukuo, Hsinking (Changchun) as well as a letter of introduction
to see Major General Itagaki[16] when Gareth arrived in the city.

Gareth toured several countries bordering the Pacific Basin where he diligently
recorded the expatriates' views of the considered intentions of the Japanese and their
designs on territorial expansion. Finally, on July 4, 1935 he arrived in Peking (Beijing)
from where he embarked on his final journey into Inner Mongolia. Innocently unaware
of what lay ahead, he was to enter a hornet's nest of intrigue and conspiracy and within a
month he would, for a fortnight, become the focus of front-page news around the world.

On leaving Peking, Gareth described his first day's journey:

At 3.30 in the afternoon (after 8½ hours), we came to a huge collection of
mud houses, with some stone in the middle surrounded by hills. It was Kalgan,
the outpost for trade between the Mongols and China. There, two magnificent cars
were waiting for us. We were to be the guests of Mr Purpis, a Latvian, known as the
"King of Kalgan" who is the chief trader in Inner Mongolia and sells about 30,000
horses each year to the Chinese Army. Our chauffeur was the former chauffeur
of the Panchen Lama, who with the Dalai Lama is the chief lama of Tibet and
Mongolia. He drove us through the dirty town to a kind of mud-wall fortress on the
outskirts of the town. It was Wostwag, the company for trading with the Mongols,
a German firm. We entered a courtyard, which was full of hides, tobacco, boxes
of silks, wool. There were many lorries, which go from Kalgan across part of the
Gobi Desert to Urga in (Soviet) Outer Mongolia. Mr Purpis, a very lively man,
very strong and vigorous, in breeches and leather boots, came to welcome us. He

gave us a wonderful dinner that night. We had a warning to beware of Mongol dogs that are said to leap at men's throats if the men are afraid. (But I do not have the slightest trouble with Mongol dogs. Either they take a liking to me or they are terrified of me and slink away. They can tell at once that I have no fear of dogs.)

Our caravan consisting of two cars and a lorry was to start off next morning at four o'clock, just about dawn. Plessen woke Müller [German journalist, Dr Herbert Müller] and myself before four o'clock. (The Baron was just like an alarm clock). He shaved, whistling and put on his shorts. We dressed, drank tea without milk or sugar; the effect of the sunrise over the hills was fine; our caravan rattled out of the fortress. Two cars were leading and one had a trunk with all kinds of goods for the Mongolians.

The evening before, a Chinese Foreign Office representative asked us to sign the following:

We, the undersigned herewith certify that we are going to visit Inner Mongolia on our own risk for any eventualities, which may happen during our travelling.

We carefully considered all warnings of the local Chinese officials who will take no responsibilities should anything happen to the undersigned:

Von Plessen

Herbert Müller

Gareth Jones.

Kalgan, 11th July 1935.

Next to me in my car was a tremendous Cossack, he had a head like a melon — only square — shaved bald; he was terrifically strong and fat; he had bandy legs from being so much in the saddle. He laughed and joked all the time. He was very much of a child. His name was Vishnevitch and after the Revolution he walked 800 miles in winter across Mongolia, from Urga to Kalgan! There were three Russians and myself in the car and the driver said: "don't be disappointed if we don't get further than twelve miles, for floods may have blocked the road". When we left the town boundary, the day gradually getting lighter, we had to show our special visas for Chahar and Suiyuan (as the Inner Mongolian Province is called) while blue uniformed soldiers, formerly of General Sung, stood there with fixed bayonets. And so we rattled on along horrible tracks into Inner Mongolia. We left the last Chinese town behind, gradually cultivated fields disappeared; we entered the Steppes and were in real Mongolia by afternoon.[17]

A few days later Gareth ventured into territory purported to be Chinese, and into the town of Dolonor bordering on Manchukuo where Japanese troops were massing, accompanied by Dr Herbert Müller. Soon afterwards, on July 28, Chinese bandits, controlled by the Japanese from Tientsin, captured them both. Müller was released within two days, in order to obtain the ransom of 100,000 Mexican dollars, which was demanded for Gareth's release. Though this was forthcoming, the bandits were curiously obdurate, and Gareth, alone and unable to remount his horse due to exhaustion, was shot three times by his captors and killed on August 12, the eve of his 30th birthday.

Anatoli, Gareth and Dr Herbert Mueller.

After his release from captivity, Müller wrote a comprehensive report of his time in the custody of the bandits which the Foreign Office received, but its details were never published in the British newspapers, perhaps due to the British Government's policy of Appeasement.[18] In this account, if he can be believed, Müller mentions a third party. Gareth, Müller and Baron von Plessen, from the German Legation in Peking, had attended the Court of the Mongolian, Prince Teh Wang:

> *From Prince Teh's residence I started on a longer journey for the northeast part of Inner Mongolia, Herr Purpis, director of the Wostwag in Kalgan, having most kindly placed a motorcar at my disposal. Mr Jones travelled with me, also my boy Liang, and the Russian chauffeur, Anatoli Petrewschtschew.*
>
> *…I am an experienced traveller and have known Inner Mongolia since 1913 and I have gone over thousands of miles there. I know the risks and hardships of travelling in those parts and, when approached by Mr Gareth Jones for advice as to a visit to Inner Mongolia, I recommended a more comfortable trip based on the Suiyan Railway although he was himself making preparations for an extended journey into Eastern Chahar. But advice from a third party prevailed and I consented, very reluctantly, to accept the company of Mr Gareth Jones, telling him quite openly that it was the first time I had taken another foreigner on such a trip and that by doing so I was acting against my principles.*

A fuller account of Gareth's final days may be found in *Gareth Jones: A Manchukuo Incident* (Colley 2001) in which it is argued that he died at the hands of Japanese-controlled Chinese bandits. Since its publication, it is now known from spy case files held at the British National Archives (released in the UK only in May 2004, though previously available in the USA under the Freedom of Information Act) that Gareth was captured from a vehicle belonging to the Soviet secret police. Furthermore, the German company Wostwag, which had a Soviet concession in Siberian furs, was, in fact, a cover for espionage in the Far East by the NKVD.[19]

The invitation to travel with Müller appears to have been extended to Gareth at Larsen's Camp, some 150 miles from Kalgan. Was the 'third party' who allegedly persuaded Müller to take Gareth with him Mr Purpis? If so, why did he encourage him to do so? Or could it have been Baron von Plessen? Quite possibly, the tenacious Gareth would have charmed him into putting in a good word on his behalf. Gareth would no doubt have been very keen to undertake the journey and it is plausible that Müller's stated reluctance to take him was real. But we only have his word for that, and it is unfortunate that the Foreign Office did little, if anything, to corroborate Müller's story by, for example, interviewing Purpis or von Plessen. Another theory is that either Purpis organised the kidnapping of the pair in order to receive a portion of the ransom money or, alternatively, he was using the trip by the two foreign journalists as cover for his Russian driver to investigate Japanese troop movements in Dolonor, East Chahar.

The pertinent question is whether either the Soviet Union or Japan would have orchestrated Gareth's death. His exposure of the disastrous effects of Stalin's Five-Year Plan of Collectivisation and Industrialisation was clearly an embarrassment to the Soviets. Irked by the recent appearance of even more anti-Soviet articles by Gareth in Hearst's newspapers did they decide to take this opportunity to silence him once and for all? Were they suspicious of the fact that he had visited Japan before journeying on to Manchukuo? Was he giving secret information to the Japanese about the Soviets' plans? Did Moscow ask Purpis to arrange for the so-called 'friendly' bandits to capture Gareth, and thereby finally silence someone who had clearly been a thorn in their side? There are many intriguing questions but as yet no satisfactory answers.

On the other hand, the Japanese, in their quest for raw materials and their desire to become a major colonial power, would have been equally anxious that Gareth did not expose their carefully laid plans to invade the northern Chinese provinces by stealth. The worldwide headlines and international interest in his capture by bandits may have foiled another "*Manchukuo Incident*". His death may not have been part of the plan — the Japanese army might have staged the kidnap with the intention of rescuing him, thereby creating the conditions for a peaceful invasion of Inner Mongolia.

A further possibility might have been some kind of subtle collusion between the two countries. The Soviets would have been only too pleased if the Japanese struck south into China rather than north into Siberia, which had been the Japanese's earlier plan. With Gareth's death however, and the international spotlight it cast on their activities in the region, the Japanese push south stalled. This meant that the necessity of maintaining a large body of Soviet troops on the Soviet-Manchukuoan border remained. So, if the plan of the Japanese was to create an incident in which they would engineer a kidnap and then rescue Gareth in order to give grounds for pushing south, wouldn't it have been in the interest of the Soviets to allow that to go ahead, so that there was less chance of them heading North? The importance of protecting the Soviet border surely would have trumped any desire for petty revenge against Gareth on the part of Stalin or Litvinov?

With today's understanding of the ways in which secret police operated during the 1930s, Gareth may be considered to have been somewhat reckless in the risks he took. Did he believe just a little too strongly that his influential connections and British passport, along with his linguistic skills and charm, would always be his protection? It may be that, as Lloyd George always feared, he did, in the end, "take one risk too many".

Notes on Chapter 35

1
  Gareth began his 'interview with Sinclair noting "Lenin once described Upton Sinclair as an 'emotional socialist without theoretical background', an analysis which would condemn Mr Sinclair among Orthodox Marxists, but which sums up in America the very causes of his strength and of his selection in the Literary Digest as the fourth outstanding man in the world following Roosevelt, Hitler and Mussolini." Los Angeles. January 1935.

2
  Gareth Vaughan Jones Papers, National Library of Wales. Correspondence Series B6/5. January 13, 1935.

3
  Peter Fleming was probably the role model for Ian Fleming, his brother, in the James Bond spy thrillers. On account of his buccaneering lifestyle, Peter became a special operation executive in World War Two.

4
  Gareth Vaughan Jones Papers, National Library of Wales. Correspondence Series B6/5. January 20, 1935.

5
  Ibid. January 27, 1935.

6
  Western Mail "America's 'Great Hawaiian Problem'", June 25, 1935, p. 11.

7
  Gareth Vaughan Jones Papers, National Library of Wales. Correspondence Series B6/5 February 17, 1935.

8
F. W. Deakin and G. R. Storry 1966. *The Case of Richard Sorge*. London. Chatto & Windus,

9
Jimmy Cox held controversial views and asked awkward questions at the Japanese Foreign Office press briefings. Raymond Lamont-Brown's book *Kempeitai, The Dreaded Japanese Secret Police* states that: "He made no effort to cover up his contempt and growing animosity for the Japanese militaristic state". In his book he also says that James 'Jimmy' Melville Cox, the *Reuters'* correspondent in Tokyo: "was arrested on 27 July 1940 by the Kempeitai on the usual non-specific charge of espionage". Two days later he was seen falling from an open window on the third floor of the Kempeitai Headquarters. They claimed that he had committed suicide because he was guilty of espionage. The foreign community very much doubted this and was fully convinced that he had been thrown out of the window to conceal damage done to his body by the Japanese secret police. "The mercurial Gaimu-daijin (Foreign Minister) Matsuoka Yosuke issued a report exonerating the Kempeitai."

10
Gareth Vaughan Jones Papers, National Library of Wales. Correspondence Series B6/5. February 20, 1935.

11
Walter Duranty. *New York Times*, 'Soviet Watchful of Japan's Moves', 'Holds Tokyo Aims to set up economic dictatorship over the Chinese', February 24, 1935, p. 8.

12
Matsuoka Yosuke took Japan out of the League of Nations on February 24, 1933, following the Manchurian (Mukden) Incident (September 18, 1931) and the Shanghai Fake War (January 28, 1932). On March 1, 1932, a manifesto announced the creation of Manchukuo. The reference is to the time when all the members of the League of Nations, except Siam, voted against Japan following the Lytton Report, which condemned Japan for having invaded Manchuria and annexing the territory from China. See endnote for a summary of the interview.

13
Gareth Vaughan Jones Papers, National Library of Wales. Correspondence Series B6/5. March 3, 1935.

14
Ibid.

15
Baron Tanaka was Emperor Hirohito's highest representative in Manchuria and adviser to the Commander in Chief, Honjo at the time that Lord Lytton and the League of Nation's Commission visited the province in April 1932. He was also involved, while in Manchukuo, in planning a military coup to kill the Prime Minister, Inukia who had negotiated with Chiang Kai-shek and wished to cut down the Japanese military spending. He reported back the situation in Manchukuo to the Emperor.

David Bergamini's sister whose family were interned by the Japanese in World War II stated:

I think that the lethal element in his [Gareth's activities] was the meeting with Baron Tanaka Tokichi, former Japanese Ambassador to USSR. He is Hirohito's highest representative in Manchuria and was working on a coup. No one in our Government seems to appreciate the simple-minded planning that went into WWII for that inter-decade by the Japanese. …Getting back to Gareth Jones – I don't think there is any question of Japanese direction of the bandit's actions. As the book on the Philippines points out, they manipulated indigenous peoples to their own criminal activities as part of subjugation act. See David Bergamini, 1971 Japan's Imperial Conspiracy p. 497 and Margaret Siriol Colley 2001, The Manchukuo Incident, p. 59.

16
As Chief of the Intelligence Section of the Kwantung Army from 1931, he helped plan the 1931 Mukden Incident along with Kanji Ishiwara that led to the Japanese seizure of Manchukuo/ Manchuria. See Behr 1987, *The Last Emperor*, London, Futura, p. 194.

17 Gareth Vaughan Jones Papers, National Library of Wales. Correspondence Series

18 There is a Foreign Office dossier on Gareth's kidnap and murder (National Archives FO 676/215). The British Security Service held a dossier on Herbert Mueller covering 34 years of his activity up until his death in 1951. His Communist leanings and connections were known to the British Government (National Archives KV2/2566).

19 After the Japanese overran Northern China in 1937, Wostwag's Far Eastern operation was wound up. Soviet defector Walter Krivinsky (who was murdered outside his Washington hotel in 1941 by 'unknown' assassins) alerted the Western security services, that Wostwag (later renamed the Far Eastern Fur Company) was indeed involved in Soviet espionage. After Hitler came to power in Germany, Wostwag's head office relocated from Berlin to London to avoid arousing the interest of the Gestapo. Purpis was by no means a small player in the Soviet secret service as MI6 notes that at least two payments totalling $250,000 were made into his Shanghai bank account from Martin's bank in London. This money is believed to have been used to set up the Oriental Trading and Engineering Company in New York. On transit to America Purpis turned up in Europe, where he was followed by the British in 1938, who discovered he was travelling on a fake Honduran passport. The next news of Purpis comes from American records, when in 1940, he was cited as the "third associate" in a Soviet Spy ring in the USA. After this, Purpis seems to have disappeared, but as an aside, it is interesting to note that in August 1945, Kim Philby whilst stationed in Washington received a copy of the 'Wostwag' dossier from Roger Hollis of MI6, who coincidentally was a reporter for the *Shanghai Post* during the 1930s and a representative of British American Tobacco. He may well have come across Wostwag in the course of his duties. Government papers on Wostwag are held at the National Archives (National Archives KV2/1902).

Chapter 36

"A Oes Heddwych? Is there Peace."

It is bitter to think of all that brilliance, vigour, and promise [was] brutally wiped out by the bullet of a miscreant.[1]

The *Western Mail* had published daily reports on Gareth's capture by bandits. Early on the morning of Friday, August 16, 1935, his father, Edgar answered the telephone and received the terrible news of his death from the Reuters' correspondent — a day never to be forgotten by his family. The news devastated his parents. Not only had they lost their beloved son, but Wales had lost a man of integrity. The news of his murder shocked the Principality.

The sparkle went out of Gareth's home, Eryl, and was darkened forever. Life went on in the house as usual, but it was never to ring with the laughter and happiness that Gareth brought to it. No longer would the family be able to look forward to his homecoming. His great knowledge, painted on the wide canvas of his short life, had been wiped out in one single stroke. Very few young men in 1935 could have had such a broad span of worldly wisdom and political foresight.

Lloyd George, shocked by Gareth's death, had made a statement, quoted in most British newspapers, "That part of the world is a cauldron of conflicting intrigue and one or other interests concerned probably knew that Mr Gareth Jones knew too much of what was going on."

Gareth's death left a void not only in his family's life, and those of his many friends, no matter what colour, or creed — the rich and the poor, but also to the profession of journalism. Reporting of Gareth's death at the time threw little light on the motives of the bandits. Paul Scheffer, the *Berliner Tageblatt's* Editor-in-Chief and close friend, wrote Gareth's obituary on August 17, 1935, with an oblique reference to Walter Duranty (who was an amputee) and, by inference, his paper the *New York Times*:

The number of journalists with his initiative and style is nowadays, throughout the world, quickly falling, and for this reason the tragic death of this splendid man is a particularly big loss. The International Press is abandoning its colours — in some countries more quickly than in others — but it is a fact. Instead of independent minds inspired by genuine feeling, there appear more and more men of routine, crippled journalists of widely different stamp, who shoot from behind safe cover, and thereby sacrifice their consciences. The causes of this tendency are many. Today is not the time to speak of them.[2]

Claud Cockburn[3] (American correspondent for *The Times*) penned an article for his own newsletter *The Week*, pointing the finger of blame for Gareth's murder directly towards the Japanese and Germans.

Suppressed, for reasons which will become grimly apparent, by three governments, there reached us today from Pekin the real facts of the kidnapping and murder of the well-known British journalist, Gareth Jones last month in the territory north of the Great Wall of China. The truth is as significant as it is startling: for it throws an unmistakably lurid light on the immediate plans of the Japanese in north-eastern Asia, and on the attitude towards these plans of two of the other governments concerned... The same information was given by Dr Müller to the British and German authorities. His interview revealed that what he and Jones had really bumped into was nothing less than the early stages of a Japanese attempt to repeat in Chahar the coup which began to shake the world when Manchuria was invaded in 1931.

The British and German authorities concerned are both the agents of governments which for the same reason — the hope of securing useful allies against the influence of Soviet Russia — are strongly averse to doing or saying anything disagreeable to certain Japanese designs... And while this amiable diplomatic game was in progress in Pekin, Gareth Jones was allowed to be murdered in Chahar, for fear of disturbing the 'good relations' between the three 'understanding' governments of Tokyo, London and Berlin.[4]

This article, shocking in its revelations, was the only one published in Britain attempting to convey the 'truth' about Gareth's death. Cockburn's report was picked up and accepted verbatim by the British Foreign Office, who made exhaustive investigations into the claims that the Japanese and Germans were solely behind Gareth's murder. The National Archives holds a government dossier on the circumstances of

Gareth's death which is over 500 pages long, but there is not a single cross reference to Gareth's exposure of the famine as a possible motive for his murder.

The only reference in the entire dossier relating to a possible Soviet connection was from an allegation by a New York socialite friend of Gareth's, one Adelaide Ferry Hooker,[5] who actually saw his bullet-ridden car in Kalgan. After hot-footing it to London, she alleged told Lloyd George's Secretary, that, "Wostwag was supposedly a German company, but was really a Russian company trading with Mongolia." Kitson of the Foreign Office followed this up; "According to 'Oriental Affairs' for Sept [1935] 'Wostwag' is believed to have good Soviet connections otherwise they would not be able to get the necessary trading permits for Mongolia, which no other foreign firm can get,". Unfortunately, this particular line of enquiry appears to have gone no further.

The political implications of Gareth's murder with regard to Japan and the USSR had not escaped Walter Duranty's personal attention. One month after Gareth's death Duranty sent an article from Moscow by special cable, to the *New York Times*, which was published on September 15, 1935, just two days after the publication of Cockburn's article in *The Week*. It provided him with a final opportunity to 'twist the knife' into his Welsh adversary while echoing the views of Lloyd George that Gareth knew too much:

> *Today it can be stated positively that the Soviet Union has no fear of a Japanese attack, but that does not mean the Soviet Union is yet in a position to interfere with Japanese expansion in China. There are frontier incidents aplenty between Inner Mongolia which is under Japanese control, and Outer Mongolia, which belongs to the Soviet sphere. Moscow newspapers this week publish a dispatch from Britain hinting plainly that the murder of the British journalist, Gareth Jones, by 'bandits' on the western fringe of Outer Mongolia was due to the fact that he knew too much about Japanese military preparations and troop concentrations in that region. It is thought here that Japan is on the verge of new action in Northern China, with the aim of consolidating the five Northern provinces, including Inner Mongolia, as a Japanese protectorate... Faced by this probability Soviet policy is definitely "wait and see," because in point of fact the deeper the Japanese get their feet into Chinese mud the better the Russians are pleased.* [6]

Duranty, like Cockburn, avoided any reference to Gareth's 1933 exposure in newspaper reports of famine conditions in the Soviet Union — thus preventing by association any possibility of blame towards the Soviets. Was this his final blow against Gareth with its clearly perceived propaganda benefits for the Stalinist régime? Duranty also states that the Soviets would be only too delighted to see Japan's further entanglement in China. Above all, Duranty mentions a 'dispatch' from Britain of action which implied that both the British and the Soviets were aware that the Japanese military were preparing for new action in north China with the aim of invading the five Northern Provinces. But, with the exception of Cockburn's article in *The Week* this 'action' was never referred to in the British press at the time.

The unwelcome publicity caused by Gareth's kidnapping and murder may have led to the Japanese territorial expansion of Manchukuo being postponed for a further two years. In July 1937, following the Marco Polo Bridge Incident, the Japanese invaded China proper entering Peking on July 29, 1937. On December 10, 1937, the city of Nanking was entered by the Japanese and there followed three months of atrocities that came to be known as the Rape of Nanking. This series of events may arguably be seen as the true beginning of the Second World War.

Gareth's ashes were brought back to his beloved Wales and they were buried in Merthyr Dyfan Cemetery in Barry.

YMA
Y GORWEDD LLWCH
GARETH JONES
MAB ANNWYL EDGAR A GWEN JONES
IEITHYDD TEITHIWR CARWR HEDDWCH
A LALLWYDD YM MONGOLIA AWST 12 1935
YN 30 MLWYDD OED
HE SOUGHT PEACE AND PURSUED IT.

[*Here lie the ashes of Gareth Jones, the dear son of Edgar and Gwen Jones, linguist, traveller, lover of peace, killed in Mongolia August 12, 1935, aged 30 years. He sought peace and pursued it.*]

The family memorial at Merthyr Dyfan Cemetery, Barry, South Wales.

Gareth's short career spanned a turbulent period in world events when nations feared the advent of a second war following so soon after the catastrophic Great War. He had been employed by David Lloyd George, a signatory of the Treaty of Versailles, and understood the acrimony that ensued following this Treaty, with the subsequent consequences, and the failure of its revision. He foresaw the outcome of many world events that were to come true only after his death. Back in 1930 Gareth was one of the first to predict that, "The success of the Five-Year Plan would strengthen the hands of the Communists throughout the world. It might make the twentieth century, a century of struggle between Capitalism and Communism."

Gareth witnessed the hostility between Germany and Poland and correctly predicted that Germany would demand the return of the Polish Corridor, ultimately

367

by means of aggression. In Hawaii, he was concerned for the security of Pearl Harbor where he wrote of the potential for attack on the oil depots by the Japanese, as a trigger for war. But most significant amongst his achievements were his eyewitness accounts of the starvation in Ukraine, now referred to as the Holodomor. His tenacity in exposing a famine in a country deprived of wheat still holds "more than a grain of truth".

Notes on Chapter 36

1
Prof. H. Stewart. 'A letter to *The Times*, August 19, 1935.'

2
Paul Scheffer, *Berliner Tageblatt*, August 16,1935, p. 1.

3
Back in 1931, whilst working in New York, Gareth introduced Jimmy Lee to Claud Cockburn, an Oxford graduate, and took them both out to lunch. Cockburn, a committed Marxist, had by 1935, returned to London and started his own 'Gestetner' newsletter, *The Week*, which was widely read in influential political circles. *The Week* was later to gain notoriety when in December 1937, Cockburn famously coined the term, "The Cliveden Set," referring to the pre-WWII appeasement policy of a group of pro-Nazi politicians, bankers, newspaper editors, and other wealthy aristocrats, who conspired to influence the policy of Neville Chamberlain's British government. The doyen of, "The Cliveden Set" was Tom Jones, the British Government's Cabinet Secretary, who first coincidentally introduced Gareth to Lloyd George.

4
The Week,September 11, 1935,

5
Frederick Kuhn Jr., a foreign correspondent with the *New York Times* (1925-40) sent Gareth's friend Miss Adelaide Hooker (daughter of Elon Hooker of the Hooker Electrochemical Company and sister-in-law to John Rockefeller III) to Kalgan, Inner Mongolia from Japan. There she met Müller and also saw the bullet-ridden Wostwag vehicle in which the Gareth had been captured. Date not recorded.

6
Walter Duranty *The New York Times*, "Russia is watching Japanese in China". September 15, 1935. p. 14.

Epilogue

"Cut off in his prime as by frost in the midst of high summer."[1]

It was not just in his mother country of Wales that the news of his death reverberated, but throughout the whole world. A brief but impressive memorial service for Gareth was held in the British Embassy Chapel in Peking. Though his stay was very short, Gareth had made many friends in the city. There were many tokens of respect and sympathy in the form of wreaths, especially from Chinese organisations and the congregation was very representative of the international community.

Countless tributes were received from people of all walks of life, both young and old. All these affirmed that although he was disarming in his modesty, which belied the fact that he was a gifted student who would have had a brilliant future ahead of him had his life not been so tragically cut short. All knew that he was a Welsh patriot and a great lover of the land and its people.

In *The Times* on August 19, 1935, Dr H.F. Stewart, a Fellow of Trinity College, Cambridge wrote:

I desire to add a pebble to the cairn of my friend and pupil, Gareth Jones. He was an extraordinary linguist; he had literary ability of no mean order; he had, to my knowledge the makings of a good teacher. An academic or official career lay open to him; yet he preferred a life of independent activity, with its attached perils. Nevertheless, through all his adventures, he kept in touch with those who live less dangerously and I had a cheerful postcard from him at Nanking a few days before his capture. His wit, his irrepressible sense of humour, his story and shrewd and penetrating comments on men and things in America, Germany and Russia were to his friends an unfailing source of delight. "Les premiers jours de printemps ont moins de grâce que la vertu naissante d'un jeune homme". [The first days of spring have less grace than the budding virtue of a young man.] It

369

is bitter to think of all that brilliance, vigour, and promise brutally wiped out by the bullet of a miscreant.

Sir Robert Webber, proprietor of the *Western Mail*, paid tribute in *The Daily Telegraph*:

> *The news of the tragic death of Gareth Jones has brought a feeling of deep personal loss to all his colleagues on the Western Mail and the South Wales Echo and Evening Express. It is like the death of a brother. He had the rare quality, which on the instant endeared him to all that met him. When we read last week that the bandits were charmed by his personality and his singing of Welsh airs, we said how like Gareth Jones. He was Gareth to everyone, young and old and nobody thought of addressing him formally. He was a delightful, loveable boy. His youthful, jubilant spirits made us forget that he was grown up and that we were talking to a most brilliant scholar. In Wales his loss will be felt in every home.*

A letter to the editor of the *Western Mail and South Wales News* from Geoffrey Crawshay and Elfan Rees on August 28, 1935 recommended a University of Wales Memorial Travelling Scholarship,

> *To the Editor*
>
> *Sir, — In his, tribute to Gareth Jones last Sunday the Rev Gwilym Davies stressed the need for generation of men and women equipped with an under-standing of other peoples in this rapidly shrinking world.*
>
> *Everyone feels the inspiration of Gareth Jones's determination, not so much to see the world as to know it, and there must be many Welshmen who would give much to follow, in however small a way, the trail that he has blazed. Unfortunately, circumstances are ever between young Welshmen and their goals. Foreign travel is still an expensive luxury and one that those who could use it best can least afford.*
>
> *At Oxford and Cambridge there is scarcely a college that is not endowed in some small way with a travelling scholarship or bursary. For each long vacation one or two fortunate undergraduates are awarded a bursary enabling them to spend a month in some foreign country.*
>
> *Since our worst fears were realised, the thoughts of many people must have been directed to an appropriate form of memorial to Gareth Jones.*
>
> *We can envisage nothing so suitable as the establishment, in his name, at the University of Wales of such scholarships for travel abroad.*

These scholarships would not only fulfil a long-felt want, but they would also constitute a form of memorial which, we venture to think, would have appealed above all others to Gareth himself. it was by his frequent visits to the Continent, often on a tramp steamer, that he laid the foundation of his mastery of languages, graduated in his knowledge of human nature and learned to become what the Americans call "a good mixer"!

We know there are very many who would like to think that every year two young Welshmen visit a foreign land in memory of Gareth Jones. It is not a task beyond the powers of the Western Mail to bring this about by organising a fund and presenting it to the University authorities.

His own death calls not for revenge but for a better understanding amongst the people of the world.

—Yours, &c.,
GEOFFREY CRAWSHAY,
ELFAN REES.
Cardiff, Aug.28. [1935]²

The *Western Mail* quickly took up the idea, with Sir Robert Webber consenting to act as its Honorary Treasurer. It published a daily list of the new donors. The newspaper was the highest contributor donating 100 guineas. Lord Davies of Llandinam gave £100 and his sisters, the Misses Davies also contributed £25, as did Paul Block. Mr Harold S. Bucquet of the Metro-Goldwyn Mayer Corporation gave a donation. There was a subscription from Mr John Lewis of the United Mine Workers of America as well as one from the Consul-General at Rio de Janeiro. Many other well-known people donated to the fund including David Lloyd George, Mr Barnett Janner, M P, and Dr Thomas Jones. Even lesser known persons gave the sum of one shilling. The proceeds from the publication of the book *In Search of News,* an edited version of Gareth's articles and in particular his Welsh ones sold for the princely sum of two shillings and sixpence, went towards the scholarship funds.

Randolph Hearst was to write the following appreciation, which accompanied his own princely contribution, published in the *Western Mail.* It was perhaps the least he could do for the late Gareth, who died 'In Search of News', but he could not resist giving his own spin on the tragic events.

Very glad to contribute £100 to Gareth Jones Memorial. He was a fine man and a great journalist. I first met him at St Donat's where you sent him to talk to me. We had a delightful conversation, and I was greatly impressed by his ability, knowledge, fearlessness and fairness. These qualities are important in any man, but particularly important in a journalist. I was greatly shocked to hear of Mr Jones' death. A memorial is all we can do to show our respect and admiration for him. You may not wish to publish my political viewpoint, but I do not see what right the Chinese have to a land to which they are so absolutely incapable of governing. As retribution for the death of this outstanding young man and of many others, I would like to see that wretched country pass into the control of some civilized people who are capable of punishing murder and restoring peace and order.

The eventual total reached over £2,061. The award is still made annually and is open to students and graduates of the University of Wales (see Appendix V for details).

Notes on Epilogue

[1] Tribute to Gareth by the Chahar Commissioner for Foreign Affairs at Gareth's Chinese memorial service in Kalgan.

[2] The *Western Mail* September 2, 1935.

Appendices

Appendix I

This appendix contains extracts from articles by Gareth Jones published in *The Times* (London) in 1930 and the *Western Mail* (Cardiff) in 1931.

The Times
From a Correspondent, Leader,
'The Two Russias, no. 1, Rulers and Ruled', October 13, 1930, p. 13.

'The Two Russias'
Conditions in the Soviet Union 1930

Below the Surface

Visitors to Tsarist Russia often returned to England impressed with the apparent loyalty of the whole population to the Emperor and entirely unaware of the rapidly growing discontent which was seething beneath the surface. Today history is repeating itself. Groups of tourists, biased from the very beginning in favour of the "workers' paradise," are being shown by competent and charming guides the façade of Soviet Russia and leave the country enthusiastic over the success of the Socialistic experiment. Not possessing the slightest knowledge of the language, and meeting few people other than active Communists, they leap to the conclusion that the majority of that they meet are ardent supporters of the present regime. The politeness of Communist Officials, and their willingness to spare no trouble in impressing their guests, disarm criticism and leave the foreign delegations blissfully ignorant of the hunger, discontent, opposition, and hatred which in the last few months have been steadily growing in intensity and are spreading through all parts of the Soviet Union and through all sections of the community.

The Two Views

In a vast country under the "dictatorship of the proletariat" where the ballot box plays little part, it is difficult to draw a conclusion as to the exact amount of support which the regime has from the population, especially when that support varies according to such consideration as the quantity of meat or grain received in a certain town or the price of butter in a certain market. The population seems, however, to be divided into two sections, the "non-active," that is "the ruled" composed of more than 90 percent of the total. Whereas most of the "active," the 10% section, consisting of the members of the Party and of youth organisations, are filled with an enthusiasm, unknown in any other group of people save perhaps the National Socialists of Germany, the Fascist and the Salvation Army. The "non-active" 90 percent are thoroughly disillusioned, have lost faith in the Five-Years Plan and dread the return in the coming winter of the conditions which reigned in 1918 and 1919.

The Five-Years Plan

...A conversation with a Red Army commander will best illustrate the attitude of the rulers of Russia; "We must be strong and show no mercy. We are not a tender-hearted set of people. We must not hesitate, for example, to crush the kulaks and send them to cut wood in the forests of the north."

The active minority firmly believes that ultimately Communism will be victorious. To attain this victory in Russia their method is the Five-Years Plan (October 1, 1928, to September 30, 1933), which has a threefold object — rapid industrialisation, complete collectivisation of agriculture, and the elimination of all capitalist elements in the country. The State Planning Commission, in collaboration with the whole country, prepares a vast plan for the whole country, for each district and for each factory. Thus the economic system is highly centralised and the means of production in industry are already almost entirely in the hands of the State. The whole energies of the ruling body are concentrated upon the execution of the Five-Years Plan, and all national activities, from education to art, are subordinated to one object, the rapid and complete socialisation of the Soviet Union.

One of the main weapons in the hands of the active section of the population is, of course, propaganda, from which one cannot escape wherever one may go. In the train one reads in large letters, "Let us reply to the furious arming of the capitalists by carrying out the Five-Years Plan in four years." Across the streets large red and white banners are stretched, upon which are inscribed: "The capitalists of the West are preparing war on the Soviet Union," or "Let us destroy illiteracy." Sitting in any co-operative restaurant one sees on all sides pictures of Lenin, Stalin and Kalinin, and such appeals as, "On May Day remember the oppressed workers of the capitalist countries." In a factory, besides excellent posters on health and accidents, there are such notices as; 'God and the drunkard are the enemies of the Five-Years Plan,' ... Outside the Tretyakovskaya Art Gallery in Moscow the following slogan strikes the visitor, "Art is a weapon of class warfare." Upon the House of Soviets the following words are written upon a banner, "To Capitalism, the international revolutionary movement brings not peace but the sword." Finally, upon the china in the Hotel Metropole, mainly frequented by foreigners, are the words; 'Workers of the world, unite.'

Besides posters, there are other more effective propaganda methods. The theatre is an implement for the socialisation of the country. The film industry, of whose success the USSR is justly proud, has as its aim the spreading of Communism. The museums, which are artistically arranged and admirably kept, all teach one lesson, the evil of Capitalism and the glories of the revolution. Even such a minor institution as a shooting range must have its political use; thus the targets are the Tsar, a priest, a kulak (a peasant owning more than three cows), a Chinaman, and a drunkard.

The Shock Brigades

How far have these attempts to convert Russia into an industrialised country succeeded? In some branches of industries the boast of the Communists are fully justified. The power development of the electrified industry are tremendous and the quality of the materials used, and of the products is far better than in other industries. The telephone system, for example, works well. The increased sales of Russian oil testify to the development of the Baku district. Aviation is progressing rapidly and a Trans-Siberian air route is being planned which will bring London, within a few days of

Japan and thus revolutionise the postal services. New factories, mines and furnaces are being constructed everywhere. The State Publishing Company has created a network of bookshops throughout the country with vast sales of books at low prices.

In spite of the success attained in some branches of Soviet Industry, Russia remains a poor and discontented country. In the last few months, the Five-Years Plan has met with a check and in many districts, especially the Donetz Basin, there have been many breakdowns. Food difficulties arising from the slaughter of animals which followed the violent collectivisation campaign in January and February, and from the Soviet policy of exporting foodstuffs to obtain credit at all costs, are already putting a brake on the progress of industrialisation, as is proved by the decision to postpone the beginning of the Third Year of the Plan from October to January. This winter the difficulties confronting the Five-Years Plan will be greater than ever for thousands of workers are already returning from the towns to the villages and many will be too weak to work.

The optimism of the active Communists and their belief that Russia will in one- or two-years' time be prosperous cannot be justified. Far nearer to the truth are the views of the rank and file, of the non-active workers and peasants.

From a Correspondent, Leader,
'The Two Russias, no. 2, Fanaticism & Disillusion', October 14, 1930, p. 15.

Lost Faith

The views of the majority of the workers on living conditions under the Five-Years Plan can be gathered from the following conversations with workers. An employee of an agricultural implement factory said, "Everything is bad now and we cannot get anything at all. We cannot get boots and we cannot get clothes. …We cannot obtain enough food and many are too weak to work." One of many thousands of miners, whose flight from the hunger and the housing shortage of the Donetz Basin the writer witnessed, expressed his opinion of what the Five-Year Plan was doing for Russia in the following words: "Everybody is going away from the Donetz Basin, because there is no food here. There is nothing in Russia. The situation is terrible. All that the Communists do for us is to promise us that when the

Five-Year Plan is over we shall all be prosperous. My life is like a flower; it will soon wither away. I want to eat and live now. What does it matter to me what will happen in a hundred years?"

Another miner who was travelling in the same compartment nodded approval and said: "A year or two ago we could got enough to eat, but now nothing at all. Now they are sending all our grain abroad and building factories. Why cannot they give us food and boots and clothing? I get 80 roubles a month. How can I live? The Five-Years Plan will not succeed. The Communists will not last very long, for we cannot stick it any longer. You see if there will not be a revolution." Nor was this miner the only Russian who was so angry with present conditions as to speak of an uprising, for other citizens, especially in the south, spoke of revolution.

Women are equally discontented with living conditions. A woman worker said: "Times are bad. From 1922 until last year everything was satisfactory, but now things have become unbearable. With the money I receive for my eight-hour day's work I can only buy a small plateful of potatoes and tomatoes or a tiny portion of fish. I earn 52 roubles (nominally about £5 a month). How can I live?" Lack of faith in the future of the Plan and disillusionment characterized the conversation of most non-active workers.

Bitter hatred of Communists and of the privileges they enjoy was often expressed. During a journey in the South a train passed ours and in were two cleanly dressed men travelling first-class. A workingwoman (a cook) who was in our compartment shouted: "There's a party man and there's another. They are both travelling soft [first-class]. They get everything and we have to starve." With this there was general agreement among the people the compartment. "The Communists get the best rooms and we get none at all. They just send somebody off to the prisons of Solovki and take their room," said a miner on another journey.

Stalin's Dream

Stalin shares the unpopularity of his Party and most Russians evaded a reply to any question about him saying, "If Lenin had only lived, then all would have been well." An anecdote told with a warning that to repeat it would render anyone guilty of a counter-revolutionary act, illustrates the general attitude towards the dictator. Stalin has a dream in which Lenin appears and says to him, "Good-day Stalin. How is Russia?" Stalin replies: "We are getting on splendidly. Our achievements under the Five-Year Plan are wonderful." Lenin asks, "But what are you going to do when the Five-Year Plan is over?" Stalin answers, "Oh, then we shall have another Five-Year Plan." Finally Lenin crushes Stalin by saying, "By that time everyone in Russia will have died and have joined me and you will be the only man left to carry out your third Five-Year Plan."

Nor do the methods used by the Party meet with the approval of the masses. The Communists have committed a tactical blunder in over-indulging in propaganda. "We do not read the notices because we know already what is written on them," was the remark of a teacher. A miner expressed himself in more vigorous terms: "I do not believe a word they say in the papers or on the placards. They are all lies, lies, lies. Nobody reads the posters, we are so tired of them."

The action of the State Political Police in exiling peasants, members of the intelligentsia, the priests and bourgeois, to Solovki, to the Urals and to Siberia, is condemned by the majority of the non-active inhabitants, for the sympathy of the average Russian is still, as in Tsarist days, with the under-dog, with the sufferer. Fear of the secret police closed the mouths of some fellow travellers. On being asked several questions, one skilled worker became silent and said: "I am afraid of talking to you. A lot of foreigners, Latvians and others, belong to the OGPU (the State Political Police). There are spies — most of the Komsomoltsi (Young Communists), for example — who report you. You may be a spy."

The present food shortage was attributed by most Russians to two causes — the agricultural revolution begun last year and the absence of a free market. A caretaker and his wife explained: "It is all the fault of this collectivisation, which the peasants hate. There is no meat, nothing at all. What we want is a free market." Upon this, the most vital problem of all, it is better, however, to let the peasants speak for themselves.

While there is no reason to believe that the poor peasants support their Communist benefactors the point of view of the average peasant was well expressed in the following conversations, one with two members of a collective farm and the other with a Cossack individual farmer. "It's a dog's life," agreed the two collective members. "It would be better to live under the earth than to live now. They force us to join collective farms. The very best people, those who worked day and night, were sent to the

Urals and Siberia, and their houses were taken from them. What is the use of living?"

The Coerced Farmer

The Cossack individual farmer also complained bitterly of the Communist policy. "It is hard to live. Just because we have our own holdings they make life a burden for us. I come here to the big town and I go to a shop to buy something. They say, "Show us your collective farm card." I reply, "But I have no collective farm card." They say, "Then we cannot sell you anything." So in time I shall have to give up my land. Otherwise I shall not be able to buy a single thing and perhaps they will just take my house away and send me to Siberia. In my Cossack station in February they took 40 of the best and most hardworking peasants away with their women and children and sent them in freezing trains to Urals."

The conversation quoted above, upon which no comment is necessary, are not chosen on account of the opposition they express to the Soviet régime, but because they are typical of views heard in many parts of Russia. They prove that the Communist Government has to face ever-growing opposition and hatred within the country. The openness with which many Russians expressed their dissatisfaction is another striking testimony to the extent to which public opinion has been roused.

From a Correspondent, Leader,
'The Two Russias, no. 3, Strength of the Communists', October 16, 1930, p. 15

In spite of widespread discontent, the government seems relatively stable for there is no organized opposition. Any attempt at forming a policy opposed to the general line of the party is immediately nipped in the bud. The OGPU (the State Political Police) is a strong body, with powers of life and death, which can ruthlessly and immediately suppress any counter-revolutionary movement. Never the less, peasant risings are possible, but these are not likely to affect seriously the position of the Government because they can be instantly crushed. Nor will the riots, which will probably take place this winter, bring about the downfall of the Soviet power, for they will be suppressed with equal thoroughness.

Many Difficulties

These glimpses of life in Soviet Russia show that the Communists are not having all their own way with the Five-Year Plan. The difficulties are formidable and they are putting a serious brake on the progress of the Plan. There are industrial difficulties, there are agricultural difficulties and there are human difficulties.

What are the industrial difficulties? The first is the weakness of workers from lack of nearly all foods except bread. Meat is exceedingly scarce. All fats are almost impossible to obtain unless one is a manual worker or a member of the Communist party. Even a manual worker is rarely able to get enough. The bad quality of the goods produced under the Five-Year Plan is another drawback. The Soviet press publishes frank letters stating that clothes often fall to pieces in not much more than a month after purchase. Tractors often break within a few hours of use. This is easily understood. A factory is told to produce 1,000 tractors by a certain date under the Five-Year Plan. The manager may be arrested, perhaps shot or his bread-card may be taken away from him if the order is not carried out. Hence those 1,000 tractors are turned out regardless of quality.

Lack of Skilled Labour

The ever-growing lack of engineers and of skilled labour is going to be a serious barrier to the success of the Plan. It is impossible to train engineers and mechanics in a year. Often a generation or more is needed to provide a trained body of workers. A South Wales collier cannot be made in six months. He is the skilled result of generations of experience. The Soviet Government is setting up industrial and engineering schools everywhere but they will find out that they cannot run an industrialised State on unskilled and untrained engineers mechanics, and workers.

The railways of the USSR are now in a state of confusion. Terrible mistakes have been made. Men have been shot for muddling the transport organisation. A millions tons of coal was left standing idle in the Donetz Basin this year because there were not enough wagons and locomotives to carry it away. Unless transport is improved and unless the railways planned are built in time, and, what is more, built well, then the Five-Year Plan will be in grave danger of failing.

It has been difficult for the Soviet authorities re cently to keep the workers in the factories. They have been leaving one district for another or returning hungry from the towns to their villages where they have parents or brothers or cousins. The flight of workers was most marked in the Donetz Basin, the coal, iron and steel district where 93,000 workers fled last summer. The Soviet Government has had to make regulations which amount to the tying of workers to their factories or mines and to the tightening of the grip of the State over the life of each citizen.

Fuel Famine

Failure in supplying factories with raw material such as cotton or flax, &c., the famine in fuel which caused so much suffering this winter, the disappointing results of the co-operative movement all these have put a brake on the fulfilment of the Plan. In agriculture the Government have had to face the opposition of masses of the peasants. There are probably at this moment many Communists being murdered in the villages by peasants want to stick to their land. The wholesale massacre of cattle and pigs which followed upon the violent campaign of collectivisation a year ago has caused a shortage of live-stock which will affect Russia for several years. By the class-warfare in the villages and extermination of the richer peasants (the Kulaks) by exile, confiscation, or sometimes by shooting, the Communists are depriving Russian agriculture of its hardest workers.

Hundreds of Men Shot

There are, finally, serious human drawbacks which will prevent the five-Year Plan making Russia into a happy prosperous country. There is, first, the clinging of the average human being to property. Secondly, managers of factories and directors of trusts and many people in good positions are afraid of taking responsibility. It has been dangerous. During the last winter hundreds of men have been shot for failures in the branches of industry in which they had leading posts. When your actions are dictated according to a set plan and when failure may bring about death, your feeling of initiative is sure to suffer. Another human drawback is the stress which is laid upon political keenness and on orthodoxy rather than on practical ability. If you are a Communist then you have a far better chance of becoming the director of a factory than a non-Communist. A good street-corner orator is not necessarily a good organiser. There is thus waste of brain-power.

The building up of an ideal State is going to be handicapped by the lack of freedom of expression which is an obstacle to the thinker, the artist, the writer, the politician, and to the man in the street. Finally the disillusionment which is spreading through the ranks of workers and peasants and which contrasts so violently with the optimism of the Communists and of youth has shattered the first fine careless rapture of the Plan.

The Soviet policy exporting foodstuffs to obtain credits at all costs to buy machines, and build factories, with a view to making the country self-supporting is partly guided by the fear of an ultimate attack by capitalist countries. The State deprives the population of most commodities badly needed at home, in order to get currency wherewith to buy tractors, textile-making machinery, and engines from abroad necessary to carry out the Plan.

Western Mail
'Russia's Future: Stupendous Plan of Communists' April 8, 1931, p. 5

With its three aims the Industrialisation of Russia, the Socialisation of agriculture, and the extermination of the private trader, the Five-Year Plan is the most thorough revolution which has ever been attempted in the history of the world.

'Forces Behind Stalin's Dictatorship' April 9, 1931, p. 14.

The dominant factor of the Five-Year Plan is the character of Stalin, the dictator. This ruthless, honest man is just the man to drive a nation. He is brutal and has no mercy. He allows nothing to stand in his way when his mind is made up.

'Russian Workers Disillusioned', April 10, 1931, p. 5.

The policy of Collectivisation aims at doing away with the millions of individually owned farms and strips, and at establishing large farms run by machinery and owned in common. The peasants are allowed to keep their cottage, one cow, chickens, perhaps a pig or two, but the tractors and the land are common property. Besides these 'collectives', vast State farms, covering hundreds of thousands of acres, are set up. These are to produce millions of tons of grain for export.

There are, finally, serious human drawbacks which would prevent the Five-Year Plan making Russia into a happy prosperous country. There is, first, the clinging of average human being to property. Secondly, managers of factories and directors of trusts and many people in good positions are afraid of taking responsibility for men have been shot for failures. The ever-growing lack of engineers and of skilled labour is a serious barrier to the success of the Plan.

'Mixture of Successes and Failures', April 11, 1931, p. 12

In 1930, the Five-Year Plan has so far been a mixture of successes and failures. It is increasing the production of Russia, but at the expense of quality and human happiness. The success of the Plan would strengthen the hands of the Communists throughout the world. It might make the twentieth century, a century of struggle between Capitalism and Communism.

Appendix II

Letters from Gareth to Newspaper Editors about the Famine

New York Times. May 13, 1933
Mr Jones Replies: Former Secretary of Lloyd George Tells of Observations in Russia

To the Editor of The New York Times:
On my return from Russia at the end of March, I stated in an interview in Berlin that everywhere I went in the Russian villages I heard the cry, "There is no bread, we are dying". and that there was famine in the Soviet Union, menacing the lives of millions of people.

Walter Duranty, whom I must thank for his continued kindness and helpfulness to hundreds of American and British visitors to Moscow, immediately cabled a denial of the famine. He suggested that my judgment was only based on a forty-mile tramp through villages. He stated that he had inquired in Soviet commissariats and in the foreign embassies and had come to the conclusion that there was no famine, but that there was a "serious food shortage throughout the country ... No actual starvation or deaths from starvation, but there is widespread mortality from diseases due to malnutrition."

Evidence from Several Sources

While partially agreeing with my statement, he implied that my report was a "scare story" and compared it with certain fantastic prophecies of Soviet downfall. He also made the strange suggestion that I was forecasting the doom of the Soviet régime, a forecast I have never ventured. [Gareth never publicly ventured his thoughts of a collapse of the USSR, so one must assume this refers to a private conversation with Duranty at the Hotel Metropole in late March 1933.]

I stand by my statement that Soviet Russia is suffering from a severe famine. It would be foolish to draw this conclusion from my tramp through a small part of vast Russia, although I must remind Mr Duranty that it was my third visit to Russia, that I devoted four years of university life to the study of the Russian language and history and that on this occasion alone I visited in all twenty villages, not only in the Ukraine, but also in the black earth district, and in the Moscow region, and that I slept in peasants' cottages, and did not immediately leave for the next village.

My first evidence was gathered from foreign observers. Since Mr Duranty introduces consuls into the discussion, a thing I am loath to do, for they are official representatives of their countries and should not be quoted, may I say that I discussed the Russian situation with between twenty and thirty consuls and diplomatic representatives of various nations and that their evidence supported my point of view. But they are not allowed to express their views in the press, and therefore remain silent.

Journalists Are Handicapped

Journalists, on the other hand, are allowed to write, but the censorship has turned them into masters of euphemism and understatement. Hence, they give "famine" the polite name of "food shortage" and "starving to death" is softened down to read as "widespread mortality from diseases due to malnutrition." Consuls are not so reticent in private conversation.

My second evidence was based on conversations with peasants who had migrated into the towns from various parts of Russia. Peasants from the richest parts of Russia coming into the towns for bread. Their story of the deaths in their villages from starvation and of the death of the greater part of their cattle and horses was tragic, and each conversation corroborated the previous one.

Third, my evidence was based upon letters written by German colonists in Russia, appealing for help to their compatriots in Germany. "My brother's four children have died of hunger." "We have had no bread for six months." "If we do not get help from abroad, there is nothing left but to die of hunger." Those are typical passages from these letters.

Fourth, I gathered evidence from journalists and technical experts who had been in the countryside. In *The Manchester Guardian*, which has been exceedingly sympathetic toward the Soviet régime, there appeared on March 25, 27 and 28 an excellent series of articles on "The Soviet and the Peasantry" (which had not been submitted to the censor). The correspondent, who had visited North Caucasus and the Ukraine, states: "To say that there is famine in some of the' most fertile parts of Russia is to say much less than the truth: there is not only famine, but — in the case of the North Caucasus at least — a state of war, a military occupation." Of the Ukraine, he writes: "The population is starving."

My final evidence is based on my talks with hundreds of peasants. They were not the "kulaks" — those mythical scapegoats for the hunger in Russia — but ordinary peasants. I talked with them alone in Russian and jotted down their conversations, which are an unanswerable indictment of Soviet agricultural policy. The peasants said emphatically that the famine was worse than in 1921 and that fellow-villagers had died or were dying.

Mr Duranty says that I saw in the villages no dead human beings nor animals. That is true, but one does not need a particularly nimble brain to grasp that even in the Russian famine districts the dead are buried and that there the dead animals are devoured.

May I in conclusion congratulate the Soviet Foreign Office on its skill in concealing the true situation in the USSR? Moscow is not Russia, and the sight of well-fed people there tends to hide the real Russia.

GARETH JONES.

London,

May 1, 1933.

The *Manchester Guardian*, May 8th, 1933.

The Peasants in Russia Exhausted Supplies

To the Editor of the Manchester Guardian,

Sir, — In a series of articles published in the "Manchester Guardian" on March 25, 27 and 28, your correspondent described his visit to the North Caucasus and the Ukraine and summed up his impressions as follows: "To say that there is famine is to say much less than the truth … The fields are neglected and full of weeds; no cattle are to be seen anywhere; and few horses; only the military and the G.P.U. are well fed, the rest of the population obviously starving, obviously terrorised."

Attempts have been made in your columns to discredit the views of your correspondent. The "Moscow Daily News" has written on him an article entitled "When is a Lie not a Lie?" May I as a liberal-minded man who has devoted four years of university life to the study of the Russian language and history, and who visited about 20 different villages in the Ukraine, the Black Earth district and the Moscow region, as recently as March of this year, fully confirm his conclusions, and congratulate him on having been the first journalist to have informed Britain of the true situation of Russian agriculture?

The villages which I visited alone on foot were by no means in the hardest-hit parts of Russia, but in almost every village, the bread supply had run out two months earlier, the potatoes were almost exhausted, and there was not enough coarse beet, which was formerly used as cattle fodder, but has now become a staple food of the population, to last until the next harvest. Many cottages had not even cattle fodder, and the peasants assured me that the occupants of those cottages were dying of hunger. In each village I received the same information — namely that many were dying of the famine and that about four-fifths of the cattle and the horses had perished. One phrase was repeated until it had a sad monotony in my mind, and that was: "Vse Pukhili" (all are swollen, i.e. from Hunger), and one word was drummed into my memory by every talk. That word was "golod" — i.e., "hunger" or "famine". Nor shall I forget the swollen stomachs of the children in the cottages in which I slept.

Communists will reply that these conclusions are based on talks with malevolent "kulaks", who are counter-revolutionary. If that is so, I can only say that almost every Russian peasant must be a kulak, for the unanimity of the peasants' hatred of the Bolsheviks was one of the most striking features of this visit to the Soviet Union. On previous visits to Russia I have also been deeply impressed by the passionate opposition of the peasantry to the Communists.

Your correspondent's views were fully confirmed by my visits to the villages but by the most reliable official foreign representatives in the Soviet Union. Moreover, one has only to speak to hundreds of peasant-beggars, who have been driven by hunger from many parts of Russia into the towns, to find confirmation of your correspondent's statements.

As a liberal and a pacifist, I wish that something could be done to relieve the suffering of the peasants in Russia, which, according to foreign observers and to the peasants themselves, is worse than in 1921. Already efforts are being made to succour many of the German colonists, whose letters to their fellow countrymen are tragic. These letters, some of which I have seen, contain such passages as the following: "We have not had for one and a half weeks anything except salt and water in our stomachs, and our family consists of nine souls." From the Volga district we read "I went out to seek him and I went out to feed him, but I couldn't find him. One cannot get lost on the road. It is marked by human bodies… There is nobody left among all our friends who has anything left… Your brother's four children died of hunger." The Evangelical Church in Germany is helping, and those who wish to assist are advised to write to the committee, "Bruder in Not" (Brothers in Need), Berlin N24.

I hope that fellow liberals who boil at any injustices in Germany or Italy or Poland will express just one word of sympathy with the millions of peasants who are victims of persecution and famine in the Soviet Union.

Yours, &c.

GARETH JONES

Reform Club, Pall Mall, London.

May 3, 1933

Appendix III

Biographical Notes

Aitkin, William Maxwell; Lord Beaverbrook (1874–1964). Canadian millionaire stockbroker who emigrated to Britain in 1910 and entered politics as a Conservative MP. Became press baron on acquiring *Daily Express* (1916) and *Evening Standard* (1929). Ennobled by Lloyd George in 1917 and was WW1 Minister of Information in 1918. In 1936 *The Daily Express* was the world's largest daily newspaper with a circulation of 2.5 million.

Amery, Leopold (1873-1955). First Lord of the Admiralty 1922-24 and colonial secretary 1924-29.

Ammende, Dr Ewald (1892-1936). Baltic politician born in Pernau (now in Estonia). Involved in relief efforts to relieve the famine in Russia. Muggeridge had no doubts he was a financed agitator of the German government.

Araki Sadao, General (1877-1966). Appointed Japanese Minister of War in December 1931 with the Constitutionalists. He supported the Strike-North faction, which favoured expansion into Communist Russia.

Baden, Prince Max of (1867-1929). Chancellor of Germany until the 9th November 1918. He endeavoured to persuade the Kaiser to abdicate and call for a cease-fire to end the Great War but failed and so he resigned from office handing the Chancellorship to Friedrich Ebert.

Ballinger, Sir John (1863-1933). Distinguished Welsh librarian and first librarian at the National Library of Wales in the 1920s.

Barnes, Ralph (1899-1940) American journalist and Moscow Correspondent for the New York *Herald Tribune.*

Barrett, Mr R T. British journalist for *The Critic* of Hong Kong.

Bernstorff, Count Johann von (1862-1939). Son of Count Albrecht von Bernstorff. German Ambassador to Washington, 1914-1917. Bernstorff's mission was to persuade the American public and leaders to stay neutral during WWI.

Block, Paul (1875-1941). A successful American immigrant from East Prussia.

He was a newspaper publisher and contemporary of W. Randolph Hearst. Gareth accompanied him to Germany in 1934 after the Night of the Long Knives. Block was a close friend of New York Mayor Jimmy Walker (qv.) and President Coolidge. He supported Franklin D. Roosevelt in his 1928 campaign for governorship of New York.

Briand, Aristide (1862-1932). Premier of eleven French Governments between 1911 and 1929. Locarno Act instigator 1925. Nobel Prize winner with Gustav Stresemann and Austen Chamberlain. Co-author of Kellogg–Briand Pact in 1928.

Brückner, Colonel Wilhelm (1884-1954). Hitler's bodyguard and chief adjutant until 1940. Found guilty of the Beer Hall Putsch in Munich (1923).

Bukharin, Nicolai (1888-1938). Editor of *Pravda* 1918-1929. Allied with Zinoviev and Rykov and Stalin in 1923 against Trotsky. Head of Comintern 1926-1929. Broke with Stalin in 1928 to lead Right Opposition. Executed in Third Moscow Trial in 1938.

Bunker, Colonel Laurence (1902-1977). American friend of Gareth. Received a Citation for Legion of Merit for exceptional meritorious conduct in the performance of outstanding services in the Pacific Area from June 1945 to June 1946. He served as personal assistant to Major General Richard Marshall and contributed to the success of missions of the General Headquarters in the Philippines and Japan.

Butler, J R M (1889-1975). Cambridge historian, author of the *Biography of Lord Lothian, 1882-1940,* London. MacMillan, 1960. Attended Gareth's Memorial Service at Trinity College, Cambridge.

Butler Thwing, Francis Wendell (1891-1964). Married Gertrude Minna Kerr, sister of Lord Lothian.

Cairns, Andrew. A Canadian wheat trade expert and secretary of the International Wheat Advisory Commission. His important report "Mr Cairns' Investigation in Soviet Union" lay dormant in the Foreign Office files for 50 years.

Carey-Evans, Sir Thomas and Lady, Lloyd George's son-in-law and daughter.

Carson, Sir Edward (1854-1935). Leader of resistance to Home Rule and organiser of Ulster Volunteers (1912). Forced British Government to exclude Protestant provinces from the Home Rule Agreement of 1914*)*.

Chamberlain, Sir Austen (1863-1937). British Foreign Minister 1924-1929. Nobel Peace Prize winner following Locarno Act of 1925.

Chamberlain, Neville (1869-1940)**.** British Prime Minister 1937-1940. Signed Munich Agreement with Hitler in 1938 which ceded Czech land to Germany.

Chamberlin, William Henry (1897-1969). An American historian and the *Christian Science Monitor* correspondent in Moscow in 1933 who also wrote for the *Manchester Guardian* . Correspondent for the *Monitor* in Tokyo in 1935.

Cockburn, Claud (1904-1981). British journalist at *The Times* who also published his own newsletter, The *Week,* devoted to exposing the hypocrisy of the British press throughout the period of political appeasement of the 1930s. He coined the name "Cliveden Set" for Lord and Lady Astor and their influential friends, who were considered to be pro-Nazi.

Collins, Michael (1890-1922). Irish politician. In 1916, he was imprisoned following the Easter Rebellion. He was head of the Republican Army during the warfare of 1920-21. As Commander-in-Chief of the Free State Army he was killed in the war against the rebels. He and Griffiths negotiated the treaty (1921) with Britain that created the Irish Free State and partition of Ireland.

Cosgrave, William Thomas (1880-1965). Irish politician. Became a Sinn Fein M.P. in 1917. He was the first President of the Free State Executive, holding the position from 1922 until his defeat in the election of 1932.

Cox, Melville James 'Jimmy' (1885-1940). British journalist, Reuters' correspondent in Tokyo who was arrested on 27th July 1940 by the Kenpeitai (Japanese military police) and died in mysterious circumstances a few days later.

Crozier, W P (1879-1944). Editor of the *Manchester Guardian* from 1931-1944 who published the articles on the famine by Gareth and Malcolm Muggeridge.

Dafydd ap Gwylim (c. 1315/1320 - c. 1350/1370). Celebrated Welsh poet and contemporary of Chaucer.

Davies, Colonel David; later **Lord Davies of Llandinam** (1880-1944). Grandson of David Davies, the first benefactor of Aberystwyth College, University College of Wales and a coalminer owner in the Rhondda. Wartime (First World War) Parliamentary Private Secretary to the Prime Minister, Mr Lloyd George. Davies wanted to see the establishment of a strong International Police force so that international agreement and peace could be obtained. The Temple of Peace, Cardiff was a gift from Lord Davies to the Welsh people. David Davies was the Founder, in 1932, of the New Commonwealth with the object of establishing an International Tribunal empowered to deal with all disputes threatening the peace of the world that did not come in the purview of the Permanent Court of International Justice.

Davies, The Rev. Gwilym CBE (1879-1955). Welsh Baptist minister, co-founder of the Welsh branch of the League of Nations with Lord Davies. He gave the eulogy at Gareth's Memorial Service in Barry in August 1935.

Dawes, Charles Gates (1865-1951). US statesman, vice-president (1925-29), Awarded the 1925 Nobel Peace Prize for his work that produced the Dawes Plan (1924) for stabilizing the German economy. Dawes Plan (1924) — a measure devised by a committee chaired to collect and distribute German Reparations after World War I. It established a schedule of payments and arranged for a loan of 800 million marks by US banks to stabilize the German currency.

Denny, Harold (1889-1945). *New York Times* correspondent in Moscow following Duranty.

De Valera, Eamon (1882-1975). Irish Statesman and Prime Minister 1932 –1948, 1951-1954, 1957-1959. He was active in the Irish Independence movement and after the Easter Rising (1916) was elected president of Sinn Féin while imprisoned in England. He opposed William Cosgrave's Irish Free State ministry and founded Fianna Fáil in 1924.

Dewall, Wolf von. The London correspondent for the newspaper, *The Frankfurter Zeitung*, also published articles in the *New York Times* and *The Spectator*. A close friend of Gareth. One time in the employment of the China Customs and Postal Service under Sir Robert Hart.

Dillon, John (1851-1927). An Irish nationalist politician. A supporter of Charles Stewart Parnell entered Parliament in 1880 and was arrested several times for his advocacy of boycotting and agrarian agitation.

Dirksen, Herbert von (1882-1055). The German Ambassador to Soviet Union in 1933 and later to Japan. A Nazi sympathiser.

Dmovski, Roman (1864-1939) Leader of the Duma in Poland. David Lloyd George said of him, "Dmovski is a fool and the most dangerous of fools is a clever fool." In August 1917, the Allies established Dmovski as leader of the Polish National Committee. They also committed themselves to a Polish state and in November recognised the Polish National Committee as the future government. Polish nationalist and anti-Semite and admirer of Italian Fascism.

Dollfuss, Engelbert (1892-1934). Chancellor of Austria. Assassinated by Austrian Nazis in an unsuccessful coup on July 25th 1934.

Dudley, Alan. Friend of Gareth's in New York from Aberystwyth College.

William Francis Dunne (1887-1953). Union organiser, politician, editor, and Communist Party activist for most of his life. Elected in 1924 as an alternate member of the Executive Committee of the Communist International, Dunne was the representative of the Workers (Communist) Party of America to the Comintern in 1925. In 1928-1929 served as a Comintern delegate in Outer Mongolia, allegedly collecting data on Japanese intrigue in the region. In 1934, Dunne was dismissed from his national leadership position. He did occasional reporting for the Daily Worker and New Masses, and organizational and publicity work for the Party throughout the Pacific Northwest region.

Duranty, Walter (1884-1957). British born *New York Times* correspondent in Moscow. 1932 Pulitzer Prize Winner. Author of 'Russian's Hungry but not Starving' article in *The New York Times,* March 31, 1933. Duranty disputed Gareth's exposure of the folly of Stalin's five year plan in the American press.

Fleming, Peter (1907-1971). Author of *One's Company*, brother of *James Bond* novelist Ian Fleming

Fischer, Louis (1896-1970). American journalist, Moscow Correspondent for *The Nation.* Denied reports of the famine published by Gareth Jones in 1933.

Frederick the Great (1712-1786). King of Prussia, 1740-86 who made Prussia into a major European power. Glorified by the Nazis.

Garvin, James Louis (1868-1947). Eminent British journalist. Editor of Sunday newspaper *The Observer* from 1908-1942.

Graham, Professor Gerald Sandford (1903-1988). Trinity College, Cambridge, friend of Gareth's. Professor of History. Sir George Parkin Scholarship at Trinity College, The University of Cambridge, 1927-1929; Other positions, Rhodes Professor of Imperial History, (1949-1970) and Fellow of King's College London, (1981). Many publications including, A *Concise History of Canada* (Thames and Hudson, London, 1968); *A Concise History of the British Empire* (Thames and Hudson, London, 1970).

Green, Robert; alias Thomas Walker. Falsified statements to fugitives from Colorado prison and wrote fictionalised stories about the famine in Soviet Union for Randolph Hearst.

Grinko, G T. An ethnic Ukrainian, served as the Vice-Chairman of the State Planning Commission of the USSR in 1930 and as an architect of the First Five-Year Plan.

Griffith, Arthur (1871-1922). Irish Statesman and president of the Irish Free State (1922).

Hayashi Senjuro, General (1876-1943). Assumed the position of Minister of War after General Araki. He supported the rival faction of the Tosei-Ha or control school, which favoured striking south into China.

Hearst, William Randolph (1863-1951) The famous American newspaper magnate, who published Gareth's articles in his US newspapers. An opponent of the League of Nations and opposed to Prohibition. A Democrat who supported Franklin D Roosevelt in 1932, but later his political allegiances moved to the right.

Heinz, Jack II, "Heinz, Jack Heinz" (1908-1987) Grandson of the founder of the H J Company and son of Howard Heinz. Gareth travelled with Jack to the Soviet Union in 1931, as his interpreter and guide. His anonymous account of the trip was published privately as '*Experiences in Russia — 1931*'. (It was based on Gareth's diaries and the foreword was written by Gareth). He succeeded his father as CEO in 1941 and voluntarily stood down in 1966. He was the last Heinz to run the company.

Herriot, Edouard. (1872 –1957). A French Radical politician of the Third Republic who served three times as Prime Minister (1924,1926,1932) and for many years as President of the Chamber of Deputies. He was leader of the first Cartel des Gauches.

Hessel Tiltman, Hugh (1891-1975). British journalist in 1930s China who reported on Manchuria, travel writer and author of publications including *Peasant Europe* and *Manchuria: The Cockpit of Asia* in 1934 (together with Colonel P T Etherton (British Consul in Kashgar 1918-22). He was three-time president of the Tokyo Foreign Correspondents' Club.

Hindus, Maurice (1891-1969). Russian-American journalist and author from Belarus. His family emigrated to the USA in 1905 after his father, who was a kulak, had died. Gareth and Jack Heinz met him in 1931 on their trip to Russia.

Hirohito (1901-1989). Emperor of Japan 1926-1989.

Hirota, Koki (1878-1948). Japanese Foreign Minister and then Prime Minister in 1936. Executed for War Crimes after World War II.

Hitler, Adolf (1889-1945). Became leader of the National Socialist German Workers Party in 1921. Chancellor of Germany in 1933-1945.

Hoare, Sir Samuel; 1st Viscount Templewood (1880-1959). British conservative politician. Foreign Secretary in 1935 when he negotiated the Hoare-Laval Pact with French Prime Minister Pierre Laval. A leading appeaser he was removed from office, along with Neville Chamberlain, in 1940.

Hoffmann, General Max von (1869-1927). Was successful on the German Eastern Front in 1917 against the Russians. By the spring of 1918, Hoffmann was assured of total cooperation by the Austrians on Eastern Front matters. In fact, threats by the Austrian Foreign Ministry to make peace with Ukraine separately in February 1918 caused Hoffmann to threaten removal of all German support on the Eastern Front. Such an ultimatum had the desired effect and the Austrians backed his invasion of Soviet Russia in March 1918.

Hooker, Adelaide (1903-1963). Daughter of Elon Hooker, who saw the Wostwag vehicle with its bullet holes in Kalgan soon after Gareth's death in 1935. She spoke to Dr Herbert Müller and subsequently gave an account to A J Sylvester, a copy of which he sent to the Foreign Office. Wife of John Phillips Marquand q.v.

Hopper, Dr Bruce Campbell (1892-1973). WW1 aviator and Harvard expert on USSR. During WW2 worked for American Secret Service organisation, OSS in Stockholm, and after the war became an advisor on Soviet matters to the CIA.

Hoover, President Herbert (1874-1964). Defeated by Roosevelt in 1932. Proposed the Hoover Moratorium of 1931.

Hywel Dda (c.880-950). A Welshman who claimed to be "King of all Wales". He summoned representatives from the whole of Wales to an assembly for the purpose of codifying the laws. This legal system became known for its wisdom and justice and was in force in Wales until the Act of Union with England in 1536.

Innitzer, Cardinal Theodore (1875-1955). Archbishop of Vienna. Appealed internationally for aid to the Soviet famine victims in 1933 and 1934.

Jones, Annie Gwen J P (1868-1965). Gareth's mother, known to the author as Nain and in the convention of the day as Mrs Edgar Jones.

Jones, Major Edgar (1868-1953). Gareth's father. Headmaster of Barry County School for Boys. Welsh Religious Adviser, BBC Wales, 1932. He was president of the Old Students Association of Aberystwyth in 1901 and in 1951. Warden of the Guild of Graduates of the University of Wales, Aberystwyth, he received an honorary M.A. in 1922, and Ll. D in 1951. He was awarded the OBE (military) and TD (Territorial Decoration) after WW1. He was Officer in Command, Glamorgan Fortress until 1913. He always kept his wartime title of Major. He received the Freedom of the Borough of Barry in 1950.

Jones, Elfin. The younger son of Dr Thomas Jones, Elfin died tragically at the age 12 years.

Jones, Miss Gwyneth Vaughan (1895-1996). Gareth's sister. Headmistress of Barry County School for Girls for 20 years from 1938.

Jones, Dr Thomas C H (1870-1955). Secretary of the Pilgrim Trust for twenty years and a leader of the Settlement Movement. He was the founder of a monthly publication, *The Welsh Outlook*. Major Edgar Jones contributed to the journal in the field of education. He was Private Secretary to four Prime Ministers including Lloyd George

Jones, Miss Winifred (1880-1952). Gareth's aunt. Always known as Auntie Winnie or to the children as Ninnie.

Kamenev, Leon (1883-1936). See Gregory Zinoviev.

Kerensky, Alexander (1881-1970). Prime Minister of the Russia in July 1917 and held power until the Bolshevik Revolution of November 1917.

Keynes, John Maynard; 1st Baron Keynes CB FBA (1883-1946). One of the foremost figures in the history of economics. He revolutionised the discipline with the publication of his book, *The General Theory of Employment, Interest and Money* (1936).

Kirov, Sergei (1886-1934). Born Sergei Kostikov. Surreptitiously opposed Stalin's extreme measures. Stalin treated Kirov like a son. He was assassinated by a young party member, Leonid Nikolayev, on 1st December 1934. Stalin claimed that Nikolayev was part of a larger conspiracy led by Leon Trotsky against the Soviet government. His death triggered off a chain of events that culminated in the Great Terror of the 1930s. This resulted in the arrest and execution of Genrikh Yagoda, Lev Kamenev, Gregory Zinoviev, and fourteen other party members who had been critical of Stalin.

Knickerbocker, Hubert Renfro (1898-1949). Author of *Five-Year Plan*. American journalist and foreign correspondent (of whom Gareth said to his parents "had red hair just like Auntie Winnie"). He was Moscow correspondent for the International News Service for 2 years from 1925, and a close friend of Walter Duranty. In 1931, Knickerbocker was awarded the Pulitzer Prize when working for New York *Evening Post* and Philadelphia *Public Ledger* for 'international correspondence on the Soviet economy.'

Kolchak, Alexander Vasilyevich, KB (1874-1920). Leader of the White Army Forces, the anti-Bolshevik Russians on the Siberian front in 1919. It was rumoured that the Tsar's incredible wealth, comprising 22 boxes of gold ingots, was given away in a dubious arms deal between Kolchak and the Japanese in exchange for weapons he never received. Executed by Bolsheviks in Irkutsk.

Krylenko, Nikolai Vasilyevich (1885-1938). In November 1917 Trotsky promoted him from ensign to commander in chief of the Russian forces to head peace negotiations with the Central Powers. Krylenko resigned in 1918 and later became public prosecutor and commissar of justice. He was tried in the party purge trials instituted by Stalin and was executed.

Layton, Sir Walter; 1st Baron Layton, CH CBE (1884-1966). British Liberal Party politician. Served in Lloyd George's Ministry of Munitions as Director of Statistics in WW1. Was considered by the ex-Prime Minister to be the most eminent economist in the world.

Lee, Dr Ivy (1877-1934). Said to be founder of modern public relations. Best known for his work with the Rockefeller family as well as Standard Oil, Chrysler, Pennsylvania Railroad, Chilean Nitrates, Lindberg, Dwight Morrow, Bethlem Steel, and other organisations. Employed Gareth at his offices in New York, but the Depression resulted in Gareth and other staff having to leave. Died of a brain tumour.

La Follette, Robert M. (1855-1925). American lawyer and politician. He opposed the American intervention in WW1. Republican Governor of Wisconsin who ran for the presidency in 1924.

Lewis, Mrs Eirian Vaughan (1899-2000). Sister of Gareth and mother of Siriol Colley (the author) and John Lewis.

Lichnovsky, Prince Karl Max (1860-1928). German Ambassador to the Court of St James in London, he wished to bring about better relations between Great Britain and Germany, but his success made his superiors in Berlin distrustful of him prior to WW1. Author of a 1916 pamphlet that deplored German diplomacy in mid-1914 which, he argued, contributed heavily to the outbreak of WW1.

Lippmann, Walter (1889-1974). Influential American writer, journalist and political commentator. Adviser to Woodrow Wilson and assisted in drafting the Fourteen Points. Brought into common usage the term *Cold War* in his book of the same name (1947).

Litvinov, Maxim (1876-1951). Soviet Commissar for Foreign Affairs 1930-39. In 1933 he was instrumental in gaining formal diplomatic recognition by the United States of the Soviet government. Dismissed in 1939 and replaced by Molotov. When the German-Soviet non-aggression pact was signed Hitler is said to have remarked that Litvinov's replacement was decisive (Litvinov was a Jew). Soviet Ambassador to President Roosevelt from 1941-43 and died a natural death.

Lloyd George, Right Hon. David OM, PC (1863-1945). Later Earl Lloyd George of Dwyfor. Chancellor of the Exchequer, 1908-1915. Minister of Munitions, 1915-1916. Prime Minister of Great Britain from 1916 to 1922. Presided over the decline and marginalisation of his Liberal Party and the rise of the Labour Party in Britain.

Lloyd Wright, Frank (1867-1959). Architect of worldwide renown, who was much admired by Gareth.

Lothian, Lord, (Philip Kerr) (1882-1940). Under-secretary of State for India; chairman, Indian Franchise Committee (1932). Lothian became the British Ambassador to the United States in 1939. "Lord Lothian had described Hitler variously in the 1930s as a visionary rather than as a gangster and was part of the Cliveden Set of appeasers. For his commitment to appeasement some called him Lord Loathsome.

Lytton, Victor Bulwer-, 2nd Earl of Lytton KG (1876-1947) Headed the League of Nations commission following the Mukden Incident in 1932 and the establishment of the state of Manchukuo. Produced the Lytton Report which condemned Japanese aggression against China in Manchuria.

Lyons, Eugene (1898-1985). American journalist and writer. Moscow correspondent for the United Press and author of *Assignment in Utopia* (the book was reviewed by Eric Blair [George Orwell]). Formerly a Communist he became highly critical of the Soviet Union after living there. Met Gareth in Moscow.

Macnamara, Thomas James (1861-1931). Educationalist and Liberal Cabinet Minister under Lloyd George (Minister of Labour) 1920-22.

Maclean, Sir Donald (1864-1932). Liberal Cabinet Minister in Ramsay MacDonald's National Government. Father of Donald MacLean, one of the British defectors to the Soviet Union from the Cambridge Spy Ring who were all at Trinity College, but some years younger than Gareth.

Martin, Basil Kingsley (1897-1969). Editor of New Statesman, friend and colleague of Malcolm Muggeridge who lodged for a time at Kingsley Martin's home. He wrote the text for *Low's Russian Sketchbook* by the cartoonist, published on November 25, 1932. He had been with a group of British journalists, sympathetic to the Soviet Union in the summer of 1932, as guests of the government. Jules Menken was among the journalists on this visit.

Masaryk, Jan Garrigue (1886-1948). Czech diplomat and politician, son of Tomas Masaryk, first President of Czechoslovakia. He served in the Austro-Hungarian Army during WW1 and joined the Diplomatic Service in 1919. He was made Ambassador to Britain in 1925 and served as Foreign Minister of Czechoslovakia from 1940-1948.

Matsuoka Yosuke (1880-1946). Headed the Japanese delegation to the League of Nations, when Japan was denounced for its conduct in annexing Manchuria. He left the meeting and in March 1933 Imperial sanction was given for Japan to withdraw from the League. Accused of War Crimes after WW2, died in prison of natural causes before his trial.

Meissner, Dr Otto (1880-1933). Instrumental in attaining Hitler's Chancellorship in January 1933. Head of the German Chancellery during Germany's Third Reich rule and the regimes of the Kaiser, and the Weimar Republic. Secretary of the Presidential Reich's Chancellery until May 1945. He was tried but not indicted for War Crimes after WW2. Acquitted of War Crimes at Nuremberg April 2nd 1949.

Meissner, Hans Otto (1909-1992). Son of Dr Meissner and a friend of Gareth's at Cambridge. Joined the SS in 1933 and NDSAP in 1936. Diplomat 1933-1945 including London in 1939 before the War. Writer and novelist in later years.

Menken, Prof. Jules (d.1947). An eminent economist at the London School of Economics in the 1930s.

Menzhinsky Vyacheslav Rudolfovich (1874–1934). Polish-Russian revolutionary, who served as chairman of the OGPU from 1926 to 1934.

Meston, The Rt. Hon. James; 1st Baron Meston KCSI VD (1865-1943). In 1925 he was elected Chairman of the Joint India Committee of both Houses of British Parliament. Vice-chairman of the Supervisory Commission of the League of Nations. He sat on the Liberal benches in the House of Lords and served as President of the Liberal Party

Milyukov, Pavel Nikolayevich (1859-1943). Russian statesman and historian who played an important role in the Russian Revolution of 1917 and served as foreign minister in the 1917 Provisional Government in Russia headed by Prince Lvov.

Mirsky, Prince Dmitri Petrovich (1890-1939). Son of a Russian Minister of the Interior, he served as a military officer during WWI, fought against the Reds in the Russian Civil War, emigrated in 1920, was appointed a lecturer at the School of Slavonic Studies (University of London) in 1922, where he taught for 10 years. He joined the Communist Party of Great Britain in 1931, returned to Russia in 1932, was arrested in 1937, soon after the death of his patron Maxim Gorky, and vanished in the Gulag system.

Muggeridge, Malcolm (1903-90). British author, broadcaster and journalist who reported the Russian famine in 1933. In his twenties, Muggeridge was attracted to communism but after living in the Soviet Union in the 1930s, he became a forceful anti-communist. An agnostic until he became a Christian in 1969 and was received into the Catholic church in 1982.

Müller, Dr Herbert (1885-1966). Gareth's companion into Inner Mongolia. Freelance journalist, archaeologist and representative of Deutsches Nachtichenburo, the German news agency.

Krupskaya, Nadezhda (1869-1939). Lenin's widow, Deputy Minister in the Commissariat of Education in Moscow from 1929-1939, interviewed by Gareth.

Orwell, George (1903-1950). British author of literary criticism, poetry and novels including *Animal Farm* and *Nineteen Eighty-Four.*

Osumi Mineo, Admiral (1876-1941). Admiral in the Japanese Navy and served twice as Minister of the Navy in the 1930s when Gareth was in Japan.

Oumansky, Konstantin (1902-1945). Soviet Press Officer in 1933 when Gareth was in Moscow. Soviet Ambassador to Washington 1939-1941. Killed in a plane crash 25, January 1945 on way to Costa Rica to present his credentials as Soviet Ambassador.

Paish, Sir George (1867-1957). British economist and statistician, adviser to the Chancellor of the Exchequer and British Treasury in 1914-16 and Chairman of the Anglo-Austrian Union. Active in the Liberal Party, standing, unsuccessfully, three times as a parliamentary candidate.

Pares, Sir Bernard (1867-1949). Diplomat and renowned Soviet expert and Professor at the School of Slavonic and East European Studies London.

Parnell, Charles Stewart (1848-1891). Irish Nationalist. Many people referred to him as "the uncrowned King of Ireland". He entered British parliament in 1875 but failed in his efforts to free Ireland from English rule.

Pentland, Lord (Henry John Sinclair) (1907-1984). Scottish businessman and peer. Became a pupil of Ouspensky of the Gurdjieff Foundation, a system of self-remembering called 'the Fourth Way'.

Petrewschchew, Anatoli. Russian driver of the Wostwag truck which transported Gareth in Inner Mongolia.

Pilsudski, Josef (1867-1935). After WW1 Józef Pilsudski emerged as Poland's national leader and was instrumental in securing Poland's independence. His attempt to create a larger Polish state failed during the Polish-Russian War of 1920. In 1926 he established an authoritarian rule until his death.

Plessen, Baron Johan von (1890-1961). German diplomat in Peking and accompanied Gareth into Inner Mongolia.

Prima de Rivera, Miguel; 2nd Marquess of Estella, 22nd Count of Sobremonte (1870-1930). Spanish aristocrat and dictator. In 1923 he seized power in the name of the king and dissolved parliament. His regime lasted until 1931 but heightened social tensions that led to the Spanish civil War in 1936.

Purpis(s), Adam (1883-?). Manager of the Wostwag trading Company based in Kalgan, a front company for the Soviet Secret Police, the NKVD, for espionage in the Far East. His assistant Arnold Deutsch was the NKVD agent who recruited Kim Philby and ran the Cambridge spies in the 1930s.

Radek, Karl (1885 –1938). Formed Right bloc with Zinoviev, Kamenev and Stalin in 1923 against Trotsky. Later editor of *Pravda*. Tried in the Second Moscow Trial. Died while in prison.

Reilly, Sydney "Ace of Spies" (1873-1925). Reilly, who, despite his name, was probably Russian, was supposedly shot dead by Bolshevik border guards in October 1925 as he tried to cross the Finnish border into Russia. But an MI6 report describes how he was, in fact, shot in the back at Stalin's insistence after days of being interrogated in the Lubyanka, the Moscow headquarters of the GPU, Stalin's secret police. Recruited by Scotland Yard in 1896 and SIS (predecessor to MI6) in 1918.

Ribbentrop, Joachim von (1893-1946). German Nazi Leader, Secret Agent in USA during World War One. Ambassador to Britain 1936-1938. Foreign Minister in Germany until 1943. Negotiated the Anti-Comintern Pact with Japan. Executed as a war criminal.

Richards, Fred, ARCA (1878-1932). A patriotic Welshman who believed that art should be an expression of the national spirit. Friend of Gareth's family.

Richard, Henry (1812-1888). A Welshman who founded the Peace Society in 1816 and was its secretary for 40 years.

Robinson, Leland Rex (1893-1966). American economist and writer. Spent time in Persia and the Caucasus as a member of a Near-East Relief Commission and wrote article on the 600,000 Armenians slaughtered by the Turks in 1915. Author of *The Turk Looks Eastward*.

Roosevelt, President Franklin (1882-1945). 32nd President of the United States from 1932 until he died in 1945.

Rowntree, Seebohm (1871-1954). Supporter of the Liberal Party; studied social conditions that were adopted as party policy. In 1908 David Lloyd George, as Chancellor of the Exchequer introduced a series of reforms influenced by Rowntree, including the Old Age Pensions Act (1908) and the National Insurance Act (1911).

Rutherford, Sir Ernest (1871-1937). Nobel prize-winning British nuclear physicist.

Sastry, Rt. Hon. V S Srivinasa PC, CH (1869-1946). President of the Servants of Indian Society 1915-1927. Member of Madras Legislative Council 1913 and Viceroy's Legislative Council 1916-1920. Visited England as member of moderate deputation and attended the Imperial Conference in 1921.

Scheer, Vice Admiral Reinhard (1863-1928). Fought Admiral Jellico at the Battle of Jutland and became German Chief of Naval Staff in 1918.

Scheffer, Paul (1883-1963). German journalist for the Berliner Tageblatt 1919-36 and good friend of Gareth. Foreign correspondent in Moscow from 1919, married a Russian. Foreign Correspondent in the USA 1930-32, and London 1932-34; Editor-in Chief back in Berlin 1934-36. Returned to the USA. At the Third Bukharin Moscow show trial in 1938, Scheffer was accused of being the head of a Nazi spy ring involved with the sabotage of Soviet grain. The only person who later believed this specific accusation was J Edgar Hoover, who had Scheffer interned, whilst in exile from Hitler, immediately after Pearl Harbor, even though he was at the time personally working for General Bill Donovan, the head of the wartime intelligence services, the Office of Strategic Services (OSS) precursor to the CIA.

Schiller, Otto (1902-2000). German agricultural attaché in Moscow. Schiller accompanied Andrew Cairns to Western Siberia, and Kazakhstan in early 1932 and in July 1932 he went to Ukraine.

Schuschnigg, Kurt (1897-1977). Austrian fascist politician who was the Chancellor of the Federal State of Austria from 1934 (after the assassination of Dollfuss) until the Anschluss in 1938.

Shaw, George Bernard (1856-1950). Irish dramatist and playwright. Member of the Fabian Society and enthusiast for the Soviet Union which he visited in 1931 with Conservative MP Lady Astor. Also, an admirer of Mussolini.

Shidehara Kijuro (1872-1951). Japan's Foreign Minister in 1930. Became Acting Prime Minister after the attempted assassination of the Prime Minister, Hamaguchi. He assumed the position of Prime Minister when General MacArthur was Supreme Commander in Japan following the cessation of hostilities in 1945.

Simon, Sir John; 1st Viscount Simon (1873-1954). British Foreign Secretary in the National Government from 1931 to 1935.

Sinclair, Upton (1878-1968). American writer and eccentric. Pulitzer Prize winner for Fiction in 1943. Ran for governorship of California in 194 on a socialist ticket EPIC (End Poverty in California) even though he was the Democratic nominee. He lost and was expelled from the Socialist Party.

Smith, Al (1873-1944). Rival of Franklin D Roosevelt for the 1932 Democratic presidential nomination. When Roosevelt won and began pursuing the policies of the New Deal, Smith became bitter and disaffected. He became a leader of the Liberty League, a leading opponent of the New Deal, and supported the Republican presidential candidates, Alf Langdon in 1936 and Wendell Wilkie in 1940.

Sorge, Richard (1895-1944). German journalist and Soviet military intelligence officer. He informed Stalin of the intended invasion of Russia by Germany on June 21st, 1941. Stalin disregarded this information. Tried by the Japanese in 1941, found guilty of spying for the Russians and executed in 1944.

Stalin, Joseph, (1879-1953). Georgian by nationality, he was active in the plot to overthrow Kerensky in 1917. On Lenin's death he assumed his place and became leader of the Union of Soviet Socialist Republics. He implemented the first Five Year Plan to modernise and industrialise the Soviet Union in 1929 and which was to result in the great famine of 1932-3 that Gareth recorded.

Stein, Günther (?). German journalist, foreign correspondent in China for the *Manchester Guardian*, the *Christian Science Monitor*, and the Associated Press. Senator Joseph McCarthy accused Stein of spying for China during the Red Scare, as part of the Sorge spy ring.

Stevenson, Miss Frances; Countess Lloyd-George of Dwyfor CBE (1888-1972).

Lloyd George's secretary, mistress and eventually his wife. She was secretary during Gareth's time with Lloyd George.

Stewart, Dr Hugh Fraser (1863-1948). British academic, churchman and literary critic. Fellow of Trinity College, Cambridge and tutor to Gareth. His son Ludovik was a friend of Gareth's.

Stoneman, William (1904-1987). American journalist and Moscow correspondent for *Chicago Daily News.*

Strang, William; 1st Baron Strang (1893-1978). British diplomat and leading adviser to the British government from the 1930s to the 1950s. During his time in Moscow (1930-33) he played an important role in the Metro-Vickers engineers trial, In 1951 William Strang was on a list of people that the Foreign Office suspected of being a Soviet mole and whose actions, whether by accident or design, enabled Donald Maclean to defect.

Stresemann, Gustav (1878-1929). Briefly Chancellor of the German coalition government in 1923, He was Foreign Secretary, until 1928. He accepted the Dawes Plan, initialled the Locarno Pact (1925) with Aristide Briand and Austen Chamberlain, and received the Nobel Peace Prize in 1926. He accepted the Young Plan that named June 30, 1930, as the final date for the evacuation of the Ruhr. Stresemann did not live to see that evacuation. The victim of a stroke, he died in Berlin in October 1929.

Sylvester, Mr A J (1889-1989). David Lloyd George's Private Secretary until Lloyd George's death and a friend of Gareth's.

Thomas, Albert (1878-1932). French socialist politician who was briefly first Minister for the French Third Republic during WW1. Following the Treaty of Versailles, he was nominated as the first director of the International Labour Organisation, created in 1919, a post he held until his death.

Thomas, J H "Jimmy" (1874-1949). Welsh/British politician stood as a National Labour candidate for Derby in the 1931 General Election and served as Secretary for the Colonies in the government of Ramsay MacDonald. Forced to leave political life after a financial scandal.

Tiltman, Hessel Travel writer and author of publications including Peasant Europe.

Trotsky, Leon (1879-1940). After leading a failed struggle of the Left Opposition against the politics of Joseph Stalin in the 1920s Trotsky was removed as Commissar of Military Affairs in 1925. Exiled from the USSR he continued to oppose Stalin until he was assassinated in 1940 by an NKVD agent.

Villari, Luigi (1876-1959). Italian historian with particular interest in international relations, traveller and diplomat. Mussolini's personal representative in London in the 1930s.

Von Tirpitz, Admiral Alfred (1849-1930). Secretary of State of the German Imperial Naval Office. 1897-1916. He was called the father of the German Navy and persuaded the German Government and Kaiser to build a fleet rivalling the British navy. His anti- British Policy soured Anglo-German relations. After the Battle of Jutland in 1916 Tirpitz turned to submarine warfare but was dismissed soon afterwards.

Von Schleicher, General Kurt (1882-1934). Chancellor of Germany November 1932 to January 1933. Murdered by the SS in 1934 during the Night of the Long Knives.

Webber, Sir Robert John (1884-1962). Welsh newspaper proprietor. Managing Director of the *Western Mail* and chairman of the Press Association in 1932-33.

Wells, H G (1866-1946). British author of satirical and science fiction novels including *The Time Machine*, *The Invisible Man*, and *The War of the Worlds* as well as biographies, history and works of social commentary. He was a member of the Fabian Society.

Williams, Sir John; 1st Baronet of the City of London (1840-1926). Welsh physician and major donor to the National Library of Wales including the Peniarth Manuscripts (collection of medieval Welsh manuscripts).

Wilson, President Woodrow (1856-1924). Committed United States to join the Allied cause in April 1917. Took active part in the peace negotiations after WW1. Leading architect of the League of Nations, but US Senate rejected both it, and the Treaty of Versailles.

Wodehouse, P G, KBE (1881-1975). British author and humourist who spent much of his life in the USA. He was interned during WW2 while living in France and made five broadcasts to the USA via German radio, leaving him open to accusations of being a Nazi collaborator. He was not charged and on release by the French in 1946 he went on to live in the USA.

Yagoda, Genrikh Grigoryevich (1891-1938). Director of NKVD (GPU) from 1934-1936. In 1934 he arrested Kamenov, Zinoviev and others accused of being in a plot to murder Stalin. He was demoted in 1936 and in 1937 tried for espionage Trotskyism and conspiracy. He was executed with Lev Kamenev, Gregory Zinoviev, as part of the Trial of the Twenty-One.

Zimmern, Sir Alfred Eckhard (1879-1957). English classical scholar, first Wilson Professor of International Politics at University College, Aberystwyth 1919-1921. He taught at Cornell University 1922 and 1923. Professor of International Relations at Oxford University 1930-1944. He contributed to the founding of the League of Nations Society and UNESCO.

Zinoviev, Gregory (1883-1936.) He formed *troika* with Kamenev and Stalin in 1922 against Trotsky. December 1934 with Kamenev he was arrested and brought before a military tribunal 'in connection' with the GPU-engineered assassination of Kirov; they were sentenced to 10 years. Finally, in August 1936 they were framed in the first of the Moscow show trials. After making a public 'confession', Zinoviev was sentenced to death for 'organizing the joint Trotskyite-Zinovievist Terrorist Centre for the assassination of Soviet government. Shot August 21, 1936.

Appendix IV

Gareth Jones Memorial Scholarship

Y WERIN
CRONFA DREFTADAETH
LEGACY FUND
Ymddiriedolaeth Gwaddol Cyfyngedig PC
The UW Restricted Endowment Trust

The object of the Scholarship is to enable the holder to travel in foreign countries with a view to facilitating his/her study of international relations. No obligation to pursue a specific scheme of study shall be attached to the award of the Scholarship.

Eligibility

Graduate of a Welsh University

Preference will be given to a graduate who signifies his/her intention to pursue or continue a scheme of study in preparation for work in journalism bearing on international affairs or for entry into State or other services relating to international affairs.

The value of the Scholarship shall be approximately £2,000, subject to available funds and payable in two instalments

The holder of the Scholarship shall, at the conclusion of his/her tenure, submit a report of their work

Applications for the award of the Scholarship must reach UWRET, University Registry, Cathays park, Cardiff CF10 3NS on or before June 1st in any given year, although some discretion may be used to extend this deadline.

This Scholarship is provided from the income of a Memorial Fund raised by public subscription to perpetuate the memory of Gareth Richard Vaughan Jones, a graduate of the University, who met his death at the hand of bandits in Inner Mongolia, 12 August 1935. £100 each was received from Lord Davies and Mr Randolph Hearst.

Bibliography

Ammende, Ewald 1934 (reprint 2006). *Human Life in Russia.* Hong Kong, Hesperides Press.

Applebaum, Anne 2017. Red Famine: *Stalin's War on Ukraine.* London, Allen Lane.

Andrew Christopher & Gordievsky Oleg 1990. *KGB Inside Story.* Harper Collins.

'Author, The' 1932. *Experiences in Russia — 1931. A Diary.* Pittsburgh: The Alton Press Inc. Written anonymously by Jack Heinz II, with a preface by Gareth R.V. Jones. A full transcription of this rare book can be found at https://www.garethjones.org/soviet_articles/experiences_in_russia_1931.htm

Behr, Edward 1987. *The Last Emperor.* London, MacDonald & Co.

Bergamini, David 1971. *Japan's Imperial Conspiracy.* New York, William Morrow.

Boyle, Andrew 1979. *The Climate of Treason – Five who Spied for Russia.* London, Hutchinson.

Bowker, Gordon 2003. *George Orwell.* London, Little, Brown & Co.

Brendon, Piers 2000. *The Dark Valley.* London, Jonathon Cape.

Butler, J R M 1960. *Lord Lothian (Philip Kerr) 1882-1940.* London, MacMillan & Co. Ltd.

Carynnyk, Marco, Luciuk Lubomyr Y & Kordan, Bohdan S (eds) 1988. *The Foreign Office and the Famine.* British Documents on Ukraine and the Great Famine of 1932-1933, Kingston, Ontario — Vestal, New York, The Limestone Press.

Chamberlin, W H 1934 (reprinted 2012). *Russia's Iron Age* Whitefish MT, Literary Licensing

Colley, Margaret Siriol 2001. *Gareth Jones; A Manchukuo Incident.* Newark, England, Nigel Colley.

Corson, W.R. & Crowley R.T. 1985. T*he New KGB, Engine of Soviet Power.* New York, William Morrow & Co.

Crocket, Richard 1989. *Twilight of Truth.* London, Weidenfeld & Nicholson.

Crowl, James William 1982. *Angels in Stalin's Paradise.* Lanham Maryland, The University Press of America.

Crozier, Andrew 1997. T*he Causes of the Second World War.* Oxford, Blackwell.

Davies, Lord 1941. *Foundations of Victory.* London, Collins.

Deakin, F.W. & Storry G.R 1966. *The Case of Richard Sorge.* London, Chatto and Windus.

Duranty, Walter 1934. *Russia Reported.* New York, Gollancz. A collection of articles first published in the *New York Times.*

Edwards, Susan 1992. *Hughesovka, A Welsh Enterprise in Imperial Russia.* Glamorgan, South Wales, Glamorgan Record Publication.

Fox, James 1999. *The Langhorne Sisters.* London, Granta Books.

Freeborn, Richard 1966. *A Short History of Modern Russia.* London, Hodder and Stoughton.

Gamache, Ray 2018 Gareth Jones: *Eyewitness to the Holodomor.* Cardiff, Welsh Academic press (2nd edition)

Gilbert, Martin 1997. *A History of the Twentieth Century: 1900 — 1933.* London, Harper Collins.

Gilbert, Martin and Richard Gott 1963. *The Appeasers.* London, Phoenix Press.

Hosking, Geoffrey 2002. *Russia and The Russians.* London, Penguin Books.

Ingrams, Richard 1995. *Muggeridge. The Biography.* London, Harper Collins.

Jones, Gareth 1936. *In Search of News.* Cardiff, The Western Mail.

- — - 2015. *Tell Them we are Starving: The 1933 Diaries of Gareth Jones.* Executive editor Lubomyr Y Luciuk. Kingston, Ontario. Kashtan Press.

Jones, Thomas, C H 1933. *A Theme with Variations.* Llandinam, The Gregynog Press.

Kershaw, Ian 1998. *Hitler. 1889-1936: Hubris.* London, Penguin Books.

Knickerbocker H R 1931. *The Soviet Five-Year Plan and its Effect on World Trade.* London, The Bodley Head.

Knightley, Philip 1988. *Philby – K.G.B. Masterspy,* London, Andre Deutsch.

Lloyd George, David 1938. *War Memoirs of David Lloyd George;* Vol. 1. New edition London, Oldham Press Ltd.

- — - 1932. *The Truth about Reparations and War Debts1932*. Garden City, New York, Doubleday, Doran & Co.

Lloyd George, Frances 1967. *The Years that Are Past, The Autobiography of Frances Lloyd George,* London, Hutchinson.

Luciuk, Lubomyr (ed.) 2003. *Not Worthy. Walter Duranty's Pulitzer Prize and the New York Times*. Kingston, Ontario, Kashtan Press.

Lyons, Eugene 1937. *Assignment in Utopia*. New York, Harcourt Brace.

Mace, James 2003. "A Tale of Two Journalists", in Luciuk (ed.) 2003)

Maggosi, Paul Robert 1996. *A History of Ukraine*. Toronto, Toronto University Press.

Muggeridge, Malcolm 1934. *Winter in Moscow*. London, Eyre and Spottiswoode.

- — - 1972. *Chronicles of a Wasted Time*. London, Collins.

- — - 1981. *Like It Was*. London, Collins.

- — - 1940. *The Thirties*. London, Hamish Hamilton. Reissued 1967 by Collins.

Mykulyn, A. 1958. 'The Russian Terrorist Regime and the Artificial Famine in Ukraine (1932-33)', *The Ukraine Review* xxx.

Nasaw, David 2003. *The Chief, The Life of Randolph Hearst*. London, Gibson Square Books.

Orwell, George 1951. *Animal Farm*. London, Penguin Books. (First Published: 1945 by Martin Secker and Warburg Ltd)

- — - 1949. *Nineteen Eighty-Four*. London, Penguin Books.

- — -1946. *Critical Essays*. London, Secker and Warburg.

Penrose, Barrie & Freeman, Simon 1986. *Conspiracy of Silence- The Secret Life of Anthony Blunt*. London, Harper Collins.

Snyder, Timothy 2010. *Bloodlands: Europe Between Hitler and Stalin*. London, Random House Group.

Sun Youli 1993. *China and the Origins of the Pacific War 1931-1941*. London, Macmillan Press.

Taylor, A J P (ed.) 1967. *Lloyd George. A Diary by Frances Stevenson,* London, Hutchinson.

Taylor, S. J. 1990. *Stalin's Apologist*. New York, Oxford University Press.

Tiltman, Hessel 1936. *Peasant Europe*. Norwich, Jarrolds Publishers Ltd.

Vaughan-Thomas, Wyn, & Alun Llewellyn 1969. *The Shell Guide to Wales*. London, Michael Joseph.

Wise, David & Thomas B. Ross 1965. *The Invisible Government.* London, Jonathan Cape.

Other Sources

Columbia University Newspaper Archives.

G. Mudd Manuscript Library, Princeton, USA, Ivy Ledbetter Lee Papers.

Political Archives of the National Library of Wales, Aberystwyth. [Public papers of Gareth Jones].

Parliamentary Archives, London. TheLloyd George Papers (1878-1945).

Hansard. 1935-1936. Speeches by David Lloyd George.

Knickerbocker, H. R. Personal Papers, Butler Library, Columbia University, New York.

Manchester Guardian Archives. [Malcolm Muggeridge 1933 Correspondence with Editor, W. Crozier]

New York Public Library, Newspaper Archives.

Public Record Office documents. 1935. No 7699. Ref FO371/19768 (Murder of Gareth Jones) and KV2/1655 (Far Eastern Trading Company / Wostwag).

British Newspaper Library, Colindale — Various newspaper publications and documents including The *Western Mail and South Wales News, The Times, Daily Telegraph, Manchester Guardian, The Financial News, The Daily Express, The New York Times, The New York American, The New York Herald Tribune* and other newspapers, which are cited in endnotes, where used.

Gareth Jones Website: www.garethjones.org

About the Authors

Nigel Colley and Margaret Siriol Colley receiving The Ukrainian Order of Merit on behalf of Gareth Jones in 2008.

Margaret Siriol Colley was born in London on June 6th 1925. Her parents were Welsh, and every holiday was spent at her grandparents' home Eryl in Barry, South Wales where she was encouraged to speak Welsh. There she heard about, and sometimes met, the eminent men and women of South Wales, and from farther afield, who gathered in Eryl each Sunday for a Welsh high tea to discuss the topics of the day.

In 1940, following the outbreak of World War II, Siriol was evacuated to Canada where she commenced her medical education at Dalhousie University, Halifax, Nova Scotia. Returning home she graduated from medical school at St Andrews University, Scotland in 1948. She was a general practitioner in Nottingham for 35 years, and in joint practice with her husband until his death in 1973. Taking up sub-aqua diving at the age of 50 she became an accomplished diver exploring oceans across the world and helping with archaeological surveys of the Earl of Abergavenny and the Mary Rose. She had four sons and ten grandchildren. Siriol Colley died in November 2011.

The murder of her Uncle Gareth devastated the whole family but its mysterious circumstances intrigued Siriol. Upon her retirement, she devoted almost 20 years to researching his story, hoping to find the reason for his premature death. She also undertook the huge task of transcribing and translating, variously from five languages, Gareth's many letters and diaries. This resulted in the publication of her first book *Gareth Jones: A Manchukuo Incident* in 2001. Interest in Gareth's life was huge and this led to the publication of her second book *More Than a Grain of Truth* four years later. It is the story of Gareth's earlier life, leading up to the events described in the first book.

In recent years Gareth Jones has been the subject of increasing media and public interest and several academic books have now been produced on the subject of his life. In 2008 he was posthumously awarded the Ukrainian Order of Merit. In 2012 the BBC produced a Storyville documentary about his life *Hitler, Stalin and Mr Jones*. A feature film, *Mr Jones*, based on his life, achieved worldwide release in 2020. Since she began her quest to restore her beloved uncle's name, and largely because of it, Gareth Jones' place in history has been assured.

Nigel Linsan Colley was born in Nottingham in June 1960, the third of Siriol's sons. After graduating with a degree in Biochemistry from York University he took a career change and worked in advertising and marketing before devoting his life to raising his children, Edmund and Rachael. This allowed him time to create the comprehensive website on Gareth Jones and to help his mother with research on her books. They visited Ukraine together in 2008 where Nigel appeared in Sergiy Bukovsky's film *The Living*.

His many lecture tours on Gareth Jones in the UK, USA, Canada and Italy included talks at St Patrick's Cathedral New York (2005), the United Nations (2009), Princeton Club, New York (2013) and the National Press Club, Washington DC, (2011 and 2017). He was a great believer in freedom of information and always gave of his time and knowledge freely to all those who showed interest in his great uncle. Nigel was a unique and unforgettable character. It is fitting that Nigel's last public engagement in November 2017, was at the laying of a wreath in memory of Gareth Jones at the University of Wales, Aberystwyth, where Gareth had been a student. Nigel Colley died in February 2018.

Naomi Field was Nigel's partner for nine years until his death in 2018. She is an archaeologist by profession with extensive writing experience. She supported Nigel in his work and research on Gareth Jones, mainly with editorial advice, as well as accompanying him to lectures and events.